Beyond Post-Communication

This book is part of the Peter Lang Media and Communication list.
Every volume is peer reviewed and meets
the highest quality standards for content and production.

PETER LANG
New York • Bern • Berlin
Brussels • Vienna • Oxford • Warsaw

Jim Macnamara

Beyond Post-Communication

Challenging Disinformation, Deception, and Manipulation

PETER LANG
New York • Bern • Berlin
Brussels • Vienna • Oxford • Warsaw

Library of Congress Cataloging-in-Publication Data

Names: Macnamara, Jim, author.
Title: Beyond post-communication: challenging disinformation, deception, and manipulation / Jim Macnamara.
Description: New York: Peter Lang, 2020.
Includes bibliographical references and index.
Identifiers: LCCN 2020001256 (print) | LCCN 2020001257 (ebook)
ISBN 978-1-4331-6919-9 (hardback: alk. paper)
ISBN 978-1-4331-6920-5 (paperback: alk. paper) | ISBN 978-1-4331-6921-2 (ebook pdf)
ISBN 978-1-4331-6922-9 (epub) | ISBN 978-1-4331-6923-6 (mobi)
Subjects: LCSH: Communication in politics—United States. |
Communication—Moral and ethical aspects—United States. |
Disinformation—Political aspects—United States. | Public relations and politics—United States. | Information society—Political aspects—United States.
Classification: LCC JA85.M33 2020 (print) | LCC JA85 (ebook)
DDC 320.97301/4—dc23
LC record available at https://lccn.loc.gov/2020001256
LC ebook record available at https://lccn.loc.gov/2020001257
DOI 10.3726/b15614

Bibliographic information published by **Die Deutsche Nationalbibliothek**.
Die Deutsche Nationalbibliothek lists this publication in the "Deutsche Nationalbibliografie"; detailed bibliographic data are available on the Internet at http://dnb.d-nb.de/.

The paper in this book meets the guidelines for permanence and durability of the Committee on Production Guidelines for Book Longevity of the Council of Library Resources.

© 2020 Peter Lang Publishing, Inc., New York
29 Broadway, 18th floor, New York, NY 10006
www.peterlang.com

All rights reserved.
Reprint or reproduction, even partially, in all forms such as microfilm, xerography, microfiche, microcard, and offset strictly prohibited.

Printed in the United States of America

Contents

Acknowledgements	xi
About the Author	xiii
Previous Books	xv
Introduction	1
Post-Truth and Distrust in a Sea of Information	2
A Perfect Storm Scenario	17
The Framework and Context of This Analysis	18
Methodology and Sources	20

PART 1   Democratic Decline, Deficit, Destabilization   29

1   *Brexit*, Trump, 'Hung Parliaments', and the Collapse of
Public Trust	31
Truth Decay	35
Fake News, Alternative Facts, Misinformation,	
and Disinformation	36
Partisanship and Polarization	38
The Crisis of Trust	39

	Particularized Trust	39
	Generalized/Social Trust	39
	Political Trust	40
	What's the Problem with Distrust?	42
	The Role of Communication in Trust	45
	Engagement and Disengagement	47
	What's the Problem with Disengagement?	49
	The Collapse of Civility	49
	Lack of Listening	54
2	Post-Truth, Post-Democracy … Post-Politics, Post-Capitalism, Post-Society?	65
	Post-Truth	65
	What Is Truth?	67
	Post-Democracy	71
	The End of Democracy?	73
	The Relocation of Democracy	76
	Post-Media	79
	Post-Journalism	81
	Post-Representation	82
	Post-Politics	83
	Post-Capitalism	83
	Post-Society	84
	Living in the Age of Post-Everything	85
3	Post-Communication	93
	What Is Post-Communication?	95
	The Growing Pervasiveness of Post-Communication	96
	Spin	96
	Merchants of Doubt	98
	Toxic Sludge Is Good for You	100
	Citizens for a Free Kuwait	101
	Weapons of Mass Destruction	102
	'Black PR'	103
	Advertorial and Pay-to-Play	103
	Native Advertising	105
	Merged Media	107
	Greenwashing	108

	Behavioural Insights—A Tool for Good or Evil	109
	Bell Pottinger	111
	Astroturfing	112
	Covering up Corporate Corruption	113
	Communication "Tricks" of Public Companies	114
	"Washington's Worst Communicator"	114
	Churnalism	115
	Yellow Journalism—Muckraking, Sensationalism and Fabrication	116
	Partisan Journalism	117
	Targeting and Micro-Targeting	119
	The Marketization and Politicization of Government Communication	121
	Social Media Influencers	124
	Fake Accounts and Trolls	126
	Weaponizing Social Media	129
	Bald-Faced Lies in Advertising	129
	Spin, Clickbait, Fabrication, Disinformation—The Escalation to Post-Truth	130
4	Technologies Turbocharging Post-Communication	143
	Social Media—The New Media Monopolies	143
	Big Data	145
	Data Analytics	148
	Cambridge Analytica and Co.	150
	Automation	151
	Algorithms	151
	Bots	154
	Artificial Intelligence (AI)	157
	Deepfakes and Fake Text—Next Gen Disinformation	159
	A Perfect Datastorm Brews	163
PART 2	Rehabilitating Public Communication & the Public Sphere	171
5	Strategies for a Communicative Society	173
	Strategy 1: Self-Regulation by Communication Professionals—Reining in Spin	175

Journalism Futures—Beyond Opinion, Partisanship and PRization	175
Remodelling Public Relations	182
Incorporating Corporate Communication	198
Transparency in Corporate and Owned Media	199
Advertising and Marketing Standards and Codes	200
Government Communication beyond Marketing	203
Political Communication to Address the Relocation of Democracy	206
Strategy 2: Responsibility and Transparency by Publishers and Platforms	207
Human Rights and Intelligence vs. Artificial Intelligence	209
Technology as a Guardian of Technology?	210
International Cooperation—Globalization for Good	212
Strategy 3: Media Literacy for Consumption and Production	213
Overcoming Dunning-Kruger and Third Person Effects	214
Inoculation through Media Literacy for Critical Consumption	215
Media Literacy for Production—Beyond Likes and Follows to Tagging and Snoping	216
Refuting Misinformation and Disinformation	217
Obfuscating as a Way to Sabotage Surveillance	217
Strategy 4: Public Media to Protect the Public Interest	218
The Case for Public Funding of Broadcasting	218
Philanthropic Guardians of Democracy	222
Media Development	223
Strategy 5: Activism and Social Movements	223
The Arab Spring	224
Occupy	225
The Umbrella Movement	225
Climate Change Mobilization	226
Anti-Gun Lobby	227
MySociety	227
LGBTQI+	227
#MeToo	228
Black Lives Matter	228
Fixers—Fixing Themselves	229

Alt-Right	229
Shareholder Activism	230
Strategy 6: Corporate Responsibility and Social Purpose in Business	231
CSR—Responsibility, or Turning Pigs' Ears into Silk Purses	232
Purpose	232
Responsibility of CEOs—Where the Buck Stops	233
The Rise of CCOs—The Case for Communication Leadership	233
Strategy 7: Research and Analysis	234
The Social Construction of New Realities	235
A New Vision and Narrative	235
Strategy 8: Refuting and Resisting	236
The Empire Strikes Back	236
Strategy 9: Self-Responsibility—It's Up to You and Me	236
Check Up, speak Up, Act Up	237
Strategy 10: Regulation and Legislation	237
Advertising and Marketing Regulation and Legislation	238
Public Relations—Uncharted Territory	240
Data Protection and Privacy	241
Regulation of Social Media Platforms	241
Algorithmic Accountability	247
Anti-Trust Action—The Big Stick	248
Freedom of Speech and of Media	248
The Need for Balance	250
Carrots and Sticks	250

6	Conclusions	271
	Complicity	271
	A Troubling Technology Track Record	274
	A Tipping Point	275
	10 Strategies to Address Post-Communication	276
	Our Shared Responsibilities—An Action List	280

Bibliography	285
Index	291

Acknowledgements

As with all books, particularly those informed by international research, the author owes a debt to many. Some directly contributed to the analysis and discussion through interviews or provision of documents or data. Others indirectly provided assistance and support through their own important research that I have drawn on, and through their collegiality in discussions and feedback.

In particular, I wish to thank the leading scholars and professionals working in various media and communication disciplines including journalism, advertising, public relations, and corporate, government, and political communication, who agreed to be interviewed. Some preferred to remain anonymous, so I thank them collectively. Those who agreed to be quoted are duly acknowledged in the text and in citations. Industry leaders who generously gave their time and knowledge and agreed to be named include (in alphabetical order by surname): Richard Bagnall, Sylvia Bell; Stuart Bruce; Peter Fray; Lucas Bernays-Held (the grandson of Edward Bernays); Bob Jensen; Alan Kelly; Stefan Kloet; Anne Kruger; Sean Larkins; Barry Leggetter; and Therese Manus. As noted in the text, these communication professionals have held a range of senior positions in media or government, corporate, or political communication in a number of countries. In addition, insights and advice were gained from senior academics including Anne Gregory at the University of Huddersfield in the UK, who is immediate past chair of the Global Alliance for Public Relations and Communication Management (the peak global body representing 280,000 practitioners), and Jisu Huh from the University of Minnesota, who is past president of the American Academy of Advertising, as well as other leading researchers in media and communication including Terry Flew; Natalia Nikolova; Maureen Taylor, and Ralph Tench.

I thank Peter Lang, New York for believing in this book, particularly Erika Hendrix who supported and guided the project.

And, as always, I wish to acknowledge and thank Dr Gail Kenning, my best friend, colleague, and wife, who shares the journey of inquiry and discovery that is research in the hope that it may make some contribution to a better world.

Jim Macnamara

About the Author

Jim Macnamara PhD, FAMEC, FAMI, CPM, FPRIA[1] is a Distinguished Professor in the School of Communication at the University of Technology Sydney (UTS). He is also a Visiting Professor at The London School of Economics and Political Science (LSE), Media and Communications Department, and the London College of Communication.

Jim conducted research inside the UK Government before, during, and following the *Brexit* vote and served as a member of the Evaluation Council of the UK Government Communication Service (GCS) headquartered in the Cabinet Office, Whitehall and Number 10 Downing Street. Since 2016 he has led a global research project into organizational listening in public communication and stakeholder engagement, which has been described as of "major international significance."[2]

He also has been commissioned to research government communication by Australia's largest state government and he has advised the European Commission (EC) Directorate-General for Communication (DG COMM) in Brussels and other government organizations and corporations in Australia, Europe, and the USA.

Before joining the academy he worked in leading communication agencies responsible for advertising and public relations for multinational corporations, in government communication, and conducted election campaigns for political candidates.

His previous books include *The 21st Century Media (R)evolution: Emergent Communication Practices*; *Journalism and PR: Unpacking 'Spin', Stereotypes & Media Myths*, and *Organizational Listening: The Missing Link in Public Communication*.

He holds a Bachelor of Arts in journalism and media studies and a Master of Arts by research in media studies from Deakin University in Australia, and he gained his PhD in media research from Western Sydney University.

Notes

1. Fellow of the International Association for Measurement and Evaluation of Communication (AMEC); Fellow of the Australian Marketing Institute (AMI); Certified Practicing Marketer (CPM); Fellow of the Public Relations Institute of Australia (PRIA).
2. Couldry, N. (2017). Foreword. In J. Macnamara, *Creating a 'democracy for everyone': Strategies for increasing listening and engagement by government*. London, UK: The London School of Economics and Political Science. Retrieved from http://www.lse.ac.uk/media@lse/research/CreatingADemocracyForEveryone.aspx

Previous Books

- *Evaluating Public Communication: Exploring New Models, Standards and Best Practice* (Routledge, UK, 2018)
- *Organizational Listening: The Missing Essential in Public Communication* (Peter Lang, 2016)
- *Journalism and PR: Unpacking 'Spin', Stereotypes & Media Myths* (Peter Lang, 2014)
- *The 21st Century Media (R)evolution: Emerging Communication Practices* (Peter Lang, 2014)
- *Public Relations: Theories, Practices, Critiques* (Pearson Australia, 2012)
- *Media and Male Identity: The Making and Remaking of Men* (Palgrave Macmillan, UK, 2006)
- *How to Handle the Media* (Prentice Hall Australia, 1996)
- *The Modern Presenter's Handbook* (Prentice Hall Australia, 1996)
- *Effective Marketing Communication and Promotion* (Information Australia, 1988)

Introduction

Warnings of political and social decline, and even collapse, are not uncommon and, when considered in context, many are found to be unwarranted, exaggerated, or at least premature. In the 1990s, Robert Putman's *Bowling Alone*[1] warned of a decline in social interaction and participation that create what Pierre Bourdieu called *social capital*[2] and which he described as necessary for citizens to live fulfilling lives and for a healthy democracy. While Putnam drew attention to important social issues, citizens living in developed countries today are more educated and are potentially more connected than ever before. As Bill Gates wrote as guest editor of an issue of *TIME* magazine in January 2018: "On the whole, the world is getting better." Gates cited a number of statistics including:

> Look at the number of children who die before their fifth birthday. Since 1990, that figure has been cut in half ... In 1990, more than a third of the global population lived in extreme poverty; today only about a tenth do ... More than 90% of all children in the world attend primary school.[3]

Gates was not attempting to gild the lily and claim that the world does not face significant problems—indeed the foundation that he co-founded is engaged in addressing many major social, economic, health, and education issues around the world. But he was cautioning against unwarranted pessimism and doomsday thinking that arise as a result of unbalanced reporting and a lack of historical perspective.

Francis Fukuyama's *End of History* proposed a reverse collapse in which democracy, particularly American democracy, would come to dominate and stabilize the world—although, given considerable contemporary evidence to the contrary, he has backed away from this view in more recent writing in which he refers to America as a "failed state."[4]

Post-Truth and Distrust in a Sea of Information

This analysis will attempt to be cognizant of the twists and turns of human history and present a balanced discussion. However, while being mindful of premature *moral panic* that grows out of human anxiety and critical incidents, it is noted that many of the issues that concerned Fukuyama and others in 2016 have escalated since. Consider the following that are just some of the concerning facts that set the scene and the rationale for this book.

- In September 2016 at the height of campaigning for the 2016 US presidential election that saw Donald Trump take office, *The Economist* declared that "the world has entered an era of *post-truth* politics" [emphasis added].[5]
- By year end, Oxford Dictionaries announced 'post-truth' as its word of the year, defining it as "relating to or denoting circumstances in which objective facts are less influential in shaping public opinion than appeals to emotion and personal belief."[6]
- In April 2017, *TIME* magazine published a cover story titled "Is truth dead?"[7]
- In 2020 at the height of the coronavirus (COVID-19) outbreak, the World Health Organization (WHO) declared that the world faced an "infodemic" as well as a pandemic.[8] The United Nations went further, declaring the pandemic a "disinfodemic"[9] because of the flood of disinformation that was undermining public health information and risking lives.
- A recent academic analysis argued that post-truth is more than a disregard of facts and reliance on emotional appeals by a few individual demagogues. It concluded that contemporary Western societies are suffering under "regimes of post-truth."[10] In other words, post-truth is not only the product of a few aberrant individuals, but rather a systematically constructed and increasingly institutionalized condition.

- Rhetoric and *spin* have long been characteristics of politics. But today, big business as well as politics and government are implicated in creating "post-truth society," according to the same analysis.
- Trust in government has declined to alarming levels in most developed Western democracies. For example, a 2015 Harvard University study reported that only 14% of 18–29-year-old Americans trust the US Congress and only 20% trust the federal government.[11] A 2019 report by The Open Government Partnership (OGP) Practice Group on Dialogue and Deliberation noted that "research shows that less than half the citizens of countries in the OECD have confidence in their national governments."[12] The Edelman Trust Barometer, an annual survey of more than 30,000 people in almost 30 countries, reported in 2020 that less than half of the general population (47%) trust government.[13]
- Trust in media has fallen to the same low level.[14]
- Only 55% of the general population trust business and non-government organizations (NGOs). Even among what Edelman refers to as the "informed public"—university graduates and professionals—more than 40% do not trust government or media and 30% distrust business and NGOs.[15] Trust in government and institutions rebounded during the COVID-19 emergency, but long-term trends remain alarming.
- Political parties, which exert a major influence on political representation and policy, have been deserted in droves over the past few decades and are now fundamentally unrepresentative in many countries. For example, in 2019 when members of the Conservative Party in the UK decided the next Prime Minister—not citizens in a general election[16]—the party's membership represented less than 0.4% of the electorate. Only 1.7% of eligible UK voters were members of any one of the three major political parties in 2019.[17]
- Political leadership is becoming a revolving door in many countries. For example, Australia, one of the world's most stable democracies over the past century, had six Prime Ministers in nine years between 2010 and 2019 and the national government held power by a one or two seat majority during most of that time. The UK had three Prime Ministers in three years between July 2016 and July 2019.
- Professor of political communication at Goldsmiths, Aeron Davis, concluded that we "can no longer simply dismiss the problem of declining levels of trust in news media, politicians, and governments everywhere."[18]

- Some political and social scientists warn that politics and government in major developed Western countries are collapsing into *post-democracy*.[19] Some are even forecasting the "end of democracy."[20] In the least, modern democracy is "in the midst of an existential crisis," according to Davis in his 2019 analysis of political communication.[21] He says that there are "clear signs that democracy is not just going through a temporary dip."[22] For example, in 2016 The Economist Intelligence Unit (EIU) reported that half of 167 countries evaluated annually experienced a decline in their aggregate democracy scores. Over a quarter of people in some democratic states now wonder if democracy is the best political system, according to the EIU surveys.[23]
- Based on declining trust in business, particularly large corporations, some commentators have predicted the end of capitalism, or what they refer to as *post-capitalism*.[24]
- As we enter the second decade of the 21st century, some claim that the very fabric of some societies is breaking down with a collapse of trust, increasing disengagement and inequities, and marginalization of large numbers of people,[25] leading to what could be called *post-society*. The anti-social hoarding of food and household items such as toilet paper that followed the spread of coronavirus (COVID-19) in early 2020 suggested that this might already be underway.

These and other alarming events, warnings, and characteristics of our social and political world, which are examined in more detail in Chapter 1, reveal a paradox in public communication, which is the focus of this analysis. The term public communication is used here to refer to all communication that occurs in the *public sphere* between organizations such as government departments and agencies, corporations, NGOs, and non-profit organizations on one hand, and their *stakeholders* on the other. The term stakeholders is used in this analysis to refer to all groups and individuals who can affect or are affected by an organization's activities, based on the theory of multiple constituencies of organizations advanced by R. Edward Freeman and others.[26]

Media and communication are central to politics, as Davis has noted.[27] Public communication, as defined above, is also central to marketing that drives business and commerce. More resources are invested in public communication by governments, corporations, NGOs, and even non-profit organizations (NFPs) today than ever before. For instance, global spending on advertising exceeded US$630 billion in 2018, and is forecast to increase to more than US$750 billion by 2021.[28]

Industry studies indicate that more than $230 billion was spent on advertising in North America alone in 2018, with more than US$100 billion spent in Western Europe, and Asia-Pacific countries including China spending more than US$200 billion in 2018.[29] Spending on public relations (PR) grew by 34% between 2013 and 2016 to almost £13 billion in the UK alone,[30] and is reported to be growing by more than 20% a year in fast-developing markets such as Brazil.[31] An annual study by the University of Southern California (USC), Annenberg reported that 86% of PR firms predicted revenue growth in 2018. Half forecast annual growth of 15% or more.[32] Even more is spent on practices referred to as *corporate communication* (a term used by government bodies such as the European Commission as well as public companies), public affairs, organizational communication, and public diplomacy. Many millions of dollars, euro, pounds, and other currencies are also spent on public consultation, customer relations, promotional events, social media engagement, and other forms of public communication.

Yet, at the same time, public communication appears to be failing to an unprecedented extent, as evidenced by the 2016 UK referendum decision to leave the EU after 40 years of membership against all predictions and a major Remain campaign (*Brexit*); the shock election of Donald Trump; the 'hung parliament' resulting from the 2017 UK general election; and declining support in a number of member countries for the EU, one of the most significant social and political initiatives of the past century. Action on climate change has been delayed and even rejected by many leaders and industry and business groups, despite overwhelming scientific evidence. Clearly, something is wrong in the public sphere of major democratic countries. Public communication is not working in an alarming number of cases and on a number of important issues.

Another key characteristic of contemporary developed societies suggests that there is, in fact, a double paradox. Organizations have more data available to them than ever before in human history, including more data about the attitudes, behaviours, media consumption, channel preferences, interests, habits, desires, and concerns of people, referred to as *human data*.[33] Availability of such an array of human data should create unprecedented understanding of people and facilitate engagement and communication between organizations and their stakeholders.

However, upheavals such as *Brexit* and the shock election of Donald Trump illustrate that many organizations including governments, political parties, and even many analysts and pollsters seem to have no clue about public opinion and public concerns. Or they simply don't care. The petabytes and zettabytes of statistical and textual data available to governmental, political, and business organizations also should inform policies and management decisions that result in understanding and support. In short, the large amount of data available about people including their attitudes, interests, habits, concerns and needs should lead to enhanced public communication. But, despite the mountains of data available to governments and other types of organizations, distrust, disengagement, and disillusionment have increased among citizens in many countries.

In fact, the collection and use of vast amounts of data—referred to as *big data*[34]—is contributing to public distrust in many instances. It does need to be acknowledged that collection and use of personal data is beneficial for citizens and society in many respects. For example, human data such as residential and work location, family status, age, health, income, and so on inform the provision of services such as public transport, schools, and hospitals, as well as the design and marketing of products. Anonymized aggregated data from populations also can identify trends and patterns that inform authorities and policy makers on matters ranging from child care to policing. However, there have been a growing number of misuses, leaks, hacks, and flagrant abuses in relation to data in recent years. In 2016, the UK National Health Service (NHS) Care.data initiative established to extract data from doctors' surgeries into a central database was scrapped amid controversy and public outrage at the lack of transparency and a lack of patient awareness of opt-out provisions.[35] The Australian Bureau of Statistics suffered reputational damage and a loss public trust when its 2016 national census data containing detailed personal information was compromised in a cyberattack.[36]

One of the most widely known and controversial misuses of data also occurred in 2016 when UK data analytics and political consulting firm Cambridge Analytica gained access to at least 50 million Facebook users' personal accounts and used the data to target voters during the UK EU referendum and the 2016 US presidential election.[37] Subsequent studies indicate that this use of Facebook data influenced the results of the elections.[38] Some reports suggest that the personal data of 87 million Facebook users was obtained by Cambridge Analytica.[39] Facebook handed over (presumably sold for a handsome fee) the personal data of its users despite repeated promises by founder Mark Zuckerberg that the company would protect users' personal data. In fact, reports indicate that hundreds of millions of Facebook users' passwords were accessible and searchable as far back as 2012 when the social media megalith first drew the ire of the US Federal Trade Commission (FTC).[40]

Even though Cambridge Analytica closed its operations in 2018 in the wake of investigations and legal actions, more than 100,000 documents were reportedly uncovered in early 2020 showing that the company had been involved in manipulating voters in 68 countries. Carole Cadwalladr reported that the leaks "lay bare the global infrastructure of an operation used to manipulate voters on an industrial scale."[41]

The highly publicized Facebook-Cambridge Analytica scandal is far from the only or the largest data security breach in recent years. *WIRED* magazine revealed in 2018 how 340 million personal records held by Florida data broker Exactis were exposed on a publicly accessible server. The two Terabytes of data relating to 230 million individuals and 110 million businesses contained addresses, phone numbers, e-mail addresses, and other highly personal information including the number, age and gender of individuals' children. In this case there was no evidence that hackers obtained and used the data. The breach of security occurred because the data was stored in an ElasticSearch database (https://www.elastic.co) that enabled easy access via the internet using readily available search tools. Vinny Troia, who founded the New York-based security company Night Lion Security, discovered the data in a simple internet search. These instances came on the back of the release of voter registration records of 93 million Mexican citizens; a 2017 leak of personal data of 145 million people by Equifax; and release of a list of 2.2 million "high risk" people suspected of crime or terrorism from the World Check Risk Screening database.[42] *WIRED* reporter Andy Greenberg says: "Massive leaks of user databases that are accidently left accessible on the public internet have nearly reached epidemic status. And other databases are left vulnerable to hacking or intentionally traded."[43]

As a result of public concern and criticism about the collection and use of data about people, the European Commission has introduced the General Data Protection Regulation (GDPR), and a number of organizations have formed to campaign for tighter controls in relation to data, such as We The Data (http://wethedata.org). Also, organizations such as the Data and Society Research Institute in New York (https://datasociety.net) conduct regular research into the collection of data, data analytics, and the growing use and implications of bots, algorithms, and other applications of artificial intelligence (AI).

Data analytics experts increasingly use *natural language processing* and *machine learning* to target people based on deep insights into their personal as well as professional lives. Algorithms, which are lines of computer code inside what are referred to as 'black boxes' because they are not transparent, automate many daily processes from news feeds, searching online, and calling an Uber to gaining approval for a loan. The increasing capabilities and application of AI is ushering in a whole new world of *datafication*, digital intelligence, and communications by, with, and through powerful machines. Are we ready for such technologies? Do we have the values, principles, guidelines, and standards that can guide the use of new technologies in ethical socially responsible ways? Far from enhancing communication in the true sense of the term, there are indications that powerful new technologies may only add to disinformation, deception, and manipulation. Aeron Davis notes that, far from facilitating society, new information and communication technologies (ICTs) along with globalization and neoliberalism are "the great disruptors" of contemporary societies.[44] In a seminal 2019 book, *The Costs of Connection: How Data Is Colonizing Human Life and Appropriating It for Capitalism*, Nick Couldry and Ulises Mejias warn that developed societies have entered a new era of colonialism in which citizens are being connected primarily to support and serve capitalism. In the process of being "colonized by data" communication becomes focussed on capturing, trading, and exploiting personal data for profit.[45] In short, communication is used *against* society rather than *for* society.

Such developments behove us to think hard about, or even rethink, the nature and purpose of communication. The origin of the noun communication and the verb communicate is:

> *communicatio / commūnicātiō* / noun (Latin) denotes sharing, from *communis* meaning common or public. The related Latin verb *communicare* means to make common or share.[46]

Contrary to popular usage of the term, communication is not simply transmitting information, speaking, or even persuasion. While persuasion can be part of the process, communication is about exchanging information and views to try to come to shared understandings, perceptions, and values. James Carey defined communication as "a symbolic process whereby reality is produced, maintained, repaired, and transformed."[47] In adding that communication is "an ensemble of social practices," Carey also said that "these practices constitute reality or (alternatively) can deny … it."[48] John Dewey reminded us that "society exists … in communication."[49] Conversely, society is impossible without communication in its true sense.

This book identifies and critically examines a development that underlies recent landmark events and which is coming to characterize public communication today. It argues that a key cause of *Brexit*; the election of Donald Trump; the public backlash in the 2017 UK general election that resulted in a 'hung parliament'; the decline of public trust in government, business, and even NGOs and non-profit organizations; and the seeming normalization of fake news and post-truth politics is the evolution of *post-communication*.

This analysis defines post-communication, not as a simple temporal transition compared with an earlier idealized period or mythical golden age, but as an evolution in which the principles, properties, and characteristics that are traditionally identified with communication are superseded and replaced by antithetical features. As in many uses of the prefix 'post', this signifies a deterioration or even a collapse of public communication from its normative purpose of informing, meaning making, and creating understanding to disinformation, deception, and exploitive manipulation. As Boston University philosopher Lee McIntyre says in relation to the term post-truth, the prefix post is not meant simply to indicate that we have evolved "past" the following noun in chronological terms, but that the noun (the named thing) "has been eclipsed—that it is irrelevant."[50] In the very least, this analysis shows that the existence of truth and communication is under threat without urgent and appropriate intervention.

While rhetoric and spin have long been a feature of politics, and misinformation and disinformation have been disseminated throughout human history, this analysis presents evidence that these dysfunctional practices are proliferating in political and government communication today. Also, corporate and marketing communication are increasingly characterized by disinformation, deception, and exploitive manipulation. This proliferation is being aided by largely unregulated social media and increasingly powerful ICTs such as data analytics, machine learning algorithms, bots, and other artificial intelligence (AI) applications. However, technologies do not do things of their own accord—not even robots. This analysis also looks at human behaviours in relation to public communication and finds much to be concerned about. Post-communication is ultimately the creation of humans.

The term post-communication is not new, but it has received little attention since it was used in 1966 as the title of a study of rhetoric and rhetorical criticism by Robert Cathcart.[51] Echoing the traditions of classical Greek and Roman oratory and the writings of Aristotle, Cicero, and Quintilian, Cathcart described rhetoric as "a communicator's intentional use of language and other symbols to influence or persuade selected receivers to act, believe, or feel the way the communicator desires."[52] Other studies note that rhetoric can be "invitational"[53] for multiple speakers to exchange views in dialogue and debate, or "manipulative."[54] Cathcart's definition tends towards the latter, as it describes one-way persuasion. Furthermore, his use of the term post-communication narrowly refers to retrospective reflection, analysis, and evaluation to identify ways to make rhetoric more effective in persuading others "to act, believe, or feel the way the communicator desires." Such definitions and discussion conflate communication and one-way persuasion that, when taken to extremes, leads to propaganda and exploitive manipulation. This is particularly the case when, as critics warn, rhetoricians often feel justified in deploying all the powers of oratory, symbolism, and communication technologies available to them.

As noted above, technologies applied in public communication are advancing rapidly, often ahead of policy development and legislation, and reaching previously unforeseen levels of utility and sophistication. Data analytics to profile people and target them based on intelligence, techniques such as behavioural economics and behavioural insights,[55] and the use of bots, algorithms, and other advancements in artificial intelligence (AI), put more resources and potentially more power in the hands of political, governmental, and commercial organizations and therefore warrant close scrutiny.

There have been a number of critiques of the current state of public communication focused on post-truth, some of which are polemical and somewhat colloquial, such as Evan Davis's *Post-Truth: Why We Have Reached Peak Bullshit and What We Can Do About It* (Little Brown, UK, 2017) and James Ball's *Post-Truth: How Bullshit Conquered the World* (Biteback Publishing, London, 2018). There also have been many books reviewing the election of Donald Trump, *Brexit*, and related issues including:

- *The Making of the President 2016: How Donald Trump Orchestrated a Revolution* by Roger Stone (Skyhorse, New York, 2017);
- *How Trump Won: The Inside Story of a Revolution* by Joel Pollak and Larry Schweikart (Regnery, Washington DC, 2017);
- All Out War: The Full Story of How Brexit Sank Britain's Political Class by Tim Shipman (William Collins, London, 2016); and
- Brexit: What the Hell Happens Now? Everything You Need to Know about Britain's Divorce from Europe by Ian Dunt (Canbury Press, UK, 2016).

This book takes a different approach to these and other critiques in that it looks beyond the high-profile social media antics and public performances of individuals such as Donald Trump, the leaders of the *Brexit* campaign, and troll farms in Russia or China. As David Runciman states in his 2018 book *How Democracy Ends*, "it's not just Trump." Runciman argues: "His election is symptomatic of an overheated political climate that appears increasingly unstable, riven with mutual mistrust and intolerance, fuelled by wild accusations and online bullying, a dialogue of the deaf drowning each other out with noise."[56] In warning that democracy could end, Runciman says "we may not even notice that it is happening because we are looking in the wrong places."⁵⁷ This analysis turns the lens in a different direction to other analyses—a direction that will be uncomfortable for many living and working in the bosom of neoliberal capitalism and particularly those working in media and other professional communication roles.

In taking a different view and focussing on the public communication 'industry', as well as some related issues such as media literacy, this analysis challenges and rejects the doctrine of *selective depravity* that is frequently used as a guiding principle when examining aberrant or depraved behaviour. This is one of three doctrines, or belief systems, that are applied in theology to describe the nature of human kind, the others being the doctrine of "man's *natural goodness*" [gendered term in original] and the contrasting doctrine of *total depravity* based on the notion that humans are born with original sin and can only be saved by baptism, prayer, and adherence to religious rituals.⁵⁸ In a secular context, the doctrine of selective depravity was applied to PR by Marvin Olasky in a controversial 1980s article about various paradigms of PR. In discussing dysfunctions of the practice, Olasky summarized the doctrine of selective depravity as "don't blame us, it's them—the immoral outsiders who cause the trouble."⁵⁹ As theologian, R. J. Rushdoony said: "By isolating depravity in a particular class, race, or group, it implicitly locates virtue in all others, particularly in the defining group."⁶⁰ In relation to the issues discussed in this analysis, the doctrine of selective depravity leads to a conclusion that the descent into post-communication is caused by aberrant others at whom we can point the finger; the rest of us are OK. We can continue on as before because we are not the culprits.

It is true that systematic and sinister disinformation campaigns are being conducted by hostile states as part of political warfare, as discussed in a 2019 report by the RAND Corporation titled *Hostile Social Manipulation: Present Realities and Emerging Trends*.⁶¹ But this analysis focusses closer to home. It presents evidence that our own professionalized communication and information industries of advertising, marketing, PR, political and government communication, and even journalism, aided and abetted by technology giants such as Google, Facebook, and data analytics firms are complicit in post-communication. Furthermore, it argues that in some instances media and public communication professionals are systematically contributing to the corruption of the public sphere with post-communication.

Associate professor in the Department of Media and Communications at the London School of Economics and Political Science, Lee Edwards, almost stole my thunder for this analysis when she wrote in a 2018 blog post that "in societies soaked in promotional culture, Cambridge Analytica's work is the thin end of the wedge that industries such as public relations, advertising, and marketing have managed to insert into all areas of our lives." She went on to argue that:

> The origins of the current scandal lie not in lax oversight by Facebook, or in the amorality of Cambridge Analytica and its clients, but in the histories of promotional industries that have normalized the idea of manipulation in their professional practice, while marginalizing ethics and the public interest.[62]

Edwards proposed that, given recent scandals and rising concern about fake news and disinformation, deception, and manipulation, "one might expect the promotional industries to be doing a bit of soul-searching." But she lamented that "a search of industry association websites reveals precious little comment" other than placing blame "squarely on the shoulders of tech companies."[63] Sadly, and perhaps tellingly, there was only one short comment on Edwards' article. It went ignored by the vast and growing persuasion industry. Edwards' research will be further examined in discussing ethics and self-regulation of PR in Chapter 5.

In an even wider sense, those who create, like, retweet, and share online content without verifying its authenticity and accuracy are also complicit. Stanford University's Robert Proctor describes the current period of politics and public communication as the *age of agnotology*, referring to the study of culturally induced ignorance or doubt created by the distribution of inaccurate or misleading information. Proctor was one of the first to call out that "we're all complicit in spreading it."[64] Couldry and Mejias agree in relation to the collection and use of data, saying "we must acknowledge that we are, most of us, deeply complicit in the order of data colonialism, whether we like it or not."[65] This point is a key theme in this analysis. Founder and president of the Data and Society Research Institute, danah boyd, said in a 2019 address to the Digital Public Library of America conference: "Slowly and systematically, a virus has spread, using technology to systematically tear at the social fabric of public life."[66] She also raised the question of whether ignorance is "strategically manufactured"[67]—a notion that is explored in this analysis.

Lest it be thought that the 2016 US presidential campaign, *Brexit*, and the scandals related to use of Facebook data are already history and no longer relevant, a study by the Knight Foundation reported that 80% of the disinformation accounts that were active in 2016 were still in operation in late 2018.[68] While the study identified a peak of misinformation and disinformation during the 2016

US presidential election with 6.6 million tweets linking to fake and conspiracy news publishers in the month before the election, the flood of disinformation and deception continues today, as will be shown in Chapter 3.

A second key objective of this book is to look beyond analyzing problems facing democratic societies to try to identify strategies to redress the problems identified. Some suggest that we need to learn to live with post-truth. Just get used to it. For example, while exhibiting great prescience in his 2008 book titled *True Enough*, Farhad Manjoo sub-titled it and advanced his main argument as *Learning to Live in a Post-Fact Society*.[69] Conversely, in his 2018 book *Post-truth*, Lee McIntyre argues that the lesson is "one must always fight back against lies." However, McIntyre confines solutions to individual actions. Despite titling the final chapter of his otherwise excellent review 'Fighting post-truth', McIntyre says "we should learn how to vet news sources properly and ask ourselves how it is that we 'know' that something we are hearing is fake" or not.[70] Elsewhere in his book, McIntyre advocates that individuals use fact-checking websites such as PolitiFact, FactCheck, and Snopes to confirm the veracity of information.[71] This analysis indicates that far broader and more concerted actions are required to address the mess that democratic societies are in. In his wide-ranging analysis, *Crisis of Democracy*, Adam Przeworski warns against simplistic solutions and points to economic, social, and cultural factors that are affecting democracy today.

Aeron Davis has proposed three possible approaches to achieving democratic renewal, or a combination of the three. He says one option is to identify nations that appear to be more democratic, happier, more sustainable, and less divided and conflicted, and use such models as a template. This could be termed a *comparative approach*. Davis himself notes that there are difficulties with this approach, as not all countries are comparable. For example, countries that come out on top in democracy-rating studies, such as those of Freedom House, and happiness studies (e.g., the World Happiness Report[72]), are typically the Scandinavian nations of Sweden, Norway, and Denmark, along with Finland, Iceland and Switzerland. These have relatively small populations and, therefore, are more easily engaged and administered. Their populations are also mostly well educated. A second approach proposed by Davis is to identify the principles that should be applied to improve democracy. These might logically include transparency in government, fully independent media, and concerted action to address inequalities. However, this *first principles approach* is acknowledged by Davis as likely to encounter considerable debate and disagreement about what principles should apply. For example, the USA has quite different attitudes towards the right to bear arms and social welfare measures such as public health services than European countries. A third even broader approach proposed by Davis in the conclusions of his 2019 book is to "look critically at the theoretical foundations and norms of democracy itself."[73] This could be described as a *redefinition approach*, or a back to basics approach. This suggests asking critical questions about the nature of the public sphere and the capability of 'ordinary' citizens to contribute constructively to increasingly complex policy issues. While it is productive to constantly question our assumptions and theories, Davis poses a 'straw man' argument to some extent in suggesting that "we should admit that the Greek Agora or Habermassian-style public spheres of a past Europe are not real models to compare with."[74] Few today believe that the Agora of ancient Greece is a democratic model to follow, given that it excluded women and slaves who comprised a majority of the population of the city state. Also, Habermas's original concept of a deliberative public sphere has undergone considerable revision in his own more recent writing and in others' interpretations, as discussed in the following.

Solutions, it must be acknowledged, depend on what sort of democracy one believes is necessary and realistic. As Davis notes, there has been a long-running debate over whether "liberal, limited, rational choice models of representative democracy" are satisfactory, or whether republican style "participatory democracy" with higher levels of direct involvement by citizens is what works best.[75] Then there is the question of whether 'best' is practical. Do people really want to participate directly in democratic processes—and will they when it comes to the crunch? Beyond the broad frameworks that Davis mentions, at least 10 models of democracy have been proposed including liberal, representative, deliberative, monitory, direct or participatory, agonistic, dialogic, and communicative democracy.[76] There is general agreement that Habermas's original deliberative public sphere is normative and impractical—even naïve, according to some.[77] However, in fairness to Habermas, it is important to read his more recent descriptions of deliberative democracy applicable to large, complex modern societies including his two-track system in which he focusses less on the role of mass media and more on citizens participating, often informally, in multiple overlapping spheres[78]—a concept that is similar to the notion of *public sphericles*.[79] The models of democracy that can work in nations with small populations, such as the Nordic countries, are inevitably different to those that are practical in large, diverse societies such as the USA. However, given descriptions of the USA as a "failed state," something better than its current iteration of liberal democracy is desirable. Also something substantially better than the quagmire of UK post-*Brexit* politics and Australia's police raids on media newsrooms and gagging of journalists (see Chapter 5) seems essential.

In their sociological analysis, Couldry and Mejias refer to a number of strategies for addressing what they describe as *data colonialism*, including media literacy, civic activism, and regulation and legislation. However, they argue, rightly, that addressing the negative impacts of datafication requires more. They say "we must set our sights higher," calling for a broader vision and approaches. Their proposals, as well as others are examined in Chapters 5 and 6.

Based on interviews with researchers, thought leaders, and media and communication professionals; an extensive review of recent academic and professional literature; and critical analysis; this text proposes 10 strategies to reverse the corruption of public debate and dialogue that many see as essential for the survival of democracy and for an equitable stable civil society. These strategies focus on public communication because of its centrality in politics and society, as noted previously and throughout this analysis. Other scholars contribute a sociological and comparative politics perspective, such as Couldry and Mejias's critique of capitalism, neoliberalism, and colonialism, and Przeworski's focus on economic, social, and cultural factors that are contributing to populism, polarization, and post-truth.

It could be argued that attempting to identify and discuss 10 areas for focus in relation to public communication is too broad a task to undertake in a single volume. While researching and writing this book I apprehensively imagined the voices of critics saying that it attempts to cover too many issues and too many fields of practice. The following pages discuss fake news; alternative facts; misinformation; disinformation; post-truth; truth; trust; distrust; disengagement; advertising; marketing; PR; journalism; political, corporate, and organizational communication; and a range of information and communication technologies. However, there is a compelling logic and rationale for the multidimensional and interdisciplinary approach taken. This analysis starts by examining fake news, alternative facts, and disinformation in politics because they are phenomena of current and considerable public concern. But, in addition to the deceptions and manipulation created by political disinformation, it shows that marketing and corporate communication including related practices such as advertising and PR propagate deception and manipulation—often on an even larger scale than politics. A third consideration is that disinformation, deception, and manipulation spread unchecked when independent media and journalism fail to effectively perform their Fourth Estate role, which is the case in many countries. A fourth factor that makes this analysis timely and even urgent is the rapid and exponential increase in scope and scale of disinformation, deception, and manipulation that can be wreaked upon society through the use, and misuse, of new technologies. This is particularly the case when self-regulation is lacking and regulation is minimal. Data analytics, bots, algorithms, and artificial intelligence are each topics for specialized analysis, as many authors have done and commendably continue to do. Nevertheless, the following analysis shows that these concepts and practices are interconnected. Narrowing the lens to focus on a single discipline or field of practice, or a small selection or sample of activities, obscures both the breadth of the problem of post-communication and the interrelated causal elements that interact in the public communication ecosystem.

This approach borrows from the aviation crash investigation field. Aviation safety experts have shown that catastrophes involving aircraft are almost always the result of a series of failures and rarely caused by the breakdown of a single system or part. For example, investigations into hull failure have revealed as many as 20 links in a chain of events that lead to a fatal result, with an average of four contributing factors. Investigations into controlled flight into terrain (CFIT) accidents have identified that at least 10 causal factors are involved and go on to conclude that "if any one of these 10 causes had not been present … the accident would not have happened."[80] Apart from cases of intentional high impact attacks, catastrophic failure is always multi-causal.

In the context of this analysis, if journalism is independent and equipped and resolved to do its job, political spin, marketing, and PR will not be able to significantly corrupt the public sphere. Conversely, if advertising, marketing, and PR practitioners act ethically, weakened journalism will not pose such a threat to society. If social media platforms operate responsibly, threats to privacy and harmful content such as hate speech will not proliferate as much as they do. But, equally, media literacy and self-responsibility are required on the part of individuals because all risks cannot be eliminated. While self-regulation is an important element in media and culture industries, media organizations may not sufficiently safeguard consumers without appropriate regulation and even legislation by government. And so on. Societies are facing serious threat and potentially catastrophic collapse because of a series of simultaneous failures, and it only through multiple elements doing their part that the total system can be made to function effectively.

For example, this analysis has some critical things to say about PR. But in an interview that I was very keen to do, Lucas Bernays Held—a PR practitioner and the grandson of Edward Bernays, who is described as the "father of public relations"[81]—legitimately argued:

Even if 100% of all PR professionals were to conduct themselves in strict accordance with the highest standards of truth, the problem of disinformation and misinformation would remain. This is not to say that it is not essential that they act with probity; rather, that this alone won't solve the problem.[82]

A Perfect Storm Scenario

This multi-faceted, transdisciplinary analysis is brought together and is relevant now because elements that can combine to produce a perfect storm are amassing in our techno-sociopolitical world. As discussed in the following chapters, in the space of one decade developed Western societies have seen:

- The collapse of traditional media business models and the atrophying of independent journalism;
- Unprecedented growth in new forms of largely unregulated social media platforms, networks, search engines, streaming services, and other forms of 'new media';
- Rapid growth of PR and new forms of 'strategic' corporate and government communication;
- A shift from recognizable (i.e., transparent) mass media advertising to hidden persuasion through *native advertising*, sponsored content, and paid social media influencers, as marketers and media organizations seek new ways to reach fragmented audiences and circumvent ad blocking technologies and cognitive resistance in order to generate revenue;
- Escalating growth in surveillance and dataveillance through digital technologies ranging from cameras and 'cookies' to intelligent personal assistants (IPAs) and face recognition software;
- Accumulation of vast amounts of personal data that, despite assurances of data security and privacy, are being traded and used for commercial exploitation and political manipulation;
- Rapid continuing development of disruptive ICTs such as bots, learning algorithms, and other advances in AI;
- The intrusion of neoliberalism and the economic principles of capitalism and marketization into government, which leads to citizens being conceptualized as *target audiences, customers,* and *consumers* rather than constituents, resulting in erosion of democratic participation and engagement, and thus the legitimacy of democratic governments and institutions.

The Framework and Context of This Analysis

While many of the issues discussed in this book relate to political science and sociology, this analysis is undertaken within the context of human communication theory and specifically within the frameworks of political, government, and corporate communication and related practices such as advertising and PR. It is also informed by media studies related to traditional and social media. This approach is based on a large body of literature that shows communication between people and between organizations and people in the public sphere is the lifeblood of politics and human society as well as the operations of institutions and commerce—particularly in democratic societies that are the setting for this analysis.

Analysis of what is called post-communication and proposed strategies to address the problems discussed are specifically informed by a number of concepts and theories in relation to why people are susceptible to false information and deception, and how they deal with such issues, drawn from sociopsychological, sociocultural, and phenomenological approaches to communication studies. These include:

- *Selective exposure*—many internet users consume information in *echo chambers* and *filter bubbles*, hearing only information that aligns with their existing views;[83]
- *Selective attention*—even when alternative information is available, people often select information that aligns with and reinforces their existing beliefs;
- *Confirmation bias*—the resulting confirmation of existing beliefs that occurs as a result of selection exposure, selective attention, or illusory correlations;
- *Cognitive dissonance*—the well known psychological concept first proposed by Leon Festinger to describe how people seek out information that is consonant with their existing beliefs and behaviours and resist or reject information that is dissonant with their existing beliefs or behaviours;[84]
- *Motivated reasoning*—a tendency to seek out information that supports a person's existing beliefs or what they want to believe. Motivated reasoning seeks out consonance and, therefore, is a strategy to mitigate cognitive dissonance;[85]
- *Belief persistence*—a tendency for people to hold on to beliefs even in the face of contrary information;
- *Cultural cognition*—a theory proposed by Dan Kahan, which posits that people's beliefs derives from their cultural worldviews, even when empirical

evidence indicates the contrary. This makes it similar to confirmation bias, belief persistence, and motivated reasoning;[86]
- *Reactance*—a tendency to react against requests or arguments that appear to pressure a person or restrict a person's free speech and freedom to choose;[87]
- *Third person effect*—a common view among people that they are not affected by influences such as advertising, propaganda, media portrayals of violence, or disinformation, but others are;[88]
- *Attribution error*—influences such as motivated reasoning, confirmation bias, and other personal and situational factors lead to people wrongly attributing blame or praise.[89] For example, if others are duped by a hoax they are often seen as gullible and stupid (i.e., it is their own fault), whereas if oneself is duped, we tend to see ourselves as innocent victims and blame the perpetrators;
- *Inoculation theory*—a body of theory on ways to inoculate or immunize people against certain influences such as false information and propaganda;[90]
- *Backfire effects*—the finding from some studies that correction of misinformation or disinformation can cause reinforcement of existing beliefs rather than a change of beliefs.[91] Other studies have challenged this theory, as discussed in Chapter 6.

Study of disinformation, deception, and manipulation through media, particularly social media, and responses to these dysfunctions, is likely to cause some rethinking of *media effects* theory as well as *uses and gratifications* theory—a long-held set of views on what people do with media as opposed to the common media effects focus on what media do to people. As well as using media for news and information, entertainment, relaxation, escape, relieving loneliness, social connection, identify construction, and surveillance of the environment, contemporary research suggests an expansion of uses to include activism, social and political disruption, and even new practices of *informational terrorism*.

Many authors have written on the issues discussed in the following pages. But my experiences and vantage points, along with primary research, arguably afford some different perspectives that can contribute to understanding and new directions. I spent the first 20 years of my professional life working in media and communication as a journalist and then as a public relations practitioner for corporate and government organizations. I then founded and headed a research company that specialized in media and communication research for more than a decade. In particular, the research firm tracked media reporting and evaluated the communication campaigns of big business and government nationally and internationally.

After selling this company to a large media group, I joined the academy to focus on in-depth media and communication research, particularly developments such as social media and the rise of *strategic communication* in government as well as corporations and other types of organizations.

Methodology and Sources

As well as drawing on many years of experience working inside the media and public communication practices that are critically examined in the following pages, this book is informed by five years of primary and secondary research conducted between early 2015 and the end of 2019. In 2015, I initiated an international research study that closely examined the public communication of large corporate, government, and non-government organizations in Australia, the UK, and the USA. This focussed particularly on how and how well organizations engage with and listen to their various stakeholders such as customers, employees, members, local communities, and citizens. The rationale of this study (The Organizational Listening Project) was that without listening, engagement, participation, and dialogue, the democratic public sphere and indeed all communication become meaningless and pointless. Following the 2015 research, I was fortunate in 2016 to receive funding to study public communication coordinated by the UK Government Communication Service (GCS) while I was on research sabbatical at The London School of Economics and Political Science. I went to live in London in May 2016, unknowingly on the eve of a momentous event. Just one month after I arrived and my wife and I settled in to an apartment in Bloomsbury within walking distance of LSE and a short Tube ride to Whitehall, the EU referendum was held resulting in the long and bumpy road to *Brexit*. During the ensuing seven months (June–December 2016) I conducted interviews, content analysis of documents, and ethnography with senior officials and staff inside the UK Cabinet Office and Number 10, Downing Street where the GCS is co-headquartered, and with more than a dozen UK government departments and agencies.

In the same period, I was invited as an independent researcher to advise the Directorate-General for Communication (DG COMM) of the European Commission in Brussels, which afforded access to communication strategies, plans, and activities conducted across the then 28 member states of the European Union (EU). I found officials perturbed, but discrete about the UK's impending exit from the EU. As it turned out, they had other equal or even bigger problems, with trust in and support for the EU weak and weakening in a number of member countries. For example, the quarterly *Eurobarometer* survey in Spring 2016 found that only 36% of Europeans trusted the European Union compared with 40% in Spring 2015.[92]

At the same time, the election campaign juggernaut of Donald Trump raged across the US hustings, leading up to his inauguration on 20 January 2017 as the 45th President of the United States of America. I was a keen observer of this seismic shift in US politics and political communication and interviewed a number of communication and media professionals in New York and Washington, D.C.

Subsequently, after publishing findings from my 2015 and 2016 research,[93] I was invited to meet with a range of community groups, community organizers, activist organizations, charities, foundations, and think tanks in the UK, USA, and Europe. Several common themes and concerns emerged from those meetings and my three years of research to that time.

In addition, before taking up my research sabbatical in the UK and again in 2017 after my return to the University of Technology Sydney, I was contracted to undertake research examining public communication by the state government of New South Wales (NSW) in my home country, working with the Department of Premier and Cabinet.

Then, between 2017 and 2019 I was invited back several times by the UK Government Communication Service to review attempts to improve engagement and communication with UK citizens as the plans for *Brexit* rolled out—not an easy task given that more than 48% of citizens who voted against *Brexit* and many young people who did not vote expressed opposition to withdrawal from the EU. I was also invited back to Brussels to share in discussions of the European Commission's *Strategic Communication Plan 2016–2020* and was involved in reviewing and evaluating a number of EC communication campaigns as part of a consortium working with Deloitte, Brussels and Coffey International in London.

In 2018 and 2019, as well as continuing my research interest in government and political communication, my focus turned to business and the practices of large corporations, a sector that also suffered a decline of public trust as democratic societies edged precariously towards the third decade of the 21st century.

This analysis draws from this research, which included more than 300 interviews with communication professionals in government, politics, business, NGOs, and activist organizations in Australia, the UK, the USA, and Europe during the five years, as well as seven months of full-time ethnography inside major government departments and agencies in the UK, and content analysis of more than 600 strategy and policy documents.

As with all research, this analysis is also informed by many years of reading academic and professional literature across a number of disciplines including political, government, and corporate communication, PR, journalism, media studies, marketing, and digital communications technology. The research of many others has been informative in undertaking this analysis.

Most recently and specifically, this book is informed by in-depth interviews with 30 senior scholars and leading professionals working in journalism, PR, and political, government, and corporate communication in Australia, Europe, the UK, and the USA to discuss the issues of disinformation, deception, and manipulation. In addition to open-ended conversations, four key questions were put in interviews and explored in analysis as follows:

1. To what extent are disinformation, post-truth politics, and the collapse of public trust in media, government, politics, and business major threats to be addressed, or are these simply contemporary manifestations of what has occurred throughout human history [*What is the extent of the problem?*].
2. To what extent will new information and communication technologies such as data analytics, algorithms, bots, and AI redress or exacerbate the decline of public trust and corruption of the public sphere through disinformation, deception, and manipulation? [*Will technology provide solutions or exacerbate the problem?*]
3. To what extent are disinformation, deception, and manipulation the work of a few individuals and groups such as Donald Trump and his supporters, Russian trolls, etc., or are the causes more widespread? [*Who is responsible for the problem?*]
4. What, if anything, should be done, and by whom, to protect people against disinformation, deception, and manipulation; rebuild trust in government, institutions, politics, media and business; and facilitate open authentic dialogue and debate in the public sphere? [*What should be done by whom?*]

Some interviews and documents are de-identified either because of Human Research Ethics Committee requirements or based on the request of the individuals involved in signed consent forms. However, most conclusions and data supporting them are referenced in endnotes throughout this book in the interests of transparency and credibility.

Modesty and critical thinking requires acknowledgement that many of the strategies proposed are not new or exclusive to this analysis. Some have been discussed for some time in articles and books and a few have been advocated as a 'silver bullet' that can transform society. The approach proposed in this analysis seeks to avoid simplistic solutions and recognize the complexity of the challenges facing contemporary democratic societies. It is reasonable to say that there are 'wicked' problems facing societies. Thus, a single solution is unlikely. All of the strategies discussed will be required, and probably more, to restore dialogue and debate that involve true *communication* as it defined and identified as central to democracy and civilized society.

Notes

1. Putnam, R. (1995). Bowling alone: America's declining social capital. *Journal of Democracy, 61*(1), 65–78; Putnam, R. (2000). *Bowling alone: The collapse and revival of America community*. New York, NY: Simon & Schuster.
2. Bourdieu, P. (1986). The forms of capital. In J. Richardson (Ed.), *Handbook of theory and research in the sociology of education* (pp. 241–258). New York, NY: Greenwood Press.
3. Gates, W. (2018, January 4). Why I decided to edit an issue of TIME. *TIME* magazine. Retrieved from http://time.com/5086870/bill-gates-guest-editor-time, paras 2–3.
4. Fukuyama, F. (2016, December 13). America: The failed state. *Prospect*. Retrieved from http://www.prospectmagazine.co.uk/magazine/america-the-failed-state-donald-trump
5. Yes, I'd lie to you. (2016, September 10). *The Economist*. Retrieved from http://www.economist.com/news/briefing/21706498-dishonesty-politics-nothing-new-manner-which-some-politicians-now-lie-and
6. Oxford Dictionaries. (2016). Oxford Dictionaries word of the year: Post-truth. Retrieved from https://en.oxforddictionaries.com/word-of-the-year/word-of-the-year-2016
7. Is truth dead? (2017, April 3). *TIME* magazine. Retrieved from https://time.com/4709920/donald-trump-truth-time-cover
8. World Health Organization. (2020). Novel coronavirus (2019-nCoV). Situation report 13. Geneva. Retrieved from https://www.who.int/docs/default-source/coronaviruse/situation-reports/20200202-sitrep-13-ncov-v3.pdf
9. Posetti, J., & Bontcheva, K. (2020). Disinfodemic: Dissecting responses to COVID-19 disinformation – Policy Brief 2. UNESCO. Retrieved from https://en.unesco.org/covid19/disinfodemic
10. Harsin, J. (2015). Regimes of posttruth, postpolitics, and attention economies. *Communication, Culture & Critique, 8*(2), 327–333, p. 327.

24 | *Introduction*

11. Harvard University. (2015). *Trust in institutions and the political process*. Boston, MA: Institute of Politics. Retrieved from http://www.iop.harvard.edu/trust-institutions-and-political-process
12. The Open Government Partnership (OGP) Practice Group on Dialogue and Deliberation. (2019, May). *Deliberation: Getting policy-making out from behind closed doors*, p. 6. Retrieved from https://www.opengovpartnership.org/documents/deliberation-getting-policy-making-out-from-behind-closed-doors
13. Edelman. (2020). *2020 Edelman Trust Barometer*. Retrieved from https://www.edelman.com/trustbarometer
14. Edelman, 2019.
15. Ibid.
16. Boris Johnson became Prime Minister of the UK in July 2019 based on a vote by members of his political party, not a general election.
17. Audickas, L., Dempsey, N., & Keen, R. (2018). Membership of UK political parties. Commons Briefing Papers SN05125. London, UK: House of Commons. Retrieved from https://researchbriefings.parliament.uk/ResearchBriefing/Summary/SN05125. While this official record reports UK Conservative Party membership as 180,000 in 2019, Boris Johnson's 2019 election as UK Prime Minister was based on 92,153 votes to Jeremy Hunt's 46,656, which was an estimated turnout of 87.4% of Conservative Party members. This would put the party's membership at 159,320, according to Stewart, H. (2019, July 23). Boris Johnson elected new Tory leader. *The Guardian*. Retrieved from https://www.theguardian.com/politics/2019/jul/23/boris-johnson-elected-new-tory-leader-prime-minister
18. Davis, (2019). *Political communication: A new introduction for crisis times*. Cambridge, UK: Cambridge University Press, p. 205.
19. Crouch, C. (2013, February 5). Five minutes with Colin Crouch. London, UK: London School of Economics and Political Science [Web log post]. Retrieved from http://blogs.lse.ac.uk/politicsandpolicy/five-minutes-with-colin-crouch
20. Jan, A. (2003). *The end of democracy*. Canada: Pragmatic Publishing.
21. Davis, 2019, p. 7.
22. Ibid., p. 42.
23. Economist Intelligence Unit. (2016). *Democracy index 2016/2017* (9th /10th ed.). London, UK.
24. Mason, P. (2015). *Postcapitalism: A guide to our future*. London, UK: Allen Lane; Streeck, W. (2016). *How will capitalism end? Essays on a failing system*. London, UK: Verso.
25. Spinney, L. (2018, January 17). End of days: Is Western civilisation on the brink of collapse? *New Scientist*. Retrieved from https://www.newscientist.com/article/mg23731610-300-end-of-days-is-western-civilisation-on-the-brink-of-collapse
26. Freeman, R. (1984). *Strategic management: A stakeholder approach*. London: Pitman, p. 25. While Freeman is mostly recognized for developing stakeholder theory, Ian

Mitroff, an American organizational theorist and Professor Emeritus at the Marshall School of Business and the Annenberg School for Communication at the University of Southern California, published a book titled *Stakeholders of the Organizational Mind* in 1983.

27. Davis, 2019, p. 129.
28. Statista. (2019). Global advertising spending from 2014 to 2021. Retrieved from https://www.statista.com/statistics/273288/advertising-spending-worldwide
29. E-marketer. (2018, May 4). Global ad spending. Retrieved from https://www.emarketer.com/content/global-ad-spending
30. PRCA (Public Relations Consultants Association). (2017). PR census 2016. Retrieved from http://news.prca.org.uk/publications
31. ICCO [International Communications Consultancy Organization]. (2013). *ICCO world report*. Retrieved from http://www.akospr.ru/wp-content/uploads/2014/01/World-Report_en.pdf
32. University of Southern California, Annenberg. (2018). *2018 global communications report*. Los Angeles, CA: Author. Retrieved from https://annenberg.usc.edu/research/center-public-relations/global-communications-report
33. Described as "The fastest-growing type of data, covering the entire spectrum of human-generated information, shared across social networks, blogs, news sites and inside the business". See Datasift. (2020). Human data glossary, para. 14. Retrieved from https://datasift.com/glossary
34. Any collection of data so large and complex that it becomes difficult to process using standard data management tools or applications. (Datasift, 2020, para. 5.)
35. Goodlee, F. (2016). What can we salvage from care.data? *BMJ [British Medical Journal]*, *354*, i3907. Retrieved from https://www.bmj.com/content/354/bmj.i3907
36. Westbrook, T. (2016, August 10). Australia's controversial census in chaos after cyber attack. *Reuters*, Technology News. Retrieved from https://www.reuters.com/article/us-australia-census-crash-idUSKCN10L0FM
37. Hindman, M. (2018, March 30). How Cambridge Analytica's Facebook targeting model really worked—according to the person who built it. *The Conversation*. Retrieved from https://theconversation.com/how-cambridge-analyticas-facebook-targeting-model-really-worked-according-to-the-person-who-built-it-94078
38. Gunther, R., Beck, P., & Nisbet, E. (2018). *Fake news did have a significant impact on the vote in the 2016 election*. Columbus: Ohio State University. Retrieved from https://cpb-us-w2.wpmucdn.com/u.osu.edu/dist/d/12059/files/2015/03/Fake-News-Piece-for-The-Conversation-with-methodological-appendix-11d0ni9.pdf
39. Goodwin, B., & Skelton, S. (2019, July 1). Facebook's privacy game—How Zuckerberg backtracked on promises to protect personal data. *Computer Weekly*, para. 7. Retrieved from https://www.computerweekly.com/feature/Facebooks-privacy-U-turn-how-Zuckerberg-backtracked-on-promises-to-protect-personal-data

40. Vaidhyanathan, S. (2019, July 26). Billion-dollar fines can't stop Google and Facebook. That's peanuts for them. *The Guardian*. Retrieved from https://www.theguardian.com/commentisfree/2019/jul/26/google-facebook-regulation-ftc-settlement; The Reputation Institute. (2019, April 30). Facebook's corporate reputation in freefall [Web log post]. Retrieved from https://www.reputationinstitute.com/blog/facebooks-corporate-reputation-free-fall
41. Cadwalladr, C. (2020, January 5). Fresh Cambridge Analytica leak 'shows global manipulation is out of control'. *The Guardian*, para. 2. Retrieved from https://www.theguardian.com/uk-news/2020/jan/04/cambridge-analytica-data-leak-global-election-manipulation
42. Greenberg, A. (2018, June 27). Marketing firm Exactis leaked a personal info database with 340 million records. *WIRED*. Retrieved from https://www.wired.com/story/exactis-database-leak-340-million-records
43. Ibid., para. 11.
44. Davis, 2019, p. 46.
45. Couldry, N., & Mejias, U. (2019). *The costs of connection: How data is colonizing human life and appropriating it for capitalism*. Stanford, CA: Stanford University Press, p. x.
46. Peters, J. (2008). Communication: History of the idea. In W. Donsbach (Ed.), *The international encyclopedia of communication* (n.p.). Malden, MA: Blackwell. Retrieved from https://onlinelibrary.wiley.com/doi/abs/10.1002/9781405186407.wbiecc075
47. Carey. J. (2009). *Communication as culture: Essays on media and culture* (Rev. ed.). New York, NY: Routledge, p. 19. (Original work published 1989)
48. Ibid., p. 65.
49. Dewey, J. (1916). *Democracy and education*. New York, NY: Macmillan, p. 5.
50. McIntyre, L. (2018). *Post-truth*. Cambridge, MA: MIT Press, p. 5.
51. Cathcart, R. (1981). *Post-communication: Rhetorical analysis and evaluation*. Indianapolis, IN: Bobbs-Merrill. (Original work published 1966)
52. Cathcart, 1981, p. 2.
53. Foss, S., & Griffin, C. (1995). Beyond persuasion: A proposal for an invitational rhetoric. *Communication Monographs*, *62*, 2–18.
54. Heath, R. (2006). A rhetorical theory approach to issues. In C. Botan & V. Hazelton (Eds.), *Public relations theory II* (pp. 63–99). Mahwah, NJ: Lawrence Erlbaum.
55. While it emerged from economics, this field of research and practice draws heavily on psychology to identify irrational (i.e. emotional) as well as rational 'triggers' of behaviour which can be activated to achieve economic or other goals.
56. Runciman, D. (2018). *How democracy ends*. New York, NY: Hachette, pp. 1–2.
57. Runciman, 2018, p. 3.
58. Rushdoony, R. (2016, June 10). Doctrine of selective depravity: Parts 1–111. *Chalcedon Magazine*. Retrieved from https://chalcedon.edu/magazine/doctrine-of-selective-depravity-parts-i-iii

59. Olasky, M. (1989). The aborted debate within public relations: An approach through Kuhn's paradigm. *Journal of Public Relations Research*, 1(1–4), 87–95, p. 88.
60. Rushdoony, 2016, para. 11.
61. Mazarr, M., Casey, A., Demus, A., Harold, S., Matthews, L., Beauchamp-Mustafaga, N., & James Sladden, J. (2019). *Hostile social manipulation: Present realities and emerging trends*. Santa Monica, CA: RAND Corporation, p. ix.
62. Edwards, L. (2018, March 26). Cambridge Analytica: A symptom of a deeper malaise in the persuasion industry. London School of Economics and Political Science, *Polis* [Web log post], para. 6. Retrieved from https://blogs.lse.ac.uk/polis/2018/03/26/cambridge-analytica-a-symptom-of-a-deeper-malaise-in-the-persuasion-industry
63. Ibid., para. 7.
64. Agnotology: Understanding our ignorance. (2017, January 29). ABC, *Future Tense*. Retrieved from https://www.abc.net.au/radionational/programs/futuretense/agnotology:-understanding-our-ignorance/8123452#transcript
65. Couldry & Mejias, 2019, p. 194.
66. boyd, d. (2019, April 26). Agnotology and epistemology fragmentation. *Points*, Data and Society Research Institute, para. 1. Retrieved from https://points.datasociety.net/agnotology-and-epistemological-fragmentation-56aa3c509c6b
67. Ibid., para. 4.
68. Hindman, M., & Barash, V. (2018, October). *Disinformation, 'fake news' and influence campaigns on Twitter*. Miami, FL: Knight Foundation, p. 3.
69. Manjoo, F. (2008). *True enough: Learning to live in a post-fact society*. Hoboken, NJ: Wiley.
70. McIntyre, 2018, p. 163.
71. Ibid., p. 117.
72. Helliwell, J., Layard, R., & Sachs, J. (Eds.). (2019). *World happiness report*. New York, NY: United Nations Sustainable Development Solutions Network. Retrieved from https://worldhappiness.report/ed/2019
73. Davis, 2019, p. 214.
74. Ibid.
75. Ibid., p. 19.
76. Carpentier, N. (2011). *Media and participation: A site of ideological democratic struggle*. Chicago, IL: Intellect; Dobson, A. (2014). *Listening for democracy: Recognition, representation, reconciliation*. Oxford, UK: Oxford University Press; Habermas, J. (1989). *The structural transformation of the public sphere*. Cambridge, UK: Polity. (Original work published 1962); Keane, J. (2009). *The life and death of democracy*. New York, NY: W. W. Norton & Co.; Mouffe, C. (2005). *On the political*. London, UK: Routledge.
77. Davis, 2019, p. 22.
78. Habermas, J. (1996). *Between facts and norms*. Cambridge, UK: Cambridge University Press.

79. Gitlin, T. (1998). Public spheres or public sphericles? In T. Liebes & J. Curran (Eds.), *Media, ritual and identity* (pp. 170–173). New York, NY: Routledge.
80. Committee on Aircraft Safety Certification Management. (1998). Causes of incidents and accidents, Chapter 3 in *Improving the continued airworthiness of civil aircraft*. Washington, DC: National Academy Press, para. 2. Retrieved from https://www.nap.edu/read/6265/chapter/5
81. Guth, D., & Marsh, C. (2007). *Public relations: A values-driven approach* (3rd ed.). Boston, MA: Pearson Education, p. 70.
82. L. Held (personal communication [interview], August 28, 2019).
83. Bryant, J., & Davies, J. (2008). Selective exposure. In W. Donsbach (Ed.), *The international encyclopedia of communication, 10*. Blackwell. pp. 4544–4550.
84. Festinger, L. (1957). *A theory of cognitive dissonance*. Palo Alto, CA: Stanford University Press.
85. Lodge, M., & Taber, C. (2000). Three steps toward a theory of motivated political reasoning. In A. Lupia, M. McCubbins, & S. Popkin (Eds.), *Elements of reason: Cognition, choice and bounds of rationality* (pp. 183–213). Cambridge, UK: Cambridge University Press.
86. Kahan, D., & Braman, D. (2006). Cultural cognition and public policy. *Faculty Scholarship Series, 103*, 146–170.
87. Quick, B. (2016). Psychological reactance. In D. Kim & J. Dearing (Eds.), *Health communication research measures* (pp. 173–181). New York, NY: Peter Lang.
88. Davison, W. P. (1983). The third person effect in communication. *Public Opinion Quarterly, 47*, 1–15.
89. Heider, F. (1958). *The psychology of interpersonal relations*. New York, NY: Wiley.
90. Compton, J. (2013). Inoculation theory. In J. Dillard & L. Shen (Eds.), *The SAGE handbook of persuasion: Developments in theory and practice* (2nd ed., pp. 220–236). Thousand Oaks, CA: Sage Publications.
91. Nyhan, B., & Reifler, J. (2010). When corrections fail: The persistence of political misperceptions. *Political Behaviour, 32*(2), 303–330.
92. European Commission. (2016). *Standard Eurobarometer 86 Autumn 2016*. Brussels. Retrieved from http://ec.europa.eu/commfrontoffice/publicopinion/index.cfm/Survey/index#p=1&instruments=STANDARD&yearFrom=1974&yearTo=2016
93. Macnamara, J. (2015, June). *Creating an 'architecture of listening' in organizations: The basis of trust, engagement, healthy democracy, social equity, and business sustainability*. Sydney, NSW: University of Technology Sydney. Retrieved from http://www.uts.edu.au/sites/default/files/fass-organizational-listening-report.pdf; Macnamara, J. (2016). *Organizational listening: The missing essential in public communication*. New York, NY: Peter Lang.

PART 1

Democratic Decline, Deficit, Destabilization

The following chapters critically analyze public communication and the public sphere in contemporary democratic societies. The rise of fake news, disinformation, and the alleged emergence of post-truth society, aided by disruptive information and communication technologies such as data analytics, bots, and algorithms are examined and their impact on society explored. In addition, and importantly, this analysis looks beyond technology to examine human behaviour and practices that are creating what is referred to as *post-communication*, and identifies areas for change to reverse the corruption of the public sphere with disinformation, deception, and manipulation.

1

Brexit, Trump, 'Hung Parliaments', and the Collapse of Public Trust

Two cataclysmic political events with far-reaching and ongoing consequences occurred on opposite sides the Atlantic in 2016. The election of Donald Trump as the 45th President of the United States of America and the UK referendum vote to leave the European Union (EU) after 40 years of membership, referred to as *Brexit*, redefined politics and public communication in two of the world's leading democracies.

The June 2016 vote by UK citizens to leave the EU against the strong recommendation and confident campaigning of the government shocked the ruling Conservative Party and the then Prime Minister David Cameron, who subsequently resigned. It was even unexpected by many involved in the Leave campaign including *Brexiter* Boris Johnson, who later became Prime Minister. It was also contrary to the predictions of most polls and opinion surveys. For example, the 2016 *British Social Attitudes* survey published just a few weeks before the referendum reported that 60% of UK citizens were in favour of remaining a member of the EU and only 30% supported Britain's withdrawal.[1]

Donald Trump was regarded as unelectable by both the Republican and Democratic parties and by almost all pollsters and political pundits. His election shocked the world. Francis Fukuyama, who in 1992 argued that American democracy would be adopted globally as a model political system, wrote: "Donald Trump's evolution from a buffoonish fringe candidate taken seriously by no one to the President-Elect of the United States is one of the most unexpected and traumatic events in recent US history."[2] Since, Trump's presidency has caused dismay among leaders around the world, social and political scientists, and many citizens.

These are far from the only recent political events worthy of note. Just 18 months before the controversial *Brexit* vote, a referendum narrowly maintained Scotland as a member of the UK, and a popular push for Scotland to secede from the UK continued unabated. The Scottish independence referendum saw 44.7% of Scottish citizens—almost half—vote to leave the UK. In June 2016 Scotland's First Minister Nicola Sturgeon said that a second referendum on Scottish independence was "highly likely"[3] and she repeated her commitment to a second referendum in December 2019 predicting that 2020 will be an "historic year" in UK politics.[4]

Just one year after the shock *Brexit* vote, the new British Prime Minister, Theresa May, took the UK to a general election declaring support for *Brexit* and expecting a large majority. As is now part of recent turbulent political history, the UK Conservative Government led by May suffered a drubbing at the ballot box, failing to gain a majority and being forced to broker a coalition of convenience with Ireland's Democratic Unionist Party (DUP) to form a government. May subsequently resigned as Prime Minister in July 2019 to be replaced by Boris Johnson based on a vote among the Conservative Party's 159,320 members.

Australia, one of the most stable democracies for more than a century, had six Prime Ministers in nine years between 2010 and 2019.[5] In 2010 the Liberal-National Coalition and Labor parties each won 72 seats in the House of Representatives—four short of the required majority. The then Labor Government led by Julia Gillard from 2010 to 2013 retained the power to govern only when several independent and Green Party members agreed to support Labor. The country entered 2016 with a Liberal-National Coalition Government holding power by just one seat, with 76 Members of Parliament (MPs) in the 150-member House of Representatives. This was the third time in five years that Australians were split and faced the prospect of a 'hung parliament'. In the 2019 Australian federal election, the Liberal-National Coalition retained a majority and power to govern by just two seats, gaining 77 seats in the by-then 151 member House of Representatives. Much like the *Brexit* vote, the elected

Liberal-National Coalition gained 51.51% of the two-party vote count compared with Labor's 48.47%.

The EU, one of the major democratic initiatives of the past century, is under threat and losing support—not only from the UK, but from two-thirds of the citizens in its other 27 member states who do not feel well informed about or understand what the EU provides. Many are beginning to question the benefits of membership versus the costs.[6]

From one perspective these events may appear to be democracy at work. Some such as *Brexit* and even the election of Donald Trump may even look like democracy on full throttle. *Demos*—the people—speaking and making decisions that even the most entrenched elites or intractable bureaucracies could not ignore or overturn. However, these and other events that will be examined in this book have a dark underside—a shadow in Jungian terms with sinister features and characteristics.

In his 2018 book *Post-truth*, Lee McIntyre says that UK citizens were subject to a "largely fact-free campaign over *Brexit*." For example, advertising on the sides of hundreds of buses claimed that the UK was sending €350 million (Euros) a week to the EU, which McIntyre described as a "bogus statistic."[7] In a hearing of the International Grand Committee on Disinformation and 'Fake News' in the Irish Parliament on 8 November 2019, Carole Cadwalladr said that the EU referendum vote was "fraudulent and illegitimate" because of disinformation and illegal campaign activities perpetrated by the Leave campaign.[8]

Furthermore, it has to be remembered that the UK decision to withdraw from the EU was based on 51.89% of those who voted to leave, with 48.11% voting to remain in the EU. This is a very small majority and means that close to half of the voting population were opposed to the government's subsequent decision to leave the EU. From the outset, the UK referendum result was going to be problematic. Technically and legally, 50% plus one vote constitutes a majority, but it leaves a lot of the people disappointed and even angry. But there is even more to this issue than that.

In considering *Brexit* as an act of democracy it needs to be recognized that Britain had 46,500,001 registered voters at the time and, of these, only 33,577,342 voted—72.21% of eligible voters.[9] While this was a high voter turnout by non-compulsory voting standards, it means that just 37.44% of registered UK voters decided the fate of the nation's relationship with the EU. In fact, even that is still an overstatement because, contrary to popular belief and the statements of many UK politicians, a referendum is not binding on government. The

UK Parliament did not have to accept the referendum result. As the UK Supreme Court ruled on 24 January 2017, invoking *Article 50 of the Treaty on Europe Union* (TEU) required an Act of Parliament, the passing of which depended on a majority of MPs voting to leave the EU and endorsement by the House of Lords. Given the narrowness of the referendum margin, the UK Government could have deferred a decision, or called a second referendum at any time between 2016 and 2020.

A second referendum was supported by many because of a further consideration. Many young people did not vote in the 2016 referendum, but they will be the people who live with the implications of the decision. While 90% of people over the age of 65 voted in the EU referendum, only 64% of 18–24 year-olds voted. At the time, 70% of 18–24 year-olds supported the UK remaining in the EU, with just 30% in favour of leaving, according to polls.[10]

Even further, a BMG Research poll in 2019 found that 74% of people who were too young to vote in the 2016 *Brexit* referendum, but who have since reached voting age, would vote to remain if a second ballot had been called.[11]

Whether these disenfranchised citizens do vote in future referenda and elections is increasingly doubtful. Stephen Coleman's insightful study of *How Voters Feel* in Britain describes citizens' experience of voting—one of the most formal and significant acts of exercising political voice—in disturbing terms. He notes that "moments of voting are remarkably fleeting." Furthermore, he reported from his study of UK citizens that the event of voting "seems curiously socially disconnected," taking place in "impersonal spaces … devoid of … registers of intimacy," explaining that "acts of voting are surrounded by an eerie silence" and a "pervasive hush."[12] He noted that elections and voting are predominantly understood and assessed in terms of "instrumental effectiveness"[13] and concluded that democratic practice has deteriorated to "a discourse of arid proceduralism."[14] Coleman argues that "the sustainability of any cultural practice depends to a large measure on how it feels to participate in it" and adds that "the way in which politics in general, and voting in particular, are conducted is incongruent with the sensibilities of citizens as rational and emotional makers of meaning."[15] Coleman says "the rules of the political game seem too much like imposed rules and someone else's game" and concludes that the disposition of citizens towards traditional political engagements such as voting is "inflected by the weight of thwarted experience."[16]

Perhaps this "arid proceduralism," "instrumental effectiveness," and lack of emotional engagement is why controversial figure Russell Brand publicly stated in a BBC *Newsnight* interview with Jeremy Paxman: "I've never voted, never will, as the UK's political system has created a disenfranchised, disillusioned underclass that it fails to serve."[17] Brand went on to comment in *The Guardian* a few days later: "I fervently believe that we deserve more from our democratic system." He said of his radio comments: "It was the expression of the knowledge that democracy is irrelevant."[18]

In his later writing Coleman describes representative institutions such as congresses and parliaments as "remote, unintelligible, self-serving, and insensitive to mundane experience" of citizens.[19] He adds:

> Nowadays, political representatives are commonly accused of not listening to the people they represent; having partisan loyalties that casually override local mandates; taking citizens for granted; and emerging from such a narrow social base that they neither resemble nor empathize with the people they are supposed to be speaking for.[20]

Disengagement from traditional politics and civic life, particularly among young people, is noted with concern by a number of researchers and this trend can be traced to lack of trust as well as a lack of listening, which will be discussed further in this chapter and in Chapter 3. For instance, a 2013 Australia Institute study of young people aged 17–25 found that they "don't feel as though they are being represented by politicians—they don't feel as though they are being listened to."[21] In a 2018 research report, the RAND Corporation identified "erosion of civil discourse" and "alienation and disengagement of individuals from political and civic institutions" as well as "policy uncertainty" and even "political paralysis" as the major consequences of what it labelled "truth decay."[22]

Truth Decay

The RAND Corporation study identified four main "drivers" of truth decay as (1) cognitive biases; (2) the rise of social media; (3) limitations of the education system to keep up with changes in the information ecosystem; and (4) political and social polarization. Each of these characteristics and drivers are examined in this analysis. In particular, partisanship, polarization, and public trust, which were highlighted in the RAND study,[23] are critically explored in some detail in this chapter. Furthermore, the RAND study identified four trends contributing to *truth decay* as (1) disagreement about what constitutes facts; (2) blurring of opinion and facts; (3) an increasing volume and influence of opinion versus facts, and (4) declining trust in previously respected sources of information.[24] These concerns are also further examined in the following.

Fake News, Alternative Facts, Misinformation, and Disinformation

Some classify fake news and all forms of untruth simply as misinformation, while many others lump fake news, alternative facts, misinformation, and disinformation into one category and treat them as synonyms. However, it is useful to unpack the various terms to appreciate the extent of deception and manipulation as well as the degree of culpability involved.

Misinformation can and often does occur accidentally. Media all too frequently publish incorrect information in the rush to meet deadlines. Social media contain considerable misinformation, much of it accidental because of ignorance or gullibility. While media misreporting and the accuracy of social media comment are concerning, these are not the same as fake news and they do not constitute disinformation. This is not to excuse misinformation, but most of us at one time or another has distributed misinformation because of honest mistakes, unwarranted trust in others, or occasional carelessness. Misinformation is often retracted, apologized for, or at worst it is countered by dominant sources of reliable information.

The term fake news has become popular, mainly because of its frequent use by Donald Trump during his presidency, although the concept is far from new and its meaning is far from unambiguous. As noted above, some use the term fake news as a synonym for disinformation and note that distribution of false information has been part of human culture for centuries.[25] In Trumpian post-communication, the term is invoked as a label to discredit and dismiss information—even when it is true. This is a political manoeuvre and is itself a form of fake news and deception.

A recent examination of 34 research articles discussing fake news revealed six different types of media content and practice that the authors presented as a typology of fake news. This observed that for centuries media have distributed (1) news satire and (2) news parody, genres that are well understood as forms of political commentary and entertainment that are not true. A more sinister practice often referred to as fake news is (3) fabrication, in which stories are made up by unscrupulous journalists or others for commercial, political, or ideological purposes. The sordid history of *yellow journalism* in the late 19th century[26] and partisan journalism are examples. In social media, reported claims that Pope Francis endorsed Donald Trump in the 2016 presidential campaign and that Democrat candidate Hilary Clinton operated a child sex ring out of a Washington, D.C., pizza restaurant, referred to as Pizzagate, are contemporary examples of news fabrication. In the typology of fake news developed by Edson Tandoc and colleagues, fake news also includes (4) manipulation such as 'photoshopping' of photos and the production of deepfake videos and, interestingly, (5) *native advertising* and PR, as well as (6) propaganda.[27] All of these practices are critically examined in some detail in Chapter 3.

Alternative facts—a term popularized by Donald Trump as a replacement for whatever he deems to be fake news and by climate change deniers—involves fabrication. Therefore, the term is largely synonymous with fake news, particularly type 3 in Tandoc et al.'s typology.

Others see the term fake news as an oxymoron. For example, former editor of major newspapers and founder of PolitiFact in Australia, Peter Fray,[28] says: "News is news; if it's fake, it's not news."[29] Fray's perspective is based on journalistic standards that recognize that news is generally "expected to include accurate and real information," even though it involves processes of selection and interpretation that include some subjectivity.[30] In a journalistic sense, satire and parody are not regarded as news, but as distinct genre that do not mislead or deceive because of established conventions and cultural markers.

This ambiguity and politicization of the terms fake news and alternative facts limit their value as concepts or categories for analysis. While reminding us of the history and family tree of fake news, Tandoc et al.'s typology defocusses examination of deception and manipulation by including satire and parody. Here, for specificity, fake news is considered to begin with and be fundamentally about *fabrication* of information. To be even more specific, it is also recognized that fabrication can range from relatively innocuous instances (e.g., harmless hoaxes such as April Fool's Day tricks and manipulation of images as a joke) to deceptions and manipulations designed to cause harm to an individual, or social, political, or economic disruption and damage.

These intentional harmful examples are referred to in this analysis as disinformation, and it is argued that it is better to call disinformation what it is, rather than use euphemisms or buzzwords that normalize and trivialize what is a form of *informational terrorism*. If this term sounds extreme, it is worth considering that the English word disinformation originates from the Russian *dezinformatsiya*, which was derived from the name of a KGB black propaganda department,[31] giving a clear indication of its sinister nature and purpose. It is defined in the *Great Soviet Encyclopedia* of 1952 as "distributing false information with the intention to deceive public opinion."[32]

In a contemporary context, the UK Government defines disinformation as "the deliberate creation and dissemination of false and/or manipulated information that is intended to deceive and mislead audiences, either for the purposes of causing harm, or for political, personal or financial gain."[33]

It is clear from these and other definitions that intentionality is fundamental to the distinction between misinformation and disinformation. The latter also usually has a greater potential to cause harm or inequity.

While disinformation has always existed in human society, large-scale political disinformation came to international public attention following the 2016 election of Donald Trump when Russia was accused of distributing misleading and false information that disrupted the election campaign and potentially influenced the result, according to a number of studies. The Mueller Report concluded that "the Russian Government interfered in the 2016 presidential election in sweeping and systematic fashion."[34] Ron Deibert, Director of The Citizen Lab in the Munk School of Global Affairs and Public Policy at the University of Toronto, similarly stated in a university blog post that "Russian entities operated a sweeping and systematic social media 'active measures' campaign designed to sow division and support Donald Trump leading up to the election."[35]

However, the spread of disinformation extends well beyond Donald Trump and Russian troll farms. As shown in the following chapters, disinformation as well as its less malevolent but still corrosive cousins of partisan journalism, commentary, and opinion masquerading as news and facts, spin, and propaganda have become pervasive and are being spread and amplified by a range of emerging information and communication technologies. In a vicious cycle, partisan journalism, commentary, opinion, spin, propaganda, and disinformation reflect partisanship and polarization in society and, in turn, they are being used to increase partisanship and polarization.

Partisanship and Polarization

Political phenomena such as *Brexit*; the election of Donald Trump and the ongoing war on truth and balance that has waged since; the re-emergence of far right Neo-Nazi and neo-fascist movements in Europe; and the revolving door of Prime Ministers and vitriol of politics in Australia and the UK are evidence of a schismatic polarization in contemporary democratic societies. While polarization can have many causes including economic, social, and cultural differences and disparities, a key cause of polarization is partisanship not only among politicians but within the machinery of public communication. While the noun 'partisan' mean a strong supporter in some contexts, which is a relatively benign and even positive meaning, the adjective 'partisan' and the noun 'partisanship' mean "prejudiced in favour of a particular cause."[36] Partisan is also defined in some contexts as "a person who shows a biased, emotional allegiance."[37] Following chapters will examine the implications of partisanship in an era of unregulated social media and increasingly powerful communications technologies, such as data analytics, behavioural targeting, and artificial intelligence (AI) including machine learning algorithms. Partisanship and polarization create distrust and disengagement or at least selective engagement in place of trust and engagement, which are important elements for a stable, fully functioning society.

The Crisis of Trust

In the *Handbook of Social and Political Trust*, editor Eric Uslaner identifies three types of trust. He refers to (1) *particularized trust*, which involves faith in certain people based on affinity; (2) *generalized trust*, also called social trust or "basic trust,"[38] which is an open propensity to trust that does not depend on homophily or past experience; and (3) *political trust*, which involves trust in political institutions such as the executive, the legislature; and the judiciary (the three spheres of government) and political parties. Uslaner also includes "the bureaucracy" (e.g., the civil service) and the police in discussion of political trust, although there are important distinctions that will be discussed in the following.[39]

Particularized Trust

Particularized trust has to be earned or acquired in some way. It may be earned through good deeds and demonstrations of goodwill. But often it is gained on the basis of biases, discrimination, and comfort within an in-group. *Echo chambers* in social media often form and are sustained because of particularized trust. Particularized trust does not facilitate open communication and engagement between individuals and groups with diverse views and interests. Thus, Uslaner argues that a deeper form of generalized trust is important.

Generalized/Social Trust

Generalized trust is based on a person's perception of the nature of humankind—whether one believes in a 'natural goodness' of humans or the contrasting 'doctrine of total depravity' with original sin and a propensity for evil, as discussed in the Introduction.[40] At its extreme, generalized trust leads to naivety, and at a minimum it results in optimism.

Trust requires a willingness to be *vulnerable* and to accept *risk*. *Uncertainty* is another pre-condition of generalized or what some call social trust.[41] Drawing on the ethics work of Annette Baier, Pippa Norris, and others, Mark Warren provides the following definition of generalized or social trust.

> An individual's judgement that another person, whether acting as an individual, a member of a group, or within an institutional role, is both motivated and competent to act in the individual's interests and will do so without overseeing or monitoring.[42]

Generalized or social trust is fundamentally important to human society. For example, trust is necessary to reduce complexity.[43] If one does not have at least some level of trust, one is required to investigate and think critically about every phenomenon one encounters in life and every decision one is required to make. To do so would be overwhelming. As psychologists point out, people need to be *cognitive misers* and reserve deliberation and elaboration for matters that most concern them and that involve most risk. Warren notes that in human society "trust relationships are highly efficient, since they do not involve the high costs of monitoring and sanctioning" that are required in an environment of distrust.[44] Imagine if we could not trust motorists to drive on the correct side of the road, or trust our neighbours not to burgle our home while we are at work. Of course, some people do not live up to our trust expectations, but breaches of such trust are anti-social and relatively infrequent in civilized societies. Generalized or social trust has pragmatic as well as moral underpinnings. Warren concludes that "humans can hardly be conceived of as social beings without trust, nor is it easy to conceive of societies that could function without trust relations."[45]

Political Trust

Political trust is different to generalized social trust, because trust in people and trust in politics and government are based on different foundations. Uslaner says "the former reflects long-term optimism, the latter short-term outcomes and the evaluations of particular leaders."[46] Also, he and others argue that political trust is heavily dependent on factors such as the state of the economy, while generalized social trust is more stable.

A further important distinction needs to be made between trust in what Warren refers to as the "political parts" of government compared with government departments and agencies and the professional staff who work in them to provide services such as public transport, health services, and so on. The political parts of government including political parties, elected politicians, the executive arm of government (e.g., Ministers and Secretaries), and the legislature hold considerable power and operate in an environment of conflict in relation to policies, values, and ways of organizing society. Wherever power resides, trust needs to tread cautiously. English philosopher, jurist, and social reformer Jeremy Bentham posed the question: "Who ought we to distrust, if not those to whom is committed great authority, with great temptations to abuse it."[47]

In contrast, government departments and agencies staffed by civil servants (also called public servants in some countries, which is symbolic) are protected from political agendas and patronage to a considerable extent through legislation in many countries and required to be non-partisan and act in the public interest. The boundaries are sometimes crossed, as will be examined in Chapter 3 in the case of alleged 'Weapons of Mass Destruction' in Iraq that led to the second Iraq War. However, while healthy democracies accept and even require a level of distrust leading to regular scrutiny of the political branches of government, it is generally recognized that trust in government departments, agencies, and institutions such as the police are essential for stability and a fully functioning society.

While generalized or social trust is based on "a psychological state comprising the intention to accept vulnerability based upon positive expectations of the intentions or behaviour of another,"[48] political trust is contingent and situation specific. Unlike generalized trust, which is situation-independent (i.e., A trusts B, full stop),[49] an expected behavioural action or object is inherent in political trust. Jack Citrin and Laura Stoker summarize this expected action or object, or what some refer to as a "three-way relationship" in political trust,[50] as follows.

> Trust ... is relational and domain specific. That is, A trusts B to do X. Trust always has an object or target (B), which could be a person, group, or institution, and a domain of action (X) where trust is given or withheld. The foundation of trust is that A judges B to be trustworthy, that he or she will act with integrity and competence and with A's interests paramount.[51]

While a level of generalized or social trust may be essential, even a pre-requisite, for society, the literature highlights that political trust is contingent and variable. It depends extensively on previous experiences, knowledge, and contextual and situational factors.

The integrative ABI model of trust that is used in interpersonal communication and psychology identifies the essential elements, or antecedents of trust, as *ability*, *benevolence*, and the *integrity* of the trustee. Ability refers to the "skills, competencies, and characteristics that enable a party to have influence within some specific domain."[52] Benevolence focuses on the extent to which a trustor attributes good intentions to the trustee. Integrity is "the trustor's perception that the trustee adheres to a set of principles that the trustor finds acceptable."[53]

Researchers examining political trust say that it manifests when citizens appraise the government and its institutions, policy making in general, and/or the individual political leaders as *promise-keeping*, *efficient*, *fair*, and *honest*.[54] Writing in the *British Journal of Political Science*, Arthur Miller and Ola Listhaug argue that "political trust … is the judgment of the citizenry that the system and the political incumbents are *responsive*, and will do what is right even in the absence of constant scrutiny."[55] Some political science literature suggests that *competence* is also a key element of political trust[56] and competence is shown in management studies research to be even more important than demonstration of integrity in terms of creating trust in organizations.[57]

While the ABI model in its original form focuses mainly on interpersonal communication, some researchers argue: "Just as perceptions about an individual's ability, benevolence, and integrity will have an impact on how much trust the individual can garner, these perceptions also affect the extent to which an organization will be trusted."[58]

What's the Problem with Distrust?

Following the 2015 World Economic Forum, the chairman of Baker & McKenzie USA, Eduardo Leite, wrote in a blog post: "In business, trust is the glue that binds employees to employers, customers to companies—and companies to their suppliers, regulators, government, and partners."[59] Under the title 'Why trust matters in business' he added:

> Most companies appreciate that high trust levels lead to a stronger reputation, sustainable revenues, greater customer advocacy and increased employee retention. It is also likely that companies with higher levels of trust will bounce back from future crises far quicker than others.[60]

Leite further stated: "Lack of trust is something we should all be worried about, because trust matters. For many companies, particularly professional services firms like the one where I work, trust is at the centre of the business model."[61] Leite's comments are supported by management research shows that trust is a key driver of relationships within and between organizations affecting employee loyalty, productivity and retention, and business partnerships.[62]

Charles Tilly's important study of *Trust and Rule* identified trust is a necessary condition for democracy and warned that "a significant decline in trust threatens democracy."[63] Political scientist Stephen Coleman similarly argues that trust is a vital element of democracy and identifies two levels of trust pointing to (1) "trust between citizens so that they are confident that if they keep to their side of the bargain (e.g., paying taxes), then others will too," and (2) "citizens must have a generalized trust in the outcomes of democratic processes or they will defect from those processes."[64]

Paradoxically, a level of distrust can be a good thing and is at least somewhat necessary in relation to politics. Trust and distrust is not a binary scale. Rather, trust exists along a continuum from total trust to total distrust. While many identify a decline in political trust and trust in government as part of a concerning "democratic deficit,"[65] a "crisis of democracy,"[66] and a "democratic malaise,"[67] some argue that lack of political trust need not be detrimental to democracy. Scholars use labels such as sceptical, critical, and vigilant to describe non-trusting citizens who can potentially strengthen democracy because their lack of trust stimulates scrutiny and engagement. As William Mishler and Richard Rose say in *The Journal of Politics*:

> Democracy requires trust but also presupposes an active and vigilant citizenry with a healthy scepticism of government and a willingness, should the need arise, to suspend trust and assert control over government—at a minimum by replacing the government of the day.[68]

Nevertheless, severe lack of trust, or high distrust, can lead to a number of problems that undermine personal relationships, business, civil society, and democracy. Even before the presidency of Donald Trump, studies found that a majority (52%) of Republicans say that they "never" trust the US Government to do what is right. Almost half (46%) of Republicans said that they trust government "only some of the time." Only 2% of Republicans reported that they trust government "most of the time" in the 2010 Cooperative Congressional Election Study (CCES).[69] Democrats were more trusting, with 29% saying that they trust government "most of the time." However, this study was done shortly after the election of Democrat Barack Obama as US President (2009–2017). After a surge of trust and unity following 9/11, an analysis of political trust and polarization by political scientists Marc Hetherington and Thomas Rudolph noted that "the warm glow of national unity experienced in the months following September 11 did not last for long."[70] Over a 12-year period from 2002 to 2013, research studies show a sharp polarization of political trust in the USA. With the election of a Republican government under George W. Bush, trust of Democrat voters fell to just 18% by 2008, while Republican voters retained high levels of trust—around 60% between 2002 and 2004. However, over the following decade, Republican trust fell to less than 10% in 2010 and 2011, while Democrats' trust increased to close to 40% in 2010.[71] Hetherington and Rudolph conclude that partisanship is fuelling this polarization and declining trust in government. They say that "partisans increasingly dislike the opposing political party" and add: "It might not be too much of a stretch to say that they actually hate the opposition."[72]

Young people in particular are untrusting, which is alarming. A 2015 Harvard University study found that less than one-third of 18–29 year olds trust the President—and that was in relation to President Obama. Only 14% of young Americans trust Congress; only 12% trust Wall Street; and only 11% trust major media.[73] The situation became worse under President Trump, with the Pew Research Center reporting that in 2017 trust in the US President had reached its lowest level since recording started in the 1960s.[74]

In a 2019 paper, Naom Ebner referred to Donald Trump's campaign and his administration's constant references to fake news and alternative facts as part of the *Trust War*, and he says that this approach is in direct conflict with human communication and strategies such as negotiation. He notes that negotiation embraces "constructive ambiguity to bridge over parties' differences of perception, but this concept is not equivalent to the notion of alternative facts."[75] The public's declining trust is well-justified according to fact-checking analysis. *The Washington Post*'s Fact Checker column reported in December 2019 that Donald Trump had told 15,413 untruths during his presidency—"an average of 14.6 lies for each of his 1,055 days in office" to that time.[76] In the same year PolitiFact bestowed its "Lie of the Year" award on Trump for the third year in succession.[77]

Notwithstanding the argument that a level of distrust leading to monitoring and critical analysis of the political side of government—politicians, political parties, the legislature, the executive and, to some extent, the judiciary—democratic systems need to limit distrust to maintain confidence and to avoid the requirement for frequent interventions such as elections, independent inquiries, impeachments, protests, and so on.

Also, beyond trust in a particular government or administration, it is important that citizens trust *the system*—the political system of a country as a whole and its social systems and institutions. Political scientists and sociologists warn that the ultimate loss of trust is lack of trust in the institution of government and the institutions that comprise government such as the legislature, the judiciary, and related services such as police.[78] Social stability relies on the fact the system is seen as containing tried and tested internal controls that protect the public interest even when individuals prove to be untrustworthy.

The Role of Communication in Trust

As well as behaving in trustworthy ways, would-be trustors such as governments, political organizations, and corporations must present themselves as trustworthy. To do so, public communication serves as a *trust intermediary* between organizations and the public.[79] Public communication is part of creating legitimacy and acceptance, as well as creating toleration of change and risk. But not any old public communication as it is often conceived and enacted in contemporary societies. Public communication should be truthful and transparent (e.g., disclose its sources and interests) in order to be ethical. Propaganda is not ethical communication. Communication can legitimately seek persuasion, but communication and public relations (PR) scholars point out an important difference between persuasive communication and propaganda. For example, Garth Jowett and Victoria O'Donnell say that "the purpose of propaganda is to promote a partisan or competitive cause in the best interest of the propagandist, but not necessarily in the best interest of the recipient."[80] In an earlier text they said:

> Propaganda is a form of communication that is different from persuasion because it attempts to achieve a response that furthers the desired intent of the propagandist. Persuasion is interactive and attempts to satisfy the needs of both persuader and persuade.[81]

It does not help the PR industry that the title of the second book by Edward Bernays, who is described as the "father of public relations,"[82] was *Propaganda*. In it Bernays advocated "manipulation of the … opinions of the masses" and said that "those who manipulate this unseen mechanism of society constitute an invisible government which is the true ruling power of our country."[83] It is also instructive that a later book by Bernays was titled *The Engineering of Consent*.[84] To be fair, Bernays identified three roles of PR—information, persuasion, and "efforts to integrate attitudes and actions of an institution with its publics and of publics with that institution."[85] But many studies show that, despite normative theories, PR is mostly focussed on the first two roles identified by Bernays, particularly persuasion.[86]

Ethical human communication is defined as a *two-way, transactional* process, as distinct from a one-way, top-down transmission of information or propaganda. Early models of information processing, such as the widely cited 1949 Shannon and Weaver *mathematical theory of communication*,[87] simplistically suggested a linear flow of information from a source via a channel to a receiver with the assumption that messages arrive and are understood and acted on—what David Berlo rephrased as the source-message-channel-receiver (SMCR) model.[88] In reality, human communication is a far more complex, contextual, contingent, and collaborative undertaking. As noted in the Introduction, communication—*communicatio* in Latin, derived from the Latin root *communis* meaning common or public and the Latin verb *communicare* meaning to create or build[89]—is a process of meaning making and meaning sharing involving negotiation and accommodation.

The foundations of ethical human communication are found in the philosophies of Martin Buber,[90] Mikhail Bakhtin,[91] and more recently David Bohm,[92] who emphasize the importance of *dialogue*, as well as in concepts such as openness to others as described by Hans Georg Gadamer.[93] Openness should extend to wanting to know what others think and feel and "recognizing that I must accept some things that are against me" in order to achieve mutuality and reciprocity.[94] These and other important concepts in relation to ethical human communication are explained in detail in books and seminal articles on human communication by Robert Craig, Stephen Littlejohn, Karen Foss, and others.[95]

The fundamental role of communication in politics and society has been identified by many philosophers and social scientists including John Dewey who said "society exists not only by … communication, but it may fairly be said to exist in … communication."[96] In short, society cannot exist without communication. Raymond Williams also wrote effusively about the importance of communication in creating and sustaining communities and societies, saying "society is a form of communication."[97] Noted 'Chicago School' sociologist and founder of American cultural studies, James Carey, similarly pointed out that communication is "the process whereby a culture is brought into existence."[98]

So it can be said in relation to politics, particularly democracy. *Vox populi*—the voice of the people (the *demos*)—and its right and potential to influence the policies and decisions of government and the exercise of power and authority (the *krátos*) are fundamental principles of democracy.

Understanding effective communication as sharing meaning and a capability to influence policy and decisions highlights another important feature of human communication. Communication must involve mutual *listening* as well as speaking. Listening must be open and responsive, not only conducted to gain 'intelligence' for targeting stakeholders and citizens and designing persuasive campaigns, as is often the focus of political, governmental, and corporate listening.[99] Listening in politics can include social and market research, stakeholder and citizen engagement such as public forums, public consultation, and monitoring of public opinion through traditional and social media. Public communication should include incoming information as well as outbound information—what Tom van der Meer calls *democratic input* as well as *government output*.[100] A common misconception in political, government, and corporate communication is to conceive communication as distributing information and messages. This is only half of the process of communication.

Methods, tools, and the implications of listening—as well as not listening—are examined in more detail in Chapter 3 in discussing the nature and forms of *post-communication* and how it can be reversed to create meaningful public debate and dialogue.

Political and public communication literature also highlights the central role of communication in contributing to *reputation* and *relationships*, of which trust is a key ingredient, as well as creating an informed public and enabling public participation through *engagement*, *dialogue*, and what some prefer to call *conversations*.[101]

Engagement and Disengagement

Trust and distrust are closely connected with *engagement* and *disengagement*. However, the term engagement is used loosely and superficially in marketing, PR, and government and political communication, often attached to simple actions such as clickthroughs to web pages and likes and follows in social media. In an article on public engagement, Minjeong Kang discusses "conceptual confusion caused by marketers' use of the term engagement to describe any interaction … with their customers" and the tendency of marketers to "spin" using a variety of basic metrics such as clicks, visits, and downloads to claim engagement.[102] This has led to engagement being described as "a prototypical buzzword."[103] For example, throughout the period of research for this book, I followed Donald Trump and Boris Johnson online. I did so to monitor the extreme and egregious comments that they make with bewildering regularity and insensitivity. To count my follow as engagement is misleading, as the following definitions of the concept show.

Engagement is extensively discussed in psychology and organizational psychology literature in which leadership and HR specialist Tamara Erickson describes it as commitment involving a level of passion and investment of discretionary effort.[104] More specifically, engagement is comprised of three key elements, according to organizational psychologists:

1. A psychological bond formed through a combination of cognitive processing of information and what scholars call *affective commitment* (i.e., emotional attachment such as a sense of belonging, feeling valued, etc.);
2. *Positive affectivity*, a deeper level of positive emotional connection beyond liking or attraction, such as absorption, enthusiasm, excitement, pride, and/or passion; and
3. *Empowerment* of those engaged, which psychologists and political scientists say is most effectively achieved through *participation* of some kind.[105]

In an organizational context, Bruce Bimber and colleagues describe engagement as "how much people perceive that they are able to shape the agenda and the direction of their organization."[106] In PR literature, Maureen Taylor and Michael Kent describe public engagement as:

> … a two-way, relational, give-and-take between organizations and stakeholders/publics with the intended goal of (a) improving understanding among interactants; (b) making decisions that benefit all parties involved, not simply the organization; and (c) fostering a fully functioning society.[107]

It is important to look beyond superficial understandings of engagement and recognize the emotional as well as cognitive dimension of engagement and, even more importantly, the role of participation. While participation can include a range of actions such as voting, becoming a member of a committee, writing letters as an advocate, or protesting, one of the most common forms of participation for most citizens is engaging in *dialogue*, or what James Carey referred to as *conversations*.

Engagement is important for organizations—corporate, government, non-government and non-profits. Brian Solis devoted a book to the subject titled

Engage in which he said organizations need to "engage or die."[108] A 2013 McKinsey survey of senior executives found that engagement with customers rated among their top 10 priorities.[109] Governments now routinely call for and promote citizen engagement.[110] But people tend to engage with other people and organizations when they have a substantial level of generalized trust and, ideally, some level of particularized and political trust. Conversely, people tend to disengage from individuals, organizations, and institutions that fail to earn and maintain their trust.

What's the Problem with Disengagement?

In short, lots. As shown in Figure 1.1, disengagement occurs at both ends of the *trust-distrust continuum*. Total trust leads to uncritical, unquestioning, naïve actors. Total distrust creates disconnected actors, who no longer care because they have given up on the person, organization, or institution that caused their distrust. In the case of democracy, disengagement can involve failing to vote or casting invalid or 'donkey' votes;[111] lack of participation in political discussion and debate; disinterest in becoming informed about political and civic issues; and becoming disconnected and marginalized in society. At its extreme, disengagement can mobilize citizens towards alternatives. While alternatives may be reasonable choices in relation to products or services in a competitive marketplace, in a social and political context they may include political radicalism such as extreme Alt-right movements, white supremacist parties, or even terrorism. Thus, neither total trust nor total distrust are healthy for human relationships or organization-public relationships. Nor are they healthy at a macro level for democracy and civil society.

In the middle of the trust-distrust continuum is scepticism, characterized by monitoring,[112] critical thinking, and questioning. Scepticism that is mild and leans towards trust results in optimism, while scepticism that edges towards cynicism and distrust leads to pessimism. A healthy relationship and society could be considered to be represented by 3–7 on the trust-distrust continuum shown in Figure 1.1.

The Collapse of Civility

An important ingredient for productive engagement, dialogue, and conversations that Dewey, Carey, and other philosophers consider central to human society and

| 0 | 1 | 2 | 3 | 4 | 5 | 6 | 7 | 8 | 9 | 10 |

| DISTRUST | *Pessimism* | SCEPTICISM | *Optimism* | TRUST |

DISENGAGED
(disconnected, don't care, given up, or mobilized to alternatives)

ENGAGED
(Monitoring, critical thinking, questioning)

DISENGAGED
(uncritical, unquestioning, gullible, naïve)

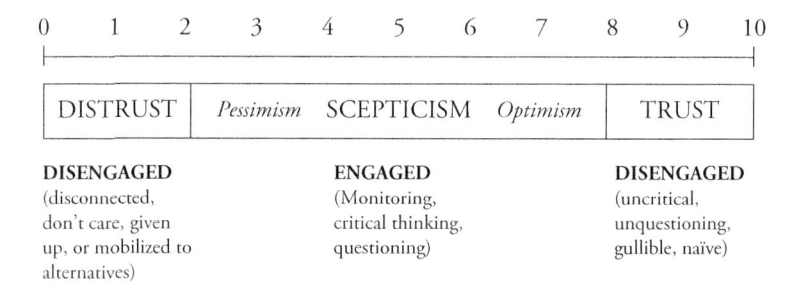

Figure 1.1. The trust-distrust continuum

culture is civility. The 2018 RAND Corporation study titled *Truth Decay* identified "erosion of civil discourse" as one of the "consequences of truth decay" and a driver of disengagement.[113] In a 2019 book examining incivility, Robert Boatright cited a Marist Poll that found 70% of Americans believe that the level of civility in American politics declined between 2016 and 2017 and a Weber Shandwick survey that found 75% of Americans agreed that there is a "crisis of civility." In the same study, over half of the respondents said that they were not interested in following politics or engaging in public affairs because of incivility.[114]

The 2019 Australian federal election was reported to be one of the "nastiest" and most vitriolic ever, with reported instances of highly personal *ad hominem* attacks,[115] vandalized campaign posters, anti-Semitic e-mails, and even arson attacks.[116] The Prime Minister Scott Morrison described Nazi imagery painted over a billboard featuring Treasurer Josh Frydenberg as "deeply disturbing" and a sign of "ugly hatred" in the election campaign.[117] Partisanship and polarization in politics are also reported in many other countries, with the growth of Alt-right white nationalist movements, neo-facism, Neo-nazism, and xenophobia.

Of course, what one person sees as incivility, another may see as free speech and passionate debate. In the same text as Boatright's comments, Kate Kenski and colleagues noted that civility and incivility are not well-defined. They also noted that civility and incivility occur at a personal level, as well as publicly. It is the latter that is of most concern in relation to public debate and dialogue, although personal incivility is likely to spill over into public debate.

Most political scientists, sociologists, and communication scholars agree that a level of civility is important for productive engagement and an effective public sphere, and they offer some important guidelines that are salutary in examining the current "clamorous, gridlocked public sphere."[118] Importantly, civility does not rule out rigorous and lively debate. Zizi Pappacharissi says "civility standards should promote respect for the other, enhance democracy, but also allow human uniqueness and unpredictability."[119] This suggests that open-mindedness and some level of tolerance are required, but importantly it also emphasizes that a key element of civility is respect. Kenski and her colleagues go on to define incivility as "features of discussion that convey an unnecessarily disrespectful tone toward the discussion forum, its participants, or its topics."[120] This emphasizes that incivility involves *disrespect* that is *unnecessary*. In other words, disrespect in and of itself is not problematic. People have the right to disrespect certain institutions and even people—for example, those who commit crimes such as sexual abuse. But when disrespect is unnecessary and publicly communicated it becomes a corrupting negative force in public debate and undermines civil society.

Turning back to the positive—*civility*—Cherie Strachan and Michael Wolf make the important point that "public civility and interpersonal politeness sustain social harmony and allow people who disagree with one another to maintain ongoing relationships."[121] This point is important because it highlights the practical and pragmatic importance of civility for society. People will disagree. That is inevitable in diverse societies with differing political, religious, and cultural beliefs and practices. The maintenance of a public sphere in which discussion and debate can continue necessitates a capacity to agree to disagree and maintain social relations—even when differences are substantial and emotions run high. Noted political philosopher John Rawls in his theory of a just liberal society argued that people have a "duty of civility" and he described this as involving "a willingness to listen to others and a fair-mindedness in deciding when accommodations to their views should reasonably be made."[122] In discussing civility as *politeness* and *responsiveness* involving skills and choices, Anthony Laden concludes that civility is "a cooperative skill."[123]

In this sense, public diplomacy literature offers a useful contribution to the principles and theories of human communication discussed previously in this chapter—particularly what is described as the *new public diplomacy*. Whereas diplomacy is primarily conducted between governments, and public diplomacy has traditionally been focussed on using media and communication to influence international relations, Harvard University professor Joseph Nye describes the new public diplomacy as:

> … no longer confined to messaging, promotion campaigns, or even direct governmental contacts with foreign publics serving foreign-policy purposes. It is

also about building relationships with civil-society actors in other countries and facilitating networks between non-governmental parties at home and abroad.[124]

Public diplomacy is mentioned because, as Cherie Strachan and Michael Wolf note, "cultivating [a] more civil, deliberative public sphere will not be easy."[125] This is particularly the case when many organizations and institutions that have previously played a role in mediating, moderating, and mitigating public debate and discourse have declined in influence and lost public trust and support in contemporary societies. As reported in many studies, the past decade has seen a severe withering of the influence of mass media, the Church, political parties, unions, and even some major NGOs and charities have been involved in scandals that have eroded public trust and support. In place of the moderating and mediating influence of such organizations and institutions, citizens in democratic societies are facing an unchecked barrage of political and commercial spin, PR, advertising, and marketing. The difference between a public diplomacy approach and a PR approach is outlined in Table 1.1. This shows an acceptance of difference and even conflict in public diplomacy and mechanisms for dealing with *dissensus*, whereas PR seeks consensus, usually through orientation of others to the views of the proponents of PR achieved through persuasion. Also, PR theory provides little by way of mechanisms for dealing with power differentials, conflict, and irreconcilable differences. This is not to deny a role for PR, but when PR overshadows or replaces public diplomacy and civility exercised in ongoing respectful discussion and debate, societies are heading down a slippery slope.

Drawing on Habermas, political scientists emphasize the importance of *deliberation* as a key component of discussion and debate in the public sphere. Through becoming informed and thinking things through, participants in discussion and debate shift from emotional and 'off the top of the head' responses to considered views with understanding of others' perspectives. In recent writing, Strachan and Wolf state:

> Advocates of deliberation point out that when people continue to engage with one another despite their differences, they not only learn *how to listen* [emphasis added] but also may use new insights to develop shared solutions, sometimes referred to as the "third way" or "win-win" solutions.[126]

While drawing attention to key concepts, the above claim can be argued to be back to front. Rather than learning how to listen after engaging with one another, learning how to listen is more logically and ethically recognized as a pre-requisite for meaningful engagement and communication.[127] Starting and developing a

Table 1.1. Comparison of public diplomacy theory and public relations theory. Based on Macnamara, J. (2012). Corporate and organizational diplomacy: An alternative paradigm to PR. *Journal of Communication Management, 16*(3), 312–325

Public diplomacy	Public relations
Prioritizes *interpersonal* communication, supported by mediated communication	Relies mostly on *mediated* communication except in the personal influence model
Recognizes and respects competing interests and accepts tensions and *conflict as the 'norm'* of human relations rather than breakdown—including recognition that some interests and conflicts may be irreconcilable (i.e., *agonistic*)	Sees conflict as a breakdown of communication and/or relationships and views symmetry as a necessary goal based on belief in the possibility of consensus and harmony
Maintains *ongoing dialogue* at all cost (except in war)—even in the face of complete disagreement and hostility. This is facilitated by patience and the following features	Maintains dialogue while consensus / concurrence / win-win symmetrical resolution is possible but, if not, sees "withdrawal from dialogue"[a] and "no deal" as ethical[b]
Develops and prioritizes *negotiation skills*	Primarily focuses on communication and *promotion* skills
Establishes *mechanisms for dealing with disparities in power* (e.g., powerful nations often agree to 'one vote one value' in international negotiations despite size; organizations can work through arbitration bodies, etc.)	Has no effective mechanisms for dealing with disparities in power; relies on organizations pursuing "enlightened self-interest"[c] and the "professional values" of practitioners[d]
Establishes and follows *protocols* for dealing with conflict and hostility including diplomatic etiquette and reciprocal arrangements such as return visits, equal size delegations, and turn-taking and equal time in discussions and negotiations	Has no formal protocols for dealing with conflict; again relies on professional values

[a] Grunig, J. (2001). Two-way symmetrical public relations: past, present and future. In R. Heath (Ed.), *Handbook of public relations* (pp. 11–30). London: Sage Publications, p. 16.
[b] Hon, L., & Grunig, J. (1999). Guidelines for measuring relationships in public relations. Gainesville, FL: Institute for Public Relations, p. 17. Retrieved from http://www.instituteforpr.org/measuring-relationships
[c] Grunig, L., Grunig J., & Dozier, D. (2002). *Excellent organizations and effective organizations: A study of communication management in three countries*. Mahwah, NJ: Lawrence Erlbaum, p. 472.
[d] Grunig, J. (2000). Collectivism, collaboration, and societal corporatism as core professional values in public relations. *Journal of Public Relations Research, 12*(1), 23–48, p. 26.

discussion or debate without listening is a recipe for communication failure. Productive conversations, dialogue, and debate require civility, which is grounded in respect or at least an absence of unnecessary disrespect, openness, listening, and tolerance rather than partisanship which leads to polarization.

Lack of Listening

The five-year study of how and how well organizations listen to their stakeholders that I led between 2015 and 2019, as noted under 'Methodology and Sources' in the Introduction, found that 80–95% of communication-related resources in major corporate, government, and non-government organizations are applied to disseminating the organization's messages through advertising, PR, publications, presentations and so on (i.e., speaking). Furthermore, of the 5–15% of resources devoted to functions such as market and social research, customer relations, stakeholder engagement, public consultation, complaints processing, and so on, most is instrumental. That is, it is conducted to gain 'intelligence' and 'insights' to inform *targeting* of people, whether as customers or voters, or some other object of persuasion.[128] Research shows that corporate, government, and non-government organizations routinely fail to listen to their stakeholders.

Listening is defined in this study and other literature as (1) recognizing others as having a right to speak and something to say (*recognition*); (2) *acknowledging* what they say; (3) paying *attention* to what they say; (4) *interpreting* what they say fairly and ideally with empathy; (5) trying to *understand* them; (6) giving *consideration* to what they say; and (7) *responding* in some appropriate way. Thus, listening is much more than hearing or receiving information, which is a physical phenomenon. Importantly, these "seven canons" of listening[129] do not include agreement or acceptance. All discussants retain the right to disagree. Appropriate response might include denial of a request, for example, which is ethical and appropriate if there are good reasons that justify denial or disagreement. But giving attention, consideration, and response informed by the other 'canons' are essential for meaningful engagement.

Examples of the extent and seriousness of the lack of listening that pervades neoliberal capitalist democracies are readily available. For example, upon taking up the office of Prime Minister of the UK after the historic referendum vote to leave the EU that led to the resignation of former PM David Cameron and a dozen Ministers, Theresa May referred to *Brexit* as "a revolution in which millions of our fellow citizens stood up and said they were not prepared to be ignored anymore." She went on to say: "Our democracy should work for everyone, but if you've been trying to say things need to change for years and your complaints fall on deaf ears, it doesn't feel like it's working for you."[130]

Acknowledgement by the Prime Minister of a leading democratic country that citizens' complaints "fall on deaf ears" is quite some admission. But, even worse, lack of listening by organizations has been shown to lead to physical human suffering and even deaths, as tragically illustrated in 2013 when the Mid Staffordshire NHS Foundation Trust Public Inquiry into deaths in hospitals drew the following conclusion in its report.

> Building on the report of the first inquiry, the story it tells is first and foremost of appalling suffering of many patients. This was primarily caused by a serious failure on the part of a provider Trust Board. It did not listen sufficiently to its patients.[131]

Even more recently, the 2017 Grenfell Tower fire in London that claimed more than 70 lives and injured many others has been directly attributed to a "failure to listen."[132] Warnings of inadequate fire safety standards were posted on the website of the Grenfell Action Group four years before the disaster, and reports identifying the dangers of combustible cladding on buildings were submitted to the UK Parliament as early as 1999.[133]

In an out of court settlement in June 2019, the Australian Government admitted that it had not considered more than 2,000 submissions from citizens and community groups in relation to a controversial coal mine plan to use 12.5 billion litres of water from Australia's sparse inland river system, and that it had "lost" many more submissions.[134] The Australian Conservation Foundation, which took the federal government to court with the support of the Environmental Defenders Office in Queensland, described the government's decision making process in relation to the Adani North Galilee mine as "a complete farce."[135]

These and many other examples show that democratically elected governments are fragrantly disregarding the voice of electors and citizens. In doing so, they are—quite foolishly at times—contributing to an undermining of trust in their administrations and in democracy itself as a system. Corporations also have a chequered history of failing to listen or blatantly ignoring information that is in the public interest, as well as distributing disinformation.

Notes

1. NatCen Social Research. (2016). *British social attitudes study, No 33*. Retrieved from http://www.bsa.natcen.ac.uk/latest-report/british-social-attitudes-33/euroscepticism.aspx

2. Fukuyama, F. (2016, December 13). America: The failed state. *Prospect*. Retrieved from http://www.prospectmagazine.co.uk/magazine/america-the-failed-state-donald-trump
3. De Freytas-Tamura, K. (2016, June 24). Scotland says new vote on independence is 'highly likely'. *The New York Times*, Europe edition. Retrieved from https://www.nytimes.com/2016/06/25/world/europe/brexit-scotland-independence-referendum.html?_r=0
4. Green, C. (2019, December 31). Nicola Sturgeon predicts "historic year" for Scottish independence. *iNews*. Retrieved from https://inews.co.uk/news/scotland/nicola-sturgeon-scottish-independence-2020-historic-year-1352143
5. Australia's Prime Ministers between 2010 and 2018 were Kevin Rudd (2007–2010); Julia Gillard (2010–2013); Kevin Rudd again (2013–2013); Tony Abbott (2013–2015); Malcolm Turnbull (2015–2018); Scott Morrison (2018–).
6. This has been shown in successive *Eurobarometer* surveys since 2009 (see http://ec.europa.eu/COMMFrontOffice/publicopinion/index.cfm) and is acknowledged by the European Commission (2015). Terms of reference for evaluation of corporate communication campaign. Brussels, p. 3.
7. McIntyre, L. (2018). *Post-truth*. Cambridge, MA: MIT Press, p. 5.
8. Cadwalladr, C. (2019, November 7). Presentation to the International Grand Committee on Disinformation and 'Fake News'. Dublin.
9. Electoral Commission. (2018). EU referendum results. Retrieved from https://www.electoralcommission.org.uk/find-information-by-subject/elections-and-referendums/past-elections-and-referendums/eu-referendum/electorate-and-count-information
10. Spratt, V. (2018, October 5). The truth about young people and Brexit. BBC 3, *Real Life*. Retrieved from https://www.bbc.co.uk/bbcthree/article/b8d097b0-3ad4-4dd9-aa25-af6374292de0
11. Alexander, I. (2019, March 10). Three-quarters of newly eligible voters would vote remain in second poll. *The Guardian*. Retrieved from https://www.theguardian.com/politics/2019/mar/09/new-young-voters-want-peoples-vote-strongly-remain-survey
12. Coleman, S. (2013). *How voters feel*. New York, NY: Cambridge University Press, p. 3.
13. Ibid., p. 4.
14. Ibid., p. 192.
15. Ibid., p. 5.
16. Ibid., p. 3.
17. "Russell Brand: I've never voted, never will." (2013, October 23). *BBC Newsnight*. Retrieved from http://www.bbc.com/news/uk-24648651
18. Brand, R. (2013, November 6). Russell Brand: We deserve more from our democratic system. *The Guardian*, Opinion, paras 2, 4. Retrieved from http://www.theguardian.com/commentisfree/2013/nov/05/russell-brand-democratic-system-newsnight
19. Coleman, S. (2017). *Can the internet strengthen democracy*. Cambridge, UK: Polity, p. 4.

20. Ibid., p. 9.
21. Lucas, C. (2013, August 7). You are not listening, say young voters. *The Sydney Morning Herald*, p. 14.
22. Kavanagh, J., & Rich, M. (2018). *Truth decay: An initial exploration of the diminishing role of facts and analysis in American public life*. Santa Monica, CA: RAND Corporation, p. xvi. Retrieved from https://www.rand.org/research/projects/truth-decay.html
23. Ibid., pp. xiii–xv.
24. Ibid., p. 3.
25. Soll, J. (2016, December 18). The long and brutal history of fake news. *Politico Magazine*. Retrieved from https://www.politico.com/magazine/story/2016/12/fake-news-history-long-violent-214535
26. McChesney, R., & Scott, B. (Eds.). (2003). *The brass check: A study of American journalism*. Urbana: University of Illinois Press; Spencer, J. (2007). *The yellow journalism: The press and America's emergence as a world power*. Evanston, IL: Northwestern University Press.
27. Tandoc E., Lim, Z., & Ling, R. (2018). Defining 'fake news'. *Digital Journalism*, 6(2), 137–153, p. 147.
28. Peter Fray has held many senior media positions including editor in chief of the *Sydney Morning Herald*, deputy editor of Australia's national newspaper *The Australian*, founder and head of PolitiFact Australia, and professor and co-director of the Centre for Media Transition at the University of Technology Sydney. Fray returned to journalism in 2020 as editor in chief of an independent Australian media group overseeing publications including *Crikey* and *The Mandarin*.
29. P. Fray (personal communication [interview], September 12, 2019).
30. Tandoc et al., 2018, p. 140.
31. Jowett, G., & O'Donnell, V. (2005). *Propaganda and persuasion*. Thousand Oaks, CA: Sage Publications, pp. 21–23.
32. Bittman, L. (1985). *The KGB and Soviet disinformation: An insider's view*. Washington, D.C.: Pergamon-Brassey's, pp. 49–50; Shultz, R., & Godson, R. (1984). *Dezinformatsia: Active measures in Soviet strategy*. Washington, D.C.: Pergamon-Brassey's, pp. 37–38.
33. Government Communication Service. (2019). *RESIST: Counter disinformation toolkit*. London, UK, p. 6. Retrieved from https://gcs.civilservice.gov.uk/guidance/resist-counter-disinformation-toolkit
34. Mueller, R. (2019, March). *Report on the investigation into Russian interference in the 2016 presidential election*, Volume 1. Washington, D.C.: Department of Justice, p. 1.
35. Deibert, R. (2014, May 14). Endless Mayfly: An invasive species in the social media ecosystem. *Ronald Deibert* [Web log post], para. 1. Retrieved from https://deibert.citizenlab.ca/2019/05/endless-mayfly

36. "Partisanship". (2019). Oxford dictionaries. Retrieved from https://en.oxforddictionaries.com/definition/partisanship
37. Partisan. (2019). Dictionary.com. Retrieved from https://www.dictionary.com/browse/partisanship
38. Erikson, E. (1959). Growth and crisis of the healthy personality. In E. Erikson (Ed.), *Psychological issues: Selected papers*, *1*(1), 51–107. New York: NY: International Universities Press, p. 57.
39. Uslaner, E. (2018). The study of trust. In E. Uslaner (Ed.), *The Oxford handbook of social and political trust* (pp. 3–13). New York, NY: Oxford University Press, pp. 4, 6.
40. Rushdoony, R. (2016, June 10). Doctrine of selective depravity: Parts 1–111. *Chalcedon Magazine*. Retrieved from https://chalcedon.edu/magazine/doctrine-of-selective-depravity-parts-i-iii
41. Kelton, K., Fleischmann, K. R., & Wallace, W. A. (2008). Trust in digital information. *Journal of the American Society for Information Science and Technology*, *59*, 363–374.
42. Warren, M. (2018). Trust and democracy. In In E. Uslaner (Ed.), *The Oxford handbook of social and political trust* (pp. 75–94). New York, NY: Oxford University Press, p. 75.
43. Luhmann, N. (1968). *Vertrauen: ein mechanismus der reduktion sozialer komplexität* [Trust: A mechanism for reducing social complexity]. Stuttgart: Ferdinand Enke.
44. Warren, 2018, p. 75.
45. Ibid.
46. Uslaner, 2018, p. 11.
47. Bentham, J. (1999). *Political tactics*. Oxford, UK: Clarendon Press. (Original work published 1816)
48. Rousseau, D., Sitkin, S., Burt, R., & Camerer, C. (1998). Not so different after all: A cross-discipline view of trust. *Academy of Management Review*, *23*(3), 393–404, p. 395.
49. Uslaner, E. (2002). *The moral foundations of trust*. New York, NY: Cambridge University Press.
50. Hardin, R. (1992). The street-level epistemology of trust. *Analyse & Kritik*, *14*, 152–176, p. 154.
51. Citrin, J., & Stoker, L. (2018). Political trust in a cynical age. *Annual Review of Political Science*, 49–70, p. 50.
52. Mayer, R., Davis, J., & Schoorman, F. (1995). An integrative model of organizational trust. *Academy of Management Review*, *20*, 709–734, p. 717.
53. Ibid., p. 719.
54. Blind, P. (2006, June). Building trust in government in the twenty-first century: Review of literature and emerging issues. Paper presented to the 7th Global Forum on Reinventing Government Building Trust in Government, Vienna, Austria.

55. Miller, A., & Listhaug, O. (1990). Political parties and confidence in government: A comparison of Norway, Sweden and the United States. *British Journal of Political Science, 20*(3), 357–386, p. 358.
56. Abravanel, M., & Busch, R. (1975). Political competence, political trust, and the action orientations of university. *The Journal of Politics, 37*(1), 57–82.
57. Connelly, B., Crook, T., Coombs, J., Ketchen, D., & Aguinis, H. (2015). Competence- and integrity-based trust in interorganizational relationships: Which matters more? *Journal of Management, 44*(3), 919–945.
58. Schoorman, F. D., Mayer, R. C., & Davis, J. H. (2007). An integrative model of organizational trust: Past, present, and future. *Academy of Management Review, 32,* 344–354, p. 345.
59. Leite, E. (2015, January 19). Why trust matters in business. Address to the World Economic Forum, Davos-Klosters, Switzerland, para. 6. Retrieved from https://agenda.weforum.org/2015/01/why-trust-matters-in-business
60. Ibid., para. 7.
61. Ibid., paras 3, 5.
62. Tomlinson, E., & Mayer, R. (2009). The role of causal attribution dimensions in trust repair. *Academy of Management Review, 34,* 85–104.
63. Tilly, C. (2005). *Trust and rule.* New York, NY: Cambridge University Press, p. 133.
64. Coleman, 2013, p. 125.
65. Curran, J. (2011). *Media and democracy.* Abingdon, UK: Routledge, p. 86; Norris, P. (2011). *Democratic deficit: Critical citizens revisited.* New York, NY: Cambridge University Press.
66. Van der Meer, T. (2017a). Political trust and the crisis of democracy. *Oxford research encyclopedia of politics.* Oxford, UK: Oxford University Press. Retrieved from http://oxfordre.com/politics/view/10.1093/acrefore/9780190228637.001.0001/acrefore-9780190228637-e-77
67. Zmerli, S., & Van der Meer, T. (Eds.). (2017). *Handbook on political trust.* Cheltenham, UK: Edward Elgar.
68. Mishler, W., & Rose, R. (1997). Trust, distrust and skepticism: Popular evaluations of civil and political institutions in post-communist societies. *The Journal of Politics, 59*(2), 418–451, p. 419.
69. Hetherington, M., & Rudolph, T. (2018). Political trust and polarization. In E. Uslaner (Ed.), *The Oxford handbook of social and political trust* (pp. 579–597). New York, NY: Oxford University Press, p. 580.
70. Ibid.
71. Ibid., p. 581.
72. Ibid., p. 582.
73. Harvard University. (2015). *Trust in institutions and the political process.* Boston, MA: Institute of Politics. Retrieved from http://www.iop.harvard.edu/trust-institutions-and-political-process

74. Pew Research Center. (2017, May 3). Public trust in government: 1958–2017. *US Politics & Policy*. Retrieved from http://www.people-press.org/2017/05/03/public-trust-in-government-1958-2017
75. Ebner, N. (2019). Begun, the trust war has: Teaching negotiation when truth isn't truth. *Negotiation Journal, 35*(1), 207–210.
76. Moran, L. (2019, December 17). The number of lies Donald Trump has now told in office is mind-boggling. *The Huffington Post*. Retrieved from https://www.huffingtonpost.com.au/entry/donald-trump-lies-washington-post_n_5df898c3e4b03aed50f4725d?ri18n=true
77. Harvey, J. (2019, December 17). Guess which of Trump's fibs won him PolitiFact's 'Lie Of The Year' award. *The Huffington Post*. Retrieved from https://www.huffingtonpost.com.au/entry/trump-politifact-lie-of-the-year_n_5df82d1fe4b047e888a2f037?ri18n=true
78. Luhmann, N. (1995). *Social systems*. Stanford, CA: Stanford University Press; Sztompka, P. (2006). New perspectives on trust. *American Journal of Sociology, 112*(3), 905–919.
79. Hoffjann, O. (2011). *Vertrauen* in public relations [trust in public relations]. *Publizistik, 56*, 65–84; Wiencierz, C., & Röttger, U. (2017). The use of big data in corporate communication. *Corporate Communications: An International Journal, 22*(3), 258–272.
80. Jowett, G., & O'Donnell, V. (2006). *Propaganda and persuasion* (4th ed.). Thousand Oaks, CA: Sage Publications, p. 30.
81. Jowett, G., & O'Donnell, V. (1986). *Propaganda and persuasion*. London, UK: Sage Publications, p. 13.
82. Guth, D., & Marsh, C. (2007). *Public relations: A values-driven approach* (3rd ed.). Boston, MA: Pearson Education, p. 70.
83. Bernays, E. (1928). *Propaganda*. New York, NY: Liveright, p. 9.
84. Bernays, E. (1955). *The Engineering of consent*. Norman: University of Oklahoma Press.
85. Bernays, E. (1952). *Public relations*. Norman: University of Oklahoma Press. Section 1. Retrieved from https://www.amazon.com.au/Public-Relations-Edward-L-Bernays-ebook/dp/B00E87Z3M6
86. Watson, T., & Noble, P. (2007). *Evaluating public relations: A best practice guide to public relations planning, research and evaluation* (2nd ed.). London, UK: Kogan Page, p. 14.
87. Shannon, C., & Weaver, W. (1949). *The mathematical theory of communication*. Urbana: University of Illinois.
88. Berlo, D. (1960). *The process of communication: An introduction to theory and practice*. New York: Harcourt/Holt, Rinehart & Winston.
89. Peters, J. (2008). Communication: History of the idea. In W. Donsbach (Ed.), *The international encyclopedia of communication* (n.p.). Malden, MA: Blackwell. Retrieved from https://onlinelibrary.wiley.com/doi/abs/10.1002/9781405186407.wbiecc075

90. Buber, M. (1958). *I and thou* (R. Smith, Trans.). New York: Scribners. (Original work published 1923, 2nd ed. 1987); Buber, M. (2002). *Between man and man* (R. Smith, Trans.). London, UK: Kegan Paul. (Original work published 1947)
91. Bakhtin, M. (1984). *Problems of Dostoevsky's poetics* (C. Emerson, Ed. & Trans.). Minneapolis: University of Minnesota Press. (Original work published 1963); Bakhtin, M. (1986). *Speech genres and other late essays* (C. Emerson & M. Holquist, Eds., V. McGee, Trans.). Austin: University of Texas Press. (Original work published 1979)
92. Bohm, D. (1996). *On dialogue* (L. Nichol, Ed.). New York, NY: Routledge.
93. Gadamer, H. (1989). *Truth and method* (2nd ed., J. Weinsheimer & D. Marshall, Trans.). New York, NY: Crossroad. (Original work published 1960)
94. As cited in Craig, R., & Muller, H. (Eds.). (2007). *Theorizing communication: Readings across traditions*. Thousand Oaks, CA, Sage Publications, pp. 217–250.
95. Craig, R. (1999). Communication theory as a field. *Communication Theory, 9*, 119–161; Craig, R., & Muller, H. (Eds.). (2007). *Theorizing communication: Readings across traditions*. Thousand Oaks, CA: Sage Publications; Littlejohn, S., Foss, K., & Oetzel, J. (2017). *Theories of human communication* (11th ed.). Long Grove, IL: Waveland.
96. Dewey, J. (1916). *Democracy and education*. New York, NY: Macmillan, p. 5.
97. Williams, R. (1976). *Communications*. Harmondsworth, UK: Penguin, p. 10. (Original work published 1962)
98. Carey, J. (2009). *Communication as culture: Essays on media and culture* (Rev. ed.). New York, NY: Routledge, p. 111. (Original work published 1989)
99. Her Majesty's Government. (2019). Government communication plan 2019/20. London, UK: Government Communication Service, p. 13. Retrieved from https://gcs.civilservice.gov.uk/communication-plan-2019; Government Communication Service. (2018). External affairs operating model, p. 5. Retrieved from https://gcs.civilservice.gov.uk/guidance/external-affairs
100. Van der Meer, T. (2017b). Democratic input, macroeconomic output and political trust. In S. Zmerli & T. van der Meer (Eds.), *Handbook on political trust* (Chapter 17, n.p.). Cheltenham, UK: Edward Elgar.
101. Baxter, L. (2011). *Voicing relationships: A dialogic perspective*. Thousand Oaks, CA: Sage Publications; Bimber, B., Flanagin, A., & Stohl, C. (2012). *Collective action in organizations: Interaction and engagement in an era of technological change*. New York, NY: Cambridge University Press; Carey (2009); Carpini, D. (2004). Mediating democratic engagement: The impact of communications on citizens' involvement in political and civic life. In L. Kaid (Ed.), *Handbook of political communication research* (pp. 395–434). London, UK: LEA; Dahlgren, P. (2009). *Media and political engagement: Citizens, communication and democracy*. Cambridge, UK: Cambridge University Press.

102. Kang, M. (2014). Understanding public engagement: Conceptualizing and measuring its influence on supportive behavioural intentions. *Journal of Public Relations Research, 26*(5), 390–416, p. 400.
103. Satell, (2013, November 17). 4 failed marketing buzzwords that you really shouldn't use. *Forbes*. Retrieved from http://www.forbes.com/sites/gregsatell/2013/11/17/4-marketing-buzzwords-that-you-really-shouldnt-use
104. Erickson, T. (2008). *Plugged in: The generation Y guide to thriving at work*. Boston, MA: Harvard Business School.
105. Macey, W., & Schneider, B. (2008). The meaning of employee engagement. *Industrial and Organizational Psychology, 1*(1), 3–30; Meyer, J., & Smith, C. (2000). HRM practices and organizational commitment: A test of a mediation model. *Canadian Journal of Administrative Services, 17*, 319–331; Rhoades. L., Eisenberger, R., & Armeli, S. (2001). Affective commitment to the organization: The contribution of perceived organizational support. *Journal of Applied Psychology, 86*, 825–836.
106. Bimber, B., Flanagin, A., & Stohl, C. (2012). *Collective action in organizations: Interaction and engagement in an era of technological change*. New York, NY: Cambridge University Press, p. 32.
107. Taylor, M., & Kent, M. (2014). Dialogic engagement: Clarifying foundational concepts. *Journal of Public Relations Research, 26*(5), 384–398, p. 391.
108. Solis, B. (2011). *Engage: The complete guide for brands and businesses to build, cultivate, and measure success in the new web*. Hoboken, NJ: Wiley, p. 2.
109. Brown, B., Sikes, J., & Wilmott, P. (2013, August 14). Bullish on digital: McKinsey global survey results. Retrieved from http://www.mckinsey.com/insights/business_technology/bullish_on_digital_mckinsey_global_survey_results
110. Dorgelo, C., & Zarek, C. (2014, June 27). Using citizen engagement to solve national problems [Web log post]. Open Government Initiative, The White House. Retrieved from http://www.whitehouse.gov/blog/2014/06/27/using-citizen-engagement-solve-national-problems; Transform. (2010, September 29). *Directgov strategic review*: Executive summary. London, UK, p. 2. Retrieved from https://www.gov.uk/government/uploads/system/uploads/attachment_data/file/60995/Directgov_20Executive_20Sum_20FINAL.pdf
111. Whereas an invalid vote is one that marks a voting card inappropriately, such as writing comments on it, a 'donkey vote' refers to a voter in a preference voting system ranking candidates in the order that they appear on the ballot paper, rather than by considered choice.
112. This relates to John Keane's concept of *monitory democracy* as discussed in Keane, J. (2009). Monitory democracy and media-saturated societies. *Griffith Review, 24*, Retrieved from https://griffithreview.com/articles/monitory-democracy-and-media-saturated-societies
113. Kavanagh & Rich, 2018, p. 192.

114. Boatright, R. (2019). Introduction: A crisis of civility? In R. Boatright, T. Shaffer, & S. Sobieraj (Eds.), *A crisis of civility: Political discourse and its discontents* (pp. 1–6). New York, NY: Routledge, pp. 1–2.
115. The News Corp newspaper, the *Daily Telegraph* in Sydney, published a front page lead story, two inside pages, and an editorial on 8 May 2019 under the headline "Mother of Invention", alleging that the then Leader of the Opposition, Bill Shorten, had been "slipshod" and "slippery" in an ABC *Q&A* program in telling a story about his mother's struggle to gain an education while raising children. Shorten described the story as "a new low" and the story, which was also published in a number of other News Corp media, was widely condemned as unwarranted and unfounded. "Congratulations to The Daily Telegraph on a great own goal". (2019, May 9). Editorial, *Sydney Morning Herald*. Retrieved from https://www.smh.com.au/politics/federal/congratulations-to-the-daily-telegraph-on-a-great-own-goal-20190508-p51l9q.html
116. Oriti, T. (2019, May 14). Is this Australia's 'dirtiest' election campaign. ABC, *The World Today*. Retrieved from https://www.abc.net.au/radio/programs/worldtoday/is-this-australias-dirtiest-election-campaign/11111384
117. Macmillan, J. (2019, May 5). Targeting of candidates during federal election campaign 'deeply disturbing', 'utterly unacceptable'. *ABC News*, para 1. Retrieved from https://www.abc.net.au/news/2019-05-04/federal-election-campaign-pm-condemns-targeting-of-candidates/11080410
118. Lukensmeyer, C. (2019). Preface. In R. Boatright, T. Shaffer, & S. Sobieraj (Eds.), *A crisis of civility: Political discourse and its discontents* (pp. 1–6). New York, NY: Routledge, p. xxii.
119. Pappacharissi, Z. (2004). Democracy online: Civility, politeness, and the democratic potential of online political discussion groups. *New Media & Society*, 6(4), 259–283, p. 266.
120. Coe, K., Kenski, K., & Rains, S. (2014). Online and uncivil? Patterns and determinants of incivility in newspaper website comments. *Journal of Communication*, 64(3), 658–679, p. 660.
121. Strachan, J. C. & Wolf, M. (2012). Political civility. *PS: Political Science and Politics*, 45(3), 401–404, p. 402.
122. Rawls, J. 1996). *Political liberalism*. New York, NY: Columbia University Press.
123. Laden, A. (2019). Two concepts of civility. In R. Boatright, T. Shaffer, & S. Sobieraj (Eds.), *A crisis of civility: Political discourse and its discontents* (pp. 9–30). New York, NY: Routledge, p. 21.
124. Nye, J. (2010). The new public diplomacy. Project Syndicate. Retrieved from http://www.project-syndicate.org/commentary/nye79/English
125. Strachan, J., & Wolf, M. (2019). Can civility and deliberation disrupt the deep roots of polarization. In R. Boatright, T. Shaffer, & S. Sobieraj (Eds.), *A crisis of*

civility: *Political discourse and its discontents* (pp. 113–141). New York, NY: Routledge, p. 113.
126. Strachan & Wolf, p. 114.
127. Macnamara, J. (2016). *Organizational listening: The missing essential in public communication.* New York, NY: Peter Lang.
128. Macnamara, 2016, p. 236.
129. Ibid., pp. 41–43.
130. May, T. (2016, October 5). Speech to the Conservative Party Conference 2016. Birmingham, UK, paras 19, 45. Retrieved from http://www.independent.co.uk/news/uk/politics/theresa-may-speech-tory-conference-2016-in-full-transcript-a7346171.html
131. Her Majesty's Stationery Office. (2013). *Report of the Mid Staffordshire NHS Foundation Trust public inquiry.* London, UK, p. 3. Retrieved from http://www.midstaffspublicinquiry.com/sites/default/files/report/Executive%20summary.pdf.
132. Ghelani, D. (2017, June 22). Grenfell Tower: "There are only the deliberately silent, or the preferably unheard". *Media Diversified*, paras 1, 5. Retrieved from https://mediadiversified.org/2017/06/22/grenfell-tower-there-are-only-the-deliberately-silent-or-the-preferably-unheard
133. House of Commons. (1999). *Potential risk of fire spread in building via external cladding systems.* London, UK: Select Committee on Environment, Transport and Regional Affairs First Report, London. Retrieved from https://publications.parliament.uk/pa/cm199900/cmselect/cmenvtra/109/10907.htm
134. Australian Conservation Foundation. (2019, June 12). ACF wins legal challenge to Adani's water scheme approval as Federal Government concedes case. News release. Retrieved from https://www.acf.org.au/acf_wins_legal_challenge_to_adanis_water_scheme_approval_as_federal_govt_concedes_case
135. Australian Conservation Foundation. (2019, June 12). We Won! *Facebook*. Retrieved from https://www.facebook.com/AustralianConservationFoundation

2

Post-Truth, Post-Democracy … Post-Politics, Post-Capitalism, Post-Society?

As developed societies have evolved from modernism to postmodernism—a much-debated conceptual and philosophical shift[1]—it has become increasingly popular to use the term *post* as a prefix in front of various nouns. While postmodernism involves a chronological difference from modernism, the significance of the prefix exists beyond its temporal meaning. When placed in front of important concepts, post refers to an evolution or mutation of the original in which its properties and characteristics are superseded and replaced by what are often antithetical features. In many instances, 'post-something' denotes deterioration or even collapse. This is the interpretation of many in contemporary societies who use the prefix post to reflect deep concerns in relation truth, journalism, democracy, politics, capitalism, and human society itself.

Post-Truth

In September 2016 *The Economist* declared that "the world has entered an era of post-truth politics."[2] This pronouncement was triggered by the controversial presidential campaign of Donald Trump—although Trump was far from the first politician to tell 'porky pies' and base statements and policies on fantasy rather than

> ## A Word about Hyphens
>
> The writing style guide of the American Psychological Association (APA) that is widely applied in academic literature and used in this text declares that hyphens should not be used in words beginning with the prefix 'post'. Postmodernism, for example, is usually not hyphenated. However, the sources of a number of the *post* concepts that are examined here have used hyphens, including dictionaries as well as leading media. Accurate citing suggests retention of the original terms. Furthermore, correct English in many countries requires hyphens to avoid repeated consonants, such as in *posttruth*. Even further, some of the terms discussed in the following are relatively new and unfamiliar. So, in the interest of readability and standardization, this text uses hyphens in terms in which post is added before a familiar noun to create a new term.

facts. *The Economist* was not the first to use the term post-truth either. In a 1992 article titled 'A government of lies', playwright and novelist Steve Tesich criticized the administration of George Bush Snr for creating a "post-truth world."[3] A 2004 book examining deception in contemporary life referred to the early 2000s as "the post-truth era."[4] In 2016 the term post-truth was picked up by headline writers and media commentators across the USA and in the UK, Europe, South America, and Asia. By year end, Oxford Dictionaries announced post-truth as its word of the year, defining it as "relating to or denoting circumstances in which objective facts are less influential in shaping public opinion than appeals to emotion and personal belief."[5]

While concern about post-truth existed long before Donald Trump, during his election campaigning and his presidency Trump took post-truth to a new level. However, in an academic analysis Jayson Harsin argues that post-truth is more than a simple disregard of facts and reliance on emotional appeals by a few individuals. He refers to "regimes of post-truth."[6] Harsin says a convergent set of developments have created the conditions of a "post-truth society," pointing to the fragmentation of traditional media and the loss of media *gatekeepers*;[7] the pursuit of celebrity, infotainment, and *tabloidization* in popular media (i.e., journalists are complicit as well as critical in relation to post-truth); the growth of professionalized PR and *spin*; algorithms that govern what appears in social media and search engine rankings; internet practices such as *clickbait*; and other economic, technological, social, cultural, and political developments. Like Harsin, a 2018 RAND Corporation study titled *Truth Decay* referred to "truth decay as a *system*" [emphasis added].[8]

Looking beyond individuals such as Donald Trump and exemplars such as Russian trolls and hackers is essential to fully understand the phenomenon of post-truth and its contributing factors in contemporary societies. Uncovering and critically examining regimes of post-truth and systems responsible for truth decay is the focus of Chapter 3.

To set the scene for that analysis, a number of warnings of the outcomes of unchecked post-truth and truth decay are noted because they provide the reasons why action is needed. A number of social and political scientists propose that a society that does not have truth-telling as a core value lurches towards a decline or collapse of democracy and potentially civil society. Also, it is important to begin from an understanding of the nature, role, and importance of truth, trust, and related concepts.

What Is Truth?

To discuss post-truth in an informed and rational way one needs to have an understanding of the nature of truth as a comparative benchmark. While truth is often assumed to be found in facts, it is a far more slippery concept than many think. 'What is truth' is a question that has troubled philosophers since Plato and Aristotle. Answers to the question are framed by perspective and relativism, but it is a concept on which we need to have some agreed principles before we can discuss and make judgements about post-truth and related concepts such as alternative facts.

In coming to a discussion of truth we need to be cautious about generalizations for several reasons. First, while people living in developed societies have been raised to place emphasis and credibility on facts and empirical evidence, paradoxically we learn a lot about reality from fiction. Fiction by definition is not true. The term refers to invention, fabrication, and imaginary events. But fiction in the form of literature, movies, and TV drama is where most people find out what life in prison is like (e.g., *The Shawshank Redemption*), or what happens in an emergency ward of a hospital (e.g., the TV series *Emergency*), or what war is like (e.g., *Apocalypse Now* or *1917*). While news and documentaries seek to present truth and reality based on facts and recording of actual events, it is a social reality that more people learn about history and events beyond their personal experience from fiction than from documentaries or news reporting. So any categorical dismissal of untruth is not justified or realistic.

A second important factor is that postmodern views in relation to *ontology* (the study of the nature of existence and reality) and *epistemology* (the study of how knowledge is constructed) question whether there is a single objective truth in relation to many issues in the human world. As some authors note, one could argue that postmodern scholarship has contributed to the perception of Donald Trump and his aides and advisers that alternative facts should be given attention and credence as well as what others deem to be facts and truth. While the *scientific method* of research applied in the natural sciences and positivist scholarship in the social sciences have argued that there is a single truth in each situation to be discovered and applied universally, postmodern scholarship in the arts, social sciences, and humanities argues that truth is relative. These disciplines see truth as dependent on one's perspective and a result of human interpretation and social constructionism. Contrary to what some say, this is not a rejection of well established truths such as the laws of physics. But truth in relation to history, for example, depends on whose account one reads and from whose perspective one perceives events. An oft-quoted truism is that history is written by the victors. The vanquished in most instances have a different view of truth. Similarly, in culture and religion there are many competing claims for truth, such as differing beliefs about the existence and nature of God. In recent times, even scientifically established truths about gender and sexuality have been questioned, with factors beyond physiology needing to be considered. While proponents of positivism and *scientism*[9] see their truth-seeking as independent, objective, value-free, and rational, postmodern interpretivist perspectives challenge such claims and argue that all humans including scientists and journalists, who claim the mantle of objectivity, are subjective, value laden, and emotional as well as rational, and that all reality is interpreted.

Contrary to some claims, this does not mean that humanistic approaches to research and knowledge construction are subjective in the pejorative sense of the term, or that they are biased and skewed by irrational responses, 'soft' methodologically, or that anything goes when it comes to truth. The interpretivist paradigm of research and knowledge construction proposes that through thinking and debate humans achieve *intersubjectivity*—a shared subjectivity or consciousness in relation to various realities. In this sociological sense, truth is an isomorphism. Furthermore, and importantly, reflexivity is applied to methodologically moderate how individual subjectivity, values, and emotions affect knowledge construction, as well as critical analysis of theories and hypotheses.

In philosophy there are at least three ways of understanding and identifying truth. A common view is based on *coherence theory*, which philosopher Donald Davidson describes as coherence between one's beliefs and those of many others that creates reason to conclude that one's beliefs are true.[10] It could be argued that Donald Trump's election and popularity among a sizeable proportion of Americans is evidence of coherence and that this justifies his statements about truth. However, while postmodern interpretivist approaches to knowledge construction recognize subjectivity and affective as well as rational cognitive processing of information, many of the statements of Donald Trump and his apparatchiks fail to meet the test of *intersubjectivity* beyond like-minded followers gained through populism and polarization (see the following description of postmodern truth). His 'truths' also fail to incorporate reflexivity and critical analysis in most if not all instances. Nevertheless, coherence theory identifies things that are considered true because a significant number of people believe they are true.

Another more widely accepted explanation of truth that merges philosophy with science is *correspondence theory*. Correspondence theory contends that when human propositions about reality correspond or align with reality or states of affairs as revealed through empirical evidence or observation over a period of time, they are deemed to be true. *Semantic theory of truth* proposed by Alfred Tarski is viewed as a successor to correspondence theory by some, but it focusses specifically on language and metalanguage used to describe reality that is beyond the level of analysis required here.[11]

A third explanation refers to *postmodern truth*, which identifies truth as intersubjective interpretations, as referred to above.[12] However, even though postmodern concepts propose that truth is relative and involves subjectivity because of human interpretation, which is influenced by values and emotion as well as rationality, this is different to truth as defined in coherence theory because postmodern interpretivist knowledge construction involves reflexivity and critical analysis. Truth within postmodern thinking is also eked out by the techniques of qualitative interpretivist research. Rather than using deductive quantitative methods that externally generalize based on statistical calculations, interpretivist research achieves validity through inductively exploring authentic views and experiences via fair and *balanced* inquiry. When done carefully and sensitively, this provides *credibility* and *transferability* of knowledge to other situations—albeit not generalized to all situations.[13] Plurality is recognized in postmodern perspectives. As Neuman says in *Social Research Methods: Quantitative and Qualitative Approaches*: "Qualitative researchers are more interested in *authenticity* than in the idea of a single version of truth. Authenticity means giving a fair, honest and balanced account of social life."[14] The scientific method is undoubtedly reliable for understanding the natural world, but humanistic methods are essential to understand the human world—the world of lived human experience.

In this analysis, correspondence theory of truth as well as postmodern thinking are applied. This steers a middle ground, or what could be called an extended correspondence theory because it seeks to identify truth based on correspondence of claims and propositions with reality as it is revealed in events and empirical evidence, as well as recognizing and respecting individual perspectives and values when they are supported by reflexivity and critical analysis. Thus, it combines scientific and humanistic thinking.

This brief discussion of the nature of truth does, however, illustrate the complexity of the issue and raises the spectre that even academics might be part of the problem of post-truth society. That may sound like heresy to post-positivist scholars, but in challenging scientific knowledge as the only or primary method for understanding the human world and advocating relativity and interpretation, academics may have inadvertently created a basis for Trump's truths. Scholars as eminent as Bruno Latour have observed that the challenge to scientific certainty mounted by postmodernist scholars has, at least in part, created an environment for multiple interpretations of truth and in which "everything is questioned and little is taken at face value."[15] Latour says:

> PhD programs are still running to make sure that good American kids are learning the hard way that facts are made up, that there is no such thing as natural, unmediated, unbiased access to truth, that we are always prisoners of language, that we always speak from a particular standpoint, and so on, while dangerous extremists are using the very same argument of social construction to destroy hard-won evidence that could save our lives.[16]

As controversial as it is to say, this perspective further contributes to one of the central arguments presented in this analysis—that we are all complicit in post-truth. All of us. Even academics and scientists, who are among the most trusted sources of information in non-trusting contemporary societies.[17] In a recent profile, feminist philosopher Donna Haraway said of her views and those of Bruno Latour and other postmodernist philosophers such as Nancy Hartsock: "Our view was *never* that truth is just a question of which perspective you see it from" [original emphasis].[18] However, she acknowledged that her writing on "situated knowledges" and how truth is "made" became "politically explosive during the so-called science wars of the 1990s—a series of public debates among 'scientific realists'

> The term democracy originates from Greece in the 5th century BCE referring to the political systems that existed in Greek city-states, notably Athens. The term *dēmokratía* means rule of the people, which was derived from *dêmos* meaning people and *kratos* denoting power or 'rule'. It is an antonym of *aristokratia* meaning rule by an elite.

and 'postmodernists', which echo in the controversies of today."[19] Lee McIntyre lucidly explores the role of postmodern thinking and what he calls *perspectivism* in a chapter titled 'Did postmodernism lead to post-truth?'[20] It puts academics along with everyone else in the muddy trenches of the war on truth.

Post-Democracy

The right of citizens to information in order to become informed, as well as their access to express their voice through the often problematic concept of *free speech*, are specifically enshrined in the principles of democracy. Indeed, democracy depends on an informed public. Therefore, post-truth and post-communication are inextricably linked to the functioning of democracy and go to the very heart of how our societies work—or don't work.

As has been widely discussed, the informing of citizens as well as expressions of voice and free speech take place in what is somewhat loosely referred to as the *public sphere*. In democratic societies this is meant to be a pluralistic, vibrant, and constructive realm of representation, discussion, and debate. While the public sphere was envisaged as a forum or fora for direct interpersonal interaction in pre-modern societies, such as the much-cited but massively over-stated *agora* of ancient Greece,[21] in contemporary societies media collectively function as a primary site of the public sphere. In addition, various other public fora such as political conventions and communication channels such as letters and submissions to inquiries, reviews, and public consultations form part of the public sphere for information exchange and debate on issues of public interest. Jürgen Habermas, who coined the term public sphere and championed a deliberative version of it based on rational debate, expressed concern in the late 1980s that traditional media have failed to provide viable sites for the effective functioning of the public sphere because of their focus on entertainment, celebrity, and sensation.[22] He also has expressed misgivings about social media stepping up to provide the necessary platforms for people to engage in constructive debate and decision making.[23]

For several decades, political scientists, sociologists, and media and communication scholars have expressed concern at what they term "the democratic deficit,"[24] referring to the failure of democratic institutions to provide an inclusive and effective public sphere, and the disengagement and disillusionment of citizens that have occurred as a result. Even though democracy in one form or another is established in more than 200 countries worldwide,[25] The Economist Intelligence Unit (EIU) Democracy Index declared that just 4.5% of the world's population were living in a "full democracy" in 2018. The United States of America, long-held as a beacon for democracy, was rated a "flawed democracy" by the EIU in 2018 for the third year in succession. Just 18% of Americans approved the way Congress was doing its job in 2018, according to Gallup polls—down from 40% in 2000.[26]

As a result of a deteriorating rather than an improving public sphere, UK political scientist Colin Crouch describes the current state of politics and government in the major developed Western countries as *post-democracy*. He defines post-democracy as follows.

> A post-democratic society is one that continues to have and to use all the institutions of democracy, but in which they increasingly become a formal shell. The energy and innovative drive pass away from the democratic arena and into small circles of a politico-economic elite.[27]

Crouch see post-democracy as one that, for example, continues to have elections and allows freedom of speech and even freedom of assembly, but in which political participation becomes mostly spectatorship, with decision making and power held by political and financial elites. He argues that post-democracy is a withered and emaciated political system that is emerging in place of democracy. For instance, in his book *Coping with Post-Democracy*, Crouch says:

> While elections certainly exist and can change governments, public electoral debate is a tightly controlled spectacle, managed by rival teams of professionals expert in the techniques of persuasion, and considering a small range of issues selected by those teams. The mass of citizens plays a passive, quiescent, even apathetic part, responding only to the signals given them.[28]

Crouch is not alone in his concerns. In *How Voters Feel*, Stephen Coleman makes a number of alarming observations about elections, as noted in Chapter 1.

Coleman reported from his research that elections and voting are predominantly understood and assessed in terms of "instrumental effectiveness," such as voter turnouts, percentage swings, and winning, leading to his conclusion that democratic practice has deteriorated to "a discourse of arid proceduralism."[29] Coleman concluded that there is an "affective deficit"[30] in contemporary democratic politics, which is largely responsible for the disenchantment and disengagement, or stoic resignation at best, that characterizes voting and attitudes towards politics in many democratic countries.

In their analysis of what they call the "fourth revolution" in democracy, John Micklethwait and Adrian Wooldridge say that there is a need to reinvent the state in Western democracies.[31] These and similar criticisms of the state of democracy today are examined in the following chapters. Some even predict the end of democracy.

The End of Democracy?

A 2003 book by Abib Jan titled *The End of Democracy*[32] critiqued Western liberal democracy from a Muslim perspective. While having merit, it received relatively little attention in the West because of its particular viewpoint. The phrase 'the end of democracy' reportedly dates back to Thomas Jefferson who is alleged to have said: "The end of democracy and the defeat of the American Revolution will occur when government falls into the hands of lending institutions and moneyed incorporations." Jefferson's fears could be seen to have become reality with the far too cosy relationship that developed between Washington, D.C. and Wall Street leading to the global financial crisis of 2008–2009 and the policies of successive UK Governments to make London one of the world's financial capitals. So in Thomas Jefferson's terms, democracy has ended, right? Well, no, because Jefferson never said that. Archival records of the writings of Jefferson show that he never used the phrase 'the end of democracy.' These words were added by Naom Chomsky in his 1994 book[33] paraphrasing and drawing conclusions from a letter written by Jefferson to William Branch Giles in 1825 in which Jefferson referred to:

> … vast accession of strength from their younger recruits, who having nothing in them of the feelings or principles of '76 now look to a single and splendid government of an Aristocracy, founded on banking institutions and monied [sic] in corporations under the guise and cloak of their favoured branches of manufactures, commerce and navigation, riding and ruling over the plundered ploughman and beggared yeomanry.[34]

Chomsky summarized Jefferson's loquacious early 19th century prose to say that Jefferson "warned that that would be the end of democracy and the defeat of the American Revolution."[35] Historical analysis cautions us against sweeping and generalized claims.

Nevertheless, questions about the future of democracy have been asked by scholars, commentators, and pundits during the late 1990s and increasingly in the 21st century. For instance, three years after Chomsky's 1994 analysis, Ian Morris and Kurt Raaflaub edited and published a volume of colloquia and conferences papers under the theme 'Democracy 2500?' They included a question mark. But one has to ask whether anyone can look that far into the future with any real perspicacity or clarity, particularly given the rate of change that is occurring in developed societies. This analysis attempts to be more specific, grounded in contemporary events and focussed on identifying imperatives for today and the immediate future.

In the same year that Jan published his book, Simon Hix from the department of government at The London School of Economics and Political Science (LSE) wrote a working paper titled 'The End of Democracy in Europe?'[36] Hix also included a question mark. But his paper, which focussed on democracy in Europe and the European Union (EU) in particular, was never published under that title. Hix's research has appeared in a number of publications, but none retained the fundamental question from his original title. Perhaps reviewers found it preposterous or insufficiently supported.

The question has resurfaced more recently. For example, following the election of Donald Trump as US President, *Newsweek* journalist Neil Buchanan posed the question in relation to Trump's election campaign statements and announcements. These included Trump's infamous campaign warning that he might not accept the results of the election if he lost, and indications that he would act unilaterally in implementing some of his policy proposals such as building "a great wall along our southern border" and deporting millions of Hispanic immigrants and Muslims. The approval of Congress for such major decisions did not seem to matter to Trump at the time. Reflecting on Trump's ascension to power, Buchanan asked: "Are we witnessing the end of democracy?"[37]

Some have been more definite and definitive. In his 2018 book *How Democracy Ends* and in various articles, David Runciman explores various scenarios. Runciman argues that it is a mistake to compare the current "crisis of democracy"[38] with the past examples of populism and public distrust of government and look for solutions from the 20th century. He says "it is likely that democracy will fail in the 21st century in ways that we are not yet familiar with … we need to consider what it means for democracies to fail forwards, tumbling into an unknown future." He points to "the rise of heartless, conscienceless super-capable machines"—technologies and their uses and effects that are explored later in this analysis—as examples of new challenges.[39]

As part of seeking balance in this discussion, one has to be sceptical towards predictions of the end of things—referred to as *endism* by John Seely Brown and Paul Duguid, who critique the tensioned binary of "digerati hype and end-user gloom" in their millennium book *The Social Life of Information*.[40] *Eschatology* (the study of end times) is a major branch of study within Christian theology focussed on the apocalypse and various predictions of the end of the world. But it also crops up in many other systems of thought. For example, Marxism and neoliberalism are both grounded in an "end-of-history" narrative.

As Brown and Duguid and many others point out, endism is a much over-predicted phenomenon. Notable examples include Phillip Meyer's widely cited 2004 prediction of the "end of newspapers,"[41] a prediction by George Gilder in 1994 that the internet would mean the "end of television,"[42] and a prediction by Roland Rust and Richard Oliver in the same year of the end of mass media advertising.[43] When video cassette recorders (VCRs) entered the market in the 1970s, doomsayers predicted the end of cinema.[44] However, some 40 years on the movie industry is producing more blockbusters for the big screen than ever before and attracting viewers generating billions in revenue. Television and newspapers, while undergoing massive change, continue to exist and most rational analyses suggest that they will for some time yet. While advertising has become more targeted, global advertising expenditure has grown from just over US$500 billion a year in 2015 to US$630 billion in 2018 and is a predicted to top US$750 billion by 2021, with television still taking a substantial share.[45]

Other examples of *endism* include sociologist Franco Ferrarotti's analysis of the social impact of mass media in a book titled *The End of Conversation*,[46] while Francis Fukuyama has gone further and postulated that we are reaching the "end of history."[47] Fukuyama argues that human history is comprised of a struggle between ideologies and that, with the fall of the Berlin Wall in 1989 and the collapse of the Soviet Union in 1991, the world has settled on liberal/neoliberal capitalist democracy and pursuit of new economic, political, and social systems will cease. The global explosion in conversations through interactive social media and proliferation of social movements challenge Ferrarotti's view, and many have criticized Fukuyama's sweeping claim, pointing to the rise of fundamentalist Islam and growing criticism of neoliberal capitalism by environmentalists, activists, and social reformers. Recent events suggest that Fukuyama's version of the end of history was substantially wrong.

Nevertheless, disinformation and the alleged emergence of a post-truth society are not good for democracy. As former US President Barack Obama told a political rally in Florida in November 2018: "When words stop meaning anything, when truth doesn't matter, when people can just lie with abandon, democracy can't work."[48]

The Relocation of Democracy

Rather than an end of democracy, evidence suggests that what many societies are witnessing is a relocation of democracy. The traditional and primary sites at which democracy has been exercised through the 19th and 20th centuries were major political parties that recruited members, pre-selected representatives, and developed policy platforms; trade unions; the major Churches that galvanized people on moral and spiritual issues; and mass media (i.e., major newspapers and radio and TV networks). Today, many politicians still take their cue from these traditional institutions. For example, in Number 10, Downing Street—the office the UK Prime Minister and his media staff—planning of announcements, events, and visits by the PM and ministers is done using The Grid. This is a large spreadsheet listing known events, announcements, and other activities that are likely to be of interest to media into which media advisers schedule activities so as to avoid clashes with other newsworthy events. To some extent, The Grid is simply a schedule to ensure that all parts of the government know what is happening and coordinate announcements. However, for critics it is much more than that. Many see it as artefact of *mediatization*. Politicians and their advisers play to the media—that is, they plan events, make decisions, and even decide policy that they know from experience will appeal to editors and news reporters and, therefore, generate headlines and media coverage.

However, as has been widely reported, the audience and influence of newspapers, TV, and radio have declined substantially over the past two decades. The Pew Research Center reported that 68% of Americans accessed their news mainly from social media in 2018,[49] and that trend is common across almost all developed countries.[50] Playing to the increasingly unread, unseen, unheard, and untrusted mass media, even the partisan conglomerates of News Corp, is not reaching the majority of citizens today.

Political parties have suffered a similar decline in membership and support. For example, as noted in the Introduction, membership of the three major political parties in the UK—Conservative, Labour, and Liberal Democrat—totalled just 1.7% of eligible voters in 2019 and has been as low as 0.8 of eligible voters in recent years.[51] Political parties were dominant in what Jay Blumler and Dennis Kavanagh call the *first political age*, which Aeron Davis notes was the "golden age" of parties.[52] But that is long past, as TV came to dominate political communication in the *second political age*, followed by the *third political age* characterized by ubiquitous 24/7 communication via the internet and social media, referred to by Blumler and Kavanagh as a "Hydra-headed beast."[53] Aeron Davis argues in his 2019 discussion of "political communication for crisis times" that Western democratic societies have now entered a *fourth political age*. He says this is characterized by the weakening of state institutions, the loss of trust in political organizations, "hollowed-out legacy news media," information overload, audience fragmentation, polarization, and the rise of complex policy issues that few can fully understand.[54] He also notes that "politics is full of professional communication intermediaries, in public relations, marketing, advocacy, and so on."[55] In writing about the influence of the internet on political communication, Stephen Coleman says: "It may well be that political parties as we knew them in the 20th century are now obsolete."[56]

It seems clear that the heyday of traditional political parties has indeed passed. They will no doubt continue to exist, because organized politics—that is the organization of groups of politicians to win and form governments—requires a great deal of administration, fund-raising, coordination, and promotion of ideology and policies beyond individual endeavours. However, political parties have much to answer for in relation to the loss of public trust and the moral decay in contemporary democracies. Much political criticism is focussed on individual politicians such as Donald Trump, Boris Johnson, and the likes of Fraser Anning in Australia—and deservedly so given frequent exposes of lying, fraudulent business practices, sexism, racism, anti-Semitism, and what *The Guardian* called "vile and offensive" statements.[57] However, apart from the relatively small number of independent politicians, it is political parties that select, endorse, and support politicians and political leaders. Given their decreasing membership and poor record in selecting and promoting politicians and political leaders, it is unsurprising, and probably necessary, that citizens turn elsewhere for representation.

Trade unions remain supportive of Labour/Labor parties in a number of countries including the UK, Australia, and New Zealand, but their membership and influence also has declined from the days when manufacturing dominated the economies of developed and developing countries. While trade union membership in the UK increased slightly in 2018, this followed the lowest membership since UK Government reporting began, with union membership declining to 6.23 million in 2016. Even in 2018, less than a quarter of employees in the UK were members of a trade union.[58] Similarly, in the USA, just 10% of workers are members of a labour union today, compared with more than 20% in the 1980s.[59]

Likewise the major churches, due to increasing secularism in many Western societies and scandals such as the conviction of priests for sex offences against children.

One of the lessons for politicians and government officials today is to look hard at the reference points that they are using as representations and reflections of public opinion. Many of the institutions and reference points that political leaders have relied on are in decline in terms of public support and trust. At the same time, new sites of participation and discourse have been forming, often to the surprise of the establishment, but often ignored and regarded as fringe groups. These new sites of participation range from small community groups to national and even multinational movements involving hundreds of thousands and even millions of people.

The past decade has seen the rise of many social movements and community-based democracy organizations engaging in contemporary issues such as *Occupy*; the *Umbrella Movement* in Hong Kong, which resurged in 2019 with marches involving more than one million people; *Black Lives Matter*; *#MeToo*; and *MySociety*. These groups, movements, and emerging leaders are where the eyes and ears of politicians need to be focussed—not on the coterie of journalists working in the bubble of Brussels, Westminster, or Washington, D.C.; partisan columnists and blowhards; ageing political parties that are unrepresentative of society today; or lobby groups glued to the interests of elites. The potential of social movements and activist groups to contribute to a revitalization of democracy and civil society is examined in Chapter 5.

The election of Donald Trump, *Brexit*, and the rise of a number of social movements comprise what UK political communication scholar Stephen Coleman has called "the insurgence of the unheard."[60] In an essay in *Spiegel Online*, George Diez described the rising populism that elected Donald Trump as a "rearguard battle of the defeated."[61] He explained that those who voted for Trump felt defeated and beaten down. They saw Trump's scorn for the political establishment and his belligerent style as an alternative to institutions and a system that had failed them. Unfortunately, in the case of Trump they were deluded as well as disillusioned.

The real revelation from *Brexit* was not the decision made by the citizens of the UK. It was the shock and bewildered disbelief that followed these events within the halls of power and established institutions—the *krátos* in the language from which the word and the concept of democracy is drawn. Like the election of Donald Trump, *Brexit* showed that the *dêmos* and the *krátos* were disconnected. The *krátos* was out of touch with the *dêmos*. And the *dêmos* were not happy. In the words of actor Peter Finch playing a TV newsreader tired of dishing out infotainment and sensation in the film *Network*, they were saying "I'm mad as hell and I'm not gonna take it anymore."[62] Like the flabbergasted network bosses in the film, UK political leaders did not know what to do. The comfortable conventions by which they operated were no longer working. They were facing disruption in a form and on a scale that they had not seen before.

Walking into the Cabinet Office, Whitehall on the morning of 24 June 2016—the day after the EU referendum—was like walking into a funeral parlour or crematorium. A pervasive silence filled the air. The sense of loss and bewilderment was palpable. In the following weeks, the Prime Minister David Cameron resigned and 13 Ministers lost their jobs in the leadership reshuffle that followed. The leader of the Leave campaign Boris Johnson retired to his backbench role as Member of Parliament (MP) for Uxbridge and South Ruislip to contemplate his next move, before being strategically included in the Cabinet of the new Prime Minister Theresa May as Secretary of State for Foreign and Commonwealth Affairs in July 2016—a case of keeping your friends close and your enemies even closer. Such disruption of a government elected only one year before with an increased majority illustrates a changing tide in politics and how even governments with a seemingly tight grip on power can be toppled.

Almost three years later in March 2019 an estimated one million people marched in the streets of London in protest against the UK Government's handling of *Brexit*, referred to as the 'Million march'. In July 2019 Johnson pounced, taking over the UK Prime Ministership from Theresa May, but still the saga continued on for many more months of polarized debate. What was started by the Conservative government of David Cameron as a referendum that was expected to put the 'European Union question' to rest, raged out of the control for three years. Democracy is on the move and politicians, political parties and many political journalists and commentators are still to catch up.

Post-Media

The concerns of Habermas and many others about the ineffectiveness of media in providing a forum for information, deliberation, and debate and checks and balances on power, along with audience fragmentation and massive technological, economic, and structural changes in digital communications, have led some to speculate that we have entered a *post-media* world.[63] Leaders in advertising in particular point out that those they call consumers now have internet search tools to directly access information from a range of sources, well as a range of ad blocking technologies available to them that enable them to find information without relying on mass media that push information to audiences.

Michael Kahn, CEO of Performics Worldwide, the global performance marketing arm of Publicis Media, says that online information seekers are increasingly averse to accepting pushed advertising and promotional content particularly on mobile devices, which are fast becoming the most popular communications device. One study reported that almost 40% of people block digital advertising content and a further 42% say that they intend to do so in future.[64] Kahn says that brands must adopt and capitalize on an "owned-and-earned-first mentality," which is almost a complete reversal of the long-used PESO media strategy, which prioritized *paid* media (i.e., advertising) above *earned* media coverage such as editorial publicity, *shared* social media content and comment, and *owned* media such as organization websites. In what Kahn more accurately terms a "post-paid media" approach, marketers advocate greater use of owned media such as websites, organization publications such as newsletters and reports, and even fully controlled digital publishing, along with earned media publicity and social media comment.[65] This shift to owned and earned media enabled by low-cost digital technology and the loss of *gatekeepers*[66] includes what is called *native advertising*, which involves commercial and promotional messages being embedded into what appears to be independent editorial or comment. Ethical concerns have been raised about such practices and they are arguably examples of post-communication. (See further discussion of 'Native Advertising' in Chapter 3.)

Kahn also says that *profiling* of individuals built from data analytics and the techniques of psychographics that enable personalization through identification of the personal interests, tastes, preferences, and habits of citizens, who marketers like to narrowly describe as consumers, is the way of the future in marketing communication. However, the use of data analytics has progressed well beyond identifying citizens' interests and preferences. In 2017, *The Guardian* published a major exposé of how the Leave campaign that led to *Brexit* and the Trump election campaign applied dystopian uses of surveillance, data mining, and data analytics to manipulate public opinion. *The Guardian* compared these to *psyops* (psychological operations) used in warfare.[67]

The disguising of promotional messages and manipulative rhetoric in what appears to be non-commercial and non-political media content is part of the "regime of post-truth" that Jayson Harsin discusses. Examples of these practices will be critically examined in Chapter 3. The escalation in the use of data analytics, techniques such as behavioural insights, and growing use of automation and artificial intelligence are further examined in Chapter 4.

Post-Journalism

A number of writers refer to *post-journalism* and many use the prefix post, not in the sense of transforming or transcending, but to denote a negative and retrograde development. For example, in lamenting partisan reporting on the 2008 Obama presidential campaign in which some journalists actively supported Obama, military historian, academic, and columnist Victor Hanson wrote:

> We live now in the age of post-journalism. All that was before is now over, as this generation of journalists voluntarily destroyed the hallowed notion of objectivity and they will have no idea quite how to put Humpty-Dumpty back together again.[68]

In a widely-quoted article in *The Atlantic* in October 2009 discussing a campaign against President Obama's nomination of US Circuit Court Judge Sonia Sotomayor to the Supreme Court in which compromising videos were fed to the mass media by opponents, along with social media attacks, Mark Bowden weighed in as follows.

> I would describe their approach as post-journalistic ... Distortions and inaccuracies, lapses of judgment, the absence of context, all of these things matter only a little, because they are committed by both sides, and tend to come out a wash ... But we never used to mistake it for journalism. Today it is rapidly replacing journalism, leading us toward a world where all information is spun, and where all "news" is unapologetically propaganda.[69]

Others argue that such views reflect nostalgia and romanticization of a mythical golden age of journalism at best, and defensiveness and a power play to maintain control of information flows in society at worst. Author of *Understanding New Media*,[70] Eugenia Siapera wrote in an online post in *The Guardian*'s 'Media Network' blog in 2013 that the future of journalism did not need a new business model to sustain traditional journalistic practices, but a radicalized "move towards imagining not only post-industrial, but post-journalism."[71] She said that journalism as it has existed for the past century or so was "an institution of modernity" and argued that contemporary societies "cannot sustain a model of journalism that remains wedded to old and currently largely irrelevant norms conceived for a kind of society that no longer exists."[72] Siapera said post-journalism refers to "the kind of journalism that applies itself to the kind of society we live in," suggesting that "journalists are no longer only reporters, but data miners, media artists, writers, analysts, witnesses and so on."[73] She argued that journalism needs to be more open, collaborative, accountable, and accepting of a redefining, reordering, and reshuffling of the field as the value of various practices is established, including "data journalism, news aggregation, citizen witnessing, opinion blogs, affective news, and so on."[74] Failings of contemporary journalism will be examined in Chapter 3 and the future of journalism will be explored in Chapter 5.

Post-Representation

Along with a viable public sphere, a fundamental element of democratic societies is representation. Even in the most open democracies not everyone can personally participate in all of the decision making and policy making that affects their lives—and few people have the time or even the desire to do so. Hence we rely on representatives to carry the baton for us on many issues.

While political matters are left largely in the hands of representatives such as members of Congress and members of Parliament in liberal democracies, John Keane says that various non-government organizations (NGOs) and civil society groups monitor the performance of political representatives and governments and take direct action when it is considered necessary in what he terms *monitory democracy*.[75] Keane sees the role of what he calls 'watchdog' organizations as an important and key feature of contemporary democracies.

However, Simon Tormey, professor of politics at the University of Sydney, goes further and says we have seen the end of representative politics[76]—a view that, if correct, is concerning on one hand, but exciting and informative for the future on the other, as Tormey explains. Tormey argues that assumptions about the nature and role of political parties and party based democracy need to be rethought in the light of the Arab Spring, the Indignados uprising in Spain, the street protests in Brazil and Turkey, and spontaneous citizen uprisings such as Occupy, Anonymous, the Umbrella Movement in Hong Kong, and so on. He says

Western democracies are entering an era of "fast politics, evanescent politics, a politics of the street, of the squares, of micro-parties, pop-up parties, and demonstrations."[77] In other words, a new kind of politics is emerging. This supports this author's notion of the 'relocation of democracy', although the lack of listening by politicians and other representatives are not addressed in Tormey's account and not yet resolved.

These issues, which are matters of communication as much as politics, are examined in Chapters 5 and 6, which explore how and where the voice of individuals and groups is expressed today and how there needs to be a reconnection between the power elites of politics, business, and even NGOs and non-profit organizations on one hand with their constituents on the other.

Post-Politics

Some argue that the collapse of many institutions has gone beyond post-democracy and post-representation to an era of post-politics *per se*. This notion first emerged in the period following the end of the Cold War, which culminated in the tearing down of the Berlin Wall—a symbolic as well as a physical act of liberation. However, it remains relevant today and is perhaps more relevant than ever. Rather than being conceived as a positive development, a number of philosophers including Jacques Rancière conceive post-politics as an acceptance of capitalism and neoliberal market values as the organizing basis of society.[78] They argue that, far from being a new post-ideological politics of consensus, the apparent peace and stability that has emerged following several decades of tension between the West and the former Soviet Union and Maoist China disguised a post-democracy in which government is reduced to social administration and elites hold all power and influence. Francis Fukuyama's *End of History* refers to this post-political, post-ideological zeitgeist as it was reflected in the Third Way politics of Britain's New Labour.[79] Thus, post-democracy and post-politics are largely synonymous and are terms that reflect the concerns and pessimism of our age.

Post-Capitalism

Recognizing and reflecting on the issues and concerns briefly outlined, British journalist and author Paul Mason forecasts that we are witnessing the failure of capitalism and ultimately will see the end of capitalism—although, unlike

84 | *Beyond Post-Communication*

Crouch's negative concept of post-democracy, Mason sees post-capitalism positively as preferable replacement to the industrial capitalism of the 20th and early 21st centuries. The superstructures of most developed democracies in the world sit on—or are squashed underneath—a capitalist economic base. In his 2015 book Postcapitalism: A Guide to Our Future and in a number of articles and speeches, Mason says that "millions of people are beginning to realize they have been sold a dream at odds with what reality can deliver" and the result is rising anger at both capitalism and contemporary democracy that are inextricably linked in most developed countries.[80] He points to pro-*Grexit*[81] factions in Greece, the *Le Front National* in France, and the isolationism of the American Right, as well as collapses in capitalism such as those of 2008 and the rise and rise of neoliberalism that he says has "morphed into a system programmed to inflict recurrent catastrophic failures" on societies.[82]

Wolfgang Streeck, director of the Max Planck Institute for Social Research in Cologne and professor of sociology at the University of Cologne, is one who has argued that capitalism will end and is already in severe decay. He says that the regulatory institutions that exist have failed to curb the financial sector's excesses and that there is no political agency capable of rolling back the liberalization of markets. He points to declining growth, oligarchic rule by elites, a shrinking public sphere, and institutional corruption. There are strong signs that public opinion is turning against capitalism, with 56% of 34,000 respondents to the *2020 Edelman Trust Barometer* survey saying that "capitalism as it exists today does more harm than good in the world."[83]

Post-Society

UK Prime Minister Margaret Thatcher infamously said in an interview with *Woman's Own* magazine at Number 10 Downing Street in 1987 that "there is no such thing as society." Far from a slip of the tongue, Baroness Thatcher repeated the phrase several times in the interview with Douglas Keay, also saying: "Who is society? There is no such thing."[84] Thatcher's argument was that people were "casting their problems on society" and expecting the government to resolve them rather than "look to themselves first." While individual initiative and resilience are important, Thatcher's statement was widely criticized as advocating individualism and absconding from the responsibilities of the state.

The policies of neoliberal capitalist governments then and since are seen to have weakened trust in government and eroded social and cultural capital that bond, bridge, and bolster—even make possible—human society. Pessimists predict that the promotion of individualism and the forces of privatization are creating *post-society*—a world in which private interests dominate and survival is matter of every man and woman for themselves. Such doomsday prophesies may be extreme, but there is widespread concern that the fabric of a number of advanced societies is breaking down, evidenced by increasing disengagement from traditional politics and civil society and engagement with radicalization and extremism.

Living in the Age of Post-Everything

Underlying causes of these pessimistic and apocalyptic views are examined in the following chapter. The purpose of this chapter has not been to justify or prove the claims discussed, but simply to note the deep concerns being expressed. Even if the preceding doomsday predictions are exaggerated, there is wide agreement that things are not working the way people would like politically, socially, culturally, and economically.

Beyond trying to shine light on the challenges faced in a number of societies and their underlying causes, a key focus of this book is forward thinking. Despondency often creates a form of blindness. Some things, if not all things, come to an end. But others things begin. Sometimes, things change and morph into something else. Under the canopy of a dead forest, new life springs forth. We need to be alert to such emergent developments. And we need to be prepared to change. As the aphorism says: If we always do what we've always done, we'll always get what we've always got. Right now, many people in Western democratic states—very large numbers of people—do not like what they have got. So, to quote a line from the popular song sung by Sam Cook, Seal, and others: "Change is gonna come"—one way or another.

Notes

1. Latour, B. (1993). *We have never been modern*. Boston, MA: Harvard University Press.
2. "Yes, I'd lie to you". (2016, September 10). *The Economist*. Retrieved from http://www.economist.com/news/briefing/21706498-dishonesty-politics-nothing-new-manner-which-some-politicians-now-lie-and
3. Tesich, S. (1992, January 6). A government of lies. *The Nation*, pp. 12–13.
4. Keyes, R. (2004). *The post-truth era: Dishonesty and deception in contemporary life*. New York, NY: St. Martin's Press.

5. Oxford Dictionaries (2016). Oxford Dictionaries word of the year: Post-truth. Retrieved from https://en.oxforddictionaries.com/word-of-the-year/word-of-the-year-2016
6. Harsin, J. (2015). Regimes of posttruth, postpolitics, and attention economies. *Communication, Culture & Critique, 8*(2), 327–333.
7. The term 'gatekeeper' was coined by social psychologist Kurt Lewin and was used to refer to editors, producers and journalists who control access to and content of media by David Manning White and a number of other media scholars since. See Lewin, K. (1947). Frontiers in group dynamics II: Channels of group life, social planning and action research. *Human Relations, 1*(2), 143–153; White, D. (1950). The gatekeeper: A case study in the selection of news. *Journalism Quarterly, 27*, 383–390. Reprinted in L. Dexter & D. White (Eds.) (1964). *People, society and mass communications*. New York, NY: Free Press.
8. Kavanagh, J., & Rich, M. (2018). *Truth decay: An initial exploration of the diminishing role of facts and analysis in American public life*. Santa Monica, CA: RAND Corporation. Retrieved from https://www.rand.org/research/projects/truth-decay.html
9. *Scientism* is the belief that the assumptions and methods of research of the physical and natural sciences are equally appropriate, or even essential, to all other disciplines including philosophy, the humanities and the social sciences. It developed from empiricism and is closely related to positivism, the philosophy that the only authentic knowledge is scientific knowledge, and that such knowledge can only come from strict application of the scientific method of research (The Basics of Philosophy website— https://www.philosophybasics.com/branch_scientism.html).
10. Davidson, D. (2000). A coherence theory of truth and knowledge. In S. Bernecker & F. Dretske (Eds.), *Knowledge: Readings in contemporary epistemology* (pp. 413–428). Oxford, UK: Oxford University Press.
11. Tarski, A. (1943). The semantic conception of truth and the foundations of semantics. *Philosophy and Phenomenological Research, 4*(3), 341–376.
12. Pardi, P. (2019). What is truth? *Philosophy News*. Retrieved from https://www.philosophynews.com/post/2015/01/29/What-is-Truth.aspx
13. Lincoln, Y., & Guba, E. (1985). *Naturalistic inquiry*. Beverly Hills, CA: Sage Publications; Shenton, A. (2004). Strategies for ensuring trustworthiness in qualitative research projects. *Education for Information, 22*(2), 63–75.
14. Neuman, W. (2006). *Social research methods: Qualitative and quantitative approaches* (6th ed.). New York, NY: Pearson, p. 196.
15. McIntyre, L. (2018). *Post-truth*. Cambridge, MA: MIT Press, p. 125.
16. Latour, B. (2004). Why has critique run out of steam? From matters of fact to matters of concern. *Critical Inquiry, 30*, 225–248, p. 227. Retrieved from http://www.bruno-latour.fr/sites/default/files/89-CRITICAL-INQUIRY-GB.pdf

17. Edelman. (2019). *2019 Edelman trust barometer*. New York, NY, p. 32. Retrieved from https://www.edelman.com/sites/g/files/aatuss191/files/2019-02/2019_Edelman_Trust_Barometer_Global_Report.pdf
18. Weigel, M. (2019, June 20). Feminist cyborg scholar Donna Haraway: 'The disorder of our era isn't necessary'. *The Guardian*, Interview, para. 10. Retrieved from https://www.theguardian.com/world/2019/jun/20/donna-haraway-interview-cyborg-manifesto-post-truth
19. Ibid., para. 6.
20. McIntyre, 2018, pp. 123–150.
21. The *agora* of ancient Greece, which were physical gathering places or assembly areas, are often cited as an exemplar of democracy. However, slaves and women were not admitted to debates or discussion in the *agora*, thus more than 50% of the population was excluded.
22. Habermas, J. (1989). *The structural transformation of the public sphere*. Cambridge, UK: Polity. (Original work published 1962)
23. Habermas, J. (2006). Political communication in media society: Does democracy still enjoy an epistemic dimension? The impact of normative theory on empirical research. *Communication Theory, 16*(4), 411–426.
24. Couldry, N. (2010). *Why voice matters: Culture and politics after neoliberalism*. London, UK and Thousand Oaks, CA: Sage Publications, p. 49; Curran, J. (2011). *Media and democracy*. Abingdon, UK: Routledge, p. 86; Norris, P. (2011). *Democratic deficit: Critical citizens revisited*. New York, NY: Cambridge University Press.
25. Marsh, I., & Miller, R. (2012). *Democratic decline and democratic renewal: Political change in Britain, Australia and New Zealand*. Cambridge, UK: Cambridge University Press, p. 3.
26. The retreat of democracy stopped: Or has it just paused? (2018, January 8). *The Economist*. Retrieved from https://www.economist.com/graphic-detail/2019/01/08/the-retreat-of-global-democracy-stopped-in-2018
27. Crouch, C. (2013, February 5). *Five minutes with Colin Crouch*. London, UK: London School of Economics and Political Science. Retrieved from http://blogs.lse.ac.uk/politicsandpolicy/five-minutes-with-colin-crouch
28. Crouch, C. (2012, July). *Coping with post-democracy extract*. London, UK: The Fabian Society, para. 3. Retrieved from http://www.fabians.org.uk/wp-content/uploads/2012/07/Post-Democracy.pdf
29. Coleman, S. (2013). *How voters feel*. New York, NY: Cambridge University Press, p. 192.
30. Coleman, 2013, p. 5.
31. Micklethwait, J., & Wooldridge, A. (2014). *The fourth revolution: The global race to reinvent the state*. New York, NY: Penguin.
32. Jan, A. (2003). *The end of democracy*. Canada: Pragmatic Publishing.

33. Chomsky, N. (1994). *Keeping the rabble in line: Interviews with David Barsamian*. Monroe, ME: Common Courage Press. Chomsky's book quoting (or misquoting) Jefferson is available in full online at https://zcomm.org/keeping-the-rabble-in-line.
34. Jefferson, T. (1903). *The complete anas of Thomas Jefferson* (F. Sawvel, Ed.). Ann Abor, MI: Hathi Trust Digital Library.
35. Chomsky, 1994, p. 245.
36. Hix, S. (2003). The end of democracy in Europe. Working paper. Retrieved from http://personal.lse.ac.uk/hix/Working_Papers/Hix-End_of_Democracy_in_Europe.pdf
37. Buchanan, N. (2016, November 25). Are we witnessing the end of democracy? *Newsweek Europe*. Retrieved from http://europe.newsweek.com/neil-buchanan-are-we- witnessing-end-democracy-524169?rm=eu
38. Van der Meer, T. (2017). Political trust and the 'crisis of democracy'. *Oxford Research Encyclopedia of Politics*, pp. 1–23. Retrieved from https://oxfordre.com/politics/abstract/10.1093/acrefore/9780190228637.001.0001/acrefore-9780190228637-e-77
39. Runciman, D. (2018). How democracy ends. *Cambridge Alumni Magazine, 83*. paras 5–7. Retrieved from https://www.cam.ac.uk/howdemocracyends
40. Brown, J., & Duguid, A. (2000). *The social life of information*. Boston, MA: Harvard Business School Press.
41. Meyer, P. (2004). *The vanishing newspaper: Saving journalism in the information age*. Columbia, OH: University of Missouri Press
42. Gilder, G. (1994). *Life after television*. New York, NY: W.W. Norton & Company, p. 49.
43. Rust, R., & Oliver, R. (1994). The death of advertising. *Journal of Advertising, 23*(4), 71–77, p. 71.
44. Lewis, J. (2001). *The end of cinema as we know it: American film in the nineties*. New York, NY: New York University Press.
45. Statista. (2019). Global advertising spending from 2014 to 2021. Retrieved from https://www.statista.com/statistics/273288/advertising-spending-worldwide
46. Ferrarotti, F. (1988). *The end of conversation: The impact of mass media on modern society*. New York, NY: Greenwood.
47. Fukuyama, F. (1992). *The end of history and the last man*. New York, NY: Free Press.
48. Thomas, K. (2018, November 2). Obama says democracy can't work 'when people can just lie with abandon' at Florida rally. *Global News*. Retrieved from https://globalnews.ca/news/4626146/obama-florida-rally
49. Matsa, K., & Shearer, E. (2018, September 10). News use across social media platforms 2018. Pew Research Center, Reports. Retrieved from https://www.journalism.org/2018/09/10/news-use-across-social-media-platforms-2018
50. It should be noted that traditional media, particularly newspapers, remain popular in some countries such as India.

51. Audickas, L., Dempsey, N., & Keen, R. (2018). Membership of UK political parties. Commons Briefing Papers SN05125. London, UK: House of Commons. Retrieved from http://researchbriefings.parliament.uk/ResearchBriefing/Summary/SN05125
52. Davis, A. (2019). *Political communication: A new introduction for crisis times.* Cambridge, UK: Polity, p. 6.
53. Blumler, J., & Kavanagh, D. (1999). The third age of political communication: Influences and features. *Political Communication, 16*(3), 209–230, p. 213.
54. Davis, 2019, pp. 7–8.
55. Ibid., p. 10.
56. Coleman, S. (2017). *Can the internet strengthen democracy?* Cambridge, UK: Polity, p. 75.
57. Davidson, H. (2019, June 21). Peter Dutton condemned for 'vile and offensive' Nauru rape claims. *The Guardian.* Retrieved from https://www.theguardian.com/australia-news/2019/jun/21/peter-dutton-condemned-for-vile-and-offensive-nauru-claims
58. Department of Business, Energy and Industrial Strategy. (2019, May 30). Trade union membership: Statistical bulletin. Retrieved from https://assets.publishing.service.gov.uk/government/uploads/system/uploads/attachment_data/file/805268/trade-union-membership-2018-statistical-bulletin.pdf
59. Organization for Economic Cooperation and Development. (2020). Trade union. *OECDStat.* Retrieved from https://stats.oecd.org/Index.aspx?DataSetCode=TUD
60. Coleman, 2017, p. 118.
61. Diez, G. (2016, November 7). Democracy at a dead-end in America. *Spiegel Online.* Retrieved from http://www.spiegel.de/international/world/trump-is-the-product-of-the-erosion-of-liberal-democracy-a-1120133.html
62. The line was delivered as part of what is known as the 'I'm mad as hell' speech delivered by actor Peter Finch in the 1976 film *Network* about a fictitious TV network also starring Faye Dunaway, William Holden, and Robert Duvall. The line was a challenge to audiences to rebel against what the network was dishing up as news and information.
63. Brogan. C. (2008, November 10). Communications in a post-media world [Weblog post]. Retrieved from http://chrisbrogan.com/communications-in-a-post-media-world
64. GlobalWebIndex. (2016). 37% of mobile users are blocking ads [Web blog post]. Retrieved from https://www.globalwebindex.net/blog/37-of-mobile-users-are-blocking-ads
65. Kahn, M. (2016, July 13). How brands can survive in a post-paid media world. *CMO* [Web log post]. Retrieved from http://www.cmo.com/opinion/articles/2016/6/22/how-brands-can-thrive-in-a-postpaid-media-world.html#gs.gkeE=Ec
66. The term 'gatekeeper' was coined by social psychologist Kurt Lewin and was used to refer to editors, producers and journalists who control access to and content of media by David Manning White and a number of other media scholars since. See Lewin,

K. (1947). Frontiers in group dynamics II: Channels of group life, social planning and action research. *Human Relations*, *1*(2), 143–153; White, D. (1950). The gatekeeper: A case study in the selection of news. *Journalism Quarterly*, *27*, 383–390. Reprinted in L. Dexter & D. White (Eds.) (1964). *People, society and mass communications*. New York, NY: Free Press.
67. Caldwalladr, C. (2017, May 7). Follow the data: does a legal document link Brexit campaigns to US billionaire? *The Guardian*. Retrieved from https://www.theguardian.com/technology/2017/may/07/the-great-british-brexit-robbery-hijacked-democracy#comments [since taken down because of a legal complaint].
68. Hanson, V. (2008, November 7). Post-journalism. *National Review Online*, The Corner, para. 5. Retrieved from http://www.nationalreview.com/corner/173630/post-journalism/victor-davis-hanson
69. Bowden, M. (2009, October). The story behind the story. *The Atlantic*, para. 39. Retrieved from http://www.theatlantic.com/magazine/archive/2009/10/the-story-behind-the-story/307667
70. Siapera, E. (2012). *Understanding new media*. London, UK: Sage Publications.
71. Siapera, E. (2013, February 15). From post-industrial to post-journalism. *The Guardian*, Media Network [Web log post], para. 7. Retrieved from http://www.theguardian.com/media-network/media-network-blog/2013/feb/14/post-industrial-journalism-changing-society
72. Ibid., para. 5.
73. Ibid., para. 1.
74. Ibid., paras 5–7.
75. Keane, J. (2009). *The life and death of democracy*. New York, NY: W. W. Norton & Co.; Keane, J. (2011). Monitory democracy: The secret history of democracy since 1945. In B. Isakhan & S. Stockwell (Eds.), *The secret history of democracy* (pp. 204–218). Basingstoke, UK: Palgrave Macmillan.
76. Tormey, S. (2015). *The end of representative politics*. Cambridge, UK: Polity.
77. Tormey, S. (2015), Description. See http://au.wiley.com/WileyCDA/WileyTitle/productCd-0745681964,subjectCd-PO17.html
78. Ranciere, J. (2004). Introducing disagreement. *Angelaki: Journal of the Theoretical Humanities*, *9*(3), 3–9.
79. Fukuyama, F. (1992). *The end of history and the last man*. New York, NY: Free Press.
80. Mason, P. (2015). *Postcapitalism: A guide to our future*. London, UK: Allen Lane.
81. The movement advocating the exit of Greece from the European Union, paralleling the exit of the UK referred to as *Brexit*.
82. Mason, P. (2015, July 17). The end of capitalism has begun. *The Guardian*, Economics, para. 18. Retrieved from https://www.theguardian.com/books/2015/jul/17/postcapitalism-end-of-capitalism-begun

83. Edelman. (2020). *2020 Edelman trust barometer*. New York, NY, p. 12. Retrieved from https://www.edelman.com/trustbarometer
84. Keay, D. (1987, September 23). Interview for *Woman's Own*. London, UK: Margaret Thatcher Foundation. Retrieved from http://www.margaretthatcher.org/document/106689

3
Post-Communication

As noted in the Introduction, Robert Cathcart coined the term *post-communication* in 1966 as the title of a study of rhetoric and rhetorical criticism.[1] In this Cathcart described rhetoric as "a communicator's intentional use of language and other symbols to influence or persuade selected receivers to act, believe, or feel the way the communicator desires in problematic situations."[2] Cathcart's use of the term post-communication referred to critical reflection, analysis, and evaluation undertaken after communicative acts such as speaking in order to identify strengths, weaknesses, and ways in which rhetoric could be improved. Hence, it was used in a temporal sense in one respect. However, in his discussion of analysis and evaluation, Cathcart conflated rhetoric and communication with *one-way* persuasion to achieve "the communicator's desires"—by which he clearly meant the desires and objectives of a particular actor. 'Communicator' is a singular subject in his definition and discussion, while others are described as "receivers." No doubt Cathcart was influenced by information processing models circulating at the time such as Shannon and Weaver's one-way transmissional model[3] and David Berlo's one-way source-message-channel-receiver (SMCR) model of information processing that were applied to communication.[4]

Influence and persuasion are recognized as legitimate and ethical objectives of communication in some circumstances and, as such, they are sought and practiced in interpersonal communication and in public communication, such as road safety and health campaigns. However, Cathcart's definition of rhetoric and his generalized conflation of communication with *one-way* persuasion are problematic in several respects. First, his definition of rhetoric implies that the rhetorician knows what is best and, therefore, leads to a view that dialogue and debate can be avoided. The reality that rhetoricians might not know what is best is conveniently overlooked or cynically ignored. Second, one-way persuasion is only half the process of communication, which is widely defined and advocated in contemporary literature as a two-way dialogic process for exchanging and negotiating meaning (see 'The Role of Communication in Trust' in Chapter 1). Third, the potential for rhetoricians to deploy an ever-expanding arsenal of rhetorical techniques and technologies leads to imbalances in resources and power far beyond those that concerned Plato,[5] and potentially results in propaganda and manipulation.

Therefore, at a time of problematic practices in public communication, which will be explored in this chapter, and rapid advances in powerful information and communication technologies (ICTs) that will be examined in Chapter 4, it seems appropriate to revisit and repurpose Cathcart's concept of post-communication and his focus on analysis and evaluation of communication.

It must be acknowledged that, despite a continuing pejorative view of rhetoric in popular culture, scholarly understanding of rhetoric has broadened beyond Cathcart's definition. Recent texts advocate that rhetoric can be balanced and productive by ensuring that both sides of debates have the ability to present their case persuasively. Emeritus professor of communication Karen Foss notes that rhetoric may be intended to persuade, but she says that it also may be an "invitation to understanding" through two-way debate, which is referred to as *invitational* rhetoric as opposed to manipulative rhetoric.[6] Bob Heath has applied this argument to public relations (PR) in his *rhetorical theory of public relations*,[7] although many remain unconvinced that PR is about balanced discussion and interaction. More will be said about PR and its role in the malaise affecting contemporary Western societies in the following discussion. Invitational rhetoric presumes that both sides, or all sides, in debate and discussion have equal access to the tools of persuasion and equal skills of persuasion. However, even a quick glance at the numbers of professional media advisers, press secretaries, PR practitioners, and *strategic communication* consultants employed by governments and corporations shows that this is far from the case. For example, in addition to special advisors (a euphemism for media and campaign staff) directly employed by ministers, the UK Government Communication Service (GCS) employs more than 4,000 communication professionals in national government departments and agencies, and local government employs thousands more. Corporations and major lobby groups similarly have large resources and budgets for public communication through advertising, PR, websites, direct marketing, events, and social media.

What Is Post-Communication?

The term postcommunication (without a hyphen) has been used recently in positive ways, such as a Facebook site that refers to itself as *The Postcommunication* and promotes living harmoniously through applying a set of guidelines in social media and communication generally.[8] The site is promoted by a group called Slowbyte that claims to "propose new ideas to interpret and satisfy the social and cultural needs arising from globalization."[9] However, in this analysis it is Cathcart's use of the term that is conceptualized in a contemporary context due to its direct relevance to the practices of rhetoric and persuasion; language, symbols, and technologies of communication; and the importance of analysis and evaluation.

Like post-truth, post-communication is not a simple temporal transition. As briefly discussed in the Introduction and in discussion of the prefix post in Chapter 2, the term post-communication is used in this analysis to refer to an evolution in which communication has been transmogrified from its normative purpose and function, with its principles and characteristics superseded and replaced by antithetical features. Specifically, the term is used in relation to public communication to denote the transition from ethically informing and dialogically interacting to disinformation, deception, and manipulative persuasion aided by the adoption of new technologies without commensurate regulation, self-regulation, and ethical frameworks. Post-communication refers to a breakdown of communication and a disregard for and discarding of its key principles, as described in Chapter 1, to the extent that all there is left is a pretence of communication.

Nor is discussion of post-communication a comparison with an earlier idealized period of unfailing communication, or a naïve overly optimistic notion of communication. As John Durham Peters says poetically, drawing on William James: "That we can never communicate like the angels is a tragic fact, but also a blessed one."[10] He explains that giving up on the dream of instant unfailing communication is not to be driven into a nightmare of solitude or ignorance. He says communication, in all its fractures and mediations, is all we have. It is what makes us human. Interestingly, Peters goes on to say that, despite the potential for misunderstanding in human communication, "most of the time we understand each other quite well; we just do not agree."[11]

Also, is has to be recognized that breakdowns in and corruption of communication, both interpersonal and public, are not new. There has been misinformation, various forms of fake news as discussed in Chapter 1, and intentional distribution of disinformation throughout human history. The noted existentialist Albert Camus (1913–1960) lamented that "dialogue and personal relations have been replaced by propaganda or polemic."[12] James Carey warned in 1989 that "language—the fundamental medium of human life—is increasingly defined as an instrument for manipulating objects, not a device to establish the truth but to get others to believe what we want them to believe." Carey added that "the instrumentalization of communication has not merely increased the incidence of propaganda; it has disrupted the very notion of truth, and therefore the sense by which we take our bearings in the world is destroyed."[13]

The Growing Pervasiveness of Post-Communication

Despite its perennial nature, recent events indicate that post-communication is escalating with "regimes of post-truth"[14] funded by the deep pockets of governments and large corporations. Three key factors are causing this escalation of post-communication and, therefore, of related concerns. The first is the scale at which post-communication can be created and distributed in the age of the internet and social media. Second, many of the ICTs that have been used in the past decade pale into insignificance compared with the ICTs coming on stream, such as ever more powerful data analytics and the use of artificial intelligence (AI) in public communication. Third, evolution in practices such as advertising, marketing, PR, and political campaigning are pushing the boundaries of what has been considered legitimate and ethical, and sometimes crossing those boundaries. This chapter examines a number of practices and uses of technology that are deployed for creating disinformation, deception, and manipulation and which are corrupting the public sphere.

Spin

The term spin is commonly applied to statements and speeches by politicians and their media advisers, press secretaries, and special advisers (known in the trade as SPADs), as well as to PR activities and outputs. The term is pejorative, alluding to the process of fabrication as undertaken in the manufacture of thread and textiles. It also carries connotations of twisting and stretching—in the case of communication, the twisting and stretching of truth.

The phenomenon of spin has been widely studied and criticized over the past two to three decades. For example, it has been the subject of more than a dozen books including:

- *Spin control: The White House Office of Communications and the Management of Presidential News* (John Maltese, 1994);
- *PR: A Social History of Spin* (Stuart Ewen, 1996);
- *Spin Man: The Topsy-turvy World of Public Relations: A Tell-all Tale* (Thomas Madden, 1997);
- *The Father of Spin: Edward L. Bernays and the Birth of Public Relations* (Larry Tye, 1998, 2002);
- *Spin: How to Turn the Power of the Press to Your Advantage* (Michael Stirick, 1998);
- *Spin Cycle: How the White House and the Media Manipulate the News* (Howard Kurtz, 1998);
- *Open Scotland? Journalists, Spin Doctors and Lobbyists* (Philip Schlesinger, David Miller & William Dinan, 2001);
- *Inside Spin: The Dark Underbelly of the PR Industry* (Bob Burton, 2007);
- *A Century of Spin: How Public Relations Became the Cutting Edge of Corporate Power* (David Miller & William Dinan, 2008);
- *A Persuasive Industry? Spin, Public Relations and the Shaping of the Modern Media* (Trevor Morris & Simon Goldsworthy, 2008);
- *Stay on Message: The Spin Doctor's Guide to Effective Authentic Communication* (Paul Ritchie, 2010).

Concern about spin prompted the establishment of organizations such as Spinwatch in the UK by non-profit company Public Interest Investigations, which "investigates the way that the PR industry and corporate and government propaganda distort public debate and undermine democracy."[15] The PR industry comes in for much of the blame for spin, although many examples cited involve communication by politicians and others including journalists, as is shown in allegations of 'weapons of mass destruction' that justified the second Iraq War, which is discussed in this chapter. Nevertheless, the PR industry is implicated in many cases, as will be shown in the following examples.

North American PR, in particular, is heavily orientated to promoting business and the interests of capitalism, which extends to neoliberal governments. For example, a Delphi study conducted by the US Institute for Public Relations (IPR) in 2019 reported that participants "overwhelmingly believe their role to be to support business objectives."[16] This geopolitical orientation does not only apply to PR conducted within North America. In the second half of the 20th century and into the 2000s, PR education was bolstered in American universities and promoted internationally as a 'cash cow' to replace declining enrolments in mass communication and journalism schools (so-called J schools) and became the "dominant paradigm"[17] worldwide, as discussed in Chapter 5.

Gina Dietrich is one PR professional who advocates publicly against spin and deceit. In her 2014 book *Spin Sucks: Communication and Reputation Management in the Digital Age* she devotes chapters and sections to "tell your story without spin" and "tell your story without sex or extortion." She also discusses "content farms," "robots that write," and other things to avoid in today's digital age—although, in the end, Dietrich mainly focusses on how to make PR successful.[18] Most PR practitioners reject the notion that they are engaged in spin but, while PR is used to promote many important causes, the following examples show that the PR industry has a lot to answer for.

Merchants of Doubt

An archetypal use of public communication to intentionally misinform and mislead the public has been the systematic undermining of science in the second half of the 20th century and early 21st century. Two examples stand out—one that began in the 1950s and continued for more than four decades. The other is in full swing right now.

In *Lies, Incorporated*, Ari Rabin-Havt outlined how corporate-funded lobbying that included misrepresentation and lying has influenced political positions and policies on guns, immigration, health care, abortion, climate change, and other important social and political issues. A noteworthy example was documented by Naomi Oreskes and Erik Conway in *Merchants of Doubt*, in which they trace the tactics used by the tobacco industry to mislead the public about the dangers of smoking tobacco over several decades. The campaign of disinformation about the link between smoking and lung cancer began at a summit in New York City in 1953 at which John Hill, one of the founders of the global PR firm Hill & Knowlton, proposed a "fight the science with alternative science" approach by sponsoring additional research. Big Tobacco CEOs agreed to Hill's plan to establish the Tobacco Industry Research Committee (TIRC) that, over the following 45 years, produced and distributed pseudo-science to deny any link between smoking and cancer. In 1998, when the TIRC was finally disbanded, internal documents revealed that the tobacco companies had known the truth all along, and they subsequently paid out $200 billion in lawsuits.[19] Rabin-Havt summarized:

The Tobacco Industry Research Committee was created to cast doubt on scientific consensus that smoking cigarettes causes cancer, to convince the media that there were two sides to the story about the risks of tobacco and that each side should be considered with equal weight. Finally it sought to steer politicians away from damaging the economic interests of the tobacco companies.[20]

The role of the co-founder of the PR firm Hill & Knowlton in the Tobacco Industry Research Committee was not the only association between Big Tobacco and PR. The acclaimed "father of public relations,"[21] Edward Bernays, worked for the American Tobacco Company to promote cigarette smoking. In one notorious example of his craft, Bernays promoted smoking among women by distributing free cigarettes to women marching in the 1929 Easter Sunday parade in New York City, describing cigarettes as "torches of freedom" to appeal to the rising sentiment of women's liberation.[22]

Merchants of doubt continue to engage in what Lee McIntyre calls the creation of "manufactured doubt"[23] and spin their web today, the most notable example of which is in relation to anthropogenic climate change. Scientists are almost unanimous in their understanding of the *Anthropocene*—the period dating from the commencement of significant human impact on the Earth's geology and ecosystems—including climate change effects such as global warming. For example, in 2012 researchers reviewed 13,950 scientific papers on climate change and found just 0.17% dissented from the overwhelming view that human activity was contributing substantially to global warming, melting of the Arctic and Antarctic ice caps, rising sea levels, and other deleterious climate changes.[24]

However, the public and media are fed a diet of disinformation from lobby groups and think tanks such as the Heartland Institute, which is funded by Exxon-Mobil and other major companies in the fossil fuel industry.[25] In the style of the Tobacco Industry Research Committee, the American Petroleum Institute (API) convened a series of meetings in Washington, D.C. in 1998 to discuss industry responses to the Kyoto Protocol treaty to reduce carbon emissions that was being negotiated at the time. Among attendees were representatives of some of the world's largest oil companies including Exxon and Chevron. In 2001 the USA withdrew from the Kyoto Protocol and, as at the beginning of the 2020s, had not re-joined. The Union of Concerned Scientists (UCS) has claimed that Exxon Mobil gave US$16 million to 43 different think tanks to write sceptical reports about climate change between 1998 and 2005.[26] Another report claims that between 2002 and 2010 a corporate network of billionaires, facilitated by Charles and David Koch of Koch Industries, a multinational corporation involved in manufacturing, refining, and distribution of petroleum and chemicals, contributed US$118 million towards 102 interest groups to discredit the science of climate change.[27]

These are not the only examples of campaigns by what Oreskes and Conway refer to as merchants of doubt. Darwin's theory of human evolution supported by considerable scientific evidence was attacked and undermined systematically for decades, and in some places is still denied by advocates of *creationism*.

Along with climate change denial, in contemporary times anti-vaccination advocates seek to undermine scientific evidence that vaccines are safe and important in preventing disease. Claims that vaccines cause autism and other health problems continue to circulate, despite the fact that the research article that purportedly established such a link was withdrawn because the research was found to be flawed. A study by Dr Andrew Wakefield and colleagues published in 1998 was subsequently revealed to be based on a small sample of only 12 children and it was revealed that some of Wakefield et al.'s research was funded by lawyers acting for parents involved in lawsuits against vaccine manufacturers.[28] The research was consequently shown to be biased and unreliable.

This shows that even scientists are sometimes complicit and even directly involved in disinformation and deception, motivated by financial support in the form of grants and contracts. For a number of years the sugar industry paid scientists to focus on the effects of fats in order to downplay the negative impacts of sugar on human health. A front organization called the Sugar Research Foundation (SRF) sponsored research by Harvard scientists that was published in the *New England Journal of Medicine* in 1967 blaming fats for increasing rates of heart disease, obesity, and other health problems, and giving sugar a clean bill of health. The article was published with no disclosure of its funding by the sugar industry, which is contrary to academic publishing standards. One of the researchers, who was the chairman of Harvard's Public Health Nutrition Department, was also a member of the SRF board.[29] The questionable research and the sugar industry's disinformation campaign was outed in a 2016 academic journal article published in *JAMA* [Journal of American Medical Association] *Internal Medicine*.[30] Fortunately, in the scientific and scholarly community, there are rigorous independent review processes that prevent such deception in the vast majority of published research.

Toxic Sludge Is Good for You

One of the most damning and high-profile contemporary critiques of PR was the book written by John Stauber and Sheldon Rampton titled *Toxic Sludge is Good for*

You: Lies, Damn Lies and the Public Relations Industry.[31] The first part of the book's title was originally drawn from a Tom Tomorrow cartoon. But it took on special meaning following an investigation by the authors of a campaign by the US Water Environment Federation (formerly known as the Federation of Sewage Works Associations) to rebrand sewage sludge as 'biosolids' and promote it as harmless, even beneficial fertiliser for farms. The authors reported: "Our investigation into the PR campaign for 'beneficial use' of sewage sludge revealed a murky tangle of corporate and government bureaucracies, conflicts of interest, and a cover-up of massive hazards to the environment and human health."[32] Their investigation led to a whistleblower in the hazardous site control division of the Environmental Protection Agency, who described the untreated sludge as "the mother lode of toxic waste."[33] The publisher's introduction and back cover of *Toxic Sludge is Good for You* says that the book "blows the lid off of today's multi-billion-dollar propaganda-for-hire PR industry." It continues: "This book reveals how public relations wizards concoct and spin the news, organize phony grassroots front groups, spy on citizens and conspire with lobbyists and politicians to thwart democracy."[34]

Citizens for a Free Kuwait

During the first Gulf War, one of the world's largest PR firms, Hill & Knowlton, was engaged in a US$10.8 million campaign to mobilize American support for an invasion of Iraq. While Hill & Knowlton has denied most of the accusations made against it,[35] Sourcewatch[36] and a number of other sources allege that Citizens for a Free Kuwait was a front organization created by the PR firm, a practice referred to as *astroturfing*.[37] Astroturfing is defined by digital communication specialist and blogger Paull Young as "the practice of creating fake entities that appear to be real grassroots organizations, when in fact they are the work of people or groups with hidden motives and identities."[38] In addition to creating Citizens for a Free Kuwait as a largely citizen-less organization,[39] a key element of the campaign to mobilize American public opinion in support of war against Iraq was testimony by 'Nurse Nayirah' to the Congressional Human Rights Caucus in October 1990 that she had witnessed Iraqi soldiers killing hundreds of premature babies at the Al-Addan Hospital in Kuwait City. The public was told that the identity of Nurse Nayirah was concealed to protect her family. However, it was later disclosed that Nurse Nayirah was Nayirah al-Sabah, daughter of the Kuwaiti Ambassador to the US, and her story was revealed to be untrue. Why would she make up such stories? It has been reported subsequently that she was recruited and coached by Hill & Knowlton as part of its campaign for Citizens for a Free Kuwait.[40] It is difficult to know if all the allegations made about the campaign are true—and it does need to be recognized that many of the activities undertaken by Hill & Knowlton in the campaign were legitimate free speech practices such as arranging interviews for visiting Kuwaiti government officials. But it is well established that PR was used to manipulate American public opinion in favour of the war in Iraq and that part of this was disinformation. A number of other cases of astroturfing are cited later in this chapter.

Weapons of Mass Destruction

One of the worst examples of spin and pseudo-science of all time may well be the claim that justified and the second Iraq war—that Iraq possessed weapons of mass destruction and constituted a threat to its neighbouring countries and regional security. This so-called evidence was used to gain congressional, parliamentary, and public support for the 2003 military invasion of Iraq by US, UK, and other allied forces. BBC radio reporter Andrew Gilligan reported controversially in May 2003 that Number 10 Downing Street had demanded that the September 2002 dossier on Iraqi weapons be "sexed up."[41] On the day that Gilligan's report was aired, the director of communications for the UK Labour Government and adviser to Prime Minister Tony Blair, Alistair Campbell, issued a firm denial, saying: "Not one word of the dossier was not entirely the work of intelligence agencies." Subsequent official inquiries revealed that this claim was simply not true. As Nick Davies disclosed in *Flat Earth News*, intelligence agencies reported that Iraq was likely to use chemical and biological weapons only if it was attacked and that Iraq "may be able" to deploy such weapons within 45 minutes of an order to do so. "May be able" was changed by Downing Street to "are able" and, by the time the information was reported in *The Evening Standard* and *The Sun*, it was headlined as '45 minutes from attack' and 'Brits 45 minutes from doom'.[42] Official government communication misled the nation and supported a political agenda to invade Iraq. In the interests of fairness to PR, it should be pointed out that Alistair Campbell, known as a master spin doctor, was in fact a journalist before going to work for the UK Labour Government of Tony Blair, starting his career with Mirror Group newspapers and later reporting for *The Sunday Independent*, *The Daily Mirror*, and *Today*.

An *Independent Review of Government Communications* known as the Phillis Review was conducted in the UK in 2004 and its recommendations to separate political communication from government communication were implemented in full. These included establishment of a Government Information and

Communication Service (GICS) headed and staffed by civil servants independent of prime ministerial and ministerial campaign managers and special advisers. This helped restore public trust in government communication. However, professor of corporate communication and regular adviser to the UK Government on communication, Anne Gregory, has argued that this independence has dissipated since 2011 when the permanent secretary heading government communication was made redundant and major changes were made to what has been subsequently named the Government Communication Network (GCN) and, since 2013, the GCS.[43] From her close observation and research, Gregory believes that UK government communication has become politicized again. The 'Get ready for Brexit' campaign discussed later in this chapter is an example, according to some. There is also evidence of politicization of government communication in the United States and other countries.

'Black PR'

An extreme sub-field of PR is referred to as 'black PR'—not to be confused with the National Black Public Relations Society (https://www.facebook.com/NBPRS) or references to pioneers and practitioners of colour in the PR field. The term black PR draws on the categorization of propaganda as black, white or grey.[44] Black PR, a form of black propaganda, is described as:

> … a process of destroying someone's reputation and corporate identity … In summary, BPR is all about professional smear strategies, industrial espionages, propaganda and information hacking because data accessibility is crucial for every BPR campaign.[45]

While originally linked to negative PR tactics in the former Soviet Union and Russia, black PR has spread and continues today. For example, the *South China Morning Post* reported in 2014 that "popular online services such as WeChat and Weibo have become the new battleground for black PR," used by firms to "tear down their rivals."[46] It could also be argued that some of the practices in the USA, UK, and other democratic countries discussed previously and some of the following examples constitute black PR.

Advertorial and Pay-to-Play

A long-standing dubious practice in PR and traditional media, particularly newspapers and magazines, is the purchase of media space or time at advertising rates and placement of information designed to look like editorial. Such content is referred to as *advertorial*. While some media prohibit advertorial being typeset in the same or similar layout and fonts as editorial, many examples closely resemble editorial. In some cases, advertorial content is labelled to signal that it is not independent editorial. However, this is rarely done explicitly by labelling such content as advertising. Most often advertorial content is thinly disguised under labels such as special feature or special supplement. Also, such labels are also often printed in very small fonts in page headers or footers where they are easily missed by readers. The result is that many media consumers cannot distinguish paid promotional content from independent editorial—which is the intention.

A study of reader response to print media advertorial found that more than two-thirds of readers who were exposed to labelled advertorial failed to recall the presence of the label and the study concluded that the advertorial format "fools readers into greater involvement with the advertising message and that the presence of advertorial labels may not be particularly effective in alerting consumers to the true nature of the message."[47] Advertorial has been referred to as a form of "information pollution."[48]

Most journalists are understandably opposed to advertorial content, as it misrepresents information and confuses readers, as shown by the research. However, it has to be said that advertorial is not solely the fault of PR practitioners. In many cases, the advertising departments or supplements sections of media organizations dangle the promise of advertorial, sometimes even with discounts on regular advertising rates, to make their revenue targets. This is yet another example of complicity among communication professionals that contributes to biased and partisan information in the least, and sometimes to disinformation, deception, and manipulation. Advertorial has expanded recently through what is referred to as native advertising, which is discussed in the following section.

In some cases, journalists and media commentators are directly paid to spruik sponsored news and information. In 2001, the International Public Relations Association (IPRA) exposed the practice of *Zakazukha* in Russia in which media routinely sought payment for publication of press releases. However, payola to media is not confined to countries that lack free independent media. For example, in Australia, what became labelled as the 'cash for comment' scandal erupted in 1999 when it was revealed that top-rating Sydney radio announcer John Laws and others were routinely accepting payment for 'plugs' of commercial products and services on air.[49] These practices are not something that only happens in Russia or in the past.

In 2019 the *New York Times* revealed how the high-profile US financier Jeffrey Epstein, after getting out of jail for sex offences in 2009, rehabilitated his reputation and career, before being charged with further offences relating to sex trafficking of underage girls in July 2019. Epstein gained fame in the decade from 2009 to 2019 through extensive media publicity, including articles in *Forbes*, *The National Review*, and *HuffPost* that promoted him as a titan of business, and websites alleging he was a philanthropist and benefactor. However, is was subsequently revealed that the media articles were produced by a PR firm employed by Epstein, which not only wrote the articles but paid a reporter to attach his by-line and submit them as independent news. Incredibly, no fact-checking was done by editors of several leading publications.[50] This case of "pay-to-play" media content illustrates the complicity of mainstream journalism as well as the lack of ethics within some sectors of the PR industry. Epstein was found dead in his cell at the Metropolitan Correctional Center in New York City on 10 August 2019.

Native Advertising

Desperate to make up for declining audiences and avoidance of advertising through ad blocking software that have led to declining revenue, the advertising industry has turned to what is referred to as *native advertising*, as well as a number of other terms including *brand placement, branded content, paid content*, and *sponsored content* (see Table 3.1). Native advertising has been hailed as the possible "salvation" of the troubled advertising industry.[51] Writing in *Mashable* in 2013, Todd Wasserman noted that the up-beat advertising and marketing industry view is that native advertising is "a bold new path for brands and publishers," although another view is that "it's the hoary advertorial dressed up in 21st century clothes."[52] *The New York Times*, which has published a number of articles questioning these techniques, reports that "almost all of the publishers running branded content say they abide by the traditional church-and-state separation" of editorial and advertising, but it added that "sponsored content runs beside the editorial on many sites and is almost indistinguishable."[53]

Native advertising in its various forms is undertaken because it minimizes or avoids *persuasion knowledge*—that is, media consumers' recognition of content as intentional commercial or political persuasion, which reduces the effect of persuasion.[54] While product placement in media content, particularly in movies, has long been practiced and studied, the growing plethora of new advertising and marketing techniques designed to at least partially "hide the truth,"[55] or even fully

Table 3.1. Terms used for paid promotional content or messages embedded in media programming

Product focussed	Brand focussed	Advertising focussed	Entertainment focussed	Other and Related
Product placement	Brand placement	Native advertising	Branded entertainment*	Paid content
Product plugs	Branded content	Natural advertising	Advertainment	Paid syndication
In show plugs	Branded entertainment*	Advertiser funded programming	Edutainment	Paid integration
Showing the can	Brand integration	Sponsored content	Celebrity endorsements	Paid co-creation
Product integration	Brand casting	Sponsored messages	Advergames	Advertorial
	Branded storytelling	Content integration		Editorial integration
				Embedded marketing communication

* Listed under both brand focussed and entertainment focussed.

conceal marketing and promotional messages in media editorial and entertainment content, have been largely hidden under the corporate carpet.

Major PR firms as well as advertising agencies have been quick to jump in on the trend. In 2013 the New York head office of the world's largest PR consultancy, Edelman, issued a report titled *Sponsored Content: A Broader Relationship with the US News Media*. The report acknowledged that there are ethical issues in sponsored content, but went on to report that Edelman was "teaming up with the advertising arm of publishers on sponsored content partnerships," which it noted were also referred to as "paid content" or "native advertising."[56] Edelman identified three key formats, which it termed "paid syndication" involving paid posts, articles, and graphics appearing alongside editorial or as advertorial; "paid integration," which involves product placement and paid content that are "weaved into the narrative" of content; and "paid co-creation" referring to a new category of content such as news sites or apps jointly created with media for promotional purposes.[57]

The American Press Institute welcomed sponsored content, which it acknowledged had a number of "pseudonyms" including native advertising, as a new much-needed revenue stream for media and claimed that "sponsored content (done well) is properly labelled."[58] However, Edelman's description of various types of paid content above, particularly "paid integration," refute this claim.

The US Federal Trade Commission (FTC) issued a set of guidelines on native advertising in 2015 in which it reaffirmed that "advertisements or promotional messages are deceptive if they convey to consumers expressly or by implication that they're independent, impartial, or from a source other than the sponsoring advertiser—in other words, that they're something other than ads."[59] Despite this, a range of native advertising, sponsored content, paid content, and ambiguously labelled media partnerships continue. A 2018 report published by UK media regulator Ofcom identified native advertising as the third largest source of online advertising revenue after video and banners, responsible for more than £1 billion (US$1.2 billion) in advertising spend, with other forms of sponsored content generating a further £124 million (US$150 million) in advertising revenue.[60]

Merged Media

The global CEO of the major PR group Red Havas, James Wright, proudly coined and promoted the term "merged media" in a blog post and an article published on LinkedIn in 2019. In the article, Wright reported a survey that found "60% of public relations leaders, CEOs and students surveyed in 2019 say that within five years the average person will not be able to make a distinction between paid, earned, shared, and owned media when consuming information."[61] As noted in Chapter 2, paid media (advertising), earned media (editorial publicity published or broadcast on its merits as news or useful factual information), shared media (social platforms), and owned media (corporate websites and publications produced by organizations) are referred to by the acronym PESO. The acronym is so arranged because paid media space and time (advertising) has dominated media communication by organizations for the past century and has been quite separate and distinct from other media content such as news, current affairs, business and financial reporting, and even product reviews. As noted previously, the US FTC and regulatory bodies in other countries stipulate that paid media messages must be identified as such. Wright declared that merged media, which completely blurs the lines between paid promotional messages and independent news and information, is the "future of PR." In fact, he went even further to say that the future of PR is "the insertion of relevant content into the cultural ethos to drive desired outcomes."[62] It is somewhat gratifying that Wright restricted the future of the practice to distributing *relevant* content. However, it is telling and concerning that the global CEO of a major PR firm based in New York sees no problem with the corruption of all independent news and analysis with promotional messages, and the shaping of culture to achieve "desired outcomes" that clearly are those of corporations and other clients. Such statements by PR industry leaders give cause for concern and contradict the widely promoted theories of PR as establishing dialogue and building mutually beneficial relationships between organizations and their stakeholders.

Greenwashing

With the rise of environmental awareness in recent decades, many companies have turned to their PR firms and advertising agencies to make them look 'green'. While some promote truthful messages about environmental impact—for example, reporting environmental impact with evidence is part of Triple Bottom Line reporting such as that undertaken by members of the Global Reporting Initiative (https://www.globalreporting.org)—many organizations exaggerate or even fabricate their green credentials. The term *greenwashing* was introduced by Jay Westerveld in an undergraduate term paper written in 1983, which was later published in a New York literary journal, after he visited an island resort claiming that guest re-use of towels helped protect the environment. Westerveld found no evidence that the resort reduced its environmental impact—in fact it was expanding and increasing its environmental footprint.[63] A litany of exaggerated and false environmental claims have been made by oil companies, automotive manufacturers, and consumer product companies since and continue today.

There are regulations in most countries in relation to false environmental claims, but in many cases these are not enforced, or lack teeth. For example, until recently the US FTC guidelines were voluntary and since tightening its *Green Guide* and commencing enforcement, the FTC has prosecuted only a handful of companies.

Many companies now avoid blatant greenwashing and, instead, use generic terms such as organic, natural, and fresh to connote environmental friendliness. Such terms have become weasel words in advertising, PR, and marketing used to mislead and deceive. For example, many poisons are organic and natural—i.e., they are found in nature. Hydrochloric acid is natural, produced by organisms in human stomachs to help digest food. Likewise, carbon dioxide is natural, found extensively in the atmosphere. But, as we are learning all too well, being natural does not prevent acids and CO_2 causing major environmental damage. In extreme examples of marketing spin, cigarette brands have been promoted as fresh (e.g., Alpine and Peter Stuyvesant) and even the fattiest meat that can clog arteries can be organic. Greenwashing techniques are yet another way that organizations distribute disinformation as part of our daily information diet in contemporary societies.

Behavioural Insights—A Tool for Good or Evil

In the early 2000s, economists began to realize that financial decisions by people were not always based on cognitive processing and rational analysis but, instead, many decisions were influenced by or primarily based on emotion (affective processing). In 2002, psychologist Daniel Kahneman was awarded the Nobel Memorial Prize in Economic Sciences for integrating insights from psychological research into economics, especially in relation to human decision making. Why this realization took so long is somewhat perplexing. It demonstrates the myopia that can occur in disciplines of study that do not look outside their field to consider other explanations for phenomena. Initially this new field of study was referred to as *behavioural economics*. But, given that its epistemological base was psychology, social anthropology, and some elements of neuroscience rather than economic science, it has increasingly become known as *behavioural insights*.

In 2008, Richard Thaler, who visited Kahneman at Stanford University in the late 1970s and was influenced by his research, and legal scholar Cass Sunstein popularized behavioural insights in their book *Nudge: Improving Decisions about Health, Wealth, and Happiness*. They used the colloquial term 'nudge' to refer to the processes of identifying and applying triggers of behaviour identified through research and testing.

In 2010, the UK Government set up a behavioural insights team, known as the Nudge Unit, and became a leader in applying the practice. Number 10 Downing Street subsequently divested the unit in 2014 as a social purpose company jointly owned by the Cabinet Office, employees, and Nesta (https://www.bi.team). The Behavioural Insights Team (BIT), as it is now known, headed by British psychologist David Halpern, uses random controlled trials (RCTs) to test messages and strategies in order to identify those that are most effective in triggering behaviour change.

Other countries are also turning to behavioural insights to inform policy making and influence citizens' behaviour. In the US, Harvard University's John F. Kennedy School of Government has established the Behavioural Insights Group (BIG), and the White House set up a Nudge Unit in 2014 known as the Social and Behavioral Sciences Team,[64] although it is not clear what happened to the team under the Trump Administration. The official SBST website (https://sbst.gov) was intact in 2019, but listed as "frozen" as of January 2017. In Australia the New South Wales State Government has established a Behavioural Insights unit (BIU) in the Department of Premier and Cabinet.[65]

Behavioural insights has created considerable excitement among government and corporate communicators because of its potential to unlock the secrets to human behaviour change. Such research can be very useful, and socially important, in informing campaigns to promote healthy lifestyles, road safety, and compliance messages such as paying tax, avoiding drink driving, and so on. However, behavioural insights also can be a tool used by unscrupulous individuals or organizations to get people to do what they want. The technique can potentially be used for exploitation and manipulation that is anti-social such as encouraging people to buy fatty fast food, borrow money that they cannot afford to repay, join extreme groups, or vote for political candidates who would be unlikely to gain support based on rational thought.

Potential abuses do not provide a reason to avoid the use of behavioural insights. But the research practice needs to be recognized as another advanced tool in the armoury of would-be persuaders and its use should be transparent and ethical. The US IPR published a useful plain-English primer on behavioural science in 2019 discussing the application of behavioural insights, including ethical considerations.[66] However, the codes of ethics applying to advertising and PR in most countries make no mention of how this 'scientific' technique for creating behaviour change should be applied. Like many other communication, marketing, and promotion techniques, it is left to self-regulation and the social responsibility of users.

Bell Pottinger

On 12 September 2017, London PR firm Bell Pottinger, reported to be the largest in the UK at the time, entered administration and subsequently collapsed following a global scandal over its promotional activities for South African clients that involved stirring up racial tensions through disinformation and corrupt practices.[67] At the centre of the scandal was a £100,000 (US$125,000) per month contract with Oakbay Investments, a firm controlled by the controversial Gupta family that had close relations with the government of South African President Jacob Zuma. Zuma was forced to resign in 2018 when he faced 18 charges of corruption, including more than 700 counts of fraud and money laundering.[68]

This was not the first time that the PR firm founded by former PR adviser to Margaret Thatcher, Lord Tim Bell, and Piers Pottinger had been in trouble. It had been criticized numerous times for conflict of interest edits to Wikipedia pages referring to its clients and, according to the Bureau of Investigative Journalism, the company was employed by the Pentagon to work in Iraq making fake terror and news videos at a cost of more than half a billion US dollars.[69]

When the PR firm's activities in South Africa became public, most of its clients terminated their contracts and its second largest shareholder Chime Communications, which is owned by the giant WPP group and the US firm Providence, handed back its 25% shareholding. A review by law firm Herbert Smith Freehills concluded that the firm had breached ethical standards and lacked appropriate policies for managing controversial accounts. The CEO James Henderson subsequently resigned and the Chartered Institute of Public Relations (CIPR) expelled Bell Pottinger from its membership.

The Bell Pottinger case stood out for the scale of the scandal that resulted. But it is far from the only example of PR companies and advertising agencies engaged in disinformation, deception, and manipulation. The propagandized re-imaging of convicted sex offender Jeffrey Epstein discussed previously is another notorious recent example. UK management consultant specializing in risk and reputation management, Ella Minty, wrote in her blog *Power & Influence* in 2019:

> Bell Pottinger is hardly alone in this ethical quagmire. The destabilizing power of those who are very good at what they do (whether we like it or not) in the world of PR and comms has never been so strong nor their reach so high.[70]

Minty pointed to other controversial activities of PR firms including the appointment of leading global PR firm Burson Marsteller to promote a Saudi Arabia led military alliance referred to as the "Muslim NATO." While reportedly formed to combat terrorism and militancy in northern and western Africa, human rights organizations allege that the group was engaged in oppressing rebels in Yemen, and some of its leaders have been linked to war crimes.[71]

Astroturfing

Minty also pointed to an expansion of astroturfing that takes advantage of relatively unregulated social media platforms. For example, Facebook banned Israeli firm Archimedes Group and took down several hundred of its accounts in May 2019. Facebook found that the group had created numerous fake accounts, often pretending to be locals in order to influence local elections and political discourse in Africa, Latin America, and Southeast Asia.[72] A *Times of Israel* investigation revealed that the group, which was found to be involved in "coordinated and deceptive behaviour" was linked to Adler Chomski Communication Marketing Ltd, one of Israel's largest advertising firms, and Grey Content Ltd, which is a major supplier of advertising services to the Israeli Government.[73]

Political strategists are also heavily involved in disinformation, deception, and manipulation through fake social media accounts and other media tactics. A controversial example is Australian Lynton Crosby who has managed a number of election campaigns in several countries including the 2012 London Mayoral election; the 2015 and 2017 UK general elections; the pro-*Brexit* campaign; and Boris Johnson's campaign for the UK Prime Ministership. In 2019, *The Guardian* reported that Crosby's firm CTF Partners had engaged in online disinformation campaigns on anonymous Facebook pages to promote the interests of its clients including the Saudi Arabia Government and "major polluters." *The Guardian* alleged that CTF Partners "employs the latest tools in digital management ... to run professional-looking 'news' pages reaching tens of millions of people on highly contentious topics, without apparently disclosing that they are being overseen by CTF Partners on behalf of paying clients."[74] Lynton Crosby was appointed an Officer of the Order of Australia (AO) in 2005 and knighted for his political service in the 2016 New Year Honours list.

Veteran public affairs professional and executive chairman of Media House International, Jack Irvine, told the international trade journal *PRWeek* in 2019 that, even though professional bodies such as the CIPR and the PR and Communication Association (PRCA) condemn the practice, astroturfing is widely used. Irvine said "there's a lot of dirty work going on in the PR world."[75]

Covering Up Corporate Corruption

As well as occurring in politics, much of that dirty work is going on in the corporate and financial sector. The irresponsible promotion of sub-prime loans and other banking practices in the USA that led to the collapse of Lehman Brothers, large write-downs by other major banks including Morgan Stanley and Goldman Sachs, and a global financial crisis in 2007–2008, are well known as examples of public deception by big business. Despite the rancour that followed this deception, the giants of the Australian banking industry were found to have extensively and systematically deceived people just over a decade later. In early 2019, The Royal Commission into Misconduct in the Banking, Superannuation and Financial Services Industry in Australia, commonly known as The Banking Royal Commission, handed down a scathing report on banking practices. The Royal Commission, established in late 2017, received 10,323 submissions—a number that of itself indicates the level of concern, frustration, and dissatisfaction in the community. More than 60% of the submissions related to banking practices, with 12% in relation to superannuation, and 9% discussing financial advice.[76]

Apart from the financial and management implications of the findings of the Australian Banking Royal Commission, what is relevant to this analysis is that the commission found that the nation's major banks had systematically misled their customers. Key findings included cases of customers being charged for services that they had never received and even "scandalous cases" of "people being charged fees even after they had died."[77] In short, the major banks and some other financial institutions such as insurance companies lied to, misled, and cheated customers on a massive scale. The ABC reported that "the scandal would cost wealth managers and the major banks AUD$850 million [almost US$600 million] in compensation."[78]

While most of the findings of the Australian Banking Royal Commission are matters of malfeasance by corporate management and issues for financial regulators to address, many questions emerge in the context of this analysis. First, did the heads of corporate communication and PR of the major banks know about this corruption and abuse of customers? Given that most of the banks involved had heads of communication appointed at C-suite management level, it seems very unlikely that they would not. Second, if they knew, what did they do to stop the disinformation that enabled the deception, and counsel management on truth-telling and transparency? Third, and most concerning, to what extent did the banks' corporate communication professionals play an active part in covering up the corruption over a period of years. Finally, if they didn't know, why? What was wrong in the structure of these large corporations that their public communication was so dislocated from what the Royal Commission found to be common practice?

Under the leadership of High Court Justice Kenneth Hayne, the Royal Commission's report referred some of the nation's biggest companies to regulators for possible criminal or civil action for the way they treated their customers, and made 76 recommendations for structural and practice change in the Australian financial services industry.[79] In all, the Royal Commission made 24 referrals to regulators for possible action over misconduct, which *The Guardian* reported could lead to 20 prosecutions.[80] The regulators were also criticized in the report for lack of oversight.

Communication "Tricks" of Public Companies

An indication that public communication professionals in corporations are not only aware, but actively involved in or even playing a leading role in deception and manipulation of stakeholders, is that the "tricks" of investor relations and corporate communication are openly discussed in trade media. Under the headline '5 tricks companies use during earnings season', *Investopedia* reported in 2019 that:

> There are a number of "tricks" or actions that some public companies will use or set in motion to pull the wool over the investment community's eyes come earnings season—particularly when a company misses estimates or otherwise disappoints investors.[81]

These include what is referred to as "strategic release timing," such as the release of bad news in media quiet periods such as late on Fridays after stock markets close or during holiday weekends; "burying bad news" after good news; and planning announcements that will overshadow or draw attention away from poor results.[82] Such strategies comply with the letter of the law relating to disclosure of financial information, but they can hardly be seen to be in the public interest. It is also difficult to see how they are ethical in either a deontological sense (duty to do right) or teleological (consequences) context.

"Washington's Worst Communicator"

While many have focussed on Donald Trump as a lightning rod of political disinformation, staff who have gone to work for him provide examples of professional communicators engaged in disinformation, deception, and manipulation. One notable example is Sarah Huckabee Sanders, who served as White House press secretary for President Trump in 2018 and the first half of 2019. An analysis of her role published in *The Guardian* labelled her "Washington's worst communicator" and described her communication on behalf of the White House as "World Cup-quality lying."[83] According to the report, by her own admission Sanders "just made stuff up when she briefed the press."[84] In late 2019 Sanders joined Fox News as a political commentator, which speaks volumes for the ethics and integrity of Fox as a media organization.

Churnalism

Journalists are quick to point the finger at PR and press secretaries as the perpetrators of disinformation, deception, and manipulation. However, there is considerable evidence that the buck stops in many places including in the newsrooms of many media organizations. Investigative journalist Nick Davies coined the term *churnalism* in his 2009 book *Flat Earth News* to describe media reporting that churns out minimally rewritten wire service stories and media releases prepared by PR practitioners. In some cases, media have been shown to regurgitate PR material verbatim. Davies based his claim on a study conducted by researchers at Cardiff University involving content analysis of Britain's four 'quality' daily newspapers—*The Times, The Guardian, The Independent* and *The Daily Telegraph*—and *The Daily Mail*, the highest circulation popular newspaper in the UK. The study collected 2,207 media articles published during a two-week period and, with the help of staff on *The Guardian* news desk, attempted to capture all of the incoming material that was passed to reporters during the two weeks including wire service stories and PR releases. The Cardiff University study found almost 60% of printed stories were comprised wholly or mainly of wire service copy and/or PR material.[85] Davies also quoted other studies that revealed churnalism on a global scale.

A literature review by Lynne Sallot and Elizabeth Johnson in 2006 estimated that more than 150 studies have examined the interrelationship between PR and journalists since the 1960s.[86] In fact, such studies have been conducted since the early 20th century and many more have examined the extent of the influence of PR on media reporting since 2006. In *Journalism and PR: Unpacking 'Spin', Stereotypes & Media Myths*, I concluded that at least 200 studies have examined the interrelationship between journalism and PR and summarized the findings of more than 20 of these.[87] Research unequivocally shows that independent journalism is not as independent as often claimed. To the contrary:

116 | *Beyond Post-Communication*

> Extensive data from quantitative studies conducted over the past 100 years show that somewhere between 30 and 80% of media content is sourced from or significantly influenced by PR, with estimates of 50–80% common.[88]

The variation in the above figures is not an indicator of uncertainty. Rather, it reflects variations in the operations of different types of media, with quality newspapers using less PR material, while trade media and magazines (e.g., travel and women's magazines), and TV infotainment programs use high levels of what Oscar Gandy identified as "information subsidies."[89]

Another important clarification is that, while the substantial reduction in journalists' positions in the past two decades is of concern, this is not the primary cause of the *PRization* of media as some claim. Research shows that high levels of PR material have been present in media reporting since the 1920s and continued through the 1980s when newspaper circulations and journalism employment were at their highest.[90] The weakened state of journalism in the 21st century is problematic in terms of the health of the public sphere, as will be discussed further in Chapter 5. But what is evident in research is that many journalists do not act independently as they claim to do, and journalism has not adequately fulfilled its role as *gatekeepers*[91] against misinformation and disinformation and as a "watchdog of society."[92]

Furthermore, as well as not filtering out misinformation and disinformation and challenging so-called fake news with facts and investigative reporting, in some cases journalism has actively contributed to post-truth society. While complaining about the alternative facts distributed by Donald Trump and others, many journalists have only too willingly republished the extravagant claims and statements made in his posts in social media, particularly on Twitter. It can be no surprise that, as a consequence, in 2016 less than one-third of Americans trusted media 'a great deal' or even 'a fair amount' to report fully, accurately and fairly. In 2018, trust in media in the USA had recovered slightly, according to Gallup surveys, but still less than half of Americans trusted their media.[93] Young citizens are particularly untrusting of media, which does not auger well for the future of journalism or politics. Gallup concluded: "Younger adults have come of an age in an era marked by partisan media and fake news."[94]

Yellow Journalism—Muckraking, Sensationalism and Fabrication

The term *yellow journalism* is mostly associated with a form of reporting that was prominent in the late 19th century characterized by "hysterical headlines, gimmicky features, fakery, and muckraking."[95] Yellow journalism reached a crescendo in the USA between 1895 and 1898 during a circulation war between the publications of William Randolph Hearst and Joseph Pulitzer, most notably the *New York Journal* and the *New York World*.[96] In the UK, similar sensationalist reporting is referred to as *tabloid journalism*.

While much has been done to bring ethics and social responsibility to journalism, unfortunately media in many countries including developed Western democracies continue to be active participants in creating fake news and disinformation. Long-time professor of journalism and mass communications Tom Goldstein says that "fabrication was a fixture of journalism for much of the 19th and 20th centuries."[97] There is ample evidence that fabrication and fake news is a continuing characteristic of media in the 21st century. For example, in 2017 the actor Rebel Wilson was awarded more than AUD$4.5 million in damages plus interest and court costs in a defamation case against Bauer Media, the publisher of two of Australia's leading women's magazines, *Woman's Day* and the *Australian Women's Weekly*, when the court found that the group had published claims about Wilson that they knew to be false.[98] Wilson's damages were later substantially reduced because of a failure to demonstrate financial loss resulting from the published lies, but the original finding of defamation stood. Bauer Media were back in the headlines in 2018 when a TV presenter and former Commonwealth Games medal-winning swimmer spoke out against fabricated articles about her. British tabloid newspapers are renowned for publishing countless fabricated stories about the British Royal Family.

Some try to deflect criticism of media by segregating allegedly *quality* media from tabloid newspapers, TV infotainment, and magazines, and dismissing the latter categories as less significant. However, this ignores the reality that more people consume information from popular media than from elite publications. Furthermore, even leading publications such as the *New York Times* have their scandals, such as the resignation of Jayson Blair in 2003 after it was discovered that he had plagiarized and fabricated numerous articles. This is not to deny that quality independent journalism exists. It is merely to say that contemporary democratic societies do not have enough of this important element in the public sphere.

Partisan Journalism

Apart from the extremes of muckraking and fabrication, an often forgotten feature of the history of journalism is that it has not always subscribed to independent fact-based reporting and analysis. Through many periods of even recent history, journalism has been partisan with publications owned and controlled at various times by the Church, trade unions, and business interests. In *Comparing Media Systems*, Daniel Hallin and Paolo Mancini identify three models of media in operation around the world that they describe as the *liberal* model, the *democratic corporatist* model, and the *polarized pluralist* model. They pay close attention to the relationship between media and political parties and report that the polarized pluralist model features partisan reporting. Hallin and Mancini see this partisan model operating in Mediterranean countries of southern Europe including France, Italy, Spain, Portugal, and Greece and in some emerging democracies.[99]

However, many are expressing concern that partisan journalism is increasingly becoming a characteristic of mature Western democracies. Fox News and its partners in the Murdoch controlled Fox/News Corp network in the USA, UK, and Australia[100] are known for blatantly advocating conservative and even strongly right-wing views and supporting conservative political parties in elections. For example, *The Sun* in the UK, part of Murdoch's extensive media empire, championed *Brexit* and openly campaigned for Theresa May to become Prime Minister of the UK in 2016. Murdoch media also have supported climate change deniers and helped overturn carbon taxes in countries such as Australia. In 2017 former Prime Minister of Australia, Kevin Rudd, described News Corp as a "cancer" on democracy and called for a Royal Commission into the corporation's relationship with the conservative coalition government in Australia.[101] During the 2019 Australian federal election, photos published on social media showed Piers Akerman, a high-profile columnist employed by the News Corp owned *Daily Telegraph*, standing with the then Australian Prime Minister Tony Abbott at a campaign rally wearing an Abbott campaign T-shirt, clearly revealing his political bias and the ideology of his organization. Writing in *The Monthly*, Richard Cooke described News Corp as "democracy's greatest threat" and referred to it as an "unhinged propaganda outfit" rather than a news organization.[102] When journalists point the finger of blame for disinformation, deception, and manipulation at PR practitioners and political *spin doctors*, they need to reflect on their own profession and its role in the current state of affairs.

As political bias and interference have escalated in the past two decades, many journalists have simply gone along with it, happy to have a job in a time of cutbacks. However, some journalists working for News Corp media have spoken out. Social affairs editor of *The Australian*, Rick Morton, told a seminar in Sydney during the 2019 Australian election that "the craziness has been dialled up." Morton said: "It's not always a Murdoch line; it's just that Murdoch hires editors who are very much like him." He told a seminar at the University of Technology Sydney that journalists working on the newspaper were more uncomfortable than at any time in the previous seven years.[103] Morton was not alone. News Corp journalist for 30 years and winner of five Walkley Awards and the Graham Perkin Journalist of the Year award, Tony Koch, lambasted the News Corp owned national newspaper *The Australian* saying: "No editor I worked for would have put up with the biased anti-Labor rubbish that, shamefully, the papers now produce on a daily basis."[104]

Fox News in the USA, Sky News Australia, and the American pay TV network MSNBC, which is owned by NBC-Universal News Group, are widely seen as purveyors of partisan and politically biased news and information that distort the public sphere and fail to meet the standards of quality independent journalism. In his book *Post-truth*, as well as pointing the finger at MSNBC, Lee McIntyre says "Fox has taken partisan news coverage to a new level."[105]

Targeting and Micro-Targeting

Marketing literature broadly conceptualizes people as markets, and those most likely to buy products and services as *target markets*. Marketing management texts define target markets as groups of customers or potential customers at which a business aims its marketing efforts and resources.[106] It is true that marketing seeks to understand and serve customers' needs. But targeting, which is a key strategy in marketing and is being ramped up substantially in the era of personalized marketing (see Chapter 4, 'Technologies Turbocharging Post-Communication'), reduces people to targets, which are defined in the Oxford Dictionaries as an objective, or "a person, object, or place selected as the aim of an attack."[107] Concepts such as relationship marketing and customer-focussed seldom make it beyond the text books.

Similarly, in PR literature and that of closely related and largely synonymous fields such as corporate, government, political, and strategic communication, people are widely described as *target audiences* and *target publics* despite theories describing practice as two-way communication, relationship building, and dialogue. For example, the term target audiences was used in the first PR Excellence study book[108] and, along with target publics, has become common currency in PR and related texts since.[109] Even in some of the latest PR literature, stakeholders such as shareholders and investors, members of communities, and even employees are described as targets. For instance in *The Encyclopedia of Strategic Communication*, Kirk Hallahan says: "Public relations activities can be directed to the public at large but often focus on target groups."[110] The three-volume *International Encyclopedia of Strategic Communication* published in 2018 also contains a chapter devoted to discussion of "target groups."[111]

While targeting can be understood as a tactical imperative in strategic communication, it reveals an underlying ontological perspective in which organizations are the *subject* in communication, while people such as customers, employees, local communities, and citizens are *objects*. At a philosophical level, this reflects the difference between Descartes' focus on the *ego* or *I* as the subject at the centre of experience in which the subject's perspective "has priority over all other things" compared with Heidegger's *dasein* philosophy in which the subject is a being "in the world" not separate from it, and part of an evolving everyday existence shaped by context, choices, and possibilities.[112] In a simpler sense, an online dictionary defines a subject as "the pronoun, noun, or noun phrase that does the action of the verb" and object as "the thing or person that the verb is done to, or who receives the verb."[113] This ontological dichotomy permeates PR theory, with ongoing debate about author versus audience and producer versus consumer. Despite the advent to the *prosumer*,[114] or what Axel Bruns and others call the *produser*[115]—the person who is both producer and consumer in the era of social media—a power relationship exists in public communication and skews it towards transmission and targeting.

Beyond demographic and psychographic targeting, data analytics enables *micro-targeting* of segments of the population such as young voters, people with disabilities, the elderly, families with young children, and so on. In micro-targeting, organizations combine data from public and private sources, such as demographic and geographic information available from national census data and attitude and lifestyle factors drawn from surveys and social media, to identify people susceptible to persuasion and mobilization. In one method, data collected is modelled to provide *micro-targeted propensity scores*—that is, the likely propensity of individuals to respond to and comply with targeted messages.[116] Propensity modelling and micro-targeted propensity scores (MPS) are increasingly used in political campaigning as well as commercial marketing.

It has to be said that when data are obtained legally and ethically, micro-targeting can be of mutual benefit to citizens as well as organizations. It can mean that citizens do not receive irrelevant information, while organizations such as political parties and marketers do not waste money sending information to uninterested people. However, in an environment of minimal regulation and poor self-regulation, what is legal is a broad church and citizens' rights to opt out or protect their personal data are limited and sometimes non-existent.

The Marketization and Politicization of Government Communication

Government communication in a number of Western democratic countries has drunk the Kool-Aid of commercial marketing and is progressively reinterpreting and reshaping government communication as campaigning and marketing—a move that has major negative implications for democracy. For example, most of the Communications and Engagement branch of the New South Wales government in Australia that was formerly based in the Department of Premier and Cabinet was relocated to a newly formed Department of Customer Service in 2019. This followed a successful roll-out of Service NSW (https://www.service.nsw.gov.au) that established government service centres capable of handling more than 800 types of transactions in major population areas, thereby greatly increasing access to government information and services. Given that delivery of services such as public health facilities and public transport are part of the role of government, this initiative justifiably draws on techniques from marketing and identifies people as customers. But people living in democracies have another more significant identity in terms of their rights and responsibilities. They are citizens—the constituents of electorates in democracies with rights afforded under constitutions, charters, and conventions dating back to ancient Greece and the *Magna Carta* and much refined and expanded since.

The marketization of government communication is also evident in the UK where the GCS declared 2019 the "year of marketing."[117] Despite the fact that UK citizens have reeled against the government in the 2016 EU referendum; that Scotland has been advocating for another referendum on membership of the UK; and that former Prime Minister Theresa May acknowledged that the voices of citizens "fall on deaf ears,"[118] the communication chiefs on Whitehall believe that marketing and campaigning are the way to go. The UK GCS conducted more than 160 campaigns in 2019, up from 40 in 2018, according to *PRWeek*.[119] The 2019 UK *Government Communication Plan* states: "We will improve the capability of government marketers and increase understanding of the effectiveness of marketing as a tool to deliver operational and policy objectives."[120]

UK government communication policies and plans discuss listening, but this is framed in instrumental terms. For example, in the foreword of the *UK Government External Affairs Operating Model*, executive director of the GCS Alex Aiken states: "We need to act as ambassadors, but also listening to what others have to say and using that intelligence to help build campaigns that deliver government objectives."[121] In short, listening is undertaken primarily or solely to gain intelligence that can inform the targeting of citizens in campaigns designed to achieve government objectives.

Citizens have a right to participate in policy making and the voice of the people (*vox populi*) is the ultimate source of legitimacy of governments in a democracy. As a 2019 report of The Open Government Partnership (OGP) Practice Group on Dialogue and Deliberation stated: "Citizens are staking their claim to political power, expecting politicians to be among them, not above them. And expecting them to make decisions with them, not just for them."[122] But research shows that this voice is paid tokenistic attention in many democracies in which listening by government has been shown to be lacking.[123] The *marketization* of government communication in which citizens are conceptualized as customers further relegates citizens to the status of *consumers* and target audiences or target markets.

There are also concerning examples of the *politicization* of government communication in major democracies. It has to be recognized that government communication is conceptualized as distinctly different to political communication—for good reason. While the latter includes the promotional and largely partisan communication of politicians, their media advisers, political parties, and lobbyists, government communication in most democratic countries is charged with being non-political and focussed on a dual role of engaging citizens in policy development, as well as informing citizens factually and even-handedly in relation to policy, services, and their rights and responsibilities.[124]

In the UK, the 4,000-strong GCS (https://gcs.civilservice.gov.uk) is jointly headquartered in the Cabinet Office and Number 10, Downing Street, the office of the Prime Minister and the PM's staff of advisers. Perhaps because of that, it has failed to maintain independence from political manoeuvres and machinations. The recommendations and reforms triggered by the Phillis Review of 2004 referred to earlier in this chapter under 'Weapons of Mass Destruction' have been increasingly eroded. For example, in the second half of 2019 the UK GCS developed and launched a 'Get ready for *Brexit*' campaign reportedly at a cost to taxpayers of £100 million (US$125 million). The campaign was designed to inform businesses and citizens of what they needed to do to prepare for an exit from the European Union (EU) by 31 October 2019 as promised by Prime Minister Boris Johnson. However, opposition MPs and media described the campaign as "redundant and misleading" because at the time the EU was intractable on terms requested by the UK and the UK Parliament had passed a bill vetoing a 'no deal' *Brexit*, making it impossible to leave the EU by the October deadline. The parliament called for an extension until 31 January 2020. Thus, critics argued that the Prime Minister was acting illegally by pushing for an October 2019 withdrawal and using public funds to promote his plan.[125] A number of MPs and commentators branded the 'Get ready for Brexit' campaign party political because it represented Conservative party policy, but not government policy as decided by parliament.

Also, *Guardian* columnist Suzanne Moore described the campaign as "useless" because of its lack of information, as well as politicized communication. She wrote:

> This is all billed as a public information campaign but it is devoid of information and is simply publicly-funded government propaganda. How easily we have slipped into a world where our government consistently breaks every rule in front of us: there is supposed to be a ministerial code governing taxpayer-funded communications.[126]

In the face of opposition to his plans, Boris Johnson announced that he would close parliament for more than a month leading up to the October 2019 *Brexit* deadline that he had set—an unprecedented move in democratic politics. Along with the government's marketing focus, this sent three very clear political messages to UK citizens: We're closing democracy down; we're not listening; and communication is one-way persuasion to get people to do what we want. If this sounds extreme, consider *The Guardian's* expose of how the plan to prorogue parliament was hatched in secret by Johnson and his advisers. One of Johnson's closest advisers, Dominic Cummings, was described as having "disdain for Whitehall and the way the entire system of British government works." A Whitehall source who worked with Cummings said: "If he meets resistance from ministers or officials he will just tell them to fuck off, whoever they are."[127] Such instances of ignoring parliament—the representatives of the people—voices of concern and protest, and public opinion leaves much to be desired in terms of public communication in a democracy.

John Dewey famously noted the "eclipse of the public" in terms of political representation and participation, which he saw as taken over by "political machines" and mass media in industrially and technologically advanced societies.[128] Today, in the orbit of democratic governments we are increasingly seeing the eclipse of the citizen.

Two misconceptions are driving this reduction of citizenship to a marketer-customer, producer-consumer relationship. First, those who shape government communication often confuse communication with information. Communication also must involve listening and responding to others. The second related misconception is that government communication is an *ex-post* activity undertaken after government policies and initiatives are enacted. This comes about because of a separation of policy development and government communication that has occurred in many countries. Government communication has become conceptualized as information or persuasion campaigns to *sell* government policies, decisions, and services after they are decided and developed.

UK political communication specialist Stephen Coleman has documented how citizenship is a thwarted experience for people in many Western democratic countries today.[129] Turning citizens into customers and targets will only contribute to the democratic deficit and decline of trust in government. Strategies for redressing the one-way barrage of propaganda distributed as government communication are discussed in Chapter 5 under 'Government Communication beyond Marketing'.

Social Media Influencers

A form of promotion for commercial and political purposes that has grown rapidly in recent years is the use social media influencers (SMIs) to spread information in line with the *diffusion of innovations*,[130] the theory proposed by Everett Rogers that information and influence flow down from early adopters and social leaders to followers, also referred to as a *two-step flow* of communication.

The decline in reach and influence of traditional advertising, which is typically identifiable as paid messages and thus creates *persuasion knowledge*[131] (awareness that the content is promotion), has led to marketers seeking other ways to promote products, and one of these is influencer marketing. This involves the recruitment of bloggers and social media users with a large number of followers to promote products and services in return for payment. Paid bloggers have been around since soon after the term blogs (a contraction of web logs) was coined by pioneering blogger Peter Merholz in 1999.[132] However, while many of those who are paid for their social media posts are transparent in relation to their commercial interest, a concerning trend is for social media influencers to hide the fact that they are paid promoters.

For example, in 2016 the US FTC charged Machinima, Inc., an online entertainment network that worked with Microsoft's ad agency, for deceiving consumers by paying a large group of alleged influencers to develop and post videos touting XboxOne. The videos were presented as the objective independent views of those appearing and did not disclose that they were, in fact, paid endorsements.[133]

In mid-2019 the Advertising Standards Authority (ASA) in the UK launched an investigation into the activities of 'Mrs Hinch', who was purportedly a middle-aged woman providing independent advice on household cleaning and maintenance. In reality, the online Mrs Hinch with 2.5 million followers on Instagram turned out to be 29-year-old Sophie Hinchcliffe, who was paid by Proctor & Gamble to promote its products. Corporations refer to such influencers as *brand ambassadors*, but unlike ambassadors whose identity and interests are transparent, many social media influencers are deceiving social media users and mixing paid promotional content with factual information and independent opinion, which is another form of post-communication.

Richard Bagnall, Chairman of the International Association for Measurement and Evaluation of Communication (AMEC) and CEO–Europe of media analysis firm CARMA, said "the whole issue of influencers is problematic. In many cases, so-called 'influencers' are being exposed as a massive fraud." Bagnall gave an example.

> I know of cases in which someone has generated over 50,000 followers, partly from bots, and then been able to quit work and make a living as an 'influencer', getting paid to promote products, receiving foreign trips, and even writing blogs and columns for mainstream media, despite having no real expertise or real world influence at all.[134]

He added that "the real problem is that the big brands continue to fall for it" by paying self-made social media influencers to promote their products. One of the reasons for this, says Bagnall, is that marketers and management rely on automated collection of rudimentary quantitative data such a counts of likes, follows, and shares and equate these to real world results. He says: "In evaluation terms, they are counting content *outputs* and then assuming that these numbers mean that they have achieved desired *outcomes* such as awareness or behaviour change."[135]

As well as being deceptive, paid influencers can be dangerous. A study by a team of researchers at the University of Glasgow found that just one in nine UK bloggers writing about weight management and diet provided accurate information. The study, presented at the 2019 European Congress on Obesity, reported that only one of the leading social media writers on diet and weight management was a qualified nutritionist and that most distribute misinformation or disinformation. The lead researcher, Christina Sabbagh, described the public communication of these influencers as not only misleading but as "potentially harmful."[136]

Research by the Project on Computational Propaganda in the UK, which is focussed on political disinformation, reported in 2018 that "manipulation of public opinion over social media platforms has emerged as a critical threat to public life." The research found evidence of "formally organized social media manipulation campaigns in 48 countries," particularly by political parties "spreading disinformation during elections."[137]

As reported earlier in this chapter, the global CEO of PR agency Red Havas in New York, James Wright, said in a blog 2019 post that social media has "become so massively pay-to-play, with influencer marketing blurring the earned and paid lines."[138] Such observations have led the UK to introduce regulations requiring disclosure of commercial interests online,[139] but many countries have no such self-regulation and little oversight.

Fake Accounts and Trolls

Some—in fact many—so-called social media influencers are fake. A noteworthy example was the case of *Jenna Abrams*. Her profile on Twitter showed an image of an attractive woman in her early thirties who posted about a range of topics including the importance of punctuation, use of the Confederate flag, and celebrities such as Kim Kardashian, along with support for Donald Trump and a number of conservative policies. Sounds like a not-unusual American Twitter user, right? Jenna Abrams gained 70,000 followers on Twitter and became a darling of the Alt-right and the scourge of political correctness in the US between 2014 and 2016. That might not sound like a large audience, but Abrams' posts were picked up and reported by CNN, the *New York Times*, the *Washington Post*, and the BBC.[140]

However, Jenna Abrams—the "all-American, Trump-loving, segregation-supporting, Confederate-defending Twitter star"—does not exist.[141] *The Daily Beast* exposed her in 2017 as the creation of the Internet Research Agency, a Russian government-funded "troll farm" in St. Petersburg.[142] In short, Jenna Abrams was a fake account created in Russia to distribute disinformation and mobilize public opinion in the US in ways that destabilized national politics and civil society. Whether 'she' was a human employee at the Internet Research Agency (IRA) or a bot remains unclear. The 2018 Computational Propaganda Research Project study has reported that social media manipulation uses both "account automation [bots] and online commentary teams" as well as "making increasing use of paid advertisements and search engine optimization on a widening array of internet platforms."[143] The so-called Jenna Abrams, created under the Twitter handle @Jenn_Abrams in 2014, operated for three years before being exposed.

A Knight Foundation study of Twitter reported that 2,700 IRA accounts operated during the 2016 US presidential election campaign.[144] Fake account posts were cleverly disguised using American cultural markers, such as Abrams' reference to Kim Kardashian and debates about the Confederate flag. However, close examination of social media posts often reveals signs of English as a second language and, most significantly, a consistently high volume of posts seven days a week at all hours of the day and night—not the pattern of posting by humans. Nevertheless, many social media users remain unaware that they are reading and listening to trolls and bots created for malevolent purposes.

Russian troll farms are far from the only distributors of disinformation. *Endless Mayfly* is an Iran-aligned network of inauthentic websites and online personas used to spread false and divisive information primarily targeting Saudi Arabia, the United States, and Israel. An investigation by the Munk School of Global Affairs and Public Policy at the University of Toronto reported that:

> *Endless Mayfly* publishes divisive content on websites that impersonate legitimate media outlets. Inauthentic personas are then used to amplify the content into social media conversations ... Once *Endless Mayfly* content achieves social media traction, it is deleted and the links are redirected to the domain being impersonated. This technique creates an appearance of legitimacy.[145]

The research team concluded that *Endless Mayfly* content led to incorrect media reporting and caused confusion among journalists and the public. According to their study, "even in cases where stories were later debunked, confusion remained about the intentions and origins behind the stories."[146] One of the researchers, Ron Deibert, described *Endless Mayfly* as "an invasive species in the social media ecosystem."[147] Deibert says that many actors in countries and regions around the world are now undertaking social media influence operations. He points to India where citizens "are bombarded with fake news and divisive propaganda on a near-constant basis from a wide range of sources," Myanmar where Facebook has been used to incite genocide, and several African countries where hoaxes, disinformation, and spoof articles are now commonplace.[148] The report of the Computational Propaganda Research Project at the Oxford Internet Institute concluded:

The manipulation of public opinion over social media platforms has emerged as a critical threat to public life. Around the world, a range of government agencies and political parties are exploiting social media platforms to spread junk news and disinformation, exercise censorship and control, and undermine trust in the media, public institutions, and science.[149]

The *Reuters Institute Digital News Report 2019* found that "concern about misinformation and disinformation remains high despite efforts by platforms and publishers to build public confidence." For example, the Institute reported that "in Brazil 85% agree with a statement that they are worried about what is real and fake on the internet. Concern is also high in the UK (70%) and US (67%)."[150] Interestingly, the study found that concern about disinformation was much lower in Germany (38%) and the Netherlands (31%).

A 2019 report by the IPR in the USA titled *Disinformation in Society*, based on a survey of 2,200 adults found that "nearly two out of three Americans think the spread of misinformation and disinformation is a major problem in the country." Survey respondents ranked disinformation on par with gun violence and terrorism.[151]

This view is also expressed by many senior practitioners in media and communication. Almost all media and communication professionals interviewed as part of research for this book rated disinformation as "pervasive," rather than frequent, occasional, rare, or non-existent, and as "growing rapidly" and as a "very serious" issue. And most feel it is getting worse. Bob Jensen, who worked as a communication executive in the White House and with a number of US government agencies for more than 30 years,[152] said "it is definitely worse because of scale." He reflected: "There has always been fake news and even disinformation. But today with the internet, and particularly social media, millions and millions of people can post information and billions can access it."[153] Veteran journalist and editor Peter Fray agrees. Fray notes that "misinformation and disinformation have always been present in human societies," but he sees "scale as a significant difference particularly as a result of social media."[154] He also agrees with the notion of a perfect storm creating the conditions for post-truth society if unchecked, generated through a combination of social media content; lack of self-regulation or regulation of social media platforms; the use of algorithms, bots, and data analytics in marketing and political campaigns; the growth of PR, sponsored content, and paid influencers; and other practices that privilege opinion, promotion, and propaganda over facts and science.

Director of research in the Leeds Business School at Leeds Beckett University in the UK, Ralph Tench, adds that the increasing sophistication of disinformation is part of the challenge that contemporary society faces. He says "discerning fact from fiction is just getting harder."[155]

Weaponizing Social Media

While social media platforms face justifiable criticism for their algorithmic and commercial practices, the previous sections show that it is also the users of social media who are involved in manipulation and often deception and disinformation—including media and communication professionals. Beyond the Cambridge Analytica scandal and the influence it reportedly had on the 2016 US presidential election and the UK's EU referendum, social media are continuing to be used in weaponized ways to influence citizens in elections and on political and social issues.

For example, in late 2019 when Boris Johnson decided to take the UK to a general election, his campaign team engaged two young New Zealanders whose online strategies were identified as largely responsible for Australia's Labor Party losing the "the unlosable election"[156] in May 2019. Sean Topham and Ben Guerin, who operate a digital marketing agency simply called TG, were employed by Australia's Liberal Party to run its social media campaign in what most pundits predicted to be an electoral drubbing. However, the Coalition led by Scott Morrison won a convincing victory following what one post-election media investigation called a "24-hour meme machine—a social media firehose of attention-grabbing, emotion-manipulating, behaviour-nudging messaging."[157] In a video titled 'Friedman 19 // Using Social Media Effectively' posted on YouTube, Guerin gave a "blow-by-blow account" of what he called "the battle of the thumbs." This included Guerin explaining techniques such as creating "boomer memes," unlocking "arousal emotions," and using a barrage of social media posts like "water dripping on a stone" to influence attitudes and behaviour.[158] Australia's national public broadcaster, the ABC, described the video as "a guided tour of the dark arts of contemporary information warfare."[159]

Bald-Faced Lies in Advertising

During the December 2019 UK general election, the global verification and collaborative investigation organization First Draft (https://firstdraftnews.org/about) conducted an analysis of political campaign advertising and found that 88% of Facebook ads by the winning Conservative Party (5,952 ads) contained figures or claims that had already been labelled misleading by UK fact-checking agency Full Fact. Furthermore, 54% of Conservative Party ads (3,646 ads) linked to a webpage containing misleading claims. For example, 5,132 ads stated that a Conservative government would build "40 new hospitals" in an image, caption, or link. The claim was labelled misleading by Full Fact based on published Conservative Party plans to build six hospitals—not 40. Full Fact also found that the construction of 40 new hospitals had not been included in the budget for the following parliamentary session, or even costed.[160] The analysis by First Draft revealed that Liberal Democrat advertising also was misleading, but not to the extent of the Boris Johnson led Conservative Party.

Part of the blame for blatantly false advertising can be laid at the feet of Facebook in this instance, following its decision to exempt political advertising from fact-checking. However, the culprits creating this disinformation and deception were the political party executives, who commissioned and approved the advertising, and advertising copywriters and account executives—media and communication professionals—who seem only too happy to use their skills to deceive and manipulate for a client with deep pockets.

Spin, Clickbait, Fabrication, Disinformation—The Escalation to Post-Truth

This chapter has sought to show that the perilous progression towards a post-truth society is not a sudden shift or the result of a single event such as the election of Donald Trump. It has been a long process of deterioration in public communication practices in terms of ethics and the public interest. As this chapter has shown, with numerous examples, spin has long existed and, unfortunately, continues in ever more sophisticated ways in the public communication environment today through practices such as native advertising, influencer marketing, and social media manipulation, as well as traditional PR. In the least it permeates the public sphere with exaggeration, hype, and white propaganda—sometimes even grey and black propaganda.[161]

In addition to this contaminated substrate in the public communication ecosystem, it is generally recognized that the internet brought an escalation in the scale and methods of deception. At an annoying but relatively harmless level is *clickbait*, which involves the posting of headlines and links specifically to generate large volumes of clicks by users. The links typically take users to a website that makes money based on its volume of traffic, such as a publisher earning advertising according to the number of readers, or to a pay per click advertising site.

Clickbait headlines and links skew online content to what is popular rather than substantial, and are sometimes deceptive. But clickbait is typically posted for economic gain rather than any political or social motive.

Fabrication in the form of yellow journalism, partisan journalism, and the recent phenomena of fake news and alternative facts comprise more serious forms of deception and manipulation. While these practices are sometimes defended on the grounds of free speech, and so-called fake news can sometimes be expressions of genuine beliefs, they are major concerns for political scientists, sociologists, journalism and media studies researchers, and educators—particularly when they are increasing, as signs suggest they are in contemporary society.

Beyond misinformation and the level of deception and manipulation involved in fake news and alternative facts, disinformation goes a step further because its motive is intentional political, social, and potentially economic disruption, as noted earlier. Disinformation is not only manifestly untrue, but usually damaging to its targets. It is distributed deliberately with malicious intent or to serve self-interest at the expense of others. Thus, disinformation is usually indefensible on the grounds of free speech because it breaches a number of laws in many cases.

As discussed in the Introduction, post-truth is not the same thing as, or another form of, fake news or disinformation. The condition of post-truth refers to a community or society in which personal beliefs and opinion are held as more important than facts and even scientific data. It denotes the normalization and acceptance of fake news, misinformation, and even disinformation and the resulting social and political decay. Truth is lost in a black hole of human experience, ever present but unable to be seen in a collapsing informational field of dark matter.

In short, the path to a post-truth society is a range of practices that begin with spin in minor forms such as exaggeration and hype and escalate to unethical PR

Spin	Clickbait	Fabrication	Disinformation	Post-truth
Exaggeration, hype, 'white' propaganda by politicians and organizations	Gimmicky and misleading links and headlines for economic gain	'Yellow' journalism Partisan journalism Fake news Alternative facts	Intentional spread of false information for social or political disruption	Acceptance and normalization of untruth; social and political decay

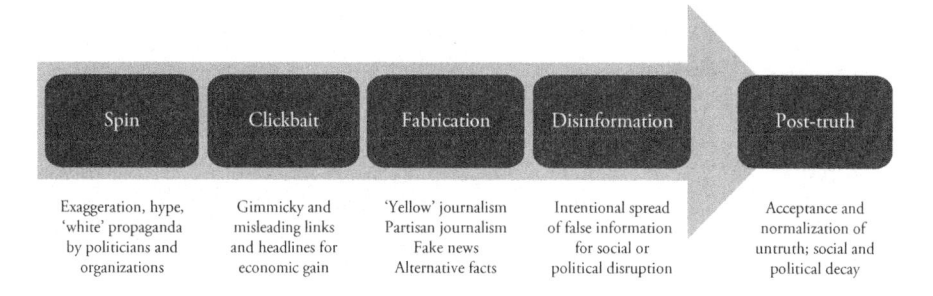

Figure 3.1. The escalating path to a post-truth society

and propaganda; the economically motivated trickery of clickbait; the systematic distribution of so-called alternative facts and the fabrication of fake news; and ultimately to the systematic disruptive and damaging practices of disinformation As discussed in the Introduction and in this chapter, this escalating range of practices that collectively create and sustain a post-truth society is referred to as post-communication. This denotes more than acts of miscommunication and ultimately even more than fake news and disinformation. Left unchecked, it is the loss of communication and, thus, the loss of the fundamental process of meaning making and sharing that forms and maintains societies.

Notes

1. Cathcart, R. (1981). *Post-communication: Rhetorical analysis and evaluation*. Indianapolis, IN: Bobbs-Merrill. (Original work published 1966)
2. Cathcart, 1981, p. 2.
3. Shannon, C., & Weaver, W. (1949). *The mathematical theory of communication*. Urbana: University of Illinois.
4. Berlo, D. (1960). *The process of communication: An introduction to theory and practice*. New York: Harcourt/Holt, Rinehart & Winston.
5. In *Gorgias*, Plato invoked his teacher Socrates to question the ethics of the Sophists and the use of rhetoric, which he saw as creating injustices and misleading people.
6. Foss, S. (1996). *Rhetorical criticism: Exploration and practice* (2nd ed.). Prospect Heights: Waveland Press. See also Foss, S., & Griffin, C. (1995). Beyond persuasion: A proposal for an invitational rhetoric. *Communication Monographs, 62*(1), 2–18, p. 2.
7. Heath, R. (2006). A rhetorical theory approach to issues. In C. Botan & V. Hazelton (Eds.), *Public relations theory II* (pp. 63–99). Mahwah, NJ: Lawrence Erlbaum.
8. Postcommunication [Facebook page]. About. Retrieved from https://www.facebook.com/pg/postcommunication/about/?ref=page_internal
9. Slowbyte. (2019). About. Retrieved from https://www.slowbyte.com/index.php/post-communication
10. Peters, J. (1999). *Speaking into the air: A history of the idea of communication*. Chicago, IL: University of Chicago Press, p. 29.
11. Ibid., p. 269.
12. As cited in Carey, J. (2009). *Communication as culture: Essays on media and culture* (Rev. ed.). New York, NY: Routledge, p. 64. (Original work published 1989)
13. Ibid., p. 64.
14. Harsin, J. (2015). Regimes of posttruth, postpolitics, and attention economies. *Communication, Culture & Critique, 8*(2), 327–333, p. 327.

15. Spinwatch. (n.d.). About us. Retrieved from http://spinwatch.org/index.php/about/about-spinwatch
16. Adi, A. (2019, June 3). *Measurement and evaluation remain a challenge for PR: According to PR2025 Delphi study*. Gainesville, FL: Institute for Public Relations, para. 3. Retrieved from https://instituteforpr.org/measurement-and-evaluation-to-remain-a-challenge-and-focus-for-pr-communications-practitioners-says-pr2025-delphi-study
17. Pieczka, M. (2006). Paradigms, systems theory and public relations. In J. L'Etang & M. Pieczka (Eds.), *Public relations: Critical debates and contemporary practice* (pp. 331–358). Mahwah, NJ: Lawrence Erlbaum, pp. 349–350.
18. Dietrich, G. (2014). *Spin sucks: Communication and reputation management in the digital age*. London, UK: Que (an imprint of Pearson Education), pp. 7, 12.
19. McIntyre, L. (2018). *Post-truth*. Cambridge, MA: MIT Press, p. 23.
20. Rabin-Havt, A. (2016). *Lies, incorporated: The world of post-truth politics*. New York, NY: Anchor Books, p. 23.
21. Guth, D., & Marsh, C. (2007). *Public relations: A values-driven approach* (3rd ed.). Boston, MA: Pearson Education, p. 70.
22. Amos, A., & Haglund, M. (2000). From social taboo to 'torch of freedom: The marketing of cigarettes to women. *Tobacco Control*, *9*(1), 3–8.
23. McIntyre, 2018, p. 79.
24. Mooney, C. (2005). *The republican war on science*. New York, NY: Basic Books, p. 81.
25. McIntyre, 2018, p. 27.
26. Union of Concerned Scientists. (2007). *Exxon Mobil report: Smoke, mirrors and hot air*. Cambridge, MA: Author. Retrieved from https://www.ucsusa.org/global-warming/solutions/fight-misinformation/exxonmobil-report-smoke.html
27. Goldenberg, S. (2013, February 14). Secret funding helped build vast network of climate change denial thinktanks. *The Guardian*. Retrieved from https://www.theguardian.com/environment/2013/feb/14/funding-climate-change-denial-thinktanks-network
28. Eggertson, L. (2010). Lancet retracts 12-year-old article linking autism to MMR vaccines. *Canadian Medical Association Journal (CMAJ)*, *182*(4): E199–E200.
29. Domonoske, C. (2019, September 13). 50 years ago, sugar industry quietly paid scientists to point blame at fat. *NPR*, The Two-Way. Retrieved from https://www.npr.org/sections/thetwo-way/2016/09/13/493739074/50-years-ago-sugar-industry-quietly-paid-scientists-to-point-blame-at-fat
30. Kearns, C., Schmidt, L., & Glantz, S. (2016). Sugar industry and coronary heart disease research: A historical analysis of internal industry documents. *JAMA Internal Medicine*, *176*(11), 1680–1685.
31. Stauber, J., & Rampton, S. (1995). *Toxic sludge is good for you: Lies, damn lies and the public relations industry*. Monroe, ME: Common Courage Press.
32. Ibid., p. 101.
33. Ibid.

34. Common Courage Press. (1995). Back cover of *Toxic sludge is good for you: Lies, damn lies and the public relations industry*.
35. PR firm Hill & Knowlton previously published details and its version of the 'Citizens to Free Kuwait' campaign on its website at http://www.hillandknowlton.com/citizensforafreekuwait, but all references to Citizens to Free Kuwait have been removed from the Hill & Knowlton site.
36. Sourcewatch. (2017). Citizens for a free Kuwait. Retrieved from https://www.sourcewatch.org/index.php/Citizens_for_a_Free_Kuwait
37. The term 'astroturfing' is derived from the artificial turf developed by the Monsanto Company and famously used at the Astrodome in Houston, Texas in the late 1960s.
38. Young, P. (2006). Astroturfing: Dark art of politics turned scourge of the blogosphere. *Blog Campaigning*, para. 1. Retrieved from http://blogcampaigning.com/2006/10/astroturfing-dark-art-of-politics-turned-scourge-of-the-blogosphere
39. PR Watch (2005) reported that, apart from US$11.9 million dollars contributed to Citizens for a Free Kuwait by the Kuwaiti government, US$10.8 million of which went to the PR firm Hill & Knowlton in fees, the only other funding of the organization totalled $17,861 from 78 individuals.
40. Deception on Capitol Hill. (1992, January 15). *The New York Times*. Retrieved from http://www.nytimes.com/1992/01/15/opinion/deception-on-capitol-hill.html
41. Davies, N. (2009). *Flat earth news*. London, UK: Random House, p. 199.
42. Ibid., p. 200.
43. Gregory, A. (2012). UK Government communications: Full circle in the 21st century? *Public Relations Review*, *38*(3), 367–375, p. 367.
44. Jowett, G., & O'Donnell, V. (1986). *Propaganda and persuasion*. London, UK: Sage Publications.
45. GNU Citizen. (2008, March 29). What is black PR? Retrieved from https://www.gnucitizen.org/blog/what-is-black-pr, paras 2–3.
46. Yu, S. (2014, January 3). How firms are using black PR to tear down their rivals. *South China Morning Post*, China Business. Retrieved from https://www.scmp.com/business/china-business/article/1396461/how-firms-are-using-black-pr-tear-down-their-rivals
47. Kim, B., Pasadeos, Y., & Barban, A. (2001). On the deceptive effectiveness of labeled and unlabeled advertorial formats. *Mass Communication and Society*, *4*(3), 265–281, p. 265.
48. Ellerbach, J. (2004). The advertorial as information pollution. *Journal of Information Ethics*, *13*(1), 61–75, p. 61.
49. Turner, G. (2001). Ethics, entertainment, and the tabloid: The case of talkback radio in Australia. *Continuum: Journal of Media & Cultural Studies*, *15*(3), 349–357.
50. Kitterman, T. (2019, July 25). Epstein puff pieces put focus on PR and pay-to-play publishing. *Ragan's PR Daily*. Retrieved from https://www.prdaily.com/epstein-puff-pieces-put-focus-on-pr-and-pay-to-play-publishing

51. Wasserman, T. (2013, September 26). Why native advertising is the opposite of porn. *Mashable*, para. 2. Retrieved from http://mashable.com/2013/09/25/native-advertising-porn
52. Ibid., para. 1.
53. Vega, T. (2013, April 7). Sponsors now pay for online articles, not just ads. *The New York Times*, Media & Advertising. Retrieved from http://www.nytimes.com/2013/04/08/business/media/sponsors-now-pay-for-online-articles-not-just-ads.html?pagewanted=all
54. Friestad, M., & Wright, P. (1994). The persuasion knowledge model: How people cope with persuasion attempts. *Journal of Consumer Research*, 21(1), 1–31.
55. de Pelsmacker, P., & Neijens, P. (2012). New advertising formats: How persuasion knowledge affects consumer response. *Journal of Marketing Communications*, 18(1), 1–4, p. 1.
56. Edelman. (2013). *Sponsored content: A broader relationship with the US news media*. New York, NY, p. 2. Retrieved from https://www.slideshare.net/EdelmanInsights/sc-report-vol1
57. Ibid., p. 7.
58. Sonderman, J., & Tran, M. (2013, November 13). Understanding the rise of sponsored content. American Press Institute, para. 33. Retrieved from https://www.americanpressinstitute.org/publications/reports/white-papers/understanding-rise-sponsored-content/single-page
59. Federal Trade Commission. (2015, December). Native advertising: A guide for business. Retrieved from https://www.ftc.gov/tips-advice/business-center/guidance/native-advertising-guide-businesses
60. Ofcom. (2018, August 2). Communications market report, London, UK. Retrieved from https://www.ofcom.org.uk/__data/assets/pdf_file/0022/117256/CMR-2018-narrative-report.pdf
61. Wright, J. (2019, July 22). What is merged media? It's the future of PR. *LinkedIn* [Web log post], para. 1. Retrieved from https://www.linkedin.com/pulse/what-merged-media-its-future-pr-james-wright
62. Ibid., para. 8.
63. Watson, B. (2016, August 20). The troubling evolution of corporate greenwashing. *The Guardian*. Retrieved from https://www.theguardian.com/sustainable-business/2016/aug/20/greenwashing-environmentalism-lies-companies
64. Nesterak, E. (2014, July 13). Head of White House 'Nudge Unit' Maya Shankar speaks about newly formed social and behavioral sciences team. *ThePsychReport*. Retrieved from http://thepsychreport.com/current-events/head-of-white-house-nudge-unit-maya-shankar-speaks-about-newly-formed-us-social-and-behavioral-sciences-team
65. NSW Government. (2019). Behavioural insights. [Web log post]. Retrieved from https://www.dpc.nsw.gov.au/programs-and-services/behavioural-insights

66. Li, T., & Flynn, T. (2019). *What you need to know about incorporating behavioural science into public relations: A primer.* Gainesville, FL: Institute for Public Relations. Retrieved from https://instituteforpr.org/what-you-need-to-know-about-incorporating-behavioural-science-into-public-relations-a-primer
67. Cave, A. (2017, September 6). Deal that undid Bell Pottinger: Inside story of the South Africa scandal. *The Guardian.* Retrieved from https://www.theguardian.com/media/2017/sep/05/bell-pottingersouth-africa-pr-firm
68. Jacob Zuma: Former South African President faces corruption trial. (2018, March 16). *BBC News.* Retrieved from https://www.bbc.com/news/world-africa-43426971
69. Rebello, L. (2016, October 3). Thatcher PR guru Lord Bell ran a $540 million false propaganda campaign in Iraq. *International Business Times.* Retrieved from https://www.ibtimes.co.uk/thatcher-pr-guru-lord-bell-ran-540m-pentagon-false-propaganda-campaign-iraq-1584495
70. Minty, E. (2019, August 15). A threat to public relations—and an opportunity. *Power & Influence* [Web log post], para. 19. Retrieved from http://ellaminty.com/commentaries/ethics-in-pr
71. Merrill, J. (2017, April 26). Saudis hire world's biggest PR firm to push 'Muslim NATO. *Middle East Eye.* Retrieved from https://www.middleeasteye.net/news/saudis-hire-worlds-biggest-pr-firm-push-muslim-nato
72. Facebook. (2019, May 16). Removing coordinated inauthentic behaviour from Israel. Retrieved from https://newsroom.fb.com/news/2019/05/removing-coordinated-inauthentic-behavior-from-israel
73. Weinglass, S. (2019, May 19). Who is behind Israel's Archimedes Group, banned by Facebook for election fakery? *Times of Israel.* paras 8, 13. Retrieved from https://www.timesofisrael.com/who-is-behind-israels-archimedes-group-banned-by-facebook-for-election-fakery
74. Waterson, J. (2019, August 2). Revealed: Johnson ally's firm secretly ran Facebook propaganda network. *The Guardian.* Retrieved from https://www.theguardian.com/politics/2019/aug/01/revealed-johnson-allys-firm-secretly-ran-facebook-propaganda-network
75. Hickman, A. (2019, August 6). Jack Irvine: 'Astroturfing is widespread in PR and tactic also used by larger agencies'. *PRWeek.* Retrieved from https://www.prweek.com/article/1593097/jack-irvine-astroturfing-widespread-pr-tactic-used-larger-agencies
76. Royal Commission into Misconduct in the Banking, Superannuation and Financial Services Industry. (2019). Website. Retrieved from https://financialservices.royalcommission.gov.au/Pages/default.aspx
77. Chalmers, S., & Worthington, B. (2019, February 4). Banking royal commission calls for compensation, crackdowns and an overhaul of financial regulators. *ABC News*, paras 5–6. Retrieved from https://www.abc.net.au/news/2019-02-04/banking-royal-commission-report-at-a-glance/10777188

78. Ibid., para. 7.
79. Commonwealth of Australia. (2019). *Final report: The Royal Commission into Misconduct in the Banking, Superannuation and Financial Services Industry*, Volume 1. Canberra, ACT.
80. Remeikis, A. (2019, February 4). Key points and recommendations of the banking royal commission report. *The Guardian*, paras 3–4. Retrieved from https://www.theguardian.com/australia-news/2019/feb/04/key-points-and-recommendations-of-the-banking-royal-commission-report
81. Curtis, G. (2019, June 25). 5 tricks companies use during earnings season. *Investopedia*, para. 1. Retrieved from https://www.investopedia.com/articles/stocks/08/earnings-tricks.asp
82. Ibid., paras 3–14.
83. Wolffe, R. (2019, June 14). Good riddance, Sarah Sanders: Washington's worst communicator. *The Guardian*, Opinion, para. 15. Retrieved from https://www.theguardian.com/commentisfree/2019/jun/14/sarah-sanders-trump-press-secretary-good-riddance
84. Ibid., para. 10.
85. Davies, N. (2009). *Flat earth news*. London, UK: Random House, p. 52.
86. Sallot, L., & Johnson, E. (2006). Investigating relationships between journalists and public relations practitioners: Work together to set, frame and build the public agenda, 1991–2004. *Public Relations Review*, *32*(2), 151–159, p. 151.
87. Macnamara, J. (2014). *Journalism and PR: Unpacking 'spin', stereotypes and media myths*. New York, NY: Peter Lang, p. 120.
88. Ibid., p. 127.
89. Gandy, O. (1982). *Beyond agenda setting: Information subsidies and public policy*. Norwood, NJ: Ablex.
90. Macnamara, 2014, p. 16.
91. The term 'gatekeeper' was coined by social psychologist Kurt Lewin and was used to refer to editors, producers and journalists who control access to and content of media by David Manning White and a number of other media scholars since. See Lewin, K. (1947). Frontiers in group dynamics II: Channels of group life, social planning and action research. *Human Relations*, *1*(2), 143–153; White, D. (1950). The gatekeeper: A case study in the selection of news. *Journalism Quarterly*, *27*, 383–390. Reprinted in L. Dexter & D. White (Eds.) (1964). *People, society and mass communications*. New York, NY: Free Press.
92. Bennett, W., & Serrin, W. (2011). The watchdog role of the press. In D. Graber (Ed.), *Media power in politics* (pp. 395–405). Washington, D.C.: CQ Press. (Original work published in 2005)
93. Jones, J. (2018, October 12). U.S. media trust continues to recover from 2016 low. Gallup. Retrieved from https://news.gallup.com/poll/243665/media-trust-continues-recover-2016-low.aspx
94. Ibid., para. 6.

95. Mayer, H. (1968). *The press in Australia*. Sydney, NSW: Lansdowne Press, p. 89. (Original work published 1964); McChesney, R., & Scott, B. (Eds.). (2003). *The brass check: A study of American journalism*. Urbana and Chicago: University of Illinois Press, pp. xvii–xviii.
96. McChesney & Scott, 2003.
97. Goldstein, T. (2007). *Journalism and truth: Strange bedfellows*. Evanston, IL: Northwestern University Press, p. 17.
98. Davidson, D. (2017, September 13). Rebel Wilson wins $4.56m damages from Bauer in record libel settlement. *The Guardian*. Retrieved from https://www.theguardian.com/film/2017/sep/13/rebel-wilson-wins-more-than-45m-in-damages-from-bauer-media
99. Hallin, D., & Mancini, P. (2004). *Comparing media systems: Three models of media and politics*. New York, NY: Cambridge University Press, pp. 10–11.
100. The Fox/News Corp media empire established by Rupert Murdoch has had various structures and identities including News Corporation (1980–2013), 21st Century Fox (2013–2019), Fox Corporation (2019–), and News Corp (2013–). Fox also owned Sky News in the UK until 2018 when it was sold to Comcast.
101. Middleton, K. (2017, November 18–24). Exclusive: Rudd calls for News Corp inquiry. *The Saturday Paper*, News. Retrieved from https://www.thesaturdaypaper.com.au/news/politics/2017/11/18/exclusive-rudd-calls-news-corp-inquiry/15109236005520
102. Cooke, R. (2019, May). News Corp: Democracy's greatest threat. *The Monthly*. Retrieved from https://www.themonthly.com.au/issue/2019/may/1556632800/richard-cooke/news-corp-democracy-s-greatest-threat
103. Muller, D. (2018, May 13). Mounting evidence the tide is turning on News Corp, and its owner. *The Conversation*, para. 10. Retrieved from https://theconversation.com/mounting-evidence-the-tide-is-turning-on-news-corp-and-its-owner-116892
104. Koch, T. (2019, May 9). For 30 years I worked for News Corp papers. Now all I see is shameful bias. *The Guardian*, para. 4. Retrieved from https://www.theguardian.com/commentisfree/2019/may/09/for-30-years-i-worked-for-news-corp-papers-now-all-i-see-is-shameful-bias
105. McIntyre, 2018, p. 71.
106. Kotler, P. (2000). *Marketing management* (Millennium Ed.). New York, NY: Prentice Hall; Pride, W., Hughes, R., & Kapoor, J. (2015). *Foundations of business*. Boston, MA: Cengage Learning.
107. Target. (2020). In Lexico [powered by Oxford]. Retrieved from https://www.lexico.com/en/definition/target
108. Dozier, D., & Repper, F. (1992). Research firms and public relations practices. In J. Grunig (Ed.), *Excellence in public relations and communication management*. New York, NY: Routledge, pp. 185–218.
109. Aldoory, L., & Sha, B. (2007. The situational theory of publics: Practical applications, methodological challenges, and theoretical horizons. In E. Toth (Ed.), *The

future of excellence in public relations and communication management (pp. 339–355). Mahwah, NJ: Lawrence Erlbaum; Heath, R., & Merkl, L. (2013). Target. In R. Heath (Ed.), *Encyclopedia of public relations* (2nd ed., vol. 2, pp. 915–917). Thousand Oaks, CA: Sage Publications.
110. Hallahan, K. (2018). Public relations. In R. Heath & W. Johansen (Eds.), *The international encyclopedia of strategic communication* (pp. 1–16). Hoboken, NJ: Wiley-Blackwell, p. 3.
111. Hutchins, A. (2018). Target groups. In R. Heath & W. Johansen (Eds.), *The international encyclopedia of strategic communication* (pp. 1–9). Hoboken, NJ: Wiley-Blackwell.
112. Çüçen, A. (1998). Heidegger's reading of Descartes' dualism: The relation of subject and object. Twentieth World Congress of Philosophy, Boston, MA, August 10–15. Retrieved from https://www.bu.edu/wcp/Papers/Cont/ContCuce.htm
113. Subject. Object. (2015). In Perfect English Grammar, paras 1, 8. Retrieved from https://www.perfect-english-grammar.com/subjects-and-objects.html
114. Toffler, A. (1970). *Future shock*. New York, NY: Random House; Toffler, A. (1980). *The third wave*. New York, NY: William Morrow.
115. Bruns, A. (2008). *Blogs, Wikipedia, second Life and beyond: From production to produsage*. New York, NY: Peter Lang; Picone, I. (2007). Conceptualizing online news use. *Observatorio Journal*, *3*, 93–114.
116. Endres, K., & Kelly, K. (2018). Does microtargeting matter? Campaign contact strategies and young voters. *Journal of Elections, Public Opinion and Parties*, *28*(1), 1–18.
117. Government Communication Service. (2019). Year of marketing. Retrieved from https://gcs.civilservice.gov.uk/guidance/campaigns/year-of-marketing
118. May, T. (2016, October 5). Theresa May's conference speech in full. *The Telegraph*, para. 45. Retrieved from https://www.telegraph.co.uk/news/2016/10/05/theresa-mays-conference-speech-in-full
119. Owen J. (2019, April 10). Exclusive: Government communications plan—Brexit the biggest priority amidst a surge in campaigns. *PRWeek*. Retrieved from https://www.prweek.com/article/1581601/exclusive-government-communications-plan-brexit-biggest-priority-amid-surge-campaigns
120. Her Majesty's Government. (2019). *Government communication plan 2019/20*. London, UK, p. 11. Retrieved from https://gcs.civilservice.gov.uk/communication-plan-2019
121. Government Communication Service. (2018). External affairs operating model. London, UK, p. 5. Retrieved from https://gcs.civilservice.gov.uk/guidance/external-affairs
122. The Open Government Partnership Practice Group on Dialogue and Deliberation. (2019, May). *Deliberation: Getting policy-making out from behind closed doors*, p. 5. Retrieved from https://www.opengovpartnership.org/documents/deliberation-getting-policy-making-out-from-behind-closed-doors

123. Macnamara, J. (2016). *Organizational listening: The missing essential in public communication*. New York, NY: Peter Lang.
124. Holmes, B. (2011). *Citizens' engagement in policymaking and the design of public services*. Canberra, ACT: Parliament of Australia. Retrieved from http://www.aph.gov.au/About_Parliament/Parliamentary_Departments/Parliamentary_Library/pubs/rp/rp1112/12rp01
125. Mason, R. (2019, September 13). MPs condemn "misleading" no-deal Brexit publicity campaign. *The Guardian*, para. 2. Retrieved from https://www.theguardian.com/politics/2019/sep/12/mps-condemn-misleading-no-deal-publicity-campaign
126. Moore, S. (2019, October 15). The 'Get Ready for Brexit' ads—Mystifying in their uselessness. *The Guardian*. Retrieved from https://www.theguardian.com/commentisfree/2019/oct/15/get-ready-for-brexit-ad-campaign-expensive-useless
127. Helm, T. (2019, September 1). How a secret plan to close parliament sparked uproar across Britain. *The Guardian*, para. 2. Retrieved from https://www.theguardian.com/politics/2019/aug/31/leaks-rows-sacking-secret-shutdown-plan-boris-johnson-dominic-cummings
128. Dewey, J. (1927). *The public and its problems*. New York, NY: Holt, title of Chapter 5 and p. 137.
129. Coleman, S. (2013). *How voters feel*. New York, NY: Cambridge University Press, p. 3.
130. Rogers, E. (2003). *Diffusion of innovations* (5th ed.). New York, NY: The Free Press.
131. Friestad, M., & Wright, P. (1994). The persuasion knowledge model: How people cope with persuasion attempts. Journal of Consumer Research, 21(1), 1–31.
132. Merholz, P. (1999). For what it's worth. *Peterme.com* [sidebar column]. Retrieved from http://web.archive.org/web/19991013021124/http://peterme.com/index.html
133. Federal Trade Commission v. Machinima, Inc., No. C-4569 (Mar. 17, 2016). Retrieved from https://www.ftc.gov/enforcement/cases-proceedings/142-3090/machinima-inc-matter
134. R. Bagnall (personal communication [interview], October 1, 2019).
135. Ibid.
136. American Association for the Advancement of science. (2019, April 29). Study scrutinizes credibility of weight management blogs by most popular influencers on social media. *EurekAlert*, para. 2. Retrieved from https://www.eurekalert.org/pub_releases/2019-04/eaft-ssc042919.php
137. Bradshaw, S., & Howard, P. (2018). *Challenging truth and trust: A global inventory of organized social media manipulation*. Working Paper 2018.1. Oxford, UK: Project on Computational Propaganda. Retrieved from https://comprop.oii.ox.ac.uk/research/cybertroops2018
138. Wright, 2019, para. 3.
139. Advertising Standards Authority. (2018, September 28). *An influencer's guide to making clear that ads are ads*. London: ASA/CAP. Retrieved from https://www.asa.org.uk/news/new-guidance-launched-for-social-influencers.html

140. Jenna Abrams: The Trump-loving Twitter star who never really existed. (2017, November 3). *The Guardian*, para. 9. Retrieved from https://www.theguardian.com/technology/shortcuts/2017/nov/03/jenna-abrams-the-trump-loving-twitter-star-who-never-really-existed
141. Ibid., para. 7.
142. Collins, B., & Cox, J. (2017, November 2). Jenna Abrams, Russian clown troll princes dupes the mainstream media and the world. *The Daily Beast*, para. 10. Retrieved from https://www.thedailybeast.com/jenna-abrams-russias-clown-troll-princess-duped-the-mainstream-media-and-the-world
143. Bradshaw, S., & Howard, P. (2018). *Challenging truth and trust: A global inventory of organized social media manipulation*. Oxford, UK: Computational Propaganda Research Project, Oxford Internet Institute, p. 3. Retrieved from https://comprop.oii.ox.ac.uk/research/cybertroops2018
144. Hindman, M., & Barash, V. (2018, October). *Disinformation, 'fake news' and influence campaigns on Twitter*. Miami, FL: Knight Foundation, p. 5.
145. Lim, G., Maynier, E., Scott-Railton, J., Fittarelli, A., Moran, N., & Deibert, R. (2019, May 14). Burned after reading Endless Mayfly's ephemeral disinformation campaign. *The Citizen Lab* [Web log post], paras 1–2. Retrieved from https://citizenlab.ca/2019/05/burned-after-reading-endless-mayflys-ephemeral-disinformation-campaign
146. Ibid., para. 4.
147. Deibert, R. (2019, May 14). Endless Mayfly: An invasive species in the social media ecosystem [Web log post]. *Ron Deibert*, article title. Retrieved from https://deibert.citizenlab.ca/2019/05/endless-mayfly
148. Ibid., para. 2.
149. Bradshaw & Howard, 2018, p. 3.
150. Newman, N., Fletcher, R. Kalogeropoulos, A., & Kleis Nielsen, R. (2019). *Reuters Institute digital news report 2019*. Oxford, UK: Reuters Institute for the Study of Journalism and Oxford University, p. 9. Retrieved from http://www.digitalnewsreport.org
151. McCorkindale, T. (2019). *2019 IPR disinformation in society report*. Gainesville, FL: Institute for Public Relations, p. 3. Retrieved from https://instituteforpr.org/ipr-disinformation-study
152. Bob Jensen, who now works as a consultant on cybersecurity, risk assessment, and crisis communication, previously spent 30 years in US Government communication roles. Most recently he was principal deputy assistant secretary of the Office of Public Affairs in the US Department of Homeland Security. Prior to that, he was deputy director of external affairs for the US Federal Emergency Management Agency (FEMA) in Washington DC, where his experiences included setting up government communication field operations and handling media and public communication following the Haiti earthquake and the Deepwater Horizon oil spill in 2010 and during Hurricane Sandy in 2012. Other positions he has held include assistant press secretary for foreign affairs of the National Security Council based

in the White House; executive officer and spokesman in Baghdad with the State Department; and director of communication for the US Department of Defense in Iraq and Afghanistan between 2006 and 2008.
153. R. Jensen (personal communication [interview], May 28, 2019).
154. P. Fray (personal communication [interview], September 12, 2019).
155. R. Tench (personal communication [interview], September 20, 2019).
156. Workman, M., & Hutcheon, S. (2019, November 8). Topham Guerin: The team that helped Scott Morrison win is now working for Boris Johnson and Brexit. *ABC News*, para. 5. Retrieved from https://www.abc.net.au/news/2019-11-08/topham-guerins-boomer-meme-industrial-complex/11682116
157. Ibid., para. 3.
158. Ibid., paras 7–9.
159. Ibid., para. 11.
160. Reid, A., & Dotto, C. (2019, December 6). Thousands of misleading Conservative ads side-step scrutiny thanks to Facebook policy. *First Draft*. Retrieved from https://firstdraftnews.org/latest/thousands-of-misleading-conservative-ads-side-step-scrutiny-thanks-to-facebook-policy
161. White propaganda is defined as partisan and promotional messaging that does not conceal its source, whereas grey and black propaganda progressively use subterfuge. See Jowett, G., & O'Donnell, V. (1986). *Propaganda and persuasion*. London, UK: Sage Publications.

4

Technologies Turbocharging Post-Communication

Accelerating and compounding the escalation from spin and clickbait to fabrication, disinformation, and malpractices such as manipulative marketing and political campaigns is the rapid evolution of information and communication technologies (ICTs) that have the potential to turbocharge what is referred to here as post-communication. I hesitate to say that technological development is unprecedented, as many do. Human history has been characterized by waves of innovation and technological change. The invention of alphabets and writing, the steam engine, and machine-powered flight triggered what could arguably be described as some of the most momentous changes in human civilisation. Notwithstanding, few could disagree that developments in computers and information transmission systems have been rapid over the past few decades and that societies are on the cusp of further disruptive change.

Social Media—The New Media Monopolies

After going public in 2004, Facebook has become the most-used media platform in history with 2.5 billion active monthly users at the beginning of 2020. Every day, more than 1.6 billion people used Facebook in 2019[1] and spent an average of more than 40 minutes on the platform daily.[2] Video sharing site YouTube, owned by Google, follows close behind with 1.68 billion monthly users worldwide and predictions for this to grow to 1.86 billion global users by 2021.[3] More than one billion people use Google products every day, including the Google search engine that provides 1.2 trillion online searches a year,[4] as well as the Google Chrome web browser and the Android operating system that Google now owns. Instagram, which passed one billion active users in 2018,[5] has surpassed Twitter's 330 million active monthly,[6] followed by Pinterest (300 million active monthly users) and Snapchat (200 million active monthly users). Blogging site Tumblr and aggregation site Reddit are also popular in the USA, Europe, and many other countries, along with instant messaging sites such as WhatsApp and Messenger.

Beyond Western (mostly American) conglomerates, Chinese social media are the major challengers, particularly WeChat with 1.1 billion monthly users in 2019; Tencent's instant messaging platform QQ, which has more than 800 million monthly users; China's video sharing site Youku Tudou with 580 million registered users; and Sina Weibo (similar to Twitter and usually referred to simply as Weibo) with 440 million active monthly users.[7]

Mark Zuckerberg built Facebook to its dominant position partly through assurances that users' data shared in the online community were safe. As recently as a 2019 'op ed' article in the *Wall Street Journal*, he asserted that Facebook would never "sell" its users' data.[8] Based on recent scandals, it is clear that this commitment has been well and truly broken on numerous occasions. Cynics suggest that once Facebook corporatized and was required to make money, it systematically set out on a strategy to build a massive user base using the lures of free access, promised privacy, and algorithms to maximize interaction on the site. Once a massive database of active users was established, with personal details and much of their life story online, Facebook had an asset that could be traded for vast profits, which it now does on a grand scale.

Other social media platforms that were once competitors offering choice to users have been subsumed into oligopolies through acquisitions and mergers. For instance, at the beginning of 2020 Facebook owned and controlled Instagram, Messenger, and WhatsApp. Facebook also had by this time purchased more than 70 other companies including Lightbox, Atlas Solutions, search engine Friend-Feed, and parts of the social network Friendster. Some of these no longer exist after Facebook stripped out assets and technologies that it wanted and then closed the companies down. Google purchased YouTube in 2006 for US$1.65 billion. The year before, Google bought Android Inc., the initial developer of the Android operating system now used on more than two billion mobile/cell phones. Control of the operating system on phones gives Google unprecedented access and influence over applications and services used on those phones. Amazon, well known as an e-commerce site but also involved in digital streaming, cloud computing, and artificial intelligence (AI) owns more than 40 subsidiaries including Audible, Goodreads, Zappos, and Shopbop and is considered one of the big four technology companies along with Google, Facebook and Apple.

This consolidation is reducing competition and affording Big Tech companies monopoly or near monopoly positions in the delivery of a range of information and communication services. Lack of competition means that these corporate giants can increasingly do what they want because the users of their products and services have little by way of choice.

Big Data

What Manuel Castells and others have labelled "the network society"[9] has led to enormous growth over the past few decades in the amount of data collected and stored in databases within organizations and in the *cloud*. Increasingly data in these databases are combined and consolidated through corporate acquisitions, mergers, and partnerships, creating what is loosely referred to as *big data*.

There are many definitions of big data, quite a few of which draw on a 2001 Gartner report that identified three Vs as key to understanding big data—*volume*, *velocity* and *variety*. While it did not use the term big data, Gartner proposed that computer-generated and stored data were characterized by "the increasing size of data, the increasing rate at which it is [sic] produced and the increasing range of formats and representations employed."[10] A recent definition described big data as "the information asset characterized by such a high Volume, Velocity and Variety to require specific technology and analytical methods for its transformation into Value" [capitalization in original].[11] The authors of this definition emphasized Gartner's three Vs with initial capitals and added value as a fourth capital V word. They also noted that others have added another V word—*veracity*—to include the importance of trust in data and the outcomes of analysis.[12]

A simpler and more common definition is that "big data is data that exceeds the processing capacity of conventional database query and analysis tools."[13] This points to the fact that big data usually cannot be analyzed using commonly available database management software and, instead, requires special systems and skills to cope with the volume, different formats, and constantly expanding and changing content of data available.

Significantly, no definition is readily available that puts a figure of the size of data sets that comprise big data. So it remains a 'fuzzy' term in relation to size, as well as in two other respects. The first of these is that use of the term generally refers to two processes: (1) the *collection* and *storage* of large quantities of data and (2) the *analysis* of data to gain insights that are of some social, economic, or political value. Storage is an IT consideration focussed on providing sufficient space on servers internally or online somewhere in the world (the *cloud*) and is largely a passive process. Data collection is also largely automated these days using IT applications, although the scale and scope of data collection is determined by policies and management decisions, such as what data to collect. Data analysis, involving data mining and then the application of computational analytic techniques to draw insights and knowledge from data, is arguably the most significant facet of the use of big data. Before examining developments in data analysis—also referred to as *data analytics*—there is a third important aspect of data that needs to be understood, but is often undervalued or even unrecognized.

Most often data is thought of in *statistical* terms—that is, as numbers such as age, weight, income, and ratings applied in scales in relation to humans; volume such as sales, profits, and percentages in relation to transactions; and length, breadth, height, surface area, distance and other measures in relation to objects. However, data consists of *textual* as well as statistical information. The opinions, perceptions, desires, expectations, and requests of customers, employees, and other people such as members, patients, students, and voters, referred to in marketing as the voice of customers (VOC), the voice of employees (VOE), and the voice of stakeholders (VOS), is expressed more often and more specifically in words than in statistics. While financial transactions and information in the physical sciences can be precisely represented in numbers, statistics about people such as demographics and psychographics are highly reductionist because they capture only a few characteristics that can be quantified. Furthermore, some numbers such as *nominal* and *ordinal* numbers merely serve as labels for categories or levels that are ascribed to people, rather than being numerical calculations or the authentic voice of those described.[14] The views, needs, concerns, and interests of people are most fully expressed in written text in the form of letters, e-mails, open-ended responses in surveys, complaints, submissions to consultations and inquiries, reports, and social media posts.

In addition to statistics and text, data increasingly includes *audio data* and *video data*. Closed circuit TV (CCTV) cameras are proliferating in major cities worldwide capturing images of people's movements and actions including who they meet and associate with and where they shop, eat, drink, and seek entertainment. Public cameras capturing video data have been justified on the grounds of traffic management, safety, security, and combatting crime—in short, they are 'for our own good'. To some extent they are. However, the potential for unwarranted surveillance is a concern for many. The American Civil Liberties Union supports the use of cameras in "high-profile public places," but warns that CCTV systems are susceptible to abuse, such as invasion of privacy and discriminatory targeting, and cites reports showing that they are not necessarily effective in deterring crime or terrorism such as suicide attacks.[15] For example, London suffered terrorist attacks in 2007 and 2017 despite having one of the most extensive CCTV systems in the world including cameras in the locations that were targeted.

In addition to video data captured by government authorities and in professionally produced films and videos, billions of videos recorded by people on phones and personal digital assistants are uploaded to social media every year. More than a few marketers are licking their lips at the prospect of accessing vast quantities of video data that provide comprehensive information about the work and social lives of hundreds of millions of people.

In a critical analysis of big data, danah boyd and Kate Crawford added a further element to definitions, which is relevant to this analysis. As well as noting that big data refers to technology (large-scale data collection and storage) and analysis, they argue that big data is in part mythology. They point out that discussion of big data incorporates "the widespread belief that large data sets offer a higher form of intelligence and knowledge that can generate insights that were previously impossible, with the aura of truth, objectivity, and accuracy."[16] Their observation and warning draws on the prophetic reference by Leslie Burkholder to "a computational turn in thought and research."[17] This is pandemic in business literature today in which big data have become buzzwords and the concept is widely touted as key to economic, political, and social progress.

A former president of the American Academy of Advertising warns that "data merger" through mergers and acquisitions of media, technology, and telecommunications companies poses a major threat.[18] Data sets that individually do not pose privacy or other concerns can lead to personally identifiable data when combined with multiple data sets. Managing director of the Norwegian Communication Association (NCA), Therese Manus, says that governments need to ensure that data is not exported to big international companies for their proprietary use; rather it should be used to benefit the people from whom it was obtained. She believes that, while the General Data Protection Regulation (GDPR) is a good start, governments need to do more through legislation—even a tax on use of public data—because multinational corporations are only just beginning to identify the potential for exploiting big data. Echoing Michael Haupt and others,[19] Manus says "data is the new oil."[20]

Data Analytics

As noted in relation to big data, it is data analysis (verb) and data analytics (noun) that provide the *insights* and what some tellingly refer to as *intelligence* that inform decisions, policies, and strategies by governments, corporations, political parties, and various other organizations. So-called *data scientists* who undertake data analysis are described as having the "sexiest job of the 21st century,"[21] which reflects the mythological status of data referred to by boyd and Crawford.

In a discussion such as this focussed on communication practices and related social and political issues, technologies cannot be examined in detail. This is not the purpose here. Other books, journals, and websites undertake that important work. What is relevant to this analysis is recognition of the role that new technologies are playing and will increasingly play and the effects—positive and negative—that they can have on public communication, dialogue, and debate.

Data analytics involves a combination of computational processes and human interpretation. Statistical analysis is one form of data analytics that processes structured quantitative data to identify correlations, relationships, patterns, trends, and make inferences and even predictions using statistical analysis methods and techniques such as hypothesis testing (also called *t* tests) and regression analysis. Statistical analysis calculates means (averages), modes, and medians and informs techniques such as statistical modelling to represent various realities based on mathematical calculations.

Textual data can be analyzed using textual analysis and similar methods such as content analysis, thematic analysis, and semantic analysis. Many books, chapters, and articles are available describing these methods.[22] With the development of *natural language processing* and *machine learning* (i.e., learning algorithms), large volumes of textual data can be analyzed more quickly than manual coding and analysis to gain insights and understanding—although algorithms, even learning algorithms, are subject to biases, as discussed in following sections of this chapter.

The large amounts of information received by organizations verbally, such as in phone calls to call centres, can be converted to text using *voice to text* (VTT) software and then analyzed using textual analysis applications.

In the past, video data has been mostly analyzed manually, or by reviewing transcripts alongside the images. However, the field of *video content analysis* is advancing rapidly. The convergence of technologies such as *video motion detection* used in office and home security systems, *video motion analysis* used in sport and fields such as physiotherapy for studying human movement, and new technologies such as *face recognition* software will see rapid development in video data analysis.

Increasingly the words written by Sting and recorded by the English band *The Police* will hold true in society: "Every breath you take; Every move you make … I'll be watching you."

Who will be watching, and listening, and what they will be allowed to hear and see, will depend on the ethics of those involved in using various ICTs, and the regulations and legislation that governments enact to protect citizens' rights and the public sphere. Analysis of the increasing amounts of data that are available can be used for the benefit of people and society, or for intelligence that aids manipulation, oppression, and the interests of power elites. In a prescient discussion of "critical questions" about big data, in which they described big data as a "socio-technical phenomenon," danah boyd and Kate Crawford ask:

> Will large-scale … data help us create better tools, services and public goods? Or will it usher in a new wave of privacy incursions and invasive marketing? Will data analytics help us understand online communities and political movements? Or will it be used to track protesters and suppress speech?[23]

Data analytics enables personalized targeting by marketers, and even *micro-targeting*. Increasingly, instead of using mass media advertising, marketers directly target people through electronic direct mail (eDM) or advertising served on their social media pages based on detailed information about their age, gender, location (even when they are travelling using geolocation technology), tastes, recent events in their life such as relationship changes, and their recent purchases, online searches, and website visits. While personalized advertising provides more relevant information than mass media advertising, zealous targeting can lead to invasive techniques and data acquisition can breach privacy.

In their 2019 book *The Costs of Connection: How Data Is Colonizing Human Life and Appropriating It for Capitalism*, Nick Couldry and Ulises Mejias argue that citizens today are being exploited by what they call *data colonialism*, which they define as "an emerging order for the appropriation of human life so that data can be continuously harvested from it for profit." This extraction is through what they call *data relations*—"ways of interacting with each other and with the world facilitated by digital tools."[24] Comparing data colonialism with historical colonialism that involved appropriation of land, bodies, and natural resources, Couldry and Mejias label data colonialism "an appropriation of social resources" and, far from seeing this as some soft form of colonialism, they argue that, while being a technological progression of capitalism, it is also a return to "more brutal forms of exploitation." Through data relations, people become "an input or resource for capitalism."[25] If this sounds extreme, they note that every time a person does something online, a small packet of data is collected by "infrastructures of connection" (such as *cookies* and *caches*), stored, often aggregated with other packets, analyzed, and then used or sold for commercial or political use.[26] There are benefits for users in this digitally connected world, but Couldry and Mejias argue that, without some controls, the costs of connection are high and, in many if not most cases, they are much greater than the benefits that individuals derive.

Cambridge Analytica and Co.

The Cambridge Analytica scandal that erupted in 2018 after it was revealed that the political consulting firm got its hands on and used the personal data of up to 87 million Facebook users during the 2016 US presidential campaign and the UK's EU referendum[27] brought to public attention how data analytics are being used for manipulation and how privacy is being breached on a large scale.

The process begins with combining multiple data sets such as demographics, psychographics, and other data such as census statistics, electoral rolls, online personality tests, and social media profiles, likes, and follows. Sometimes information revealed in social media posts is also collected. Data sets may be obtained legally for analysis, but in the case of Cambridge Analytica a huge amount of social media data was purchased from Facebook to add to the data that the company already had acquired from other sources.[28] Then a range of sophisticated "psychometric techniques" and analytic processes are used to identify predispositions of people, make predictions of likely behaviour such as purchasing or voting, and inform targeted strategic communication. Analysis techniques include the use of *singular value decomposition* (SVD) models and relatively obscure methods such as *dimensionality reduction* (also referred to as *matrix factorization*) and what one of the creators of the methodology used by Cambridge Analytica, Aleksandr Kogan, calls "a multi-step co-occurrence approach."[29]

Cambridge Analytica closed its operations in 2018 following international outrage and an investigation by the House of Commons Digital, Culture, Media and Sport Committee, which released a scathing report.[30] However, the challenge for regulators and society is that there are many Cambridge Analyticas out there. They have different names and different owners and different modus operandi. They are operated by smart people taking advantage of unprecedented access to personal information, powerful analytical technologies, and weak regulatory environments in some cases.

Automation

In addition to a desire to access more granular information that provides greater levels of precision and certainty in processes such as marketing and political communication, a goal that is driving much ICT development and taking it into new areas is the pursuit of *automation*. Manually processing the vast amounts of data available today and performing the increasing number of actions required in communication and interaction with millions of customers, potential customers, and voters, would require a huge and growing workforce of highly trained people, a lot of time, and ever-increasing costs. As is occurring in manufacturing, the media and communication industry and related fields of practice such as marketing are looking for automation to reduce time, cost, and inconsistency in outputs and performance.

The purpose here is not to examine automation in its myriad forms—that would take us well off track into areas beyond the scope of this analysis. However, understanding of the significance of emerging ICTs is facilitated by recognizing that automation is a major goal—even a *zeitgeist*—in marketing, media, and communication, as it is in business and industry generally.

Algorithms

In a digital environment, the fundamental building blocks of automation are algorithms, although the concept of algorithms is not new. Greek mathematicians used the *Euclidean algorithm* for finding the greatest common divisor of two numbers—i.e., the largest number that divides both of them without leaving a remainder—named after the ancient Greek mathematician Euclid, who described it in his *Elements* circa 300 BCE. In their simplest sense, algorithms are mathematical calculations.

Since the invention of computing, algorithms have been written into computer code that can be executed on command or even automatically to conduct a series of calculations that produce an output, which can range from matching terms in an internet search to making a decision on a loan application. Some of the formal definitions of an algorithm are complex and even circular. For example, one in the *Journal of Logic and Computation* says: "We define an algorithm to be the set of programs that implement or express that algorithm."[31] Tarleton Gillespie more coherently defines algorithms as "encoded procedures for transforming input data into a desired output based on specified calculations."[32]

For our purposes here, it is sufficient to say that algorithms are sets of instructions written in computer code that are activated to perform defined tasks. Computer programs can be understood as lots of algorithms working together, with each algorithm performing a specific function. Algorithms calculate and process digits and numerals as well as words with the development of *natural language processing*—although ultimately all data is converted into strings of the digits 0 and 1 to create binary code, the *machine language* used by computers. A common example is an internet *search algorithm*, which searches for matches of the search terms on the internet.

Other commonly used algorithms serve items in news feeds, make friend suggestions in social media, and provide recommendations on e-commerce sites such as Amazon based on *machine learning* capabilities. These are referred to as *learning algorithms* because they store key words and phrases that a user has entered or clicked on over a period of time. They then count the number of times that these stored terms appear on other sites or pages, and then automatically serve news and information from those with the highest correlation. Similarly, recommendations for new friends online are created by algorithms that identify other users with shared friends or interests.

A 2017 survey by Reuters in 36 countries found that more of the people studied get their news via algorithms and sharing on social media than by actively seeking it from recognized news sources.[33] As noted in Chapter 2, Pew Research Center studies have reported that 68% of Americans accessed their news mainly from social media in 2018.[34] This gives rise to at least three major concerns in relation to algorithms.

First, by delivering news and information and recommending friends and connections based on a user's past searches and connections, algorithms act as filters, creating *filter bubbles*. They filter out divergent and oppositional information and connections, thus creating what are also referred to as *echo chambers* in which internet users interact predominantly or only with those who echo their views and share their interests. Thus, algorithms are contributing to polarization and limiting open debate in which a range of views and positions are presented for consideration.

A second major concern in relation to the automated calculations and results of algorithms is that they do not deliver 'objective' results devoid of human subjectivity and bias as some claim. To the contrary, many algorithms involve considerable in-built bias because, while algorithmic outputs are based on mathematical calculations and empirical data, the algorithms that perform the calculations are written by humans.[35] The parameters of what they take into account and the things they count are decided by the humans who write the instructions that an algorithm executes. For example, decisions on what content to block on social media sites or in e-mail filters are based on humans encoding the criteria and terms into an algorithm.

As well as deciding what news and information many people consume, algorithms are being used for predictive policing, sentencing in courts, doing medical diagnoses, rating Uber drivers and assigning jobs to them, adjusting traffic lights and satellite navigation directions based on traffic congestion, and many other tasks. The appeal of algorithms that automate tasks is the speed with which they can make decisions and initiate actions, thus reducing the costs of human labour and, in some cases, offering benefits to users. However, depending on the programming parameters set, algorithmic programming can result in *data-driven discrimination*. Researchers at the London School of Economics and Political Science have identified a number of cases in which the data accessed by an algorithm led to serious cases of discrimination. One example involved court sentencing decisions that were based in part on an algorithm's prediction of the likelihood of an offender reoffending. Investigations by journalists and academics studying machine learning algorithms found that the algorithm was "likely to falsely flag black defendants as future criminals, wrongly labelling them this way at almost twice the rate as white defendants, while white defendants were mislabelled as low risk more often than black defendants."[36]

Often bias and discrimination are caused because the data accessed by algorithms is selective or out of date. As Professor Aram Sinnreich from American University School of Communication told a session at the 2019 International Communication Association (ICA) conference in Washington D.C., "algorithms freeze values and rights in society based on past data sets."[37]

The third problem with algorithms is their lack of transparency. The code that comprises algorithms and even the instructions that inform them, which are often written as human language text, or a mix of text and computer language such as Python or R, are referred to as a *black box* because they are locked inside password protected computers unable to be queried or reviewed by anyone other than the programmers who created them. This results in a lack of *algorithmic governance*, which concerns many media and communication researchers.[38] For instance, if an algorithm makes a decision that a person feels is wrong or unjust, there is no recourse to challenge the decision. There is no person to discuss the decision with because responsibility has been given over to an algorithm and, because the algorithm is secret inside a black box of computer code, there is no way to identify or query the criteria on which the decision was based. It literally is a case of "the computer says no."[39] This is increasingly important in an era when algorithms decide whether loan applications will be approved or not, whether Uber drivers get work or not, and whether or not information and messages reach all those for whom they are relevant.

Algorithms bring many benefits to users and to society. I must confess that I like Amazon's book recommendations that frequently introduce me to titles that I otherwise might not have found. Also, I must admit that I have found many of my favourite songs through Spotify's recommendation algorithm that becomes more finely tuned to my taste as my online music collection grows. But there is much to be concerned about when algorithms make an increasing number of decisions affecting people and society without transparency or governance.

Bots

Algorithms provide the engine for small online applets referred to as *bots*—an abbreviation of web robot. Bots are semi-autonomous or autonomous software (strings of code if you prefer) installed on internet servers to interact with visitors to websites. Bots typically include learning algorithms so that they can track users' online interactions, such as words typed, pages visited, or menus clicked, and respond with relevant information.

The most benign bots are those in personal digital assistants such as Siri and Alexa and *chat bots* that pop up on web pages and offer to help users find information or answer questions. For example, KLM Royal Dutch Airlines uses a chatbot called *Bluebot* to help users of its website book flights and answer their queries. KLM reported that 500,000 passengers had interacted with the bot and sent more than 1.7 million messages by early 2019.[40] These are relatively unsophisticated bots that are readily recognizable as machine-based and are quite limited in their capabilities. They operate by matching web users' questions that are typed into a dialogue box and then look up a library of pre-programmed responses.

Bots that operate on social media networks, often referred to as *social bots*, are more sophisticated and can mimic human behaviour to a significant extent and even act as if they are a person or an organization. Social bots are defined as "software processes that are programmed to appear to be human-generated within the context of social networking sites such as Facebook and Twitter."[41] Social bots can perform tasks such as create messages, like posts, follow internet accounts, and even act as an internet account and gain followers of their own. Such sites are referred to as fake accounts because they are not a human interacting online—they are a software application installed on a computer connected to the internet. Fake accounts operated by bots are referred to by some as *online astroturfing*,[42] drawing on the widely condemned PR and political lobbying practice of creating organizations that purport to represent grassroots support, but which have no members (named after the synthetic grass, Astro Turf).

Kearston Wesner, a professor at Quinnipiac University, has conducted research that shows bots comprise more than 50% of all internet traffic, particularly in social media. Of those, she describes 22.9% as "good bots," which perform functions such as online search, provide suggestions in websites, and make recommendations in sites such as Amazon. However, she estimates that 30% are "bad bots" that function to boost follower numbers, capture e-mail addresses and other personal details, operate fake accounts, conduct *Twitter bombing*, or create disinformation such as fake text.[43]

Bots play into popular mythology in the same way that robots do generally, being greeted with alarm and a level of moral panic that they will take over and control humans. However, the reality is the opposite. Researchers argue that the focus of attention should not be on automated behaviour by machines, but on human behaviour. Like the algorithms that scientists use to understand human DNA, bots are created by humans, they are installed on computers and networks by humans, and they work on behalf of humans to serve human interests. They extend the capabilities of humans, acting as what Katherine Hayles calls "electronic prostheses."[44] But humans are the puppeteers, creating and pulling the strings (of code in this instance). Hence, human behaviour needs to be regulated—not technology. And humans at every level in every field need to acquire contemporary media literacy and exercise diligence online.

Ralph Tench, director of research in Leeds Business School at Leeds Beckett University in the UK, says that even researchers need to be wary, warning of "evidential interference" through AI such as bots "actively responding to research instruments [and] researchers not adequately checking research that captures social robot engagement, thus influencing issues and the tone and sentiment of debate that is reported."[45]

Online applications that can identify the likelihood of posts being from a bot are becoming available—e.g., Botornot, which classifies the likelihood that Twitter accounts are bots. Also, there are tell-tale signs that a social media account is a bot, such as:

- High volume of posts—bots typically produce higher volumes of posts than humans do;
- Abnormal volume patterns—for instance, posts by bots used in campaigns often have an abrupt start and then decline or stop completely after an event such as an election;
- Bots typically retweet posts by other bots, so high volumes of retweets of the same accounts and even the same tweets can be a giveaway;
- High volume of posts seven days a week—bots typically work 24/7, whereas most organizations such as political parties and even PR agencies work Monday to Friday;
- Lack of bios and photos—bot accounts usually have little by way of bios or personal details such as schools and university attended and often do not display photos.

The above tips and many others like them increasingly need to become part of media literacy, which will be discussed in Chapter 5.

At the time of writing there were very few laws governing the use of bots. A *Bot Disclosure and Accountability Act* was passed in the USA in 2018, but little or nothing has been done in relation to the legislation, according to Kearston Wesner from Quinnipiac University.[46] In California the *Bot Disclosure Law S.B. 1001* came into force from 1 July 2019. This provides for a ban on bots that pretend to be a human and disclosure on websites and pages that use bots in the following terms.

(a) It shall be unlawful for any person to use a bot to communicate or interact with another person in California online, with the intent to mislead the other person about its artificial identity for the purpose of knowingly deceiving the person about the content of the communication in order to incentivize a purchase or sale of goods or services in a commercial transaction or to influence a vote in an election. A person using a bot shall not be liable under this section if the person discloses that it is a bot.

(b) The disclosure required by this section shall be clear, conspicuous, and reasonably designed to inform persons with whom the bot communicates or interacts that it is a bot.[47]

Such laws seek to provide transparency in relation to these types of algorithms. However, there is little or no incentive for governments to expand or enforce such laws because of the anonymity of bot creators. There is usually no one to arrest and no organization to fine or sue in the case of breaches of law, so legal action offers little or no possibility of justice or cost recovery.

Artificial Intelligence (AI)

AI is a broad term that denotes a combination of a number of the technologies discussed, including big data collection and analysis, machine learning algorithms, and advanced computational methods that lead to semi-automation or full automation. Despite much hype, there are many indications that we are only at the beginning of AI development and use. Driverless cars are much talked about, but major barriers remain before authorities and commuters will put their trust in a fast-moving human transporter controlled entirely by computers. In terms of media and communication, as recently as 2019 Facebook announced that it was working to modify its AI systems to stop sending event invitations to dead people or to wish them a happy birthday.[48] This shows that even the largest and most tech-savvy corporations in the world have not mastered AI.

The purpose of discussing AI here it not to examine the state of technical development or its potential, but to discuss attitudes and approaches in relation to the implementation of AI systems and the readiness of industry and professions to adopt and implement AI ethically and in ways that contribute to social good, rather than manipulative applications in the service of commerce and political power.

The Facebook example above shows the limitations of AI and automation at a simple day-to-day level in social media. At a more advanced level, firms such as McKinsey see AI as able to transform industry and business in ways that will reduce operating costs and speed up operations. However, even McKinsey acknowledges that there are major questions about bias and fairness in the application of AI. McKinsey consultants say that AI can help reduce bias in some processes involving human interpretation, but that it can also "bake in and scale bias" by basing decision making and processes on pre-determined parameters written into algorithms and then applying those universally. McKinsey urges developers and adopters of AI to tread carefully.[49]

However, marketing and communication industry literature indicates a headlong rush into AI with little thought other than how to serve corporate interests. For instance, the marketing director of what claims to be the largest independent marketing company in the world states that "artificial intelligence is the future of marketing" giving the example that "soon" not only chat functions but "direct-to-consumer engagement avenues will be run by AI bots."[50] The PR industry is similarly demonstrating little critical or reflective thinking in relation to AI. To the contrary, critical analyses show that PR practitioners are "cheerleaders"[51] for AI as a new powerful set of tools to exploit in the pursuit of corporate and government objectives. A Public Relations Consultants' Association (PRCA) blog post by Ian Hood, CEO and co-founder of Babel PR in the UK, welcomed AI in the following terms.

> … we have nothing to fear, and much to look forward to in the foreseeable future … the best campaigns—those that build brands and create opportunity—are those in which all of the available tools have been used to their best effect … Those who embrace and exploit all the tools, including artificial and human intelligence, will continue to win awards and deliver value to the companies they serve.[52]

It is interesting that Hood used the term "exploit" and it is clear that he sees the objective of PR to "deliver value to the companies" that PR professionals work for, without any reference to their stakeholders or society. In one of the few cautionary examinations of the use of AI in PR with a social responsibility focus, Clea Bourne from Goldsmiths, University of London, critiques the "PR profession's myopia" regarding AI, which she says is narrowly framed by "21st century neoliberal capitalism."[53] The two-way symmetrical, dialogic, and social responsibility theories and models of PR, which are reviewed with a call for "remodelling" in Chapter 5, regularly fail to materialize in practice. Comments such as those of Hood illustrate a lack of reflexivity and critical thinking among communication professionals who are shaping society and politics. And Hood is far from alone in being a cheerleader for exploiting AI in public communication. Similar uncritical thinking in relation to the application of new technologies is revealed in the following section.

At the 2019 annual conference of the Public Relations Institute of New Zealand (PRINZ) in Wellington, Hilary O'Connor, a director of Soul Machine (https://www.soulmachines.com), enthusiastically demonstrated to the audience how AI could be matched with images of real people enacting a range of emotions and responses to produce "digital humans" using a "digital brain" to interact autonomously with people. O'Connor explained how the company was "creating life-like, emotional responsive artificial humans" to work in call centres and act as "autonomously animated digital influencers."[54] While talking with a digital human might be preferable to the robotic responses of a chat bot or on-hold *muzak*, such technologies give new meaning to the concept of influencers discussed in Chapter 3 and raise further questions about who will be influencing whom on behalf of whom.

Deepfakes and Fake Text—Next Gen Disinformation

A particularly insidious form of video disinformation is *deepfakes*. At a basic level, these involve the use of advanced video editing applications such as Adobe After Effects and face-swapping tools such as FakeApp to swap faces on bodies and/or manipulate lips and mouths to have those depicted saying things that they never said. More advanced versions use AI to synthesize voice and match this to facial images.

Deepfakes have been used for fake celebrity porn for some time, but recently an even darker side of fake videos has emerged. *Buzzfeed* CEO Jonah Peretti and filmmaker Jordan Peele teamed up in 2018 to demonstrate the capability of deepfakes to fool people when they created a video of former US President Barack Obama making a public address in which he said bizarre things. *Buzzfeed* was transparent in the experiment, describing it online as a warning about what is increasingly possible with communication and media technology.[55]

It did not take long after US Congresswoman and Speaker of the House of Representatives, Nancy Pelosi, began her public criticisms of Donald Trump that several versions of a video showing her appearing to be drunk and incoherently slurring her words and stammering were posted on Facebook. The videos were edited to slow down Pelosi's speech and modify the pitch of her voice. As an editorial in *The Washington Post* declared, these were not deepfakes in a true sense, as they used simple editing techniques rather than AI to create a totally falsified image. However, the videos were clearly modified with the intention to deceive.

Apart from their appearance in the first place, three things that followed the Pelosi deepfake are most concerning. First, a version of the video was broadcast on Fox Business network, illustrating a failure of media to sift fact from fiction and serve their claimed watchdog of society role.[56] Fox's seeming delight in broadcasting the video was also an illustration of partisan journalism that is discussed in this analysis as one of the contributing factors to post-communication. Second, the President of the United States, Donald Trump, and his personal lawyer, the former mayor of New York City Rudy Giuliani, both tweeted links to the version of the fake video broadcast by Fox and used it to attack Pelosi's credibility. Third, despite widespread outing of the video as fake on social media, Facebook refused to take the video down. Facebook's response was only to downgrade the video's visibility in users' newsfeeds and attach a link to a third-party fact-checking site.[57] This response is shown to be inadequate by 2018 research that not only found Facebook to be a primary site for displaying or directing people to fake news, but also that links to fact-checking sites do not effectively counter fake news because those with polarized opinions usually do not click through to check the veracity of information and images.[58]

To give another example of the lack of reflective and critical thinking and the potential for unethical public communication practices to be systematically perpetrated, not only by 'a few bad apples' as is often claimed but by mainstream industries, a 2019 article on technologies disrupting the advertising industry welcomed deepfakes as an innovation for future advertising. A leading industry figure wrote:

> … we are in that point of history where everything can be faked. Deepfakes enable anyone with the ability of swapping one face for another in an image or a video … for most, this sounds scary and is associated with something negative. But in advertising it can be rather innovative and helpful.[59]

In the interest of fairness it must be noted that the author of the article, Angela Jeffrey, was quoting from a report written for a Greek marketing and communication firm, rather than professing her own views. But both authors and both documents reflect concerning directions in advertising given that intentionally misleading fakes are considered "helpful" and part of the future of advertising, along with personalized advertising and "ads in space" advocated in the same report.[60] I kid you not.

The purpose of citing the examples of post-communication is to show that, despite generalized claims that advertising and PR are ethically conducted, that journalism is objective and truth-seeking, and that government and political communication serve to create informed citizens and dialogically interact in the public sphere, there is extensive evidence that they are not. While some fields of public communication practice such as journalism have been undermined by factors beyond practitioners' control, external forces do not account for all or even the majority of the failings that are evident. As noted in the Introduction, the doctrine of selective depravity—that it's someone else's fault—does not cut it. It points to a few scapegoats, or a mythical 'they', and leaves whole swathes of the public communication ecosystem to continue on as it has. The extent of post-communication across the full spectrum of public communication practices drives home the argument that we are all complicit and, therefore, that there is a need for reflexivity and reflectivity leading to collective action to reverse the corruption of public debate and dialogue that is occurring.

Some go as far as arguing that technologies such as those that create deepfakes put society in danger of a total "collapse of reality" and potentially heading into a state of *post-reality*,[61] which really would be post-everything.

In an attempt to clean up their act, Facebook released a dataset in 2019 to allow users to test tools aimed at detecting deepfakes. Also, start-ups have emerged to address the problem, such as TruePic, which uses AI and blockchain technology to detect manipulated photos. The Defense Advanced Research Projects Agency (DARPA) has developed Medifor, which looks at differences in pixels to determine whether images have been 'doctored'. However, a report from the Data and Society Research Institute concludes that neither technology nor the courts can offer a full solution to deepfakes, arguing instead that social context needs to be considered, such a freedom of speech in relation to humour, parody, satire, and political commentary, as well as legitimate uses of image manipulation for anonymizing people's identity in media reporting. Also the report points out that technical solutions to automatically monitor and check images could make things worse by putting access to the identity of billions of people in the hands of a technology company.[62]

As well as fake videos, another technology-enabled form of deception and manipulation is *fake text*. While false and misleading text has been in existence since writing was invented more than 3,000 years ago, fake text refers to the large-scale creation of false text by AI-based text generators that can write sentences and whole paragraphs on almost any topic. The birth of the technology that underpins fake text is seen in *predictive text* used in text messaging on phones and in Google's *auto-complete* function. However, the technology has recently leapt past these basic applications. In 2019 OpenAI, an AI lab in San Francisco, released a machine learning language generator called GPT-2 that can conduct language modelling and use its 'intelligence' to write long-form text. A Reddit forum on the unlikely topic of cooking egg whites without a frying pan demonstrated the power of this emerging technology, with multiple participants posting suggestions and even offering to search scientific literature—except that no humans were involved. All posts were made by bots.[63] Initially, OpenAI released only a cut down version of the code, saying: "Due to our concerns about malicious applications of the technology, we are not releasing the trained model."[64] However, in August 2019 OpenAI decided to release a more powerful version trained on a dataset of eight million web pages and able to adapt to the style and content of the initial text given to it.

Technology writers have expressed concern, with one saying it "represents the kind of technology that evil humans are going to use to manipulate the population—and in my opinion that makes it more dangerous than any gun."[65] The BBC tried out the updated version and found that it could write news stories with some coherence. However, experts interviewed by the BBC such as professor of computer science at the University of Sheffield, Noel Sharkey, conducted his own tests on the text generator and reported that it still had a way to go to produce meaningful text.[66] Nevertheless, the technology is an example of the tools that are becoming available and the challenges that media professionals, law makers, ethicists, and citizens increasingly have to face.

Deepfakes, fake text, and related content are what some are call *synthetic media*. An article in an industry journal describes synthetic media "as a catch-all term used to describe video, image, text and voice that has been fully or partially generated by computers." The author goes on to say:

> The ability for AI-driven systems to generate audiovisual content is, in our minds, one of the most exciting developments enabled by recent progress in deep learning. We are about to see a major paradigm shift in media creation and consumption that will likely change the equation for entire industries.[67]

This is yet another example of communication industry professionals rushing headlong into the application of new technologies without, in some cases, even a smidgeon of critical thinking or social responsibility.

New ICTs have the potential to enhance democracy, as Stephen Coleman pointed out in his 2017 book, *Can the Internet Strengthen Democracy?* For example, governments around the world have adopted e-petitions and online public consultation via websites that arguably make participation in policy outcomes more accessible. However, research in the UK by Scott Wright found that "Downing Street e-petitions did not achieve a high level of considered judgement." While some of the fault lay with petitioners, who did not provide well-reasoned arguments or evidence to support their case, he found also that there was no space for debate. Also, most alarmingly, Wright concluded that "the vast majority disappeared into a vacuum."[68] Similar discoveries were made in my 2016 research inside the UK Government, which found thousands of submissions to public consultations, e-mails, and letters were not analyzed because the volume made manual analysis impossible and staff did not have textual analysis tools or training in textual analysis.[69] Based on his many years working in senior communication roles with US government agencies, Bob Jensen, says similar 'black holes' occur in relation to public consultation and stakeholder engagement in the United States.[70]

New ICTs can also enable new forms of activism that can have a positive effect in society in many instances. However, in an environment of inadequate self-regulation by social media platforms, big data companies, and public communication practitioners; hollowed out independent news media unable to provide an effective watchdog role; reluctance by lawmakers to act against Big Tech; and a lack of critical media literacy at many levels of society; communication technologies and public communication practices are being turned over to political and social disruption and even what this analysis has called *informational terrorism*.

A Perfect Datastorm Brews

This chapter has identified just some of the technological developments that will disrupt society over the next decade and put ever more powerful tools into the hands of governments, corporations, and individuals. It also has identified how the custodians of those technologies and those who deploy them have a track record that does not inspire trust and, in some cases, rings alarm bells.

We are arriving at the threshold of accelerating technological development without values, principles, standards, or legal frameworks that can guide that development and use in ethical, socially responsible ways.

Already we are perpetrating mass disinformation, deception, and manipulation with today's technologies. Now we are putting even more advanced information and communication technologies in the hands of criminals and children—literally in many cases.

We have foxes guarding the hen house. I refer to the likes of Facebook, Google, and Amazon, which control the computer servers in which our personal data reside and the software that make decisions that affect our lives. Those computers are somewhere in the cloud, that amorphous constellation of spinning and solid state hard drives spread across nation borders and immune from the laws of many.

Without urgent steps to balance interests, provide safeguards, and implement enforceable standards, post-communication will escalate, creating a post-truth society and potentially a post-democracy society, or even post-society.

Such warnings should not be dismissed as NeoLuddism.[71] Rather, they are a call for data science to be integrated with social science. On one hand, *technophobia*, which has existed in human society even before the Industrial Revolution, needs to be resisted. However, with the words of Arthur Koestler's *The Ghost in the Machine*,[72] Leo Marx's *The Machine in the Garden*,[73] and Lewis Mumford's *The Myth of the Machine*[74] ringing in our ears, we must avoid the blindness created by *cyberoptimism* and *cyberbole*. We must address the social and the political, not only the technological. In an editorial published in *The Guardian* in 2015, Kentaro Toyama, a former Microsoft computer scientist and more recently W. K. Kellogg Associate Professor at the University of Michigan School of Information, reported that technologies he helped develop to allegedly improve lives "had little long-term impact." He recorded the following reflection.

> When we were committed and worked with capable partners, our technology augmented their impact. But when we had corrupt or inept collaborators, the technology aggravated the dysfunction. In other words, technology doesn't add a fixed benefit. Instead, it amplifies underlying human forces.[75]

So it is that by the beginning of the third decade of the 21st century, we have entered an era of accelerating fabrication in the form of fake news and alternative facts, not only from Donald Trump but from a range of sources including once-trusted institutions and from a rapidly growing range of influencers; deceptive and manipulative practices in advertising, marketing, and political campaigning; powerful new media oligopolies flagrantly abusing privacy and human rights; a political system and public sphere characterized by partisanship and polarization as well prevarication; and powerful new technologies bearing down on us that can potentially liberate or further alienate humanity. Furthermore, we face the challenges with much depleted independent journalism; a lack of regulation and legislation in relation to social media; weak codes of ethics and a lack of standards in PR; rampant capitalism; and government grounded in neoliberalism. A perfect storm has formed on the horizon of contemporary society.

The question then is what can be done about this? This is the focus of the following chapters. To only identify and describe some of the problems facing societies is reportage. At best such analysis might become a small narrative in the history of our time. Critical thinking should extend to *praxis* if we follow the model set out by Hegel and Marx and advocated by philosophers such as Richard Bernstein[76] and political economy thinkers such as Vincent Mosco.[77] Solutions and strategies are not easy to identify, but develop them we must.

Notes

1. Statista. (2019). Number of active daily Facebook users worldwide as of 1st quarter 2019. Retrieved from https://www.statista.com/statistics/346167/facebook-global-dau

2. Statista. (2019). Average daily time spent on selected social networks by users in the United States from 2014 to 2019. Retrieved from https://www.statista.com/statistics/324290/us-users-daily-facebook-minutes
3. Statista. (2019). Number of YouTube users worldwide from 2016 to 2021. Retrieved from https://www.statista.com/statistics/805656/number-youtube-viewers-worldwide
4. Internet Live Stats. (2019). Google search statistics. Retrieved from https://www.internetlivestats.com/google-search-statistics
5. Statista. (2019). Number of monthly active Instagram users from January 2013 to June 2018. Retrieved from https://www.statista.com/statistics/253577/number-of-monthly-active-instagram-users
6. Statista. (2019). Number of monthly active Twitter users worldwide from 1st quarter 2010 to 1st quarter 2019. Retrieved from https://www.statista.com/statistics/282087/number-of-monthly-active-twitter-users
7. DeGennaro, T. (2019). 10 most popular social media sites in China 2019. *Dragon Social*. Retrieved from https://www.dragonsocial.net/blog/social-media-in-china
8. Zuckerberg, M. (2019, January 24). The facts about Facebook. *The Washington Post*, n.p. [online]. Retrieved from https://www.wsj.com/articles/the-facts-about-facebook-11548374613
9. Castells, M. (1996). *The rise of the network society*. Malden, MA: Blackwell. The term "network society" was first coined by Jan van Dijk in van Dijk, J. (1991). *De netwerkmaatschappij* [The network society]. Houten, the Netherlands: Bohn Staflen Van Loghum; reprinted as van Dijk, J. (2006). *The network society* (2nd ed.). London, UK: Sage Publications.
10. Ward, J., & Barker, A. (2013). Undefined by data: A survey of big data definitions. *Computer Science*, Cornell University, p. 1. Retrieved from https://arxiv.org/abs/1309.5821
11. De Mauro, A., Greco, M., & Grimaldi, M. (2016). A formal definition of big data based on its essential features. *Library Review*, 65(3), 122–135.
12. Ward & Barker, 2013, p. 1.
13. Dumbill, E. (2012). Making sense of big data. *Big Data*, 1(1), 1–2, p. 1. Retrieved from https://doi.org/10.1089/big.2012.1503
14. Nominal numbers serve as labels of a category (e.g., 1 = Female; 2 = Male), while ordinal numbers represent variables in an order (e.g., 1 = High school education; 2 = Undergraduate; 3 = Graduate; 4 = Doctorate; 5 = Post-doctorate).
15. American Civil Liberties Union. (2019). What's wrong with public video surveillance. Retrieved from https://www.aclu.org/other/whats-wrong-public-video-surveillance
16. boyd, d., & Crawford, K. (2012). Critical questions for big data: Provocations for a cultural, technological, and scholarly phenomenon. *Information, Communication & Society*, 15(5), 662–679, p. 663.
17. Burkholder, L. (Ed.). (1992). *Philosophy and the computer*. Boulder, CA: Westview.
18. Anon (personal communication [interview], September 30, 2019).

19. Haupt, M. (2016, May 2). Data is the new oil—A ludicrous proposition. *Project 2030* [Web log post]. Retrieved from https://medium.com/project-2030/data-is-the-new-oil-a-ludicrous-proposition-1d91bba4f294. Haupt credits UK mathematician Clive Humby with being first to use the phrase "data is the new oil."
20. T. Manus (personal communication [interview], September 26, 2019).
21. Davenport, T., & Patil, D. (2012, October). Data scientist: The sexiest job of the 21st century. *Harvard Business Review*. Retrieved from https://hbr.org/2012/10/data-scientist-the-sexiest-job-of-the-21st-century
22. Macnamara, J. (2018). Content analysis. In P. Napoli (Ed.), *Mediated communication* (pp. 191–211). Berlin: De Gruyter; McKee, A. (2003). *Textual analysis: A beginner's guide*. London, UK: Sage Publications; Neuman, W. (2006). *Social research methods: Qualitative and quantitative approaches* (6th ed.). Needham Heights, MA: Allyn & Bacon.
23. Boyd & Crawford, 2012, p. 663.
24. Couldry, N., & Mejias, U. (2019). *The costs of connection: How data is colonizing human life and appropriating it for capitalism*. Stanford, CA: Stanford University Press, p. xiii.
25. Ibid., p. 85.
26. Ibid., p. 132.
27. Goodwin, B., & Skelton, S. (2019, July 1). Facebook's privacy game—How Zuckerberg backtracked on promises to protect personal data. *Computer Weekly*, para. 7. Retrieved from https://www.computerweekly.com/feature/Facebooks-privacy-U-turn-how-Zuckerberg-backtracked-on-promises-to-protect-personal-data
28. The parent company of Cambridge Analytica, SCL, bought a data set and analysis methodology in 2014 from a start-up called Global Science Research that was founded by Aleksandr Kogan, a psychologist at Cambridge University, and his business partner Joseph Chancellor.
29. Hindman, M. (2018, March 30). How Cambridge Analytica's Facebook targeting model really worked—According to the person who built it. *The Conversation*. Retrieved from https://theconversation.com/how-cambridge-analyticas-facebook-targeting-model-really-worked-according-to-the-person-who-built-it-94078
30. House of Commons. (2018, July 29). *Disinformation and fake news: Interim report*. London, UK: Digital, Culture, Media and Sport Committee. Retrieved from https://publications.parliament.uk/pa/cm201719/cmselect/cmcumeds/363/363.pdf
31. Yanofsky, N. (2011). Towards a definition of an algorithm. *Journal of Logic and Computation*, *21*(2), 253–286, p. 253.
32. Gillespie, T. (2014). The relevance of algorithms. In T. Gillespie, P. Boczkowski, & K. Foot (Eds.), *Media technologies: Essays on communication, materiality, and society* (pp. 167–194). Cambridge, MA: MIT Press, p. 167.
33. Reuters. (2017). *Reuters Institute digital news report*. Oxford, UK: Reuters Institute for the Study of Journalism. Retrieved from http://www.digitalnewsreport.org/survey/2017

34. Matsa, K., & Shearer, E. (2018, September 10). *News use across social media platforms 2018*. Pew Research Center, Reports. Retrieved from https://www.journalism.org/2018/09/10/news-use-across-social-media-platforms-2018
35. There are claims that computers and other algorithms can write algorithms, but these claims are disputed or refer to the automated generated of basic strings of code. See https://www.quora.com/Can-computers-write-their-own-algorithms
36. Nikla, J., & Gangadharan, S. (2018, July 10). Data-driven discrimination: A new challenge for civil society. *LSE Impact* [Web log post]. Retrieved from https://blogs.lse.ac.uk/impactofsocialsciences/2018/07/10/data-driven-discrimination-a-new-challenge-for-civil-society
37. Sinnreich, A. (2019, May). Four crises in algorithmic governance. Paper presented to the International Communication Association (ICA) conference, 'Communication law and policy: Reign in your robot algorithms, governance, and hacking' session, Washington, D.C.
38. Wesner, K. (2019, May). Compelling bot speech: An analysis of California's new bot disclosure law. Paper presented to the International Communication Association (ICA) conference, 'Communication law and policy: Reign in your robot algorithms, governance, and hacking' session, Washington, D.C.
39. A sentence made famous in the TV comedy *Little Britain*.
40. O'Brien, J. (2019). 5 technology trends that are changing business communication. *Communication World Magazine*. Retrieved from https://www.iabc.com/5-technology-trends-that-are-changing-business-communication
41. Gehl, R., & Bakardjieva, M. (Eds.). (2017). *Socialbots and their friends: Digital media and the automation of sociality*. New York, NY: Routledge, p. 2.
42. Zhang, J., Carpenter, D., & Ko, M. (2013). Online astroturfing: A theoretical perspectives. Proceedings of the Association for Information Systems 2013 conference. Retrieved from https://aisel.aisnet.org/amcis2013/HumanComputerInteraction/GeneralPresentations/5
43. Wesner, 2019.
44. Hayles, N. [Katherine]. (1999). *How we became posthuman: Virtual bodies in cybernetics, literature and informatics*. Chicago, IL: University of Chicago Press, p. 291.
45. R. Tench (personal communication [interview], September 20, 2019).
46. Wesner, 2019.
47. California Legislative Information. (2019, July 1). Senate Bill 1001, Chapter 892. Retrieved from https://leginfo.legislature.ca.gov/faces/billTextClient.xhtml?bill_id=201720180SB1001
48. Lee, D. (2019, April 9). Facebook to use AI to respect the dead. *BBC News*, para. 2. Retrieved from https://www.bbc.com/news/technology-47875654
49. Silberg, J., & Manyika, J. (2019, June). Notes from the AI frontier: Tackling bias in AI (and in humans). McKinsey Global Institute. Retrieved from https://www.mckinsey.com/featured-insights/artificial-intelligence/tackling-bias-in-artificial-intelligence-and-in-humans

50. Tjepkema, L. (2019). What is artificial intelligence marketing and why is it so powerful? *Emarsys*, paras 10, 12. Retrieved from https://www.emarsys.com/resources/blog/artificial-intelligence-marketing-solutions
51. Bourne, C. (2019). AI cheerleaders: Public relations, neoliberalism and artificial intelligence. *Public Relations Inquiry*, 8(2), 109–125.
52. Hood, I. (2019). *Nothing to fear from AI*. [Web log post]. London, UK: Public Relations Consultants Association (PRCA), para. 6. Retrieved from https://www.prca.org.uk/prca-50-nothing-to-fear-from-ai
53. Bourne, 2019, p. 109.
54. O'Connor, H. (2019, July 26). Reimaging how we connect with machines. Address to Changing Mindsets, conference of the Public Relations Institute of New Zealand, Wellington, New Zealand.
55. Mack, D. (2018, April 17). This PSA about fake news from Barack Obama is not what it appears. *Buzzfeed*, News. Retrieved from https://www.buzzfeednews.com/article/davidmack/obama-fake-news-jordan-peele-psa-video-buzzfeed
56. Waterson, J. (2019, May 24). Facebook refuses to delete fake Pelosi video spread by Trump supporters. *The Guardian*. Retrieved from https://www.theguardian.com/technology/2019/may/24/facebook-leaves-fake-nancy-pelosi-video-on-site
57. Ibid., para. 4.
58. Guess, A., Nyhan, B., & Reifler, J. (2018). Selective exposure to misinformation: Evidence from the consumption of fake news during the 2016 presidential campaign. European Research Council. Retrieved from https://apo.org.au/sites/default/files/resource-files/2018/01/apo-nid126961-1162776.pdf
59. Jeffrey, A.(2019, June 17). No longer rocket science: Advertising technology is disrupting the industry. *Advertising Benchmark Index* (ABX), para. 6. Retrieved from http://blog.adbenchmark.com/advertising-technology
60. Ibid., para. 3.
61. Foer, F. (2018, May). The era of fake video begins. *The Atlantic*. Retrieved from https://www.theatlantic.com/magazine/archive/2018/05/realitys-end/556877
62. Paris, B., & Donovan, J. (2019). *Deepfakes and cheapfakes*. New York, NY: Data and Society Research Institute. Retrieved from https://datasociety.net/output/deepfakes-and-cheap-fakes
63. Schwartz, O. (2019, July 4). Could 'fake text' be the next global political threat? *The Guardian*. Retrieved from https://www.theguardian.com/technology/2019/jul/04/ai-fake-text-gpt-2-concerns-false-information
64. OpenAI. (2019, February 14). Better language models and their implications [Web log post], para. 2. Retrieved from https://openai.com/blog/better-language-models
65. Greene, T. (2019, August 21). This AI powered text generator is the scariest thing I've ever seen—and you can try it. *TNW* (The Next Web), para. 2. Retrieved from https://thenextweb.com/artificial-intelligence/2019/08/21/this-ai-powered-text-generator-is-the-scariest-thing-ive-ever-seen-and-you-can-try-it

66. Wakefield, J. (2019, August 27). 'Dangerous' AI offers to write fake news. *BBC News*, Technology. Retrieved from https://www.bbc.com/news/technology-49446729
67. Riparbelli, V. (2019, July 23). Our vision of the future for synthetic media. *Medium*, para. 1. Retrieved from https://medium.com/@vriparbelli/our-vision-for-the-future-of-synthetic-media-8791059e8f3a
68. Wright, S. (2012). Assessing (e-)democratic innovation: 'Democratic goods' and downing street e-petitions. *Journal of Information Technology & Politics, 9*(4), 453–470, p. 466.
69. Macnamara, J. (2017). *Creating a 'democracy for everyone': Strategies for increasing listening and engagement by government.* London, UK and Sydney, NSW: The London School of Economics and Political Science and University of Technology Sydney. Retrieved from http://www.lse.ac.uk/media@lse/research/CreatingADemocracyForEveryone.aspx
70. R. Jensen (personal communication [interview], May 28, 2019).
71. Refers to technophobia, based on the Luddites, a group of textile workers in England who actively resisted mechanization in England in the early 19th century.
72. Koestler, A. (1967). *The ghost in the machine.* New York, NY: Macmillan.
73. Marx, L. (1964). *The machine in the garden.* New York, NY: Oxford University Press.
74. Mumford, L. (1967). *The myth of the machine: Technics of human development.* New York, NY: Harcourt.
75. Toyama, K. (2015, June 19). In an age of machines, it's humans that matter. *The Guardian*, Opinion & Debate, p. 20.
76. Bernstein, R. (1999). *Praxis and action: Contemporary philosophies of human activity.* Philadelphia: University of Pennsylvania Press. (Original work published 1971)
77. Mosco, V. (1999). New York.com: A political economy of the 'informational' city. *Journal of Media Economics, 12*(2), 103–116, p. 104.

PART 2

Rehabilitating Public Communication & the Public Sphere

The following chapter and conclusions explore opportunities for reform in a number of areas of professional practice and policy to restore ethical public communication and an effective public sphere. While these specialized areas cannot be dealt with fully in a single analysis, each requiring ongoing research and the input of experts in those fields, the purpose here is to make the case for a coordinated collective approach, rather than pointing the finger at a few 'bad apples' or seeking a single 'silver bullet' solution. A range of strategies are proposed to address disinformation, deception, and manipulation.

5

Strategies for a Communicative Society

From five years of research that included interviewing senior professionals in journalism, marketing, advertising, public relations (PR), government communication, and politics, as well as scholars concerned about ethics, transparency, accountability, and protection of the public interest in these fields, it is clear that there is no single 'silver bullet' solution to the problems identified. This chapter identifies and discusses a number of strategies—10 in fact—to address disinformation, deception, and manipulation that are corrupting the public sphere in contemporary democratic societies. Each of these requires further research by specialists in those fields and each depends on engagement by professionals in relevant fields of practice and professional associations.

Some are not new proposals, as noted in the Introduction. However, setting them out side by side in this chapter draws attention to the interconnectedness and interdependency of the various actors in the processes of public communication and, therefore, the need for each to do their part. A holistic view and approach are necessary to identify all the relevant levers, as well as balance between strategies such as self-regulation and regulation and the responsibilities of consumers as well as producers of information.

The following discussion rejects neoliberalism and *scientism* that have led to thinking of people, progress, and social reality in terms of statistics and empirical data, such as employment rates, productivity, GDP growth, household income, and technological connectivity. Zygmunt Bauman and Leonidas Donskis refer to "the destruction of a stranger's life" by "not doubting for a moment that people are nothing but statistical units."[1] It argues that there needs to be a refocussing on moral philosophy and ethics, recognizing people as humans and society as a socially constructed framework to sustain human endeavour and welfare. Such an approach speaks to the vision that Nick Couldry and Ulises Mejias propose.

Specifically, this chapter reaffirms the fundamental principles of human communication, from the origins of the term in the Latin verb *communicare* meaning to create, build or share and the Latin noun *communis* meaning community and commonness (as in sharing or creating things in common) to the landmark work of 20th-century sociologists and philosophers such as John Dewey and James Carey. It implicitly asks what would Dewey and Carey say of current post-communication approaches, noting their descriptions of communication as the basis of human society and culture. If post-communication reflects our society and our culture, what does that say? This chapter reminds us that communication is an interactive dialogic process for negotiating and sharing meaning and co-creating social reality—not one-way transmission of information or persuasion. One-way communication is an oxymoron. Persuasion is legitimately *part* of communication. But communication also requires openness to others' views and needs through listening with empathy, negotiation, and accommodation.[2] In a critical analysis of communication theory, professor emerita in communication science at the University of Amsterdam, Betteke van Ruler, says that communication should be even more than two-way dialogue. She argues that communication should be "omnidirectional and diachronic"—that is, occurring in multiple directions and over time and space.[3] There is much to commend this view, as it reflects the complex web of interactions that occur in the public sphere and it shifts attention further away from simplistic transmissional and propagandist models.

As well as framing discussion within moral philosophy, ethics, and communication theory at a broad level, this chapter explores a number of practical steps such as the expansion and application of codes of ethics and codes of practice in fields such as advertising, PR, and political communication, as well as other alternatives such as regulation, in order to contribute to *practical theory* of public communication. Eminent communication theorist Robert Craig describes communication as a practical discipline and calls for practical theory as well as empirical social science. Craig does not mean "merely practical in the colloquial sense of technical or occupational training." Rather, he calls for theory that involves "communicative praxis … to improve communication and disseminate better communication practices." A practical theory needs to proceed beyond definitions, broad concepts and principles to provide "technical aspects of practical conduct" in Craig's words.[4] The following 10 strategies are a response to Craig's call for practical theory that informs improvements in the practices of public communication.

Strategy 1: Self-Regulation by Communication Professionals—Reining in Spin

Creating truthful, ethical and effective communication has to begin with communication professionals—journalists, advertising and PR practitioners, digital communication specialists, and others working in political, government, corporate, marketing, and organizational communication. These are primary actors in today's public sphere on whom the responsibility of lead roles fall.

Journalism Futures—Beyond Opinion, Partisanship and PRization

Many journalists and journalism scholars will be surprised to find themselves discussed along with marketers, advertising and PR practitioners, and the like. A common view for much of the past century is that journalists are truth-tellers speaking "truth to power,"[5] presenters of 'the facts', and "the fourth estate"[6] acting as "watchdogs" of society.[7] In the second edition of *The Handbook of Journalism Studies* published in 2020, Karin Wahl-Jorgensen and Thomas Hanitzsch say that "the institution of journalism has, throughout its existence, been understood as central to the health of democratic societies." They also note that "in many countries around the world, journalism remains a central institution in the *absence* of democracy" [original emphasis].[8] W. Lance Bennett and William Serrin say: "Without journalists acting as watchdogs, American democracy—at least in anything close to the form we know it today—would not exist."[9]

However, Bennett and Serrin go on to warn that journalists have a very uneven track record as watchdogs and that this role has become "overly stylized" and "ritualized" when, in fact, journalists are often a "sleeping watchdog."[10] They also say that many journalists "have sold their souls for access to public officials"[11]—a criticism made with considerable supporting evidence in a number of studies showing heavy use of official sources of news and what Oscar Gandy called "information subsidies" including those from PR practitioners and political media advisers who are often referred to as *spin doctors*.[12]

Independent journalism has been eroded by the vicious circle of *audience fragmentation*[13] in the era of social media, which has resulted in a decline of traditional media advertising that provided the main source of income for commercial media, which in turn has led to severe cutbacks in journalistic staff in almost all major networks and publications. As veteran journalist and editor Peter Fray succinctly says, the traditional media business model "blew up a decade or more ago."[14] In *Flat Earth News*, Nick Davies noted that "the media … have become structurally weakened to the point where they routinely betray their own function by passing on unchecked PR to their readers and viewers."[15] He further explained:

> Journalists who no longer have the time to go out and find their own stories and to check the material which they are handling, are consistently vulnerable to ingesting and reproducing the packages of information which are provided for them by this PR industry.[16]

However, this is not the whole story. Studies show that high use of *information subsidies* and PR and political handouts by journalists was occurring long before the slashing of journalists' jobs that occurred in the late 20th and early 21st century. In *Journalism and PR: Unpacking 'Spin' Stereotypes & Media Myths*, I summarized the findings of studies over the past 100 years that show a tensioned, often denied, but close relationship between journalists and sources, who frequently include PR practitioners, press secretaries, and political media advisers. Studies have repeatedly shown a high proportion of media content is thinly disguised and sometimes even verbatim PR material.[17]

Also, there is evidence that many so-called journalists voluntarily and even passionately engage in commentary and stating opinion, rather than reporting facts and events. "Blurring of the line between opinion and fact" was identified as a major concern in the RAND Corporation *Truth Decay* report released in 2019[18] and this was highlighted in Chapter 3 particularly in relation to News Corp publications and TV networks such as Fox and Sky. Opinion and commentary are rife in talk programs and even current affairs, notable in the rise of commentators spruiking biased, often provocative, and even offensive views on immigration, ethnicity, and gender, and using manipulative rhetoric to undermine scientific evidence on issues such as climate change. While many criticisms are directed at conservative voices, accusations of bias and injecting personal opinion into reporting are levelled from and at all sides of politics. In an 'op ed' article in the *New York Post*, former *60 Minutes* reporter Lara Logan lamented that political bias is destroying people's faith in journalism, but Logan pointed the finger at "liberals," claiming that the vast majority of journalists in the USA are Democrats.[19]

Logan's views were appropriately published as an opinion piece. But in many other instances, partisanship and polemic pass under the mantle of news and current affairs.

Peter Fray sees the rise of opinion and commentary in place of facts and critical analysis as pragmatic as much or more than it is political. In a long media career, Fray served as editor in chief of the *Sydney Morning Herald* and deputy editor of Australia's national newspaper *The Australian*, as well as founding PolitiFact in Australia, before joining the University of Technology Sydney as a professor and co-director of the Centre for Media Transition. In the spirit of Tom Peters' comment that "what gets measured gets done,"[20] Fray points to the role of clicks in deciding what gets published and what gets air time. He says "the rise of opinion is driven by the need for clickbait. With content valued and rewarded based on the number of clicks it gets, opinion wins because it is usually more attention-grabbing and popular than facts." He says this is true in the case of major public broadcasters as well as popular media and social media, as "everyone is looking for clicks."[21] Fray, who returned to investigative journalism in 2020, is critical of politically motivated partisan journalism, but he sees the focus on maximizing clicks as the major cause of the rise of opinion and commentary.

In the wake of collapsing media business models and journalist redundancies, many journalists are following a long-trod path to cross over to PR,[22] or going to work in the related and fast-growing field of what is referred to as corporate or brand journalism producing content for *owned media*, such as the burgeoning number of corporate websites, corporate and government 'news' sites, blogs, and social media pages that have a voracious appetite for content. These create well paid jobs—a not insignificant consideration for journalists faced with *precarity*[23] or unemployment. However, while providing new job opportunities, employment of journalists on a freelance, staff, or contract basis to write sponsored content takes journalists away from independent reporting and critical analysis and adds to the promotional machine that drives contemporary capitalism.

There are a number of encouraging developments in journalism, however. These include:

- *Fact checking*—Journalists employed by Florida's largest daily newspaper, the *Tampa Bay Times* (then named the *St. Petersburg Times*), started PolitiFact (https://www.politifact.com) in 2007 as an election-year project to verify statements made by politicians and rate them for accuracy using its Truth-o-meter™. Ownership of PolitiFact was transferred in 2018 to the Poynter Institute for Media Studies, a non-profit organization, and it now operates in a number of US states and Washington D.C., as well as internationally through partnerships with news organizations. For example, PolitiFact Australia (https://politifact.com.au) was launched in 2013 by Peter Fray. CrossCheck (https://firstdraftnews.org/project/crosscheck), started by First Draft and Google News Labs[24] in 2017, initially to verify claims and statements made during elections, also provides fact-checking as well as other services. (See 'Monitoring, investigation and verification of online content' below.)

- *Monitoring, investigation, and verification of online content*—After tracking online content during elections in the USA, France, the UK, Germany, Brazil, and Nigeria, First Draft (https://firstdraftnews.org), founded by Claire Wardle in 2015, is expanding its network worldwide to include proactive monitoring, investigation, and verification of online content on a wide range of topics and issues. At the time of going to press, collaborative initiatives to address what First Draft calls "information disorder"[25] were underway in Argentina, Australia, Canada, Indonesia, South Africa, Spain, and Uruguay, along with cross-border monitoring, investigation, and verification. As well as coordinating teams using its CrossCheck platform for outing misinformation and disinformation, First Draft conducts training in monitoring and verification of online content and provides ethics advice for journalists on issues such as monitoring and investigating closed groups. Australian bureau editor Anne Kruger says ongoing training is required because the tools for monitoring online content are changing regularly and gaining access to closed groups in WhatsApp and other applications raises questions about transparency. She says "investigators are sometimes accused of trolling closed groups if they use a false identity to gain entry, or even when they join in their own name."[26] Training and support by such groups help journalists investigate and expose issues in the public interest.

- *Computational and data journalism*—A 2014 report produced by the Tow Center for Digital Journalism at Columbia University was one of the first to argue that, in addition to having 'soft skills' such as maintaining networks and relationships with sources and understanding audiences, journalists in the 21st century need 'hard skills' including data literacy and even an ability to write computer code.[27] Data literacy includes skills in database searching, data mining, and data analysis to access empirical data and official records, rather than relying on claims by spokespeople, who may put their own twist on information, cover up information, or distribute disinformation. In a 2020 journalism text, Neil Thurman defines computational journalism as "the advanced application of computing, algorithms, and automation to the gathering, evaluation, composition, presentation, and distribution of news."[28] A number of universities now offer courses in computational and data journalism and see a marriage of communication and computer science as the way of the future for journalism.[29]

Such developments highlight the need for up to date education and training of journalists, both in university courses and in ongoing professional development. In addition to specialized training in online monitoring, investigation, and verification tools and methods, as discussed above, Australian First Draft bureau editor Anne Kruger says "professional journalists need to do more than simply report what people say. They must seek and present proof." She said that this applies to data provided to journalists and online by various entities, adding:

> Not enough questions are being asked by journalists about those providing data analysis. For example, many think tanks provide analysis, but do journalists know who funds them? What are their biases and motivations? Unfortunately, many don't ask the simple questions of data providers that they would ask of traditional sources of information.[30]

Some scholars and practitioners propose even greater transformation of journalism. One strand of contemporary thinking is journalism beyond the newsroom. Researchers such as Mark Deuze note that the newsroom has long been seen as the site of journalism, which has led to a routinized and institutionalized concept of journalism. Freelancing has been seen at best as an ante-room to the newsroom, or as the domain of outsiders who strive much like asylum seekers looking for a stable and secure home. Deuze and Tamara Witschge acknowledge that "it is a challenge to consider journalism as a networked practice involving a distributed variety of actors and actants" that includes "co-creating audiences" in an "emerging global start-up scene of newswork."[31] However, while seeing a continuing role for newsrooms, they critique *newsroom centricity* in conceptualizing journalism, arguing for a dynamic view that includes entrepreneurial journalism and various forms of journalism start-ups that are emerging around the world. The Beyond Journalism project that Deuze and Witschge lead is a continuation of a rethinking of journalism over the past two decades that has included discussion of *public journalism* advocated by Jay Rosen,[32] Michael Schudson,[33] and others;[34] *civic journalism*;[35] *interactive journalism*;[36] *citizen journalism*;[37] *participatory journalism*;[38] and *networked journalism*.[39]

This line of thinking suggests that, instead of seeing the precarity of newsroom journalism as a threat and fleeing to the cacoon of corporate journalism or PR, journalists should embrace their release from the shackles of media proprietors and institutionalized processes and embrace interactive, multimedia, networked journalism enabled by advanced technology and skills. Of course, that is not a simple process and it is asking a lot to expect a relatively small cadre of truth-seekers to take on the regimes of post-truth, particularly when many media consumers will not pay even a few cents for their work—an issue that will be discussed later in this chapter. But a healthy public sphere depends on journalists fulfilling the Fourth Estate role that they and political scientists have long agreed is an essential element of democracy. Despite much optimism and popular support, the Fifth Estate[40] of social media and online political engagement shows but momentary capacity to restore or create a new public sphere, particularly while major platforms behave irresponsibly and with impunity, as discussed in Chapter 4.

An insightful report exploring innovation in journalism and news media operations, including a number of case studies, is *News Media Innovation 2020* published by the Centre for Media Transition at the University of Technology Sydney. Beyond the obvious focus on digital communication, one its key conclusions is that the future of media requires understanding and putting the needs and interests of audiences first, rather than advertisers or opinionated commentators and experts.[41] This partly addresses the politics and partisanship that contaminates much media content, but audience-centricity fails to counter the effects of populism; clickbait driven by the need to attract audiences; and the underlying market logic of commercial media funded by advertising.

Another recent contribution to the debate on the future of journalism goes further to identify the implications of and question the underlying commercial base of media, particularly in the USA. In *Democracy Without Journalism: Confronting the Misinformation Society*, Victor Pickard from the University of Pennsylvania's Annenberg School for Communication argues that "run-amok commercialism" dating back to the early commercialization of the printing press in the 1800s is the core root of the crisis of journalism.[42] He says journalism has always been in crisis because the market never supported the levels of journalism—especially local, international, policy, and investigative reporting—that a healthy democracy requires. Pickard historicizes the current malaise in journalism, showing how its stems from over-reliance on advertising revenue, the uncontrolled rise of media monopolies, and a lack of public oversight. His analysis suggests that strategies to reinstate independent quality journalism must include some control of media platforms—traditional and social—as well as the presence of non-commercial media, or at least media less reliant on market logic. These approaches are examined in following sections of this chapter under 'Strategy 4: Public Media to Protect the Public Interest' and 'Strategy 10: Regulation and Legislation'.

Journalists and journalism educators also need to work out a more transparent and honest relationship with PR, instead of the "discourse of denial" and the "discourse of victimhood"[43] that they typically deploy to disavow any responsibility for subsidized news media content. As outlined in *Journalism and PR: Unpacking 'Spin', Stereotypes, & Media Myths*,[44] these refer to the long-standing practices of either denying use of information supplied by PR in news, current affairs, and other reporting, or blaming PR practitioners for exploiting, deceiving, or coercing journalists. Instead of pretending that journalists don't use PR leads, introductions, arranged events, photography, and written content, journalism education needs to provide an understanding of the role of PR in the public sphere (it draws on the right of free speech in the same way that journalists do). That does not mean acquiescing to PR. To the contrary, more open-minded education and debate will help give journalists the skills to be able to work with PR in ways that maintain their independence, such as seeking out confirming or alternative sources, fact-checking, and critical analysis.

Political scientists, sociologists, and cultural studies scholars as well as journalism and media studies academics and, perhaps surprisingly for some, many PR scholars and practitioners, are concerned about and oppose the *PRization* of journalism. In addition to their broader concerns for society, a number of senior PR practitioners interviewed noted that media credibility and trustworthiness is what makes publicity valuable. PR practitioners say that they have "a vested interest in the preservation of independent media" because "information about their organization positively reported in respected independent media is more credible than publicity in partisan media or saying it themselves through owned media."[45]

Managing director of the Norwegian Communication Association, Therese Manus, says "communication professionals are very much aware of their most valuable asset being trust." She argues that fake news and disinformation are not distributed by communication professionals, particularly in Nordic countries, and that there is recognition that "information needs to be balanced."[46] However, given that PR is generally considered to be part of *promotional culture*,[47] balance seems improbable, although there are significant differences in PR theory and practices between countries, as discussed in the following section.

Remodelling Public Relations

Much has been said and written about PR and, beyond industry literature, much of it is negative. Such is the level of criticism that Australian academics Nigel de Bussy and Katharina Wolf described PR in an education supplement in the national newspaper *The Australian* as "a profession that dare not speak its name."[48] This refers to the re-badging of PR with largely synonymous titles such as public affairs, corporate communication, communication management, and various other labels. The following quotes are but a few samples of the descriptions of PR and concerns expressed by journalists and critics.

> The PR industry … consciously fabricates news. (Nick Davies in *Flat Earth News*)[49]

> PR fabricates pseudo-evidence … pseudo-events … pseudo-leaks … pseudo-pictures … pseudo-illnesses … pseudo-groups. (Nick Davies in *Flat Earth News*)[50]

> Increasingly … [news] is unfiltered public relations generated surreptitiously by corporations and governments. (Media scholar Robert McChesney)[51]

> The growth of PR is threatening the integrity of the press. (Title of a Westminster University debate)[52]

> Spin has been the most corrosive element to hit journalism in my lifetime … the tentacles of spin reach into every part of news gathering, clouding or corrupting the facts. (Mark Day, journalist)[53]

> In some cases the line between news story and press release has become so blurred that reporters are using direct quotes from press releases in their stories without acknowledging the source. (Christine Russell writing in *Columbia Journalism Review*)[54]

> Some short-staffed newspapers are only too grateful to be stuffed full of scarcely rewritten news releases. (Tony Harcup in *Journalism: Principles and Practices*)[55]

PR had its beginnings in what is termed *press agentry*, referring to agents who acted as intermediaries between organizations and media to generate publicity, also pejoratively referred to as *flaks or flacks*.[56] In his history of American journalism, Willard Bleyer reported that a census of accredited press agents conducted by New York newspapers in the first decade of the 20th century found 1,200 press agents working to influence media and public opinion in New York alone.[57] Press agentry achieved public notoriety in the USA in the 1830s through practitioners such as the American showman Phineas Taylor (P.T.) Barnum, founder of a circus that bore his name. Barnum unashamedly coined the phrase "there's a sucker born every minute."[58]

The currency of press agents was press releases, later known as media releases in the era of radio and television and also colloquially referred to as handouts. Ivy Lee was a pioneer in the systematic use of press and media releases. Lee worked for the Rockefeller family from 1914. When several miners, two women, and 11 children were killed after an accidental shot sparked a battle between striking miners and management of a Rockefeller-owned mining company, Lee convinced Rockefeller to visit the mining camps to observe conditions first-hand and also to talk to the media. PR historian Ray Hiebert described Lee's proactive publicity strategy as "a landmark in public relations."[59] Lee also promoted the Rockefellers' major charity donations and helped rehabilitate the name and legacy of John D. Rockefeller, who prior to this time was branded a 'robber baron' by American media.

The role that was to become known as public relations, or PR for short (although many practitioners eschew this term as pejorative), was broadened and formalized in the period between the 1920s and 1950s by Edward Bernays, who is described by some as the "father of public relations."[60] Bernays continued Lee's focus on media publicity, but also advocated that the role of PR professionals is to counsel senior management on matters related to public relationships and public communication, not only do their bidding. A 1948 PR text by Eric Goldman titled *Two-way Street: The Emergence of the Public Relations Counsel* also described the role of PR professionals as advisers to management involved in two-way communication.[61] In the role of counsellor, senior PR practitioners are meant to reflect on the interests of stakeholders and society and seek to mediate between the organizations that they represent and others in order to establish and maintain functioning relationships. This is a side of PR work that is not seen outside an organization and not seen by journalists, who believe that PR exists solely to target them. A PR practitioner who can see an organization heading for trouble has a vested interest in taking a preventative approach, and some senior PR professionals spend a good deal of their time as counsellors and advisers. Nevertheless, recent research indicates that, despite claims of acting as strategic advisers, the majority of PR work is media relations and publicity generation, albeit focussed on social as well as traditional media today.[62]

In 1984, long-serving professor of PR at the University of Maryland, Jim Grunig, co-authored a landmark book with Todd Hunt that outlined four models of PR.[63] These models summarize the development of PR over the past 100 years from *press agentry* to a broader *public information* role and, most recently to what Grunig and his co-author referred as *two-way asymmetrical* communication and *two-way symmetrical* communication. Grunig advocated the two-way role of PR espoused by Bernays and Goldman, and drew from Theordore Newcomb's psychological theory of *symmetry*,[64] which is closely aligned to Fritz Heider's theory of *balance*[65] and the concept of *consonance* referred to in Leon Festinger's theory of cognitive dissonance.[66] He argued over many decades that the two-way symmetrical approach is the most effective as well as the most ethical model of PR.

Grunig claimed that the two-way symmetrical model of PR contributed to practical as well as normative theory of PR. However, critics argue that symmetrical interactions and relationships between powerful organizations such as corporations, on one hand, and stakeholders such as environmental and community groups and the general public on the other is normative—a description of what ideally ought to be—rather than what actually occurs in practice.

Subsequently, Grunig and a number of colleagues revisited the four models of PR, particularly the two-way symmetrical model, in a 15-year three-stage study conducted in the USA, Canada, and the UK between the mid-1980s and 2002 that became known as the PR Excellence Study. The study took its name from its objective, which was to identify the characteristics of excellence in PR. After a global literature review; surveys of PR practitioners and managers in 327 organizations in the three countries that gained more than 5,000 responses; and 25 in-depth interviews with senior management; the study identified 14 key attributes that it claimed correlated with organizational excellence. Not surprisingly, the practice of two-way symmetrical communication was high in the list of attributes in what became known as *Excellence theory* of PR.

The research had several flaws, however, not the least of which was that it selected its sample of 'excellent' organizations based on those identified by Tom Peters and Robert Waterman in their 1982 bestseller *In Search of Excellence*.[67] The sample of organizations espoused as excellent by Peters and Waterman was later criticized as arbitrary and inappropriate because many had poor performance in subsequent years and, in fact, quite a few went out of business not long after the Peters and Waterman study.[68]

Grunig and his co-researchers modified their model to some extent over the years following publication of the third PR Excellence theory book in 2002,[69] incorporating a *mixed motive model* advocated by Priscilla Murphy[70] and *contingency theory of PR* developed by Glenn Cameron and colleagues.[71] These scholars accepted that PR should involve two-way communication, but argued that it would not always be symmetrical or balanced. Rather, they proposed that who persuaded whom was contingent on circumstances and that a mix of *persuasion* and *accommodation* or *co-orientation* was necessary. Nevertheless, excellent PR continued to be theorized as two-way and a win-win for organizations and their stakeholders and this became the "dominant paradigm" of PR in many countries around the world for several decades.[72]

Notwithstanding, based on their extensive study of the evaluation of PR, Tom Watson and Paul Noble concluded that "the dominant paradigm of practice is the equation of public relations with persuasion"[73]—in short, it is predominantly a one-way process of advocacy undertaken to change the attitudes and behaviour of *target audiences* to those desired by an organization. This is borne out in this author's research into organizational listening that has found PR as well as other forms of corporate, organizational, and government communication overwhelmingly focussed on disseminating the messages of organizations (i.e., speaking) to achieve their objectives.[74]

In the beginning of the second decade of the 21st century, critical PR scholars cited and advocated a *sociocultural turn* in PR. UK PR scholars Lee Edwards and Caroline Hodges argue that increasing focus on sociological and cultural theories "constitutes a 'turn' in PR theory that shifts the ontological and epistemological focus of the field."[75] In simple terms, what they discuss—and advocate because the turn is nascent by even the most optimistic accounts—is that the very nature of PR (its ontology) should be taken out of organization management and relocated in a sociological and cultural context. This would shift its centre of gravity away from the service of power elites towards the interests of society—or at least to a position where balance could be achieved. Furthermore, the sociocultural turn refers to a transition from *functionalist* and *behaviourist* approaches based on systems theory and positivist social science that inform and shape the dominant paradigm of PR to a recognition of the social construction of reality, the importance of social interaction, culture, and more humanistic understandings of the world based on social theory. The sociocultural turn is also associated with postmodernism, cultural studies, feminism, and participatory approaches in politics and research. Sociocultural approaches to PR place major emphasis of ethical behaviour and social responsibility, not simply serving the interests of employers and clients. Edwards further advances sociocultural thinking about PR in her 2018 book *Understanding Public Relations: Theory, Culture and Society*.[76]

In a chapter in *The Handbook of Communication Engagement* published in 2018 titled 'Reconceptualizing public relations in an engaged society', co-editor Maureen Taylor agrees with Edwards and Hodges saying that "over time, the field of PR has moved from treating relationships with the public as a functional task tied to organizational objectives to a more co-creational approach where publics and organizations jointly create meaning and coordinate action within society."[77] Taylor's use of past tense in relation to a shift away from functionalist approaches is arguable, or at least premature, given that there are no working models of sociocultural PR and limited empirical evidence of the implementation of such approaches in practice.

The views of Edwards, Hodges, Taylor, and other critical thinkers in relation to PR, such as emeritus professor Bob Heath in the US, are more closely aligned to the views of European scholars, who Taylor notes conceptualize PR in more reflective, adaptive, and socially responsible ways "concerned with publics, the public social sphere, and public consequences of organizational behaviours."[78] Alternatively, European academics and organizations have moved away from the term PR, or not adopted PR theory in the first place. Instead, organization-public communication is commonly conceptualized in European countries as *corporate communication*,[79] *communication management*,[80] or increasingly as *strategic communication*.[81] The term *organizational communication* is also used in different ways in some European countries than it is in the USA. These terms are sometimes used simply as euphemisms for PR to avoid the negative connotations that public relations has acquired. However, there are some important differences between these fields of theory and practice—both positive and negative.

Organizational communication is the oldest body of theory in this field, dating back to the social theory of Max Weber, although the field has bifurcated into several branches or schools of thought. One focusses on how communication is the binding agent that enables human organization, based on Luhmann's theory of social systems.[82] In structural as well as social terms, this thinking is variously referred to as "communication as constitutive of organization,"[83] "communication constitutes organizations," and as "communicative constitution of organizations,"[84] abbreviated as *CCO theory*.

A narrow interpretation that is prominent in the USA, UK, and some other countries sees organizational communication as communication inside organizations, with a particular focus on employee communication.[85] Such communication would be more accurately referred to as intra-organizational communication, but this internal perspective of organizational communication remains common.

A third perspective of organizational communication that is mainly applied in European countries such as Germany and Sweden is that it includes all communication initiated by or involving an organization, both internally and externally. For example, in a review of research into organizational communication, Catrin Johansson acknowledges that the term is often applied specifically to internal communication, but says "organizational communication could also be used as a general term to cover public relations, public affairs, investor relations, labour market communication, corporate advertising, environmental communication, and internal communication."[86]

Corporate communication is also sometimes understood narrowly as the public communication of corporations. However, European uses of the term conceive corporate as relating to any *corpora* (corporate body), including non-government and non-profit organizations. Specialist literature in the field increasingly defines corporate communication broadly. For example, in *Corporate Communication: A Guide to Theory and Practice*, Joep Cornelissen defines the practice as follows.

> Corporate communication is a management function that offers a framework for the effective coordination of all internal and external communication with the overall purpose of establishing and maintaining favourable reputations with stakeholder groups upon which the organization is dependent.[87]

The words "all internal and external communication" in Cornelissen's definition are significant. In his view, corporate communication encompasses PR, internal organizational communication, external relations with stakeholders such as investors and local communities (referred to as investor relations and community relations by others), and even marketing communication such as advertising. For some, this is a case of disciplinary territoriality, and debate rages about the boundaries of various organization-public communication practices. Many definitions of PR circumscribe the same activities—although PR continues to be seen as media publicity by many. A benefit of the concept of corporate communication as defined by Cornelissen—and broad European understandings of organizational communication—is that they afford a holistic perspective. In terms of ethically managing and reforming practice, a holistic perspective that examines all public communication by an organization enables coordination and consistent standards, which can be difficult to achieve when there are multiple siloes of specialized and often competing activities.

Communication management is another term used both broadly and sometimes as a substitute for PR, or to denote a related practice. For example, the first PR Excellence study book was titled *Excellence in Public Relations and Communication Management* and this was followed by other texts with similar titles.[88] Given that PR is defined broadly as "the management of communication between an organization and its publics,"[89] use of the conjunction 'and' in the above book title begs the question of what is specifically different about communication management. That corporate communication is also defined as management of communication, as cited above, further adds to the ambiguity. Critics also point out that communication management emphasizes a managerial and functionalist perspective.

In an attempt to move away from a managerial perspective as well as perceptions that PR is tactical in most organizations largely consisting of "communication with the press,"[90] a number of scholars and practitioners have advocated *strategic communication* as an "emerging interdisciplinary paradigm" in place of or encompassing PR, corporate communication, and other related practices.[91] This paradigm or model has been promoted through the *International Journal of Strategic Communication* established by Taylor and Francis in 2007 and in a number of books such as *The Handbook of Strategic Communication*[92] and *Future Directions of Strategic Communication*.[93]

In a seminal article in the first issue of the *International Journal of Strategic Communication*, Kirk Hallahan and several co-authors noted that "strategic communication has been used synonymously for public relations in much of the literature."[94] However, they and others argue that strategic communication involves a new and evolving model of practice rather than simply a change of name. Hallahan and his colleagues noted that strategic communication has been widely understood as "purposeful use of communication to fulfil *its* mission" [emphasis added][95]—an organization-centric view in which stakeholders and publics remain targets for persuasion and change. They and others since have mounted a concerted effort to redefine and rehabilitate the term strategic within PR and communication theory, saying that "alternative and more positive notions of strategy have … emerged since the 1950s" that "reject the use of strategic only in an asymmetrical context."[96] Instead, Hallahan et al. argued that contemporary models of PR are based on two-way transactional rather one-way transmissional models of communication that recognize and engage stakeholders and publics in an inclusive win-win process. In addition, they cited and supported Derina Holtzhausen's view that strategic communication includes recognition that organizational survival means that organizations must adhere to the dominant value systems of the environments in which they operate.[97]

A number of scholars took to the stage in a session at the 2011 International Communication Association (ICA) conference in Boston and in subsequent publications to propose that strategic communication should reflect contemporary management theory in relation to strategy advocated by Henry Mintzberg and others, as well as Stanley Deetz's identification of the twin purposes of communication as *participation* as well as *effectiveness*.[98] As is now well known in management studies, Mintzberg and his co-authors argued that organizational strategy needs to evolve from traditional top-down approaches to become adaptive and *emergent* by taking into account the views of stakeholders and the environment.[99] They proposed that organizations will be more successful and sustainable if they adapt and blend their goals and objectives with those of stakeholders and the interests of society.

Within the PR/corporate communication/strategic communication field, Jesper Falkheimer and Mats Heide called on scholars and practitioners to "break the dominant approach to strategic communication" that has focused on control, persuasion, and organizational effectiveness, and "adopt a *participatory* approach."[100] In a pragmatic compromise, Simon Torp called for incorporation of the duality that Deetz identified in communication—open to participation while at the same time not abandoning the organizational imperative to effectively advocate its interests and persuade.[101] Priscilla Murphy proposed a *networked* approach[102] to developing strategic communication, while Cynthia King echoed Mintzberg et al. in advocating *emergent* strategic communication[103]—an approach that emerges out of engagement with stakeholders and publics through research, dialogue, and consultation.

However, Murphy has noted that "control has long been a troublesome issue in strategic communication."[104] As recently as the 2018 *International Encyclopedia of Strategic Communication*, the role of strategic communication professionals was described as "support of organizational thinking and action around strategy."[105] This makes it clear that strategy comes from the organization and communication professionals are there to promote it. It leaves no room for counselling organizations to alter or change their thinking or actions. Instead it puts strategic communication—and, by default, PR and its disciplinary doppelgangers—entirely in the service of power, and it renders claims of dialogue, engagement, and relationships hollow and unrealized.

Bob Heath and like-minded colleagues argue that strategic communication should be more than a re-badging of PR or an umbrella term for a range of practices. Instead they refer to it as a "meta-process" that shifts the practice of organization-public communication towards a different way of thinking.[106] In this process, strategic communication is characterized by (1) clear objectives that are focussed on outcomes and impact rather than outputs such as publicity; (2) long-term thinking; and (3) systematic planning, ideally based on research, which are all traditional characteristics of strategy and strategic planning. But, instead of being aligned only to the organization's objectives and controlled by management, strategic communication should be (4) adaptive and emergent so that (5) it is aligned to the organization's objectives *and* the interests of stakeholders and society.

A focus beyond organizational interests is identified in the contemporary concept of *social purpose* that is gaining increased attention among management in commercial as well as governmental and non-profit organizations.[107] For example, in his 2019 letter to investors, Larry Fink, the CEO of BlackRock, which is the largest money management firm in the world with more than US$6.5 trillion in assets under management, said: "Companies that fulfil their purpose and responsibilities to stakeholders reap rewards over the long-term. Companies that ignore them stumble and fail."[108] This stands in contrast to Milton Friedman's mid-20th century doctrine that the only responsibility of business is to shareholders. In 2019, the Business Roundtable in the USA, an organization representing the nation's largest and most influential businesses, issued a statement signed by 181 CEOs that said: "While each of our individual companies serves its own corporate purpose, we share a fundamental commitment to all of our stakeholders." The CEOs committed to "investing in employees," "dealing ethically with our suppliers," "supporting the communities in which we work" and delivering value to "all stakeholders."[109]

One is justified in being sceptical, or even cynical. A similar report issued a decade before in 2009 by the Business Roundtable Institute for Corporate Ethics and the Arthur Page Society, a group of senior PR leaders, championed "emerging opportunities for leaders" to rebuild public trust in business through recognition of multiple stakeholders and a focus on "mutuality."[110] In a foreword to the report, Anne Mulcahy, then CEO of Xerox and chair of the Business Roundtable's Corporate Leadership Initiative, wrote: "These turbulent times highlight the great importance of mutuality—of searching for and seizing opportunities that benefit both the public interest and business."[111]

Nevertheless, winds of change are blowing through management, stirred up by technological, social, and political disruption, and two-way communication is becoming increasingly imperative. Emergent strategy is enabled by and depends on stakeholder engagement, dialogue, and consultation that include listening, and working collaboratively in a networked participatory way.[112] Rather than simply producing and distributing *content* that promotes an organization, brand, products, or services and *storytelling* on behalf of organizations—concepts that are the focus of much marketing and PR buzz—strategic public communication as it is being reshaped and remodelled offers opportunities for leadership and innovation in stakeholder engagement and counselling senior management. However, whether practitioners in PR and those who prefer to call their role corporate, government, or strategic communication are up to this challenge, only time will tell. A number of practitioners as well as academics remain sceptical.

Lucas Held—full name Lucas Bernays Held, the grandson of Edward Bernays, who is widely claimed as the "father of public relations"[113]—says a stumbling block in PR is that "there are competing conceptions of PR." He acknowledges that from one perspective it is *advocacy*, often working for business or powerful government elites to influence stakeholders and/or society. However, from another perspective it professes to facilitate *social adjustment* of an organization to align with the expectations of its stakeholders informed by two-way engagement and relationships.[114] Held, who works for a non-profit organization in New York City, believes that PR is not a major source of misinformation or disinformation. Like Therese Manus, CEO of the Norwegian Communication Association, he argues that "credibility is an important asset" for PR practitioners. But he agrees that PR has something of an identity crisis—even a split personality. This is an issue that has plagued PR since its inception as a contemporary management practice. In a textbook published in 2012 I headlined the question: "Whose side is PR on?"[115] This is something that the field needs to resolve, as claims of *boundary spanning*—representing and serving the interests of an organization as well as its stakeholders and society[116]—are fraught with conflicts of interest and impracticality in many if not most situations.

Some PR academics have addressed this issue, most notably Kevin Moloney and Conor McGrath in a third edition of their book *Rethinking Public Relations*, which now bears the sub-title 'Persuasion, democracy and society'. In a review of this 2020 text, Richard Bailey noted that eminent US PR scholar Jim Grunig "drew an intellectual route map that in its stages distanced PR from propaganda, and made public relations intellectually respectable." Bailey continued his critique saying: "The intellectual task now, however, is to scrutinize public relations through somewhat less rose-tinted glasses, to consider its profound impact upon our democracy and society."[117] He neatly summarized the central argument of Moloney and McGrath's book saying:

> … the authors skewer the dominant public relations academic paradigm and also the fashionable argument that public relations is a strategic management function (an argument that is frequently asserted though rarely evidenced). In their view, rather than claiming that public relations leads to social harmony, industry associations should accept that its role is advocacy and counter-advocacy.[118]

Moloney and McGrath prise open what they refer to as paradoxes in PR and call out "definitional obfuscation" and "idealization." They argue that while

PR has demonstrated that it plays a key role in a free market economy as part of promotional culture, it fits less easily into idealized concepts of how democratic and pluralistic politics ought to operate.[119] By implication this view also suggests that, beyond limited deployment by activists and non-profit organizations such as charities that have scarce resources compared with big business and big government, mainstream PR fits uneasily into or even rubs against social structures.

This *standpoint* dichotomy is exacerbated by the ontological dichotomy referred in Chapter 3 in relation to subject and object. PR theory predominantly identifies the employer organization as the initiating author or auteur (the doing subject) disseminating its messages and pursuing its objectives, while stakeholders and society are *audiences* or *consumers* who receive, consume, and respond (the objects to which things are done).

A practitioner who believes that PR can never be remodelled in the likeness of the public interest and social good is Alan Kelly, an outspoken US PR practitioner and part-time teacher. Kelly founded and headed a PR agency called Applied Communications for more than 20 years before selling the business and focussing on writing about PR and proving to be something of an *enfant terrible* of the industry in his blog posts, podcasts, and speeches. Kelly agrees that PR and corporate communication should be conducted ethically. And he supports regulation of the field. However, his reasons for supporting regulation are different to most. Kelly refers to PR as part of the "influence industries" and he says that PR and related promotional practices should be transparent and frank about their role and their allegiances. He argues that PR operates "first and foremost to create competitive advantage" for those who use it.[120] He elaborates:

> Influencers are always running plays [his term for influence strategies], most especially PR people, because their essential purpose is to defend or advance the position or point of view of a client or company. PR/comms is advocacy dressed as education. And if it's advocacy, it's manipulation.[121]

Kelly believes the PR industry needs to come clean about the nature of its role and work, which he sees as predominantly advocacy to influence and manipulate, particularly on behalf of business and government. He alleges that "unlike more advanced disciplines, they [PR practitioners] have no formal or codified basis for understanding the atomic nature of their work."[122] In his book, *The Elements of Influence*, he says that PR practitioners are like chemists without a periodic table. In short, he sees the PR industry and its disciplinary doppelgangers as ambivalent and even duplicitous about their role.

Kelly claims that the PR industry obfuscates what it actually does on a daily basis because it wants to "maintain a beautified view of its work."[123] He goes further than scholarly critiques and says "decades of normalized hyperbole and hedging attribution have both compromised the Fourth Estate and laid the groundwork for fake news and post-truth." He argues that PR is heading for "it's very own 9/11 moment. Just as insurance, energy, finance, and now politics and media have hit their walls, PR is a hair's breadth away from being exposed" for the "monster they've made."[124]

In an interview in Washington, D.C. in mid-2019, Kelly reiterated his view that "PR has side-stepped the issue of defining the discipline." He said "there are poisonous elements in the mix" and expressed concern that these are being covered up under theories and codes of practice that profess mutuality and social good. Referring to fake news, disinformation, and post-truth, he said "in this country there are something like 250,000 PR practitioners and 50,000 journalists. How does that work for truth?"[125]

It is true that PR industry associations worldwide have codes of ethics, but most of these are toothless because they rely on voluntary membership and also the associations lack legal powers to enforce standards or sanctions. Many codes are also quite broad 'motherhood' statements. This has been acknowledged by the president of the UK Chartered Institute of Public Relations (CIPR), Sarah Hall, who told a PR conference in Europe in 2018: "I'd like us to first think about what kind of threshold we set our ourselves for professional conduct and ask whether it isn't, frankly, quite low."[126]

Lee Edwards, associate professor in the media and communications department of the London School of Economics and Political Science, says "the industry claims to take its social obligations seriously," but in her 2018 book on PR she adds: "In practice public interest issues tend to take second place to client and contractual obligations."[127] In a talk at the University of Waikato in New Zealand in 2019 Edwards went further, using the phrase "organized lying" coined by Hannah Arendt in the 1970s in discussing PR. In an address titled "Organized lying and professional legitimacy: Public relations' accountability in the disinformation debate," Edwards said "disinformation is part of the DNA of PR."[128] She explained: "I'm not saying the average PR and comms company is involved in fake news." But she said the PR industry has not acknowledged that the techniques and practices of PR are being used in other contexts to distort public life and, in some cases, "the biggest companies in public relations—such as [name deleted]—have been revealed to be duplicitous in what they have been doing."[129]

The industry has sought to professionalize and commonly uses the term profession to describe PR practice. But PR does not meet the criteria for being a profession in that, while knowledge and expertise exist, there are no barriers to entry (anyone can call themselves a PR practitioner and even register a PR agency); no formal certification or accreditation requirements in all but a few countries; and no legally enforceable sanctions for breaches of its codes of practice or ethics in most countries.[130] The UK is one notable exception where the former Institute for Public Relations is now the CIPR with the power to accredit members as *chartered* practitioners and some powers of censure under a Royal Charter. The CIPR is likely the most advanced PR industry organization in this respect and also supports research in partnership with universities to explore the role of PR in contemporary societies and to build practitioner resilience to help them make ethical decisions.[131] However, CIPR Fellow Stuart Bruce, who works internationally as a consultant on crisis communication and evaluation of PR and communication, says: "CIPR's chartered status affords differentiation of practitioners in the marketplace. We can say that the practices our members undertake have been approved by the Privy Council." But he says other laws such as those relating to defamation and damages limit what the CIPR can do in the case of breaches of its codes. Furthermore, he noted:

> A limitation of this approach is that, while the term chartered is well recognized and has status in the case of chartered engineers and chartered accountants, the term is not widely associated with public relations or communication and, therefore, may not mean much.[132]

Another major practical limitation is that the CIPR has around 10,000 members, but according to Bruce only around 300 have completed the professional development training and attended the one-day accreditation program to become chartered practitioners (i.e., 3%).

The Public Relations Consultants Association (PRCA), which originally represented PR consultancy firms in the UK, rebadged itself as the Public Relations and Communications Association (PRCA) in 2016 and expanded its interests internationally by opening offices in Dubai and Singapore. The PRCA claims to be the largest professional PR body with a reported 30,000 members. It offers a Diploma in Change Management and Communication and partners with Oxford University in running the PRCA Leadership Academy. While the PRCA conducts a number of workshops and discussions on ethics, it is interesting that a mid-2019 search of the terms 'ethics' and 'code of ethics' on its website revealed only a notice of an upcoming seminar, several blog posts briefly mentioning ethics, and an article titled "My life as an ethics girl in PR."[133] No code of ethics. A code may exist in the members only section, but one would expect a global PR organization to publicly state its position on ethics.

In the USA, the Public Relations Society of America (PRSA) provides an ongoing program of professional development for its members as well as codes of ethics, and the Institute for Public Relations (IPR) operates as a non-profit research institute dedicated to fostering research into PR.

In Europe, the European Association of Communication Directors (EACD) is a pan-European body operating to promote professional practice, along with national PR and communication associations throughout Europe. For example, the Norwegian Communication Association significantly updated its code of ethics in late 2019 in the light of changes in technology and concerns about fake news, disinformation, and various forms of deceptive marketing and promotion. The NCA's "ethical principles" call on members to "balance an organization's goals and society's requirements and expectations by practicing communication with openness and integrity" including transparency.[134] Managing director Therese Manus said "we don't want to make it too specific because technologies change rapidly." Manus also made an interesting point saying: "As well as ensuring it is up to date, we want to make it shorter and simpler if we can, rather than longer, because it is hard to remember and use long complex codes. They can be self-defeating."[135]

National and regional institutes and associations representing PR practitioners operate in other parts of the world including in Africa, Asia, Australia, the Middle East, New Zealand, and South America. For example, an *Institute of Public Relations and Communication Management Bill* was presented to the parliament of Kenya in late 2019, which proposes to transform the Public Relations Society of Kenya (PRSK) into an institute and give the body "a charter recognized by law." Speaking on behalf of the Ministry of Information, Communications and Technology Cabinet Secretary Joe Mucheru, Colonel Cyrus Oguna said that the legislation will help "solve the perennial problems of quacks and other entrepreneurs taking over the role of professional communication."[136] The legislation, expected to become law in 2020, was announced at the 2019 PRSK annual conference in Mombasa at the same time as the investment of 350 million Kenya shillings (U$3.4 million) in a skills development program for Kenyan government communication officers.

There are also a number of international organizations that promote standards in public relations and related fields, such as the International Communications Consultancy Organization (ICCO), the International Public Relations

Association (IPRA), and the International Association for Measurement and Evaluation of Communication (AMEC).

However, despite normative theories promoted in disciplinary literature and some exceptions in practice, PR industry bodies and practitioners mostly react defensively or turn a blind eye to revelations of malpractice, employing the doctrine of selective depravity (the 'few bad apples' argument). In most cases, there is only the flimsiest self-regulation and standards in the sector. That is not to deny that PR can be and is being used for socially important issues and causes, such as health promotion campaigns, securing blood donations for the Red Cross, and even in activist campaigns such as environmental protection. But when confronted with uncomfortable home truths, the industry too often resorts to PR for PR, although as *Forbes* magazine has noted: "The public relations industry does a terrible job of public relations."[137]

In a 2019 review of PR professional associations published in *Public Relations Dialogues*, a Canadian PR journal, the authors reported: "One major goal of associations was, and continues to be, the establishment of codes of ethics that practitioners, who are members of these organizations, vow to uphold." They concluded that efforts in relation to codes of ethics "led to a massive culture shift in the world of public relations and moved to push business and communication practices in a more ethical direction."[138] Given the examples of PR practice and comments by industry leaders and researchers cited in this analysis, claiming "a massive culture shift" in relation to ethics has occurred can only be seen as an exaggeration at best and potentially as fake news or even disinformation distributed in an official PR industry journal. Even conservative voices in PR education such as Donald Wright from Boston University are sceptical. When interviewed for the report, Wright said: "I do think that the professional associations could be better."[139]

Anne Gregory, who is a professor of corporate communication and PR at the University of Huddersfield and past president of the Global Alliance of Public Relations and Communication Management, a global federation of PR bodies, is even more frank. When asked about PR standards and self-regulation in an interview, she said many practitioners are "too willing to either accept the money from clients, or not question deeply enough to ascertain the veracity of what they are being told. So it a mix of collusion and incompetence." She added:

> The communication profession has to clean up its act and become more ethically aware. It is not just about the two issues I raised earlier [taking the money and not asking questions], but a deeper conversation about the purpose of communication for each client and asking the question 'just because we can, should we?'[140]

The PR industry and related fields of practice could look to the Global Communication Certification Council (https://gcccouncil.org) for formal certification. The GCCC an independent body that offers a communication management professional (CMP) certification and a senior communication management professional (SCMP) certification for practitioners who undergo study and pass an exam. Alternatively, national industry bodies need to pressure their governments to support a formal certification scheme and regulations, as discussed later under 'Regulation and Legislation'.

This section has gone into more detail than others for four reasons. First, PR and what are referred to as its disciplinary doppelgangers are less visible and, therefore, less recognized and understood publicly than journalism, advertising, political communication, and other public communication practices. Second, as discussed in this section, the field is bifurcating and expanding to include many sub-sets or sub-disciplines. Third, the field is almost completely unregulated. Fourth, in a progressive and honest admission, a panel discussion hosted by the IPR in New York City in August 2019 publicly acknowledged that PR has played a role in creating disinformation and contributed to the phenomenon of post-truth and what a RAND Corporation study called "truth decay." In discussing findings of the RAND study with co-author Jennifer Kavanagh, CEO of the IPR, Tina McCorkindale said: "I do think PR bears some responsibility for truth decay."[141] Director of strategic communication of the Annie E. Casey Foundation, Norris West, said that PR practitioners do not set out to conceal the truth, be he added that "they end up hiding the truth through a series of small decisions," the overall effect of which is to obfuscate the facts.[142] Professional-in-residence at the University of Florida, Patrick Ford, said a contributing cause was the "no holds barred, win at all costs" approach in business and many organizations.[143]

In summary, PR is a growing field of public communication practice that is almost completely unregulated, with mostly unenforceable codes of practice and ethics and, despite McCorkindale's claim that "bad actors comprise a small portion of the total profession,"[144] it has a track record of contributing to, if not creating, systems and regimes of untruth and deception. While legislators mostly view PR as a field not requiring legislation or regulation, it is clear that the industry needs to do a lot more in terms of self-regulation through codes of practice, education and training, and transparency. Part of being transparent is working out what PR actually is—what is its purpose and who does it serve? Sweeping normative claims that PR serves society as well as big business, governments, and other power elites, and that it builds and maintains positive relationships between organizations and their wide and increasing array of stakeholders, do not stack up in reality. Furthermore, such goals and interests may well be irreconcilable in many instances. If self-regulation does not improve, there is a case for government to introduce regulation of the field to ensure transparency, require certification or accreditation to practice, and provide sanctions for malpractice such as disbarment. A very large ball is in the court of PR industry associations and institutes around the world.

Managing director of the Norwegian Communication Association, Therese Manus, raises a counter point to the criticism that communication professionals in PR and corporate communication contribute to disinformation and deception. Noting that terms and conditions of many websites and social platforms are difficult to understand or illegible for most people, and that regulations relating to what data can be collected by whom and for what purpose are complex, she argues that communication professionals could play a positive role in helping organizations develop plain language terms and conditions and information. Also, she says communication professionals can "make sure all the right questions are asked internally during planning."[145] Thus, there are opportunities for communication professionals to play a lead role in addressing disinformation, deception, and manipulation—to become part of the solution rather than part of the problem. Whether the disparate public communication industry can respond with more than rhetoric is an unanswered question.

Incorporating Corporate Communication

As noted in the previous section, corporate communication is largely synonymous with public relations. Therefore, most if not all of the discussion about PR in the previous section applies to corporate communication. In Cornelissen's broad definition, corporate communication also includes advertising and marketing communication. However, here advertising and marketing are discussed in a separate section because specific standards, codes, and regulations apply to these practices.

Stefan Kloet, director of communication for the multinational insurance group Achmea headquartered in the Netherlands, is more optimistic than most about the use of big data, algorithms, and AI, seeing them as offering significant benefits and mostly being used ethically and responsibly. However, he agrees that professional communication practitioners including journalists and those working in PR, corporate communication, and marketing could do more to ensure truthful, balanced public communication. Kloet also believes that the social media platforms need to do more. He said Achmea and its operating companies had faced problems with disinformation such as a man posing as a physician and distributing inaccurate information about health insurance on Twitter. Achmea has an Ethics Committee that reviews and advises on ethical issues, which is a model for what corporations can do as part of their own self-regulation.[146]

Transparency in Corporate and Owned Media

One specific and fast-growing area of corporate communication practice that warrants specific mention is corporate publishing in what are termed owned media. As noted earlier in this chapter, PR practitioners and increasingly journalists and other content producers are being engaged in production of organization websites containing text, audio, and videos; blogs hosted on organization websites or platforms such as Wordpress; YouTube or Vimeo channels; and sometimes high quality, seemingly independent online publications. Owned media are often part of a PR strategy, or part of the growing practice of *content marketing*—marketing communication that is veering away from traditional advertising and PR formats to circumvent audience resistance caused by *persuasion knowledge*.[147]

Organizations are entitled to produce their own media—freedom of speech applies either constitutionally or by convention to all individuals and entities in free societies. The issue is the lack of transparency inherent in many types of owned media. Corporate blogs are usually readily identified as the voice of the organization. Similarly, online videos (e.g., on Facebook) and YouTube video channels usually are clearly identified with the organization that produced and posted them. However, less transparent are the 'media partnerships' that are willingly formed by cash-strapped media organizations and commercial organizations. For example, GE entered into an agreement with Atlantic Media, publisher of *The Atlantic*, to produce *Ideas Lab*, later renamed *GE Reports* (https://www.ge.com/reports). In its original form, GE described its owned media publication as "an interactive platform around the most critical issues impacting America's economic future," suggesting that it was independent and focused on national interests.[148] In its revised form GE is more honest, describing the web publication as "a daily news, video and social media hub covering GE's transformation into the world's largest digital industrial company."[149] Media organizations desperately looking for a new business model are enthusiastically embracing such commercial arrangements, although one wonders what it does for their credibility in the long run.

Another form of owned media are the purportedly independent websites established by PR firms or marketers to promote their clients. One example that sparked controversy in 2018 was operated by Definers Public Affairs, an agency hired by Facebook in 2017 in the midst of its PR crisis in relation to Russian disinformation activities. Media reports revealed that Definers Public Affairs owns and operates a website called NTK Network, which reporters labelled an "in-house fake news shop" because it publishes stories that promote its clients and discredit opponents.[150] In a perverse form or irony, NTK Network describes itself as is "a unique news website that brings together data points from all platforms to tell the whole story."[151] Transparent and honest disclosure should be an essential part of self-regulation in PR and corporate communication.

Advertising and Marketing Standards and Codes

Media advertising is self-regulated to a significant extent in developed countries, as well as being regulated in many. In the USA, for example, there is a long history of self-regulation of advertising to avoid offending potential customers and incurring the wrath of legislators. The National Advertising Review Council (NARC) was established in the USA in 1971 through a partnership between the American Advertising Federation (AAF); the American Association of Advertising Agencies (commonly known as the 4As), which today serves and represents more than 600 advertising agencies that control more than 85% of media advertising in the USA; and the Council of Better Business Bureaus (CBBB). In 2009, the NARC was expanded to include the Direct Marketing Association (DMA), the Interactive Advertising Bureau (IAB), and the Electronic Retailing Association (ERA). In 2012, the NARC changed its name to the Advertising Self-Regulatory Council (ASRC), and in June 2019 the ASRC merged into BBB National Programs, Inc., a non-profit organization that replaces the Council of Better Business Bureaux as administrator of national self-regulatory programs.

Today the Better Business Bureau (https://www.bbb.org) is an overarching multinational business standards body operating in the USA and Canada with branches nationwide that accredit businesses with a rating (https://www.bbb.org/bbb-accreditation-standards) based on commitments to telling the truth, honouring promises, and being transparent. The bureau also publishes a number of standards. These include the BBB *Standards for Trust* (https://www.bbb.org/standards-for-trust), a BBB *Business Partner Code of Conduct* (https://www.bbb.org/partner-code-of-conduct), and a *Code of Advertising* (https://www.bbb.org/code-of-advertising). In addition, BBB offers a dispute resolution service for consumers and businesses, with complaints settled by conciliation, mediation, or arbitration. Local BBBs resolve several hundred thousand complaints a year.

When self-regulation fails, regulation of advertising and marketing in administered by the Federal Trade Commission (FTC). Complaints about advertising are mostly processed by the FTC's Bureau of Consumer Protection, which seeks to protect citizens against unfair, deceptive, or fraudulent advertising and marketing practices. Some examples are discussed later in this chapter under 'Regulation and Legislation'.

In the UK, the Committee of Advertising Practice (CAP) and the Broadcast Committee of Advertising Practice (BCAP) produce a range of codes of practice to guide self-regulation in conjunction with the UK's advertising regulators—the Advertising Standards Authority (ASA) and the Advertising Standards Authority (Broadcast) (ASAB). These codes include the UK *Code of Non-broadcast Advertising and Direct & Promotional Marketing* (CAP Code) and the UK *Code of Broadcast Advertising* (BCAP Code) produced by the ASA and CAP.[152] In September 2018, CAP in conjunction with the UK Competition and Markets Authority (CMA) issued *An Influencer's Guide to Making Clear that Ads are Ads* covering advertorial, influencer marketing, and affiliate marketing that involves use of hyperlinks or discount codes to track sales back to media content for the purpose of paying commissions.[153]

The UK's overall national communications regulator, the Office of Communications, known as OfCom, is primarily focussed on broadcasting and telecommunications issues such as licensing, ensuring competition, and protecting the radio spectrum from abuse. However, it does also have a role in protecting the public from harmful, misleading, or offensive material, as discussed later under 'Regulation and Legislation'.

In Australia, self-regulation of advertising is managed primarily by Ad Standards (https://adstandards.com.au), formerly called the Advertising Standards Bureau, based in the national capital Canberra. This body is managed by the Australian Association of National Advertisers (AANA), the organization representing companies and organizations that commission advertising. Ad Standards functions as a secretariat with complaints about advertising referred to its Ad Standards Community Panel and the Ad Standards Industry Jury—two semi-independent bodies established to review complaints informed by advertising industry self-regulatory codes. A wide range of codes of ethics and practice exist in Australia in relation to advertising including the AANA Code of Ethics and a range of specific codes for marketing to children, advertising food and beverages, promoting gambling, and making environmental claims. The Communications Council (https://www.communicationscouncil.org.au), formerly the Advertising Federation of Australia (AFA), also publishes and promotes a number of codes of practice for advertising.

As well as national codes, self-regulation of advertising and marketing is informed by international codes of practice such as the *International Marketing*

Communications Code published by the International Chamber of Commerce that has representation in 42 countries. The ICC also publishes a number of specific guides and frameworks covering alcohol, food, and environmental marketing communication.[154]

Marketing practices, including direct marketing via electronic direct mail (eDM), are further informed by a number of national codes of practice, such as the Data and Marketing Association (DMA) code produced by the Direct Marketing Commission in the UK.[155] The American Marketing Association (AMA) publishes and promotes codes of practice including a *Statement of Ethics, a Sexual or Personal Harassment Policy, and a Conflict of Interest Policy*.[156]

In Australia, the Australian Direct Marketing Association (ADMA) updated is code of practice in 2018 to address changes in technology and public concerns. For example, one of the changes introduced was a commitment "to take reasonable steps to ensure the safety and security of customers' personal information, as well as to inform customer[s] if the safety or security of their personal information has been compromised."[157]

Beyond the content of advertising and marketing materials, the biggest issue facing the advertising industry and marketing professionals today is almost certainly the collection and use of personal data. Practitioners see the collection and use of data as essential to be competitive in an era of targeted and micro-targeted advertising and marketing. However, ethical use of personal data (human data) requires much greater attention to methods of collection, storage, and use. Examples discussed in this analysis show a lack of protection of personal data and blatant exploitation in some cases. Evolving practices such as personalized advertising and marketing based on tracking users, influencer marketing, and the use of bots and other AI tools require a step change in self-regulation. Beyond ethical considerations, public expectations are important. Even practices that meet ethical standards may create a public backlash if they are seen as invasive and exploitative, leading to reputational damage of organizations and a further decline in public trust. Codes need to be regularly updated to ensure they cover evolving uses of data and targeting of individuals.

Compared with other public communication practices such as PR and social media engagement, advertising and marketing are conducted within a relatively comprehensive self-regulatory framework. However, as with almost all self-regulation, there remains the problem that foxes are guarding the hen house in most cases—e.g., most complaints about advertising are reviewed by advertising industry representatives, or their carefully selected boards and panels. Some self-regulation panels and committees include community representatives and independent experts. Wider application of this approach will improve self-regulation in the advertising and marketing industry.

Natalia Nikolova, who heads the Advanced MBA program at the University of Technology Sydney, believes that marketing practice is not looking seriously enough at ethics. She said: "I have not heard of one major marketing or advertising agency that is making decisions about clients and campaigns based on ethics or issues such as data responsibility."[158] She points to the campaigns of Big Tobacco, the sugar industry, climate change denial, and the promotion of gambling as examples of marketers, advertising agencies, PR firms, and media companies taking the money irrespective of the negative human health, environmental, or social outcomes. She believes that the media and communication industry need to better self-regulate and commit to ethical behaviour, such as not accepting jobs that breach ethical standards or cause harm, similar to the operation of ethical investment funds. She says the success of ethical investments is evidence of changing public expectations and attitudes (see 'Shareholder Activism' in Chapter 5).

Government Communication beyond Marketing

Chapter 3 reported examples of government communication being blurred into or even reconstituted as marketing—the practice of promoting products and services to a market in which the identity and role of individuals are restricted to that of consumers and customers. This is occurring even in mature democracies in which, beyond being users of public services, people are citizens whose voice (*vox populi*) is the basis of the legitimacy of government and whose views governments are meant to listen to and consider in policy making and decision making.

In the case of governments in democratic societies, public communication needs to occur before and during policy development and decision making, not only after policies have been decided and services have been developed. Figure 5.1 illustrates the two purposes and directions of government public communication. Consultation, engagement, and listening (CEL) with and to people as citizens, voters, and electors, is expected and required as part of what is called "democratic input,"[159] as well as information and persuasion campaigns to sell services, policies, and messages. As shown in Figure 5.1, it can be argued that governments need to CEL before they SELL.

The Open Government Partnership (OGP), a collaborative initiative involving 79 countries and a growing number of governments representing more than two billion people and thousands of civil society organizations worldwide, has published a number of reports, guides, and toolkits that identify the benefits of

CEL Before Sell

Consultation, Engagement & Listening (CEL)

- Research
- Public consultation
- Stakeholder engagement and participation
- Monitoring media *(traditional and social)*
- Feedback response
- Reporting back

POLICY DEVELOPMENT

CITIZENS / ELECTORS / VOTERS

Information & Persuasion Campaigns (SELL)

- Information campaigns
- Compliance campaigns *(e.g., road safety)*
- Promotion and marketing *(e.g., tourism)*

INFORMATION & SERVICE DELIVERY

CUSTOMERS / CONSUMERS

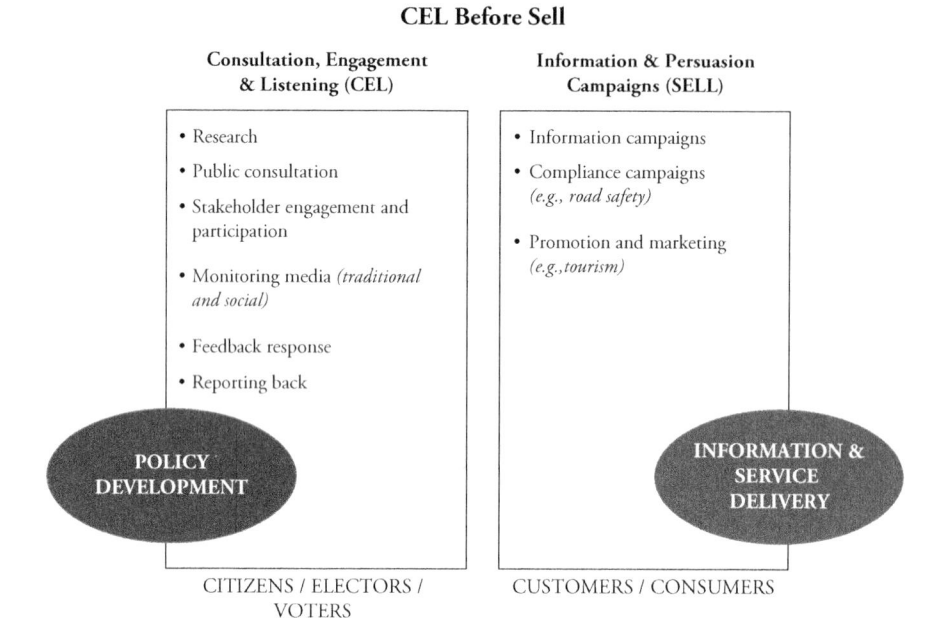

Figure 5.1. The two dimensions of government communication

engagement and *participation* in government policy making and decision making and in creating trust, cohesion, and stability in society. Engagement and participation fundamentally must involve two-way communication—not simply information and talking, and certainly not spin, propaganda, or disinformation. OGP reports and guides identify two main types of public engagement and participation as *consultation* and *deliberation*.

Public consultation is extensively undertaken by democratic governments. It is an appropriate method of public engagement when governments need to get an understanding of what people think about an issue. It may be undertaken broadly (i.e., open to all), or with specific stakeholders in some instances, such as specialized consultation on matters related to a particular industry, profession, or area. However, consultation has limitations. At its best, consultation provides information and opinions that can contribute to government decision making on particular matters. However, as an OGP guide on *Informed Participation* identifies, "once the consultation stage is done, officials retreat behind closed doors to deliberate over what they've heard and to arrive at a decision."[160] Consultations usually have a limited life span and role, after which the business of government goes on as usual. Also, as The Organizational Listening Project found, consultations are mostly passive, such as online consultation sites that invite submissions, but which predominantly attract and hear from major organizations and professional groups and leave many voices unheard.[161] At its worst, public consultation is a tick a box exercise by governments to comply with mandated procedures and to provide an impression of engagement and participation, rarely involving "collaboration," "partnership" and "delegated power" as proposed in Sherry Arnstein's *ladder of participation*[162] and the consultation spectrum of the International Association for Public Participation (IAP2).[163] A further practical limitation of public consultation is that, unless those consulted are at least reasonably well informed about and think carefully about the issues involved, the outcome can be uninformed or even ill-informed, off-the-top-of-the-head discussion—even emotional venting and ranting in the case of controversial issues. This leads to the second key type of public engagement and participation.

Public deliberation refers to methods of engagement that involve stakeholders and sometimes all interested citizens in not only sharing their views, but in discussing and debating potential solutions.[164] The OGP identifies *informed participation* as a specific methodology that creates a sense of ownership of decisions among participants.[165] Deliberation is usually undertaken in a series of discussions rather than a single shot engagement. These may be face-to-face or online, or a combination of both. As the OGP guide on deliberation says: "Public deliberation gives citizens a meaningful role, but it asks something in return: a willingness to listen to different views, weigh competing needs and interests, and carefully craft balanced solutions."[166] It also expects participants to prepare, often involving preliminary reading to gain an understanding of the history, background, and facts pertaining to the matters under deliberation.

Increased use of public consultation and public deliberation—particularly informed deliberation or what the OGP calls informed participation—can "begin to re-establish trust in government," the OGP argues. It adds: "We believe the risks of not engaging in them far outweighs the risk of doing so imperfectly."[167] This view is supported by many political scientists and sociologists worldwide and backed up by studies on several continents.

In addition, efforts to avoid the politicization of government communication need to be ongoing. History shows periodic reviews and reforms that establish government communication independent of political communication, but politics steadily infiltrates or subsumes government communication,[168] particularly under regimes that seek to control and dictate the political, economic, and social agenda through rhetoric and polemic rather than evidence and rational debate.

Political Communication to Address the Relocation of Democracy

Part of reconnecting politics and people and increasing trust as well as the accuracy and authenticity of political communication is opening up political communication to a wider frame of reference, instead of existing in a Brussels, Washington, or Whitehall bubble. Despite the growth of social media and new forms of social movements, research conducted in several countries has found that politicians primarily look to their political party; press, radio, and TV (traditional media); and polls as their sources of insights and reference points. They look to these as barometers of public opinion and as mirrors reflecting their success. However, there are three growing cracks in this approach.

Within the infrastructure of their political party, politicians mostly engage with and hear from like-minded party faithful.[169] Radical and even mildly divergent voices are usually evicted from political party meetings and conventions if they manage to gain entrance at all.

Also, as is well established, both political parties and traditional media have dwindling support in terms of membership and audiences. So politicians are often speaking to and listening to sites of declining influence and declining representativeness.

Polls, which inform election campaign strategies and guide much policy making, ask a limited number of multiple choice 'tick a box' questions with little opportunity for open-ended comments, and are typically conducted among relatively small samples—sometimes just a few thousand in a country with millions of citizens. Some still use computer aided telephone interviewing (CATI) even though telephone surveys are increasingly unanswered. Many rely on paid panels of participants for convenience and speed.[170] As such, polls regularly fail to capture the views of many citizens, particularly disengaged individuals, minority groups, young people who rarely sign up to paid survey panels, and busy people struggling to cope with work, or child rearing, or both. Furthermore, analysis of data collected in polls (short quantitative surveys) commonly reduce findings to *means* (averages) and majority views among those who participate, leaving others as minorities or outliers. Averages, as most school students know, are simply a statistical calculation of a mid-point in data set that may not exist in reality, and a majority can exclude up to 50% of a population.

When more direct political communication is undertaken it is usually restricted to meetings with major industry and professional groups such as business councils, trade associations, church leaders, and the like.

As discussed in Chapter 2, contemporary Western democracies and emerging democracies are witnessing a relocation of democracy from enactment through traditional institutions such as political parties, trade unions, and large representative organizations to a plethora of public interest, activist, and community groups and new forms of social movements. (See 'Activism and Social Movements' later in this chapter.) By and large, politicians and their political communication staff and advisers have failed to recognize the extent and significance of this relocation of democracy, or they are determined to ignore the seismic shift that has occurred in countries ranging from the USA and UK to Middle East nations and China in the case of Hong Kong. When two million people march in the streets, while the major political parties that select political representatives and develop many of their policies represent just a few hundred thousand, it is a sign that the old systems are no longer relevant. When politicians play to traditional and often partisan media organizations, to their political party and the party faithful, to a small group of peak organizations representing power elites, or to an angry rump representing minority interests, they are looking in the wrong direction in terms of democracy. Whether this flawed vision is a result being out of touch, or intentional, is debatable. But what is not debatable, in this researcher's view, is that political communication needs to be redirected to the new locations of democratic participation if politicians and political communicators want engagement and legitimacy.

If political communication does not occur between political leaders and the growing number of public interest, activist, and community organizations as well as broad social movements, civil unrest will grow. There is evidence that trust in politics and politicians is low and still falling in some countries. There are signs that frustration is turning to anger. Ultimately, some countries that are seeing large numbers of their citizens become socially as well as economically disadvantaged and marginalized are likely to look to alternative political systems. It is not impossible that a continuation of elitism in politics and economics and a widening gap between the rich and powerful and the poor and oppressed will lead to revolutionary movements. When communication breaks down completely and no longer serves its role as the enabler of civil human society, violence becomes a medium of expression and post-democracy and post-society become a frightening possibility.

Strategy 2: Responsibility and Transparency by Publishers and Platforms

Along with the exercise of self-responsibility by professionals working in media and public communication roles, reversing the growth of disinformation, deception, and manipulation of people via AI technologies and other forms of individual and social harm such as hate speech will require substantial reformist action by the major media organizations, particularly social media platforms. New media monopolies such as Facebook with 2.5 billion users in 2020, Google, and Amazon have become far more powerful than the media monopolies and oligopolies of the 20th century and reach far more people. Their potential for harm as well as good is therefore unprecedented. Governments in a number of countries are contemplating, or in the process of, introducing legislation or regulation of major social media platforms and search engines in the wake of rising community concerns about use of personal data, privacy, and their role in disseminating disinformation. Legislative and regulatory approaches are discussed later in this chapter under 'Regulation and Legislation'.

In the first instance, greater corporate responsibility and self-regulation by these new media monopolies is a key strategy to address post-communication. Self-regulation is very much in the interest of the major digital platforms, as government imposed legislation or regulation is likely to add more substantially to their operating costs through imposed governance requirements and may even restrict their operations. See discussion of anti-trust action later under 'Regulation and Legislation'.

Pressure is mounting internationally for self-regulation and responsibility by the major social media platforms and search engines such as Facebook, Google, YouTube, and Twitter, as well as major e-commerce, digital streaming, and AI companies such as Amazon and computing giants such as Apple. Facebook has taken some steps. But mostly it has been a case of too little too late. More substantive action is required, without which calls for legislation and/or regulation by government up to and including anti-trust action will grow ever louder.

In December 2019, the European Advisory Committee of Social Science One, an academic-industry partnership established to provide access to privacy protected data for research purposes, issued a statement strongly criticizing digital platforms and calling on Facebook, Google, and Twitter to give academics access to data to enable independent social science research, such as Social Science One's study of the effects of social media on democracy and elections. Led by University of Amsterdam professor Claes de Vreese, the committee said: "Digital platforms have made independent scientific research into potentially consequential phenomena such as online disinformation, polarization, and echo chambers virtually impossible by restricting scholars' access to the platforms' application programming interfaces (APIs)."[171] Such closing off of independent research and scrutiny of public companies flies in the face of corporate responsibility, claims of social purpose, and licence to operate and is unlikely to be tolerated for much longer.

Human Rights and Intelligence vs. Artificial Intelligence

In terms of a framework to inform self-regulation, a 2018 Data and Society Research Institute report on governance of AI recommended that companies need look no further than human rights. The report stated:

> In order for AI to benefit the common good, at the very least its design and deployment should avoid harms to fundamental human values. International human rights provide a robust and global formulation of those values.[172]

Specific recommendations of the report included technology companies conducting a *human rights impact assessment* (HRIA) in developing and deploying AI-based systems. This should include *algorithmic impact assessments* before and when rolling out applications. Rather than conducting these assessments alone or in secret, the report recommended that technology companies, human rights lawyers, policy makers, social scientists, and computer scientists and engineers should work together. Also, the report proposed that multinational government institutions such as the UN can play a role. A further recommendation of the Data and Society report was that technology companies should establish effective channels of communication with civil society groups and researchers to identify and respond to risks related to new technologies, particularly AI deployments.[173]

Australia's chief scientist, Alan Finkel, told a Human Rights Commission conference on technology in 2018 of a golden rule adopted by one Australian government department that he said answered the question that was the title of his address: 'What kind of society do we want to be?' He said the golden rule that served as "the mark of a … ethical custodian" is "No robot or artificial intelligence system should ever take away someone's right, privilege, or entitlement in a way that can't ultimately be linked back to an accountable human decision maker."[174] In summary, accountability including recourse is essential, along with transparency so that actions and decisions are discoverable in the first instance, and then recoverable.

Nick Couldry and Ulises Mejias reach a similar conclusion in their analysis of the *Costs of Connection*. In proposing a "decolonial vision for data," they propose:

> A vision that rejects a rationality that claims to bind all subjects into a universal grid of monitoring and categorization and instead views information and data as

a resource whose value can be sustained only if *locally* negotiated, managed, and controlled [original emphasis].[175]

They describe their "vision" as one that "rejects the idea that the continuous collection of data from human beings is a rational way of organizing human life." Instead, they call for resistance to data colonialism. But they argue that this must be more than "gestures made for effect" (such as quitting Facebook) that "leave the order of data colonialism intact."[176] Rather than a head-on attack, their somewhat abstract solution is a *paranodal* approach to escape the social pressures of digital networks. This concept refers to occupying and acting in the spaces beside and beyond (*para*) the nodes and links that comprise the visible organized structure of digital networks. Rather than being empty barren spaces, Couldry and Mejias argue that these are "inhabited by multitudes who do not conform to the organizing logic of the networks."[177] Quite who these multitudes are is not explicit in their critique, but one might assume that they are composed of marginalized groups and individuals, as well as activists and anarchists. The role that such groups can play in relation to disinformation and post-truth is discussed under 'Strategy 5: Activism and Social Movements' later in this chapter, and actions that individuals can take are spelled out in Chapter 6 in Table 6.1. Couldry and Mejias' reference to paranodal spaces also relates to the concept of the relocation of democracy discussed in Chapter 2 and earlier in this chapter under 'Political Communication to Address the Relocation of Democracy'. They state as their proposal: "Anyone who feels dispossessed by the *Cloud Empire* [original emphasis] should have opportunities and spaces to participate in collective research about the shared problems that data now poses for humanity." They confess that they do not know where these spaces will emerge. But it is highly likely that they will comprise a mixture of face-to-face and digital spaces—possibly even to the extent of building a second safer internet, which has been proposed by a number of technologists and entrepreneurs.

Technology as a Guardian of Technology?

Companies such as Facebook have reported hiring thousands of additional staff to try to moderate online content. While maintaining a human perspective and human oversight over technology is important, a Brookings Institution report on how to combat fake news and disinformation proposed that technology can play a part in identifying fake news and disinformation as well as other negative impacts of technology. In short, fight the dysfunctions of technology with technology.

The Brookings Institution report proposed that "technology firms should invest in technology to find fake news and identify it for users through algorithms and crowdsourcing."[178] It went on to explain that fake news detection can be automated, and proposed that social media companies could do more to develop their ability to produce what some refer to as "public interest algorithms."[179] Much is happening in this space. For example, the US Government has funded a project to develop "media forensics" (https://www.darpa.mil/program/media-forensics). Facebook and Microsoft launched a deepfake detection challenge in late 2019, and Google released a large database of deepfakes allegedly to fight deepfakes.

However, some are not so sure that technology will provide the solutions to the problems of technology and believe that human intervention in the form of self-regulation as well as regulation and legislation are required. For example, a review of technology initiatives in *MIT Technology Review* argued that technology will not solve the problems posed by deepfakes for three reasons. First, automated tools cannot make judgements that are often required, such as identifying the difference between harmful content and fiction, satire, or harmless humour. Second, the review argued that "deepfake-busting technology" is likely to focus on high-profile cases and not protect those who need it most. The review reported: "The biggest risk of deepfakes is not that they swing an election but that they're used to bully private citizens." Third, like CCTV cameras, deepfake detection identifies problems but it is too late to help the victims. The damage is already done.[180]

All of the senior communication practitioners and researchers interviewed agreed that social media platforms and other major internet companies need to take meaningful self-regulation steps. A former senior communication executive who worked in the White House and with the US Department of Homeland Security, the Federal Emergency Management Agency (FEMA), and the US military said "the big social media platforms are working to self-regulate," but he believes that they "have to learn how to self-regulate better."[181]

There are examples to show that responsible self-regulation and platform action against deceptive fake accounts and sites publishing and redistributing disinformation can be effective. A Knight Foundation study reported the example of The Real Strategy, an online entity responsible for initiating large-scale harassment campaigns and contributing to the Pizzagate[182] conspiracy among other falsehoods. Based on public complaints, The Real Strategy Twitter account was deleted, it was blacklisted on Reddit, and a network of supportive bot accounts were disrupted. After being referenced by more than 700,000 tweets during the 2016 US presidential election campaign, post-election analysis showed only slightly more than 1,500 tweets referring to The Real Strategy—a drop of 98%.

International Cooperation—Globalization for Good

While globalization has brought many problems to societies around the world, including colonization of local cultures and exploitation of local people employed to work in 'sweat shops', in the case of internet-based information flows and services international operations and relationships are essential for setting and maintaining any sort of standards and self-regulation measures. Internet communication flows freely across borders, with the result that authorities may not be able to take action against offensive or even illegal content because it is produced in another jurisdiction in which they cannot operate. In such cases, internet companies that operate globally have a better vantage point and access to intervene and block content and communications. Anonymous accounts and accounts established with fake identities remain a challenge, but again global social media platforms and online service providers can change their terms of service to require authentic registration by users in their internal records, even if a pseudonym is used publicly. In short, self-regulation by the major social media platforms and online service providers is potentially a more effective approach than legislation and government imposed regulation. As discussed later in this chapter under 'Regulation and Legislation', to have any effect, laws require enforcement, which can be difficult, costly, or even impossible when bits and bytes travel invisibly and sometimes untraceably across jurisdictions.

Whether the major digital platforms are prepared to self-regulate to the extent expected in society is a question. At the time of writing, a lot of promises have been made. But none have gone far enough and some promises have been hollow rhetoric. In some instances, major social media platforms have got worse in terms of disinformation and partisanship, according to some studies. Research by Avaaz reported that political disinformation was increasing on Facebook in the lead up to the 2020 US presidential election, with politically relevant disinformation gaining an estimated 158 million views in the first 10 months of 2019—"enough to reach every registered voter in the US at least once" and far more than the reach of disinformation during the 2016 presidential campaign.[183] In the midst of this growing crisis, Facebook announced that it would not fact check political advertising. However, a strong incentive is emerging in a number of countries as pressure mounts for governments to regulate the major social media platforms—even break up giants such as Facebook, Google and Amazon. (See the following section 'Regulation and Legislation'.)

Strategy 3: Media Literacy for Consumption and Production

Media literacy is widely discussed as a strategy for inoculating citizens against disinformation, deception, and manipulation. However, media literacy education has not kept pace with technological developments such as surveillance and personal data collection via websites and social media platforms, nor with the role of algorithms and bots as well as humans in the spread of disinformation, deception, and manipulation of people. Media literacy—also referred to and related to *digital literacy*, *critical literacy*, and *news literacy*—is defined by the Center for Media Literacy in the following terms.

> Media literacy … provides a framework to assess, analyze, evaluate, create, and participate with messages in a variety of forms—from print to video to the internet. Media literacy builds an understanding of the role of media in society as well as essential skills of inquiry and self-expression necessary for citizens of a democracy.[184]

This definition identifies what others refer to as two types of media literacy—media literacy for *consumption* (how to read, view and listen to media content critically), which is often referred to as an inoculation or protectionist approach, and media literacy for *production* that equips citizens to participate in various forms of media discussion as effective producers and distributors of information.[185] This second form of media literacy can be expanded to equip citizens to challenge and counter disinformation, hate speech, and other harmful content.

Media literacy related to consumption and production addresses the problems identified in this analysis from the other end—that is, rather than focussing on preventing disinformation, deception, and manipulative persuasion of people, it seeks to boost their resilience and resistance to such influences as well as their capacity to challenge and refute. Media literacy in relation to consumption can equip citizens to critically assess information and take actions such as seeking alternative and corroborating sources, while media literacy in relation to production complements and expands this by giving media consumers and internet users the knowledge and skills to post corrections and balanced content. Together these two forms of media literacy can turn thousands, even millions of citizens, into truth warriors. Thus, both types of media literacy are important.

Increasing media literacy is particularly important among children and young people. The Commission on Fake News and Critical Literacy in Schools in the UK found that only 2% of children and young people have the critical literacy skills to tell whether a news story is real or fake. Furthermore, the commission reported that half of children in the UK (49.9%) are worried about not being able to detect fake news and disinformation.[186] Media literacy therefore needs to be addressed in schools. But older sections of society are also vulnerable to phishing, data theft, and misleading and false information distributed online. Even if they are able to spot the bot, trolls, and hackers, many do not know what to do.

Sonia Livingstone at the London School of Economics and Political Science, Media and Communications Department, who is a leading researcher in relation to child safety on the internet and media literacy, warns that while it is a popular topic, media literacy is not a "silver-bullet solution." She points out that media and media practices such as dataveillance are fast-changing, so education needs to be constantly updated and ongoing. She also says that "education can never reach 100% of the population" and "people cannot learn to be literate in what is illegible." In the final point, she is referring to privacy policies and terms and conditions on sites that are written in legalese and indecipherable for most people. Nevertheless, like many, Livingstone advocates ongoing media literacy education embedded in school curriculum and available to adults.[187]

Veteran journalist and editor Peter Fray agrees that media literacy is a key strategy to combat the effects of disinformation and prevent a further slide towards a post-truth society. He says we need people —not just young people but older people as well—to "become active media consumers, not passive consumers of information. Don't rely on an algorithm."[188] Even more bluntly, he told a seminar on the future of journalism: "Get off Facebook. Fight the algorithms that want to control what you see and hear."[189]

Overcoming Dunning-Kruger and Third Person Effects

In addition to the limitations noted by Livingstone, media literacy is confronted and limited from the outset by a common psychological barrier. Many, if not most people, have an exaggerated view of their own capabilities. Referred to as the *Dunning-Kruger effect* based on experiments by David Dunning and Justin Kruger,[190] this manifests in media literacy as a belief among many that they have the ability to identify truth versus misinformation and disinformation. Such belief is often misplaced. A particularly concerning finding of Dunning and Kruger was that the greatest inflation in self-perception of abilities occurs among the lowest performers in comprehension and logical reasoning tests. This has led to the crude summary of the Dunning-Kruger effect as "too stupid to know they're stupid."[191] In terms of media literacy, this suggests that those most in need of media literacy training and development are least likely to participate in it. The Dunning-Kruger effect has similarities to *third person effect*, a commonly held belief among people that others are affected by various influences such as advertising or fake news, but they are not.

Evidence of the Dunning-Kruger effect in relation to disinformation is found in the 2019 IPR *Disinformation in Society Report* of research that found 80% of Americans feel at least "somewhat confident" in their ability to recognize information that is false or misrepresents reality.[192] Overcoming the Dunning-Kruger effect is likely to require making some media literacy measures mandatory, such as programs in schools.

Inoculation through Media Literacy for Critical Consumption

The goal of media literacy related to consumption is often referred to as inoculation. Inoculation theory, initially developed by social psychologist William McGuire, is based on research that shows people's attitudes and beliefs can be protected against change in a number ways that build resistance and resilience. McGuire proposed that exposing people to weak counter-arguments, which they refute, can create reinforcement of their existing views. Another method of inoculation is to encourage deliberative analytic (System 2) thinking rather than intuitive (System 1) cognition, which is based on heuristics and *mental shortcuts* such as habit or emotional reactions.[193] However, even System 2 thinking can fail to identify truth when it involves *motivated reasoning*, or what psychologists refer to as motivated System 2 reasoning (MS2R). This occurs when people have a strongly held belief or opinion for which they consciously or unconsciously seek justification and endorsement, such as long-held partisan political views.

Nevertheless, despite some limitations, recent research by psychologists Gordon Pennycook and David Rand using *cognitive reflection tests* (CRT) reported that in a range of cases "analytic thinking plays an important role in people's self-inoculation against political disinformation."[194] In particular, Pennycook and Rand found that analytic thinking helps people accurately identify truth in media content regardless of political ideology that might provide motivated reasoning. In their research in the USA, they found that more analytical individuals were better able to discern real from fake news irrespective of whether the content was pro-Democrat, pro-Republican, or politically neutral. They concluded that "susceptibility to fake news is driven more by lazy thinking than it is by partisan bias."[195] This research, if it is found to be generalizable and consistent, provides a strong incentive for developing media literacy in terms of critical analytical thinking.

Media Literacy for Production—Beyond Likes and Follows to Tagging and Snoping

In addition to equipping people with knowledge and skills to produce content, such as posting stories and comments that provide balanced, factual information, media literacy related to production also can include teaching internet users how to call out and correct misinformation and disinformation. In social media and websites where there are few if any official *intermediaries* such as editors, often referred to as gatekeepers,[196] media literacy of production can be aided by *apomediaries*—a term referring to those who stand at the side rather than between users and content, such as peers who provide warnings of suspicious content.[197]

Warnings and tagging of false rumours and gossip, bombast, urban legends, shoddy science, misinformation, and intentional disinformation can be done in a number of ways. Apart from posting a comment directly refuting content, a common method is to post a link to a fact-checking site as a comment on the item. This sends a signal to other readers and viewers of the content and refers them to sites such as PolitiFact (https://www.politifact.com), FactCheck (https://www.factcheck.org), or Snopes (https://www.snopes.com). Also, internet users can send an online story or comment to organizations such as Snopes or via a 'tip sheet' to CrossCheck where staff will investigate its veracity and post a refutation or correction if required. *Snoping* has become part of internet language referring to fact-checking and reporting posts, and cross-checking brings an age-old practice and skill to the digital world.

Studies by the European Research Council has found that fact-checking does not effectively counter all misinformation and disinformation because many consumers of news and information are in *filter bubbles* or *echo chambers* as a result of their highly partisan and polarized views and do not click through to fact-checking sites even when links are provided.[198] Nevertheless, tagging, snoping, and cross-checking are essential parts of the armoury to combat disinformation, deception, and manipulation.

Refuting Misinformation and Disinformation

There has been an ongoing argument for some years about whether challenging and refuting misinformation and disinformation is effective. For example, political scientists Brendan Nyhan and Jason Reifler reported that "corrections frequently fail to reduce misperceptions among the targeted ideological group." They further found "several instances of a 'backfire effect' in which corrections actually *increase* misperceptions among the group in question" [original emphasis].[199] However, a number of recent studies have found differently. Writing in *Neurologica*, psychologist Steven Novella said "more recent research suggests that the backfire effect may not exist, or at least is exceedingly rare."[200] For example, a study of more than 10,000 people published in 2019 reported that "evidence of factual backfire is far more tenuous than prior research suggests. By and large, citizens heed factual information, even when such information challenges their ideological commitments."[201] Two experiments conducted by Ulrich Ecker and colleagues published in 2019 also found that "simple retractions reduced belief in false claims, and … found no evidence for a familiarity-driven backfire effect."[202]

Novella acknowledges that the debate about the effectiveness of refuting misinformation and disinformation is likely to continue. An explanation for the differing views is probably that it depends on how corrections and refutations are done. Aggressive responses and *ad hominem* arguments are likely to trigger resentment and resistance, whereas polite, respectful responses supported with strong evidence have a much better chance of converting or at least moderating alternative views. This further reinforces the importance of media literacy that should include teaching internet users how to write effective responses and refutations to misinformation and disinformation.

Obfuscating as a Way to Sabotage Surveillance

In a 2015 book titled *Obfuscation*, Finn Brunton and Helen Nissenbaum call for a more radical approach as part of media literacy of production. They propose teaching internet users how to deliberately use ambiguous, confusing, or misleading information to interfere with surveillance and data collection projects of governments, corporations, advertisers, and hackers. In a way, they are proposing that citizens produce disinformation to combat the use of information—a perverse reversal of what has been discussed throughout this analysis. They compare their approach with the *radar chaff* deployed by World War II pilots to confuse the enemy. Brunton and Nissenbaum argue that their war-like approach is justified and

218 | *Beyond Post-Communication*

can be beneficial, saying that their recommendations teach users to "push back," software developers to keep their user data safe, and policy makers to collect data without misusing personal information. Somewhat controversially they then present users with a number of tools and techniques for evasion, non-compliance, refusal, and even sabotage of data collection systems such as ways to camouflage search queries in order to stymie the tracking that guides online advertising. Their approach to media literacy, which is the opposite of attempting to *go dark*, raises some questions and it may already be out of date given the rapid evolution of AI. However, it emphasizes that individuals need to take some responsibility for themselves and not simply be swept along or sleep walk into a world of dataveillance and manipulation.

Natalia Nikolova, an academic teaching in the Advanced MBA program at the University of Technology Sydney, and a member of its Futures Academy, believes that, along with rampant neoliberalism that has led to widespread deregulation and the privileging of economic results over all others, a failure in education generally is an underlying cause of increasing disinformation, deception, and manipulation in society. While education levels have increased in most countries over the past century, she says a lack of independent critical thinking in marginalized and 'left behind' sections of the community leads to gullibility and susceptibility to echo chambers and populist appeals. She believes that increased investment in education generally is key to redressing the effects of disinformation, deception, and manipulation.[203]

Strategy 4: Public Media to Protect the Public Interest

The role of public media that are either fully or partially funded from the public purse, such as the BBC in the UK, the CBC in Canada, the ABC in Australia, the Public Broadcasting Service (PBS) in the USA, and similar broadcasters in Europe, South America and Asia, has long been the subject of debate in media studies and politics. Many face declining government support and often criticism from the conservative side of politics for Leftist bias and inefficiency.

The Case for Public Funding of Broadcasting

Despite criticisms and claims of a drain on the public purse, the broken business model of commercial media and the Wild West nature of social media indicate that public media have to be considered a key pillar of the contemporary mediascape. As well as producing and broadcasting entertainment that provides an outlet for local creative industries and reflects diverse interests in society including those of minority groups, public media foster independent journalism free of commercial interests. To a significant extent, public media also foster journalism free of partisan political interests such as those that taint reporting by networks such as Fox News.

Furthermore, public media support the arts with programming of music, feature and documentary films, and information about exhibitions and collections that do not garner sufficient audiences to be of interest to commercial radio and TV networks. Without public media such as public broadcasting, much information and creative work would never be seen or heard. Many issues would go unreported. And many groups in society, including people living with disabilities and Indigenous people would be even more under-represented than they are in predominantly white Western societies.

There have been a number of recent events that raise alarm bells in relation to the future of public broadcasting and which signal public media as a potential battleground in the fight against disinformation, deception, and manipulation.

On 5 June 2019, Australian Federal Police (AFP) officers raided the headquarters of the Australian Broadcasting Corporation (ABC) in the downtown suburb of Ultimo in Sydney. The ABC headquarters is next door to the University of Technology Sydney (UTS), which has a close and supportive working relationship with the ABC. So, even though I was in London at the time doing research and giving guest lectures at the London School of Economics and Political Science and the London College of Communication, the raid brought home to me personally the fragile state of democracy even in stable, mature democracies such as Australia. As well as drawing justifiable outrage from Australian media, the raid sparked headlines and editorial condemnation in the UK and the USA and in many other democratic countries around the world. And justifiably so.

The Federal Police raid resulted from 2017 reporting of clandestine operations of Australian special forces in Afghanistan in which soldiers allegedly killed unarmed men and children—something that, if it did occur, deserves investigation and action. However, the police regarded the information given to the ABC by a whistleblower as secret and a spokesperson would not rule out charges being laid against the informant, the ABC, and the reporters responsible.

The credibility of the information and the circumstances would seem to have fully justified the ABC's reporting. The whistleblower, David McBride, was formerly a lawyer with the Australian Department of Defence. An investigation of the raid by *The Economist* reported that McBride first raised his concerns within the department. It was only when he concluded that his concerns were being ignored or covered up that he took the information to journalists at the ABC.[204]

Unfortunately for McBride and others like him who act in the public interest, Australian whistleblower protection laws are a "sham" in the view of lawyers involved in such cases.[205] Despite new laws introduced in 2019, whistleblowers who disclose unauthorized documents face charges and, if convicted, potentially a life sentence. *The Economist*'s review of the case stated that "the warrant against the ABC read as if it was straight out of an authoritarian rulebook. Among other things it allowed investigators to 'add, copy, delete or alter' material in the broadcaster's computers."[206] ABC journalist John Lyons personally observed and live tweeted the raid. He reported that Federal Police officers sifted through more than 9,000 e-mails and documents belonging to his colleagues who were being investigated. Lyons posted on the ABC's *Back Story* page:

> It felt a complete violation of us both as journalists and citizens—and it had nothing to do with national security. It was at that moment that I felt there was something sick about modern Australia—that an institution as important as the media had come to this.[207]

The raid raises serious questions about freedom of speech and freedom of the media in even mature democracies. Why it took two years for the raid to occur also raises questions and suggests political interference. The conservative Liberal-National federal government led by Scott Morrison, which was elected just one month before the raids, denied any involvement. However, the conservative parties have a long history of cutting funding to the public broadcaster when in office, and ministers frequently accuse the ABC of being Leftist when it turns the blowtorch of scrutiny on government. To many, this seemed like pay back.

This was not the only recent raid on Australian media. The raid on Australia's national broadcaster came just 24 hours after the AFP served News Corp journalist Annika Smethurst a warrant to search her Canberra home and her phone and computer records. This followed her reporting 14-months previously of a top-secret proposal to expand the nation's domestic surveillance agency's powers. A critical observer cannot but conclude that these are alarming attacks on a fundamental component of democracy—a free, independent media—and represent a step towards authoritarian control. These incidents indicate that a government department only has to stamp 'secret' on documents, or simply deem them to be 'a matter of national security'—a phrase increasingly coming out of the mouths of politicians and government officials—and open government, transparency, governance, media freedom, and citizens' rights are quashed.

The combination of surveillance, raids, and potential arrests on the back of what Peter Fray calls a media business model that "blew up a decade or more ago,"[208] caused former ABC journalist turned professor of journalism at UTS, Monica Attard, to describe journalists as "a threatened species."[209]

Curtailment of freedom of media deserves the strongest possible condemnation and resistance from all corners of civil society. Without free independent media, democracies lack the primary watchdog and regulatory force that exists to keep government transparent, honest, and acting in the public interest. The role of public media is particularly important because they are free of the influence of corporate proprietors such as Rupert Murdoch and free of the commercial interests of advertisers. That is not to say that public broadcasters such as the ABC in Australia, the BBC in the UK, or the PBS in the USA are without blemish. Far from it. But, despite their foibles and occasional scandals, they are sometimes all we have between citizens and political demagogues, autocrats, and fascists. This is particularly the case when some major commercial media organizations such as Fox News and Sky News in Australia and the UK have become blatantly partisan promoters of conservatism and neoliberalism.

However, governments face challenges in directing substantial additional amounts of taxpayers' money to media, especially in troubled economic times. Ministers and congressmen and congresswomen have other high priority areas such as hospitals, public transport, and schools that need more funding in many if not most countries. In addition to the competing demands of other social imperatives, the meltdown of global economies in 2008–2009 and the aftershocks that have continued since, have increased deficits and tightened budgets in many countries. As desirable as public media are in the eyes of many reformers, and as much as public service journalism has been adopted in Europe (notably in the UK), it struggles to gain widespread public and political support in the current economic environment, particularly in the USA where the idea of public service journalism has been widely questioned and mostly rejected.[210]

While supporting public media as part of the media ecosystem, Peter Fray sees dangers in having two big players such as a Murdoch owned commercial media group and a public broadcaster dominating the mediascape in a country. He says this leads to further polarization with the public broadcaster leaning to the Left to counterbalance the partisan politics and capitalist advocacy of the likes of the Fox/News Corp network and the two "going at each other." For example, Fray says Murdoch-controlled media in Australia have long tried to undermine or demolish the ABC, and ABC journalists have tended to push a progressive and reformist agenda in response.[211]

Notwithstanding, the rise of disinformation combined with the decline of commercial media in terms of audience reach and trust necessitate alternative ways of maintaining independent media. Political economy critic Robert McChesney argues that "there is no business model that can give us the journalism a self-governing society requires." His argument, which appears to be eminently logical and ever more justified in the era of post-communication, is that governments need to invest in media as a public resource. But that also means that governments, and their various agencies, need to keep their hands off public media in terms of editorial control.

Philanthropic Guardians of Democracy

Philanthropy also can play a role in providing independent critical media, as *The Guardian* demonstrates. However, even *The Guardian*, which is backed by a substantial war chest provided by its benefactors, The Scott Trust, and supported by its non-profit tax-free status, is struggling to break even, and reports indicate that the trust's funds are depleting.[212] After substantial restructuring in 2014 of Guardian News and Media and its subsidiary company, the Guardian Media Group (GMG), the trust fund had more than £800 million to support its media interests. However, by 2016 this was down to £740 million. In 2018 the total value of the Scott Trust Endowment Fund was £1.01 billion, down from £1.03 billion in 2017. So even the world's most generously supported philanthropic media organization has some question marks over its long-term viability, although thankfully it seems secure for the immediate future.

Australia saw the launch of *The Global Mail* in 2012, a free access, free of advertising, non-profit online news site funded by Wotif.com founder and philanthropist Graeme Wood. But even this strongly-supported medium ran into problems within a year and closed down in 2014. The relative scarcity of philanthropists with deep pockets, the losses of *The Guardian* that threaten to exhaust its trust fund, and the collapse of *The Global Mail*, suggest that philanthropic funding does not offer a widely applicable sustainable media business model. But philanthropy can be part of the mix.

In addition, there is a strong case that each of us needs to put our hand in our pocket and pay for quality information in the same way that we do for any other product that we expect to be useful and reliable. Former editor, editor in chief, and managing editor of a number of Australia's leading newspapers, Peter Fray, is self-critical in relation to news media allowing free news to become a public expectation. In an interview he said:

> One of the big moments in the news business—a tipping point—was when publishers and broadcasters adopted an internet strategy that made content free online. Once people got used to free online news, it became hard to go back. We're now trying to claw back the audience and convince them to pay, but that is a big challenge.[213]

Fray strongly advocates that media consumers need to be convinced to pay for quality news and analysis. "We wouldn't dream that we could get a daily cup of coffee for free. Why do we think that a news report or investigative analysis should be free," he asks.[214] It is hard to disagree.

Media Development

In developing countries and emerging democracies media development is recognized as playing a key role in enabling and strengthening democracy, economic development, political discourse, and good governance. Media development involves investment by governments, non-government organizations (NGOs), and sometimes private funding and donations, to provide media facilities, education and training for journalists and media producers, develop media literacy among citizens including digital media literacy, and ensure freedom of expression and media.[215]

The United Nations Educational, Scientific and Cultural Organization (UNESCO) works with the International Programme for the Development of Communication (IPDC), a multilateral forum in the United Nations that mobilizes the international community to support media in developing countries through grants. The IPDC publishes *Media Development Indicators* based on research that highlight gaps in media development to inform public policy and donor strategies.[216] Media development is an important avenue for increasing media literacy, as well as increasing media capacity and establishing and maintaining freedom of media, particularly in developing countries.

Strategy 5: Activism and Social Movements

What Manual Castells calls "networks of outrage and hope"[217] engaging in what Stephen Coleman eloquently calls the "insurgence of the unheard"[218] refers to the mobilization of an increasing number of activist, public interest, and community groups and social movements in democratic countries and emerging democracies. Like many of the concepts and practices discussed in this analysis, these are not new. Human history is punctuated with social and political uprisings and activism such as abolitionism to end the slave trade to the US, UK, and other countries; the temperance movement; the civil rights movement; and the suffragettes followed by first, second and third wave feminism.

Not all social movements are constructive and beneficial for society. For example, the Luddites of early 19th century England resisted the adoption of machines in textile mills. While many of their concerns were justified in terms of working conditions at a practical level and dehumanization at a more philosophical level, the Luddites became synonymous with anti-progress. Nevertheless, grassroots activism plays an important part in steering contemporary democracies.

Activism and social movements are not confined to Western societies, or even to what the Democracy Index compiled by the Economist Intelligence Unit identifies as 'full democracies'. Yo Soy 132 in Mexico, *Nuit Debout* in Paris in which hundreds of thousands of people came out in evenings in defiance of terrorist acts in the city; the Greek anti-austerity movement; Gezi Park in Turkey; and *Movimento de Junho* in Brazil have been studied with interest by scholars and noted to some extent by politicians.[219] The voice of citizens when they speak up and take action deserves ongoing research and media and political attention if democracy is to function effectively and if governments are to maintain legitimacy. Here, just a few examples of major movements are briefly noted to illustrate the range of issues that concern citizens today, and as a source for optimism and even inspiration to offset the negative features of contemporary society outlined in previous chapters.

The Arab Spring

Much has been written about the so-called Arab Spring, referring to democracy movements that spread with various degrees of success from Tunisia through Egypt and a number of other Middle East countries. The uprisings began by most accounts on 18 December 2010 when mass street protests took place in Tunisia and forced President Ben Ali to flee the country in January 2011. Similar protests started in Egypt in early February 2011, centred on Tarir Square, and gained global attention partly because of photographs, video footage, and reports distributed through Facebook, Twitter, blogs, and other social media. The Egyptian government retaliated and blocked internet communications for five days, but was forced to relent because of the damage this did to the country's financial system, businesses, and the government itself.[220] The protests led to the resignation of President Hosni Mubarak on 11 February 2011. At the same time, an uprising in

Yemen forced President Ali Abdullah Saleh to resign which led to a general election in February 2011. In Libya the long-standing regime of Colonel Muammar Gaddafi was deposed. In just over one year, rulers were forced from power in four Middle East countries, major reforms were won in several others including Jordon and Morocco, and a major civil uprising began in Syria against the ruling Syrian Ba'ath Party government that led to UN intervention and political change.[221]

Troubles in the Middle East are far from fully resolved, however, and tensions and oppression of minority groups and human rights continue today. But the democracy movements of the Middle East stand as symbolic of human will and determination to change politics. One wonders though what those who fought for democracy against oppressive Middle East regimes think of democracy as it has evolved recently in the USA, UK, and Australia.

Occupy

While politics can be a source of oppression, financial systems and economics are an even more pervasive cause of inequity in contemporary capitalist societies. A noteworthy citizen and community-based protest movement against big banks and financial institutions is Occupy, which began as Occupy Wall Street in New York City in September 2011. Occupy Wall Street protesters never did occupy Wall Street, having to gather instead in privately owned Zuccotti Park a few blocks away when police blocked them from assembling in public streets. This was described as "violation of the First Amendment right of the people peaceably to assemble" and the movement was ignored for some time by major media.[222]

However, Occupy went on to become a global protest movement against social and economic inequality spreading to more than 80 cities worldwide including Occupy London, Edinburgh, Glasgow and Cardiff in the UK; Occupy Canada; Occupy Oslo; Occupy Dame Street in Dublin; Occupy Nigeria; and *Occupy Dataran* in Malaysia, as well as Occupy protests in Spain, Switzerland, Belgium, Australia, New Zealand, South Africa, Mexico and even Mongolia.[223] It created the slogan "we are the 99 per cent" and, even though the mass protests have discontinued, the movement continues to campaign online (http://wearethe99percent.us).

The Umbrella Movement

The Umbrella Movement became the public face of Hong Kong democracy protests in September 2014 when tens of thousands stood defiantly in central Hong Kong using umbrellas to protect themselves against pepper spray by police trying to disperse them. The protests, which blocked large sections of the financial district of Hong Kong, lasted for 79 days. Rallies in support of The Umbrella Movement were held in more than 60 cities worldwide during October 2014, principally in front of Hong Kong trade missions or Chinese consulates. The organizers in Hong Kong were eventually sent to prison.[224]

Even though the Umbrella Movement dissipated, community-based democratic participation re-emerged in Hong Kong in force on 9 June 2019 when an estimated one million citizens marched in the streets of downtown Hong Kong protesting against the enactment of legislation to allow extradition of Hong Kong residents to China, which locals feared would deny them a fair trial under the rule of law. The Hong Kong Government backed down after days of protests, with the chief executive Carrie Lam issuing an apology and agreeing to suspend the controversial legislation, which was eventually dropped altogether. The strength and determination of citizens in Hong Kong was further demonstrated when, rather than be pacified with the government's deferral of the bill, an estimated "two million" people turned out in the streets of Hong Kong on 16 June 2019. Police claimed around 240,000–340,000 people marched in the two major outpourings of citizens' frustration, but the Civil Human Rights Front reported that the first rally was attended by 1.03 million people and photographs and video footage distributed worldwide told the story.[225]

Hong Kong, which is a special administrative region of the People's Republic of China (PRC), remains a volatile site of social and political protest and many fear retaliation by the Communist Party controlled Chinese Government. The Umbrella Movement and the massive protests that occurred in 2019 demonstrate the relocation of democracy discussed in Chapter 2. The youth of Hong Kong are not represented through political parties, trade unions, a church, or a sanctioned institution—they are on the streets, on social media, and on the move.

Climate Change Mobilization

The climate change movement has expanded well beyond concerned scientists and green political parties to high-profile global campaigns such as that led by Swedish schoolgirl Greta Thunberg. Just 15 years of age at the time, Greta began protesting about the need for immediate action to combat climate change outside the Swedish parliament and subsequently initiated the school strike for climate movement that formed in November 2018 and went global. For example, on 15 March 2019, an estimated 1.4 million students in 300 cities around the world joined her call for striking and protesting.[226]

Anti-Gun Lobby

Anti-gun campaigners swelled and rallied behind Emma Gonzalez, a student at the Marjory Stoneman Douglas High School in Parkland, Florida where 17 people were killed in a mass shooting in February 2018. Gonzalez called out President Trump and the National Rifle Association (NRA) in a speech in front of the White House that was televised live worldwide and gained millions of YouTube views and global support.

In New Zealand, thousands turned out in support of Muslim citizens who were attacked as they attended mosques in Christchurch in March 2019. Within days the Prime Minister Jacinda Adern initiated new gun laws to prohibit ownership of semi-automatic rifles and some other high-powered weapons, which were passed in the New Zealand parliament within the month by 119 votes to one. The shootings unleashed a national and global wave of support for the community and stricter gun laws.

MySociety

MySociety (https://www.mysociety.org) is a not-for-profit social enterprise based in the UK and working internationally that provides online services to help citizens find information and a range of what it calls "democracy tools" and "community technologies" to help citizens hold their elected leaders and officials to account and empower citizens to make improvements in their communities. One of the best known MySociety "community technologies" is FixMyStreet (https://www.fixmystreet.com) through which citizens can report problems in their area such as holes in the road or poor street lighting and apply pressure for rectification. While addressing more micro issues than climate change, guns, and oppression, initiatives such as MySociety reflect a taking back of control from unrepresentative representatives and self-serving elites, and a demand for accountability.

LGBTQI+

Long-ignored and hidden discrimination and prejudice in society have been brought to political and public attention leading to changes to law and greater social acceptance through the expanding LGBQTI+ movement (#lgbqti). This is broad movement involving many organizations and individual activists representing lesbian, gay, bisexual, queer, transgender, and intersex gender identities. Some argue that the acronym should be expanded to LGBQTIA to include asexual identities, while others prefer an open-ended approach designated by the plus sign. While LGBQTI+ and/or LGBQTIA+ address a wide range of issues, a common theme is to confront homophobia, heterosexism, biophobia, transphobia, and other prejudices that create social injustices, and advocate for the well-being of people irrespective of how they identify in terms of gender. Much has been achieved in the past few decades to reduce deep-seated prejudices and discrimination through providing a voice for these groups in society. It is only through such movements that discriminatory laws have been changed, such as the legalizing of gay marriage in Australia, Canada, New Zealand, the UK, USA, and many countries in Europe, South America, and parts of Asia.

#MeToo

The abuse of women in society, particularly by men in powerful positions, has gained worldwide focus through the #MeToo movement. The movement began in 2017 when, following allegations of sexual abuse and sexual assault against prominent movie producer Harvey Weinstein by a number of women, actor Alyssa Milano created and popularized the hashtag #MeToo on Twitter. Milano urged victims of sexual harassment to tweet about it and "give people a sense of the magnitude of the problem."[227] A number of high-profile posts and responses from American celebrities including Gwyneth Paltrow, Jennifer Lawrence, and Uma Thurman followed. What began as a protest against sexual harassment of female actors in Hollywood soon spread to a mass movement worldwide. Such movements illustrate the concepts of virality and *contagion*.[228]

Black Lives Matter

The Black Lives Matter campaign began in 2013 when the #BlackLivesMatter hashtag was established on Twitter after the fatal shooting in 2012 of an Africa-American teenager for which the white perpetrator was acquitted. The movement focussed on drawing attention to and speaking against systemic racism towards black people, police brutality, and high African-American suicide rates.

Black Lives Matter (https://blacklivesmatter.com) became nationally recognized in the USA following its street demonstrations in 2014 protesting the fatal shooting of an 18-year-old African American by police and the death of 44-year-old Eric Garner after being held in a chokehold during his arrest for selling single cigarettes from packs without tax stamps. Video viewed worldwide shows Garner saying "I can't breathe" 11 times while being held face-down on a New York City sidewalk. Subsequently, a grand jury decided not to indict the police officer responsible, although he was fired from the NYPD.[229]

Since, the Black Lives Matter has protested against the deaths of numerous other Africa Americans at the hands of police. In the summer of 2015, Black Lives Matter activists became involved in the 2016 United States presidential election. By 2016, the originators of the hashtag and call to action, Alicia Garza, Patrisse Cullors and Opal Tometi, had expanded their project into a national network of over 30 chapters. Like many other social movements, Black Lives Matter is a decentralized network and has no formal hierarchy—one of the characteristics unique to contemporary activist groups and movements.

Fixers—Fixing Themselves

Fixers was a group of more than 20,000 disadvantaged young people from England, Scotland, Wales, and Northern Ireland who banded together as a charity under the theme 'Young people using the past to fix the future'. The group sought to "fix" themselves and others by telling their stories through almost 1,000 case studies showcased in videos posted on their website and broadcast on TV networks including ITV, UTV, and STV. Unfortunately the group ran out of funding in 2019 and its operations were suspended, although its website and resources remain at the time of writing (http://www.fixers.org.uk). It was yet another example of new kinds of community organizing that are occurring among disadvantaged and disenfranchised groups that have been failed by traditional politics, traditional media, and traditional allegedly representative organizations.

Alt-Right

Alt-right organizations, while distasteful to many, are also an example of new forms of social and political movements representing the views of people. Alt-right, an abbreviation of alternative right, is a loosely connected far-right, white nationalist movement in the United States and parts of Europe that promotes white supremacism, antisemitism, patriarchy, anti-immigration policies, and even white separatism.

Breitbart News (https://www.breitbart.com), founded by conservative commentator Andrew Brietbart in 2007, is a prominent mouthpiece for the Alt-right movement. After Breitbart's death, the online site became more aggressively right-wing under the control of Steve Bannon, a former investment banker and movie producer, who was chief executive of Donald Trump's presidential campaign bid in 2016 and then served as White House chief strategist during the first seven months of Trump's term. After Bannon was disavowed by Trump in 2018 following publication of his book *Fire and Fury* and left *Breitbart News*, Alex Marlow became editor in chief. *Breitbart News* is an example of the democratization of media in the age of the internet—with both positive and negative results.

Shareholder Activism

Change is being urged and sometimes forced from inside major corporations through the relatively new phenomenon of shareholder activism. *Investopedia* defines a shareholder activist as "a person who attempts to use his or her rights as a shareholder of a publicly-traded corporation to bring about change within or for the corporation."[230]

Some shareholder activists are billionaire investors, who seek control of publicly traded companies for their own benefit, such as Carl Icahn, who earned a reputation as a *corporate raider* by taking over Texaco and American Airlines (TWA), and Bill Ackman, who waged an ultimately unsuccessful campaign against Herbalife. More common among shareholder activists are institutional investors such as hedge funds and superannuation funds that have adopted environmental, social, and governance (ESG) policies. These funds, which hold and invest large amounts of money on behalf of members of superannuation funds and small investors can exert considerable influence over companies in which they invest. Some investment funds specifically seek and manage what are termed *ethical investments*. *Investopedia* says these funds give individual investors "the power to allocate capital toward companies whose practices and values align with their personal beliefs," which may be based on environment, social justice, political, or religious principles. Simultaneously, they avoid investment in what are colloquially called *sin stocks*, such as shares in companies involved in gambling, tobacco and alcohol products, or weapons manufacture.[231]

Critics argue that social movements are not the answer to reviving democracy. One reason advanced is that "they have too little stability."[232] They do tend to come and go. But one must ask the question: why is stability or longevity important? Long-established institutions and organizations such as political parties, professional associations, and trade unions have, to varying extents, become bureaucratized, dominated by elite interests, and often subject to political infighting, and many have thus outlived their effectiveness. Social movements reflect a shift from *dutiful citizenship* to *actualizing citizenship* and from traditional political allegiances to issue-based politics, as discussed by Lance Bennett and colleagues[233] and others such as Natalie Fenton, who says "the ontology of the political" is changing.[234]

Democracy *is* relocating. From once smoke-filled cabinet rooms, boardrooms, party rooms, and trades hall rooms; church halls and town halls; and secret societies populated by white men officiating over age-old hierarchal and patriarchal practices, democracy is relocating to non-hierarchal, emergent, dynamic networks; flash mobs; hashtags; meetups; and spontaneous mass turnouts in streets and parks and even airports. Specifically, the act of democratic participation is relocating. It needs to relocate, because it is being increasingly restricted, stifled, suppressed, or ignored at the traditional sites of democratic participation other than fleeting moments of voting characterized by "arid proceduralism" and "instrumental effectiveness."[235] Governments, political parties, politicians, and purportedly representative organizations need to realign and remodel themselves and their processes, or become increasingly irrelevant.

Strategy 6: Corporate Responsibility and Social Purpose in Business

It is clear from this analysis, if not self-evident, that organizations including incorporated companies as well as other types of corporate bodies, need to act responsibly in relation to the public communication as well as their operations generally that can affect human safety, the environment, animal welfare, people's financial viability, and many other factors. As identified in Chapter 3, the practices of public communication such as advertising, PR, and other forms of marketing communication are mostly conducted on behalf of corporate, government, and large non-government organizations and serve the objectives of those organizations. While ideally maintaining a high level of independence, journalists also are explicitly or hegemonically guided by and answerable to their employers. Because of the dominance of capitalism as an economic system, even in socialist and communist states including China, corporate responsibility and social purpose in business is crucial.

The Social Responsibility of Management was the title of a book published in 1950 by Stuart Chase and colleagues.[236] It was one of the first conceptualizations of the practice of *corporate social responsibility* (CSR), sometimes referred to simply as *corporate responsibility* (CR). The expansion of corporate responsibility beyond achievement of financial objectives was notably boosted in the 1990s by John Elkington's concept of the "triple bottom line," which proposed that a company should, and would be more successful in the long-term, if it paid attention to its environmental and social impact. This approach was colloquially referred to as *people, planet, profit*.[237] Despite receiving much attention, implementation of this approach has been patchy and claims often have been little more than empty rhetoric.

CSR—Responsibility, or Turning Pigs' Ears into Silk Purses

The PR industry has promoted CSR for several decades and claims to manage this function on behalf of organizations. However, that in itself, often spells the death knell of CSR as a meaningful practice. CSR has to flow from senior management throughout the operations of the corporate body. When CSR is something that is managed by PR, it is very likely to be an add-on activity proposed and organized by the PR department or agency, not part of the core values of the organization and embodied in all its operations. Typically, CSR programs include sponsorships of local community activities or sports teams, or one-off projects such as providing computers to schools. In *The Handbook of Public Affairs*, John Holcomb notes that, despite its lauding by PR academics and in popular management books and journals, CSR is often seen as "appendage efforts such as philanthropy, often not centrally related to core functions of the firm." He prefers the terms corporate responsibility or *public responsibility*, which he says are "a more realistic terrain" and "less presumptuous territory."[238]

Purpose

As discussed in Chapter 5 in relation to remodelling PR, *social purpose*—sometimes referred to simply as *purpose* with a social dimension implicit—has become a 21st century buzzword. Whether it becomes more than a buzzword, or passes into the annals of marketing history, will depend on the commitment and long-sightedness of senior management in organizations. There are some hopeful signs of transformational change in business. As noted in Chapter 5, the Business Roundtable in the USA issued a signed statement in 2019 committing to "investing in employees," "dealing ethically with our suppliers," "supporting the communities in which we work," and delivering value to "all stakeholders."[239] In short, this concept proposes having a purpose beyond making money for shareholders, which Milton Friedman cited as the only obligation of a company.

Working against social purpose in business, particularly in the USA, is the high pressure demands of quarterly reporting by public companies and the expectations of shareholders, many of whom think and plan short-term and expect stock price rises and dividends on a regular basis. Such pressures cause public companies to focus on financial results, sometimes at the expense of the environment, employees, and society.

For social purpose to be achievable in a high octane capitalist system, public companies may need to publicly declare their position in the same way that ethical investment funds do and even engage in public education of their investors. That way, investors will know the score and set their expectations accordingly, and companies will attract investors who support their principles and approach, rather than those expecting to make a 'quick buck'.

Responsibility of CEOs—Where the Buck Stops

A large part, if not the largest part, of responsibility for corporate responsibility rests with CEOs. Responsible policies, decisions, and operations need to be part of the DNA of an organization and, while shareholders and a board of directors can apply pressure and influence strategy and plans, the CEO leads the organization. CEOs need to make a stand if corporate responsibility is to be real and not just PR.

The Rise of CCOs—The Case for Communication Leadership

In addition, there is another recent development that can support progressive CEOs. Often the reason that PR is restricted to add-on CSR activities and 'mop-up' operations after crises is that public communication is not represented at C-suite level—which some PR literature refers to as the *dominant coalition* in an organization. If PR, or corporate communication, or an equivalent function is not represented at C-suite level, able to engage in decision making on equal terms with the chief financial officer (CFO), chief operations officer (COO), chief marketing officer (CMO), chief information officer (CIO), and other senior executives, counsel on the public opinion, reputational, and social implications of decisions and actions is missing from many discussions. Also, public communication is likely to be inadequately considered, and may not be considered at all.

A promising development that can potentially increase representation of stakeholder and social interests, consider social impact, and embed effective public communication in all strategies and plans is the appointment of a chief communication officer (CCO) in organizations. The CCO can advise senior management on public communication, support the CEO in communication-related decision making, and champion the interests of stakeholders and society, helping to balance the power and influence of finance, operations, marketing, IT, and other major functions. To achieve CCO status and access, public communication managers need to have the qualifications, experience, and skills required and expected at that level, including skills in negotiation, diplomacy, research, data analysis and interpretation, and presentation.

The appointment by corporations of an Ethics Committee, such as the example in the Netherlands headquartered Achmea group cited earlier in this chapter under 'Incorporating Corporate Communication', is also a strategy that could improve corporate behaviour.

Strategy 7: Research and Analysis

Many researchers are working in universities, institutes, institutions, and centres worldwide to investigate the impact of disinformation and new information and communication technologies (ICTs) including data collection and analytics, bots, algorithms, and other applications of AI. A number of those researchers and research institutions are cited in this analysis. Their work and the work of many others is vital to understand the full implications of the practices and ICTs discussed in this analysis—not just the commercial and political benefits that corporations and governments accrue. Rigorous research is also essential to challenge the management rhetoric and PR of multinational corporations such as Facebook that present a picture framed by self-interest and often obfuscating in relation to dysfunctions.

Research—both scientific and that conducted within the social sciences and humanities—provides reliable data and well-grounded interpretations to inform policy making and decision making and challenge pseudo-science, misinformation, and disinformation. Many governments and organizations claim to take an evidence-based approach, but often this is over-ruled or overtaken by expediency, political manoeuvring, or self-interested lobbying. Funders need to support research, researchers need to be bold, and academic and media publishers need to expand the dissemination of science and facts.

As well as the discovery phase of research, a key role of academics and other researchers is critical analysis that identifies problems, gaps, and inequities, and presents recommendations for government policy makers and regulators. Also it is important that leading researchers take on roles as public intellectuals speaking out and presenting independent views and evidence in relation to matters that affect the lives of billions of people and shape society.

The Social Construction of New Realities

While our world is made up of minerals, gases, various types of physical structures, and increasingly machines that operate and interact through wires, radio waves, satellite signals, and computer code, it is also now widely that reality is also socially constructed.[240] The infrastructure of laws, policies, conventions, codes, rights, and practices that inform and govern human lives are formed through social interaction—people coming together to negotiate, form consensus, or agree to abide by majority views in order to cohabit as a society.

Research, critical analysis, and reflection based on rigorous inquiry contribute to the social construction of reality and can play a role in constructing new realities. The issues discussed in this and other analyses indicate that new realities need to be created for many who are negatively impacted, marginalized, and neglected in our society.

A New Vision and Narrative

To construct new social realities, leaders in politics, government, industry, and the professions need to develop a new vision and promote that through a compelling narrative. The narrative needs to embrace industry and business, but also balance commercial interests with social justice and equity. In their 2019 analysis of the *Costs of Connection*, Nick Couldry and Ulises Mejias call for a new vision that "rejects the idea that the continuous collection of data from human beings is a rational way of organizing human life."[241] Apart from saying what that vision should *not* be, and calling for continuing research and for information and data to be locally negotiated, managed, and controlled, including by users rather than secretly collected and used by multinational corporations and political campaigners, their incisive analysis does not describe what the vision should be in any detail. Formulating a new vision and narrative for democratic societies including those with capitalist economic systems, is perhaps the next step in research.

As a starting point, this analysis suggests that a vision for the future of information, communication, and media should be grounded in human rights as expressed by the United Nations, not only in neoliberal economics. Social good, which is now publicly recognized by business leaders as a necessary ingredient for sustainability, needs to be made concrete rather than abstract and given priority alongside personal and proprietary gain. Also, the shared responsibilities and multi-faceted approach advanced in this analysis offers a contribution to a vision that must be widely supported and adopted to be successful.

Strategy 8: Refuting and Resisting

Despite claims that refuting misinformation and disinformation can lead to reinforcement of the original messages referred to as the *backfire effect*, recent research indicates that directly challenging and correcting misleading and deceptive information can be effective. As noted under 'Strategy 3: Media Literacy for Consumption and Production', a 2019 study of 10,000 people found that "by and large, citizens heed factual information, even when such information challenges their ideological commitments."[242] Similarly, experiments conducted by Ulrich Ecker and colleagues found that "simple retractions reduced belief in false claims, and … found no evidence for a familiarity-driven backfire effect."[243]

Refutations and corrections need to be done carefully so as not to antagonize or inflame, which can lead to emotional responses and retorts. Polite, respectful responses supported with evidence have a much better chance of converting or at least moderating alternative views. This suggests that training in methods of refuting and correcting misinformation and disinformation should be part of media literacy development. (See 'Strategy 3: Media Literacy of Consumption and Production'.)

The Empire Strikes Back

Examples of formally organized resistance and initiatives to refute misinformation and disinformation include the UK Government Communication Service (GCS) *RESIST: The Counter Disinformation Toolkit* launched in 2018.[244] The GCS also has established a Rapid Response Unit—a team of communication professionals whose role is to find and refute disinformation. The aim of refutation is to create scepticism that leads to increased scrutiny and critical analysis (see Figure 1.1 in Chapter 1.) It will be interesting to track the success, or otherwise, of such initiatives.

Refutation and correction of misinformation and disinformation are also carried out by organizations such as First Draft, as discussed earlier in this chapter under 'Strategy 1: Self-Regulation by Communication Professionals—Reining in Spin'. Beyond simply fact-checking, First Draft proactively monitors, investigates and challenges misinformation and disinformation.

Strategy 9: Self-Responsibility—It's Up to You and Me

As in many aspects of life, ranging from keeping safe on the streets when crossing the road to operating machinery, taking responsibility for oneself is essential and often the primary line of defence against injury and harm. This is not to push blame and the burden of resolving complex issues on to individuals, many of whom lack the social capital and resources to take on Facebook or Google or other media monoliths. But everyone can play a part. And the current flood of disinformation and attempts at deception and manipulation requires all hands to the pumps.

Check Up, Speak Up, Act Up

There are a number of things that individuals can do, several of which have been referred to in this analysis. These include:

- Fact-checking online content that seems suspicious, surprising, or extreme. There is a golden rule in consumer protection that says "if it looks too good to be true, it probably is." The same can be concluded in relation to things that look too bad to be true, or too sensational, or extreme to be true;
- Tell others and post warnings about fallacious claims and suspected disinformation;
- Don't just get mad, get even by taking further action such as posting a refutation, correction, or link to a fact-checking site to signal to other internet users that the content may be misinformation or disinformation or that the source is not to be trusted. Also, some types of content can warrant reporting to the social media platform.

This draws on the substantial resources of what some researchers refer to as *apomediaries*. While most social media platforms lack intermediaries such as editors (referred to as *gatekeepers*), those who are beside or alongside (*apo*) rather than in between (*inter*) the creators and recipients of content can play an important part in the view of media researchers.[245] There are potentially more than 4.5 billion apomediaries available to call out and challenge disinformation and attempts at deception and manipulation—the number of internet users worldwide as at the end of 2019.[246]

Strategy 10: Regulation and Legislation

Civilized societies are characterized by a substantial legal infrastructure of regulation and legislation. Regulation and legislation are collectively two of "four levers" of government in the words of the executive director of the UK GCS Alex Aiken, along with taxation and communication.[247]

A wide range of regulations and legislation guide media and communication in most contemporary societies. Apart from a complex web of regulations and laws in relation to broadcasting and use of the radio spectrum for telecommunications services, the bodies of regulations and legislation most relevant to this analysis relate to media content, the internet, and the collection and use of data, particularly as this has expanded through digitalization. Informing, and counter-balancing these specific legal and regulatory frameworks are broad bodies of law, legal conventions, and human rights such as freedom of speech and the right to privacy.

The purpose here is not to provide a detailed analysis of the legal framework that shapes public communication in various countries, as this is beyond the space available and the focus of this discussion. Regulation and legislation have been left to last in this discussion, not because they are unimportant, but for two reasons. First, contemporary liberal and monitory democracies favour deregulation or minimal regulation and tend to see regulation and legislation as a last resort. Second, at a practical level, passing legislation or regulations does not of itself resolve any problem. Enforcement is required to effect change. This can be difficult given limited enforcement resources and competing priorities such as addressing serious crime including murder and malicious attacks such as rape. Furthermore, in the globalized world of digital communications, transactions and content flow across borders. Enforcement authorities often are not able to act in other jurisdictions and, if even if they can through international cooperation, regulations and laws differ between countries. Democracies and even many democratic socialist states rely on self-regulation to a large extent on the basis that this is more cost-efficient, prevention is better than cure, and it reflects broad principles of freedom speech and media. However, in a number of cases public communication infringes human rights and freedoms, as well as standards of decency, as this analysis has shown to an alarming extent. When this occurs there are calls for legislation or regulation.

Advertising and Marketing Regulation and Legislation

Because of its pervasiveness over the past 200 years, and its perceived power, advertising is substantially regulated in most countries. For instance, in the USA, despite its constitutional provisions for freedom of speech and of media, courts have ruled that advertising can be regulated more strictly than any other form of expression. The major regulatory body for the advertising industry is the FTC, which was originally established to prevent unfair methods of competition in commerce, but its role has been expanded through its Bureau of Consumer Protection. In the US, state authorities are also entitled to control the distribution of false or misleading advertising and advertising of illegal goods or services through departments of consumer affairs and under federal mechanisms such as the *Uniform Deceptive Trade Practices Act* and other FTC legislation such as the *Children's Online Privacy Protection Act*.[248]

The FTC has issued numerous guidelines and policy statements in relation to promotional media content and in 2015 the commission issued guidelines on native advertising titled *Native Advertising: A Guide for Business* and also reiterated its *Enforcement Policy Statement on Deceptively Formatted Advertisements*.[249] The FTC has taken legal action against organizations in relation to native advertising. For instance, in 2016 the FTC charged national retailer Lord & Taylor for having "deceived consumers by paying for native ads, including a seemingly objective article … without disclosing they were actually paid promotions."[250]

The Consumer Financial Protection Bureau (CFPB) in the USA has the authority to implement and enforce federal consumer financial law in relation to the marketing and promotion of financial services that have historically fallen outside the purview of general consumer protection agencies.

The FTC in the US introduced new requirements in late 2019 in relation to social media influencers. These require social media users who "work with brands" or "have a relationship with a brand"—whether financial, or through receipt of free or discounted products, or personal links—to transparently disclose their affiliation.[251] The FTC requires disclosures to be clearly visible and in plain language, including superimposing declaration of interests on pictures and videos. However, ensuring compliance will be the challenge given the rapid growth in social media advocacy.

In the UK, a number of regulations govern standards of advertising including the *Consumer Protection from Unfair Trading Regulations*, which prohibit false or deceptive messages, leaving out important information, and using aggressive sales techniques. Advertising to businesses is covered by the *Business Protection from Misleading Marketing Regulations*.[252] The UK also has codes applying to broadcast and non-broadcast advertising. In 2018, the overarching regulator, the Office of Communication (Ofcom) released a report on native advertising, which it identified as accounting for more than £1 billion (US$1.2 billion) of advertising spending.[253]

Advertising is regulated in Australia under the *Competition and Consumer Act* (formerly the *Trade Practices Act*), which expressly prohibits paid communication with the "intent, or likely effect, to mislead or deceive."²⁵⁴ The act is administered by the Australian Competition and Consumers Commission (ACCC).

Most researchers consider that traditional media advertising is sufficiently regulated. However, constantly evolving practices such as those examined in this analysis and the rapid rate of change in the media and communication industries mean that regulations and legislation need to be kept under constant review and updated to address new practices.

Public Relations — Uncharted Territory

In the UK, the former IPR was granted a Royal Charter signed by the Privy Council in 2005. While many other PR industry professional associations and institutes have introduced self-administered accreditation schemes, the CIPR stands alone with its quasi-legal status. However, even that does not afford regulatory powers, as discussed under 'Remodelling Public Relations'. Regulation and legislation is largely uncharted territory in terms of PR.

Few PR industry leaders support regulation or legislation. CIPR Fellow and consultant Stuart Bruce concedes that "regulation or legislation might be appropriate in specialist practices such as financial communication where there are strict requirements for disclosure in shareholder and investor relations, for example." However, he rejects industry-wide regulation or legislation saying:

> The industry has talked about regulation and legislation for years. But it's a utopian view because it is not likely to happen. Restricting the field goes against the trend towards deregulation and also conflicts with policies for open access, equal opportunity, and social mobility.²⁵⁵

In fact, perhaps not surprisingly, no PR practitioners interviewed consider regulation or legislation of PR is warranted. But surprisingly, and of concern, is that some PR practitioners interviewed also did not believe that increased self-regulation was a key part of the solution to redressing disinformation, deception, and manipulation. Instead, most practitioners put responsibility on government, fact-checking agencies, and social media platforms. However, studies show that the reputation of PR is low. For example, a UK public survey found that 92% of people polled believe PR is primarily used to deceive the public, and the same proportion believe that PR practitioners "bend the truth."²⁵⁶ The reputation and public acceptance of the practice is likely to sink further and attract public criticism if it refuses to more openly acknowledge and address malpractice and questionable practices that are much more widespread than industry leaders currently acknowledge.

Data Protection and Privacy

As more and more information about people has become available in digital form that is easily searched and valuable to various interests, one of the pressing priorities for regulators and legislators is ensuring protection of personal data and individual privacy.

The General Data Protection Regulation (GDPR) passed by the European Commission came into effect in May 2018. This has been seen as a step in the right direction by privacy advocates and even by corporations involved in collecting and using personal data. But many see this as not going far enough. The implementation of GDPR has resulted in consent boxes popping up on every website visited, requiring the user's agreement in order to continue. However, if users decline to give consent for data about them to be collected and used, the site can no longer be accessed. Complaints have been made about this 'take it or leave it' approach as it does not constitute consent without pressure or duress.

The GDPR also leaves gaps. For instance, it does not apply to data produced by algorithms and used in targeted advertising. Furthermore, many argue that national laws are not enough in a global "data-industrial complex." The 40th International Conference of Data Protection and Privacy Commissioners in Brussels, was told that national rules are not comprehensive enough to deal with complex transnational issues, and that they could even threaten global cooperation and transfers of data. "The world urgently needs a global regime for data governance," Apple chief executive Tim Cook told the conference.[257]

Regulation of Social Media Platforms

A number of academics and media and communication practitioners believe that some regulation of social media platforms is necessary to rein in disinformation, deception, and manipulation. Widely published author on digital media, Terry Flew from Queensland University of Technology (QUT), says that domination of the internet and a large part of the digital economy by a handful of platforms—which he refers to as the "platformization of the internet"—is a major cause of online manipulation, disinformation, and abuse of rights, and the resulting "crisis of trust."[258]

Speaking at the 2019 International Communication Association (ICA) conference in Washington, D.C., Kearston Wesner from Quinnipiac University said "leaving it to platforms to self-regulate doesn't work."[259] Former chair of the Global Alliance for Public Relations and Communication Management, Anne Gregory,[260] says there is a need for government legislation with penalties for privacy breaches and disinformation, although she also calls for self-regulation and responsibility by media platforms, communication professionals, and individuals.[261] Senior WPP public sector communication consultant Sean Larkins[262] said:

> The online world has become a wild west with little or no legislation in place to police it. Social media need to be brought into the same regulatory framework as broadcasters. We'd do well to bring newspapers in line with this too.[263]

In the USA, a 2019 report published by the Stigler Center for the Study of the Economy and the State concluded that "concentration of economic, media, data, and political power is potentially dangerous for our democracies" and recommended some form of regulation.[264]

The European Union (EU) adopted an *Action Plan Against Disinformation* in 2019 and released a specific election package in an attempt to prevent or minimize disruption of the 2019 elections to the European parliament. As well as working in collaboration with journalists, fact-checkers, national authorities, and social media platforms, the EU reportedly "strengthened its capabilities to identify and counter disinformation via the Strategic Communication Task Force and the EU Hybrid Fusion Cell in the European External Action Service," which (despite sounding like a nuclear power plant) includes "a rapid alert system." However, even the might of the European Commission admits that "more remains to be done."[265]

The *Online Harms White Paper* produced by the UK Government in 2019 noted that "there is a range of regulatory and voluntary initiatives aimed at addressing these problems, but these have not gone far enough or fast enough, or been consistent enough between different companies, to keep UK users safe online." In documenting a long list of online harms, the paper further noted that "many of our international partners are also developing new regulatory approaches to tackle online harms, but none has yet established a regulatory framework that tackles this range of online harms."[266] At the time of going to press, the UK Government was considering a range of initiatives recommended in the white paper including:

- Establishing a new *statutory duty of care* to make companies take more responsibility for the safety of their uses;
- Appoint an *independent regulator* to enforce compliance;
- Require companies to develop and abide by *codes of practice*;
- Require companies to submit annual *transparency reports* outlining the extent of harmful content on their platforms and what counter measures were taken.[267]

The proposed legislation will apply to all social media platforms, file hosting sites, public discussion forums, messaging services, and search engines, and the scope will cover pornographic content including revenge pornography, child sex exploitation, slavery, harassment and cyberstalking, cyberbullying, hate speech, incitement of violence and terrorism, as well as disinformation.

The Australian Government commissioned the ACCC in December 2017 to conduct a Digital Platforms Inquiry to review the impact of online search engines, social media, and digital content aggregators. The ACCC's *Digital Platforms Inquiry Report* released in June 2019 concluded that mergers were creating monopolies online and that companies such as Google had created "default bias" through deals such as making its search engine the default browser on Android devices and "self preferencing" of its own businesses in searches. The ACCC made a number of recommendations in relation to regulation of digital platforms and media as well as other initiatives including:

- Changes to merger law and a requirement for advance notice of proposed acquisitions;
- Changes to search engine and internet browser defaults;
- Development of codes of conduct for digital platforms to counter disinformation;
- Strengthening of the Privacy Act and broad reform of Australian privacy law including introduction of a statutory tort for serious invasions of privacy;
- Stable and adequate funding for public broadcasting;
- Grants for local journalism;
- Tax incentives to encourage philanthropic support for journalism;
- Improving digital media literacy in the community including school programs.[268]

Regulatory and legislative action have been taken in a number of other countries including Germany, which introduced legislation in 2017 that forces digital platforms to delete hate speech and misinformation and disinformation within 24 hours of notification. Indonesia has established a government agency to monitor online news and "tackle fake news". The Philippines has introduced a bill that proposes prison sentences of up to five years for those who publish or distribute "fake news" and disinformation.[269] Nevertheless, much of the problem with social media platforms originates in the libertarian philosophies of Silicon Valley and many see a need for US regulators and legislators to take a lead in introducing tougher regulation or legislation, particularly as the biggest offenders are US corporations.

Despite the US Government's strong commitment to deregulation and the affordances of the US Constitution, the relationship between Washington, D.C. and the "big four" information technology companies—Facebook, Amazon, Google (which includes YouTube) and Apple—has soured in the wake of Facebook's indiscretion in handing over the personal data of users to Cambridge Analytica; disclosure that its platform had been manipulated by Russian propagandists to spread disinformation and undermine democracy; its failure to take down content such as the killer's video of the Christchurch mosque massacre; and the hosting of damaging deepfake videos. Also, US legislators are concerned about biases in the algorithms used by Facebook, Google, and other social media platforms that filter news and information in ways that create *echo chambers* and polarization in society. During 2019, more than a dozen Congressional hearings produced apologies and commitments to prevent further harm from Zuckerberg and Big Tech executives and lawyers, but watchdogs and civil society advocates say that Facebook and others have not gone far enough.

In response to rising criticism of the behaviour of big technology companies, the US Department of Justice began investigating whether the likes of Google (owned by Alphabet Inc.), Facebook Inc., Amazon.com, and potentially others such as Apple Inc., are using their dominant market power to stifle competition and engaging in other behaviours that are to the detriment of consumers of their services. For example, concerns that Google harms competitors by favouring its own products in search results and on the Android platform and that it unfairly exploits its dominant position in advertising are growing internationally. In 2018, European anti-trust regulators fined Google €4.34 billion (US$5 billion) and ordered it to stop using its Android platform to block competitors. Legislators in the EU argued that Google forced device manufacturers that use the Android operating systems, to pre-install Google applications, blocking out competitors' applications.[270] This came on the back of a €2.4 billion (US$2.65 billion) fine by the EU for anti-competitive practices in 2017.[271]

In July 2019, after years of investigating Facebook's release of its users' data to Cambridge Analytica, the FTC imposed a US$5 billion fine—the largest in FTC history. US$5 billion sounds like a big fine and a significant incentive to act responsibly

However, professor of media studies from the University of Virginia, Siva Vaidhyanathan, explained in *The Guardian* that Facebook made almost US$17 billion profit in just one quarter of 2019 and pointed out that, at that rate, Facebook would earn enough to pay its fines in just 27 days of trading.[272] So fines are unlikely to be the answer.

Some US reviews have called for a new "digital authority" to regulate social media and other digital platforms.[273] But Philip Napoli believes that, while there is a case for regulation, a new authority is not needed or appropriate. Napoli says that regulation of digital platforms needs to address not only concerns about competition, but also broader "social welfare concerns". He says the Federal Communications Commission (FCC) is the appropriate body because its "regulatory mandate includes not only assuring adequate competition in the electronic media sector but also assuring that the broader public interest is being served."[274] The issue, according to Napoli, is that like media regulators in many countries, the FCC has been narrowly focussed on broadcasting and specific issues such as broadcast licences, which he described as "anachronistic" in an age of new and increasingly dominant forms of electronic media. Napoli also points out that the reason that broadcasting is regulated despite Constitutional rights and conventions for freedom of the media is that the broadcast spectrum (radio waves) are considered to be a *public resource* owned by the people. It can be similarly argued that the core assets of social media and digital platforms are user data, which Napoli says "can and should be thought of as a public resource that is owned by the people"[275]—although who owns our personal data after we have given it away online is a pertinent question. Even if Napoli's claim that user data comprise a public resource is disputed, social and digital media companies operate on the internet and the World Wide Web that were largely built with public funds.[276] Hence, there is every justification that they should be treated like broadcasting, as Sean Larkins argues.

Notwithstanding the identified harms caused by social media monopolies, caution is highly recommended in drafting and passing regulations and legislation. A headlong rush to regulation and legislation based on popular opinion and moral panic is fraught with danger. For example, in April 2019 Singapore became one of the first countries in the world to put proposed anti-fake news law before its parliament. The *Protection from Online Falsehoods and Manipulation*

Bill, passed in May 2019, proposes that the government can issue take down notices that require removal of content posted on social media platforms or news sites; demand "correction notices" alongside content it deems false; and facilitate complaints through the courts to require content to be deleted from websites.[277] Journalists, media academics, and human rights activists immediately warned that such sweeping law could put the power of censorship in the hands of government. *The Business Times* in Singapore warned that regulating social media is a "slippery slope." Writing in Singapore's business newspaper, Peter Suderman said calls for regulation are "understandable" given the reach and influence of major social platforms, but he said such calls are "mistaken and even dangerous, because at its core is a view that speech is not an individual right, but a collective good that should be subject to political control."[278] In simple terms, if governments have the power to remove content from social media and websites including news sites, how long will it be before such power is used to silence opposition and criticism, resulting in autocracy or even totalitarianism? An editorial in the *Washington Post* asked in its headline: "Is Singapore fighting fake news or free speech?"[279] Singapore's Prime Minister, Lee Hsien Loong rejected claims that the law will be used to restrict free speech and political opposition, but many remain unconvinced.

Director of research at Leeds Business School, Ralph Tench, is one who cautions against reliance on government-enacted legislation and regulation. He says self-regulation is ideal and warns that "state or judicial control is not risk free" saying it "places too high a moral responsibility and ownership on those with the power within the system." He is of the view that governments are part of the problem as much or more than they are part of the solution, saying: "Sadly, worldwide, political systems demonstrate that manipulation of fact or information is a normalized state for institutional players, especially government."[280] In short, who wants to give ultimate control to governments when governments are often among the chief perpetrators of disinformation, deception, and manipulation?

An in-between approach discussed by Australian professor of media and communications, Terry Flew, is *co-regulation* through what is termed 'soft law'. Soft law is a quasi-legal process derived from international law in which regulators set general rules and laws and industry or professional bodies "oversee the operational dimensions of their application, subject to oversight from the government regulators."[281] In short, co-regulation is a combination of self-regulation and regulation by 'hard law'. However, to have 'teeth', co-regulation requires oversight by an independent public agency that is trusted by the parties involved and by the public.

Whichever approach is taken, Flew concludes that "the days of unregulated or self-regulated digital platforms appear to be coming to an end, at least for the largest platforms."[282]

Algorithmic Accountability

A key area for regulatory and legislative attention is the use of algorithms. They are increasingly ubiquitous and, in the main, can make life easier for people by automating many basic tasks such as unlocking smart phones using facial recognition; recommending books, movies, and music based on stored user preferences; and assisting drivers of motor vehicles with lane keeping guidance and other intelligent systems. Algorithms also increasingly automate the processing of bank loan applications and credit rating calculations, saving time and costs for companies and users. However, as discussed in Chapter 4, there is increasing concern that algorithms can cause biased and discriminatory outcomes. Also, the 'black box' nature of algorithms—the secret code and data used to 'teach' algorithms that are not available for scrutiny or correction by those affected—is a major concern because it results in little or no opportunity to review or appeal decisions.

In 2019, the *Algorithmic Accountability Act* was introduced in the United States to address algorithmic and privacy harms caused by automated decision systems. The act authorizes the FTC to issue regulations that it deems necessary and also it requires companies that use algorithms to conduct automated decision systems impact assessments (ADSIA). The Act has been generally welcomed. But, as at the end of 2019, it has not been passed and enacted into law and it has been criticized as inadequate. For example, the Center for Data Innovation says the Act as drafted "misses the mark, primarily by holding algorithms to different standards than humans, not considering the non-linear nature of software development, and targeting only large firms despite the equal potential for small firms to cause harm." The Center points out that the legislation will only apply to "high-risk automated decision systems" and companies with more than US$50 million in revenue.[283]

Following an Algorithm Assessment Report released in 2018, the New Zealand government launched a draft *Algorithm Charter* that commits government agencies to "improving transparency and accountability in their use of algorithms over the next five years."[284] It was posted online for public consultation in October 2019. It is to be hoped that industry will follow suit, given that companies involved in sales and marketing are the chief users of algorithms.

Anti-Trust Action—The Big Stick

A number of voices are calling for legislators to go as far as anti-trust action to break up media giants such as Facebook, which owns Instagram, WhatsApp, Messenger, FriendFeed, and Oculus VR among many other applications and services.[285] In a stinging and highly significant statement in a May 2019 opinion article in the *New York Times*, the co-founder of Facebook, Chris Hughes, called for the US Government to break up the tech giant. Hughes is reported to have told *NBC News* after the editorial:

> The Facebook that exists today is not the Facebook that we founded in 2004 … the one that we have today I think is far too big. It's far too powerful. And most importantly, its CEO, Mark Zuckerberg, is not accountable.[286]

There are precedents for such action, such as the break up of US telephone giant AT&T in the early 1980s. The US FTC considered anti-trust action again internet oligopolies as early as 2012 when a report from the agency's Bureau of Competition recommended an anti-trust law suit against Google. However, this recommendation was dropped in 2013 after a deal was struck, much to the chagrin of some FTC investigators and commentators.[287] Governments are reluctant to take the drastic action of breaking up a company. As Teddy Schleifer wrote in critical analysis of Big Tech:

> It took Wall Street's subprime mortgage crisis to incite Congress to pass the Dodd-Frank legislation that tried to reform how our country's financial system worked. And it was only after the Watergate scandal that Washington created the Federal Election Commission to more closely govern campaign finance law.[288]

Beyond this brief review of regulatory and legislative developments and issues, this analysis leaves this area to specialists in relevant law for further discussion and recommendations. What is relevant to and evident from this analysis is (1) there are a number of other strategies and initiatives that can and should be implemented and (2) there is a need to balance regulation and legislation with the fundamental principles of freedom of speech and freedom of media.

Freedom of Speech and of Media

In the USA these important freedoms are enshrined in the First Amendment to the Constitution, which states:

Congress shall make no law respecting an establishment of religion, or prohibiting the free exercise thereof; or abridging the freedom of speech, or of the press; or the right of the people peaceably to assemble, and to petition the government for a redress of grievances.[289]

In many other countries there are no constitutional rights to freedom of speech and freedom of media. Furthermore, existing laws and the current power of authorities concern many involved in politics, media, and public communication. For example, in Australia, a country in the top 10 most democratic countries in the world according to The Economist Intelligence Unit Democracy Index, the events of June 2019 in which AFP officers raided the premises of the country's national broadcaster and the home of a journalist sent shock waves through the nation's media and journalists worldwide. On 6 June 2019, the police searched more than 9,000 computer files of two journalists, Dan Oakes and Sam Clark. The warrant was based on claims that Oakes and Clark had unlawfully obtained secret information in their 2017 reporting of the activities of Australian elite special forces in Afghanistan, which included allegations that they had killed unarmed women and children.[290]

The day before, the AFP raided the Canberra home of News Corp journalist, Annika Smethurst, who had published articles alleging that Australia's intelligence agencies were lobbying to increase the powers of the Australian Signals Directorate, an intelligence unit that monitors overseas conversations over telecommunications networks but was prevented from monitoring conversations of Australians in Australia under laws in force at the time. Furthermore, it was revealed that the Federal Police were scheduled to raid the headquarters of News Corp in Sydney following the ABC raid. This third raid was called off when live tweeting and media reporting caused outrage at what was widely seen as a direct attack on the freedom of media and public interest journalism.[291]

The reverberations of police raids on the ABC and the home of a News Corp journalist went around the world and are likely to continue for some time. In July 2019, international human rights lawyer, Amal Clooney, who was appointed the UK's first Special Envoy on Media Freedom in April 2019, spoke out saying that the ABC newsroom raid was an example of global challenges to freedom of speech. Clooney told the inaugural Defend Media Freedom conference in London that governments must "make sure that their laws respect media freedom and that their police, prosecutors, judges and citizens do the same." She noted that "all governments say they believe in a free press—the right is even enshrined in North Korea's constitution." She concluded: "What matters is enforcement of this right."[292]

The Need for Balance

The importance of freedom of speech and free media mean that balance is required. Heavy-handed over-regulation and legislation are likely to have negative overall impact of democratic societies, potentially increasing unchecked propaganda and disinformation by governments. Furthermore, the challenges raised by transnational networks, datafication, AI, and related technologies and practices discussed in this analysis are complex. As a result, hastily drafted regulations and legislation are likely to cause more problems than they solve. Further still, most media and communication professionals and legal experts argue that existing laws provide significant protections and these should be used before rushing into new legislation.

Carrots and Sticks

Having said that, governments can use a mix of 'carrots' and 'sticks'. The threat of regulation or legislation is often enough to prompt industry to improve standards and introduce greater governance. Conversely, industries often will not self-regulate adequately unless threatened with regulation and legislation. Therefore, governments must at least investigate regulatory and legal sanctions and be prepared to act if technology platforms and practices fail to responsibly self-regulate. Carrots can include freedom to develop and make profits without restrictive bureaucracy, as well as incentives in some cases, such as funding to support public interest journalism and public broadcasting, and policies to enable ethical data sharing that facilitates entrepreneurial initiatives and innovation.

Notes

1. Bauman, Z., & Donskis, L. (2013). *Moral blindness: The loss of sensitivity in liquid modernity*. Cambridge, UK: Polity, p. 10.
2. Bohm, D. (1996). *On dialogue* (L. Nichol, Ed.). New York, NY: Routledge; Broome, B. (2009). Dialogue theories. In S. Littlejohn & K. Foss (Eds.), *Encyclopedia of communication theory* (pp. 301–305). Los Angeles, CA: Sage Publications, p. 305.
3. van Ruler, B. (2020). Communication theory: An underrated pillar on which strategic communication rests. In H. Northhaft, K. Page Werder, D. Verčič, &

A. Zerfass (Eds.), *Future directions in strategic communication* (pp. 39–53). Abingdon, UK: Routledge.
4. Craig, R. (2018). For a practical discipline. *Journal of Communication, 68*(2), 289–297, pp. 289–290.
5. American Friends Service Committee & Rustin, B. (1955). *Speak truth to power: A Quaker search for an alternative to violence*. USA: Author. Retrieved from https://afsc.org/document/speak-truth-power
6. Hampton, M. (2009). The fourth estate ideal in journalism history. In S. Allan (Ed.), *The Routledge companion to news and journalism* (pp. 3–12). Abingdon, UK: Routledge.
7. Bennett, W., & Serrin, W. (2011). The watchdog role of the press. In D. Graber (Ed.), *Media power in politics* (pp. 395–405). Washington, D.C.: CQ Press. (Original work published in 2005)
8. Wahl-Jorgensen, K., & Hanitzsch, T. (2020). Journalism studies: Developments, challenges and future directions. In K. Wahl-Jorgensen & T. Hanitzsch (Eds.), *Handbook of journalism studies* (2nd ed., pp. 3–20). New York, NY: Routledge.
9. Bennett, W., & Serrin, W. (2011). The watchdog role of the press. In D. Graber (Ed.), *Media power in politics* (pp. 395–405), Sage Publications, p. 397. (Original work published in 2005)
10. Ibid., p. 400–402.
11. Ibid., p. 402.
12. Davies, N. (2009). *Flat earth news*. London, UK: Random House; Gans, H. (1979). *Deciding what's news: A study of CBS evening news, NBC nightly news, Newsweek and Time*. New York, NY: Vintage; Macnamara, J. (2014). *Journalism and PR: Unpacking 'spin', stereotypes and media myths*. New York, NY: Peter Lang; Sigal, L. (1973). *Reporters and officials*. Lexington, MA: D.C. Heath; Sigal, L. (1986). Who? Sources make the news. In R. Manoff & M. Schudson (Eds.), *Reading the news* (pp. 9–37). New York, NY: Pantheon Books.
13. Jenkins, H. (2006). *Convergence culture: Where old and new media collide*. New York, NY: New York University Press, pp. 238, 243.
14. Fray, P. (2019, September 10). A crisis for professional journalism. Presentation to Affinity Alan Knight Media Series seminar, Sydney.
15. Davies, 2009, p. 194.
16. Ibid., p. 203.
17. Macnamara, 2014, pp. 120–128.
18. Kavanagh, J., & Rich, M. (2019). *Truth decay: An initial exploration of the diminishing role of facts and analysis in American public life*. Santa Monica, CA: RAND Corporation, p. 27.
19. Logan, L. (2019, February 26). Political bias is destroying people's faith in journalism. *New York Post*, Opinion, para. 10. Retrieved from https://nypost.com/2019/02/26/political-bias-is-destroying-peoples-faith-in-journalism

20. Peters, T. (1986). What gets measured gets done. *Tom Peters! Writing*. Retrieved from https://tompeters.com/columns/what-gets-measured-gets-done
21. P. Fray (personal communication [interview], September 12, 2019).
22. Despite referring to PR disparagingly as "the dark side", many journalists and even senior editors 'cross over' to work in PR. See, for example, Bonazzo, J., & Kaminer, M. (2015, December 17). Journalists who crossed over to work in PR. *The Observer*. Retrieved from https://observer.com/2015/12/journalists-who-crossed-over-into-pr-in-2015
23. Deuze, M. (2007). *Media work*. Malden, MA: Polity.
24. Google News Labs is now part of the Google News Initiative.
25. Kwan, V. (2019, October). Responsible reporting in an age of information disorder. *First Draft*. Retrieved from https://firstdraftnews.org/wp-content/uploads/2019/10/Responsible_Reporting_Digital_AW-1.pdf?x88639
26. A. Kruger (personal communication [interview], October 9, 2019).
27. Anderson, C., Bell, E., & Shirky, C. (2014). *Post-industrial journalism: Adapting to the present*. New York, NY: Tow Center for Digital Journalism, Columbia Journalism School, Columbia University. Retrieved from https://academiccommons.columbia.edu/doi/10.7916/D8N01JS7
28. Thurman, N. (2020). Computational journalism. In K. Wahl-Jorgensen & T. Hanitzsch (Eds.), *The handbook of journalism studies* (pp. 180–195). New York, NY: Routledge.
29. Chipman, I. (2017, December 12). *What is the future of computational journalism?* Stanford, CA: Stanford University. Retrieved from https://engineering.stanford.edu/magazine/article/what-future-computational-journalism
30. A. Kruger (personal communication [interview], September 20, 2019).
31. Deuze, M., & Witschge, T. (2018). Beyond journalism: Theorizing the transformation of journalism. *Journalism*, *19*(2), 165–181, p. 170.
32. Rosen, J. (1999). *What are journalists for?* New Haven, CT: Yale University Press.
33. Schudson, M. (1999). What public journalism knows about journalism but doesn't know about 'public'. In T. Glasser (Ed.), *The idea of public journalism* (pp. 118–133). New York, NY: The Guilford Press.
34. Rosenberry, J., & St. John III, B. (Eds.). (2010). *Public journalism 2.0: The promise and reality of a citizen-engaged press*. New York, NY: Routledge.
35. Nip, J. (2008). The last days of civic journalism: The case of the Savannah Morning News. *Journalism Practice*, *2*(2), 179–196.
36. Schultz, T. (1999). Interactive options in online journalism: A content analysis of 100 US newspapers. *Journal of Computer-Mediated Communication*, *5*(1), n.p. Retrieved from https://onlinelibrary.wiley.com/doi/full/10.1111/j.1083-6101.1999.tb00331.x
37. Rosen, J. (1999). *What are journalists for?* New Haven, CT: Yale University Press.
38. Nip, J. (2006). Exploring the second phase of public journalism. *Journalism Studies*, *7*(2), 212–236.

39. Beckett, C., & Mansell, R. (2008). Crossing boundaries: New media and networked journalism. *Communication, Culture & Critique, 1*(1), 92–104; Van Der Haak, B., Parks, M., & Castells, M. (2012). The future of journalism: Networked journalism. *International Journal of Communication, 6*, 2923–2938.
40. Dutton, W., & Dubois, E. (2015). The fifth estate: A rising force of pluralistic accountability. In S. Coleman & D. Freelon (Eds.), *Handbook of digital politics* (pp. 51–66). Cheltenham, UK: Edward Elgar.
41. Park, J. (2019). *News media innovation 2020*. Sydney, NSW: Centre for Media Transition. Retrieved from https://www.uts.edu.au/sites/default/files/article/downloads/innovation%20final%2029_10%20hi%20res.pdf
42. Packard, V. (2020). *Democracy without journalism: Confronting the misinformation society*. New York, NY: Oxford University Press.
43. Macnamara, 2014, pp. 10, 15.
44. Macnamara, 2014.
45. Macnamara, J. (2014b). Journalism—PR relations revisited: The good news, the bad news, and insights into tomorrow's news. *Public Relations Review, 40*, 739–750, p. 743.
46. T. Manus (personal communication [interview], September 26, 2019).
47. Davis, A. (2013). *Promotional cultures: The rise and spread of advertising, public relations, marketing and branding*. Cambridge, UK: Polity.
48. Matchett, S. (2010, July 14). The profession that dare not speak its name. *The Australian*, Higher Education, p. 26.
49. Davies, 2009, p. 203.
50. Ibid., pp. 172–193.
51. McChesney, R. (2013). *Digital disconnect: How capitalism is turning the internet against democracy*. New York, NY: The Free Press.
52. McCrystal, D. (2008). It's more fun on the 'dark side'. *British Journalism Review, 19*(2), 47–51, p. 47.
53. Day, M. (2013, May 27). Bitter pill for spin doctors. *The Australian*. Retrieved from http://www.theaustralian.com.au/archive/media/bitter-pill-for-spin-doctors/story-e6frg9tf-1226650913146#mm-premium
54. Russell, C. (2008, November 14). Science reporting by press release. *Columbia Journalism Review*, para 2. Retrieved from http://www.cjr.org/the_observatory/science_reporting_by_press_rel.php
55. Harcup, T. (2009). *Journalism: Principles and practices* (2nd ed.). London, UK: Sage Publications, p. 32.
56. In the propaganda model of media described by Herman and Chomsky, 'flak' is one of five filters that influence media. See Herman, E., & Chomsky, N. (1988). *Manufacturing consent: The political economy of the mass media*. New York, NY: Pantheon Books. Also discussed as 'flacks' in Stegall, S., & Sanders, K. (1986).

Co-orientation of PR practitioners and news personnel in education news. *Journalism Quarterly*, *63*(2), 341–347.
57. Bleyer, W. (1973). *Main currents in the history of American journalism.* New York, NY: Da Capo Press, p. 421. (Original work published 1927)
58. Grunig, J., & Hunt, T. (1984). *Managing public relations.* Orlando, FL: Holt, Rinehart & Winston, p. 28.
59. Grunig & Hunt, 1984, p. 34.
60. Guth, D., & Marsh, C. (2007). *Public relations: A values-driven approach* (3rd ed.). Boston, MA: Pearson, p. 70.
61. Goldman, E. (1948). *Two-way street: The emergence of the public relations counsel.* Boston, MA: Bellman Publishing Company.
62. Cornelissen, J. (2017). *Corporate communication: A guide to theory and practice.* London, UK: Sage Publications, p. 4; Meng, J., Reber, B., Berger, B., Gower, K., & Zerfass, A. (2019). *North American Communication Monitor 2018-2019. Tracking trends in fake news, issues management, leadership performance, work stress, social media skills, job satisfaction and work environment.* Tuscaloosa, AL: The Plank Center for Leadership in Public Relations, p. 37; Zerfass, A., Tench, R., Verhoeven, P., Verčič, D., & Moreno, A. (2018). *European Communication Monitor 2018. Strategic communication and the challenges of fake news, trust, leadership, work stress and job satisfaction. Results of a survey in 48 countries.* Brussels: EACD/EUPRERA, Quadriga Media Berlin, p. 37.
63. Grunig & Hunt, 1984.
64. Newcomb, T. (1953). An approach to the study of communicative acts. *Psychological Review*, *60*, 393–404.
65. Heider, F. (1946). Attitudes and cognitive organisation. *Journal of Psychology*, *21*, 107–112.
66. Festinger, L. (1957). *A theory of cognitive dissonance.* Palo Alto, CA: Stanford University Press.
67. Peters, T., & Waterman, R. Jr. (1982). *In search of excellence.* New York, NY: Warner.
68. The real confessions of Tom Peters. (2001, December 3). *Bloomberg BusinessWeek.* Retrieved from https://www.bloomberg.com/news/articles/2001-12-02/the-real-confessions-of-tom-peters; Grunig, J., Grunig, L., & Dozier, D. (2006). The excellence theory. In C. Botan & V. Hazelton (Eds.), *Public relations theory II* (pp. 21–62). Mahwah, NJ: Lawrence Erlbaum, p. 26.
69. Grunig, L., Grunig J., & Dozier, D. (2002). *Excellent organisations and effective organisations: A study of communication management in three countries.* Mahwah, NJ: Lawrence Erlbaum.
70. Murphy, P. (1991). Limits of symmetry. In J. Grunig & L. Grunig (Eds.), *Public relations research annual* (Vol. 3, pp. 115–131). Hillsdale, NJ: Lawrence Erlbaum.
71. Cameron, G. (1997). The contingency theory of conflict management in public relations. Proceedings of the Norwegian Information Service, Oslo, Norway;

Wilcox, D., & Cameron, G. (2010). *Public relations: Strategies and tactics* (9th ed.). Boston, MA: Allyn & Bacon, pp. 59, 251–252.

72. Pieczka, M. (2006). Paradigms, systems theory and public relations. In J. L'Etang & M. Pieczka (Eds.), *Public relations: Critical debates and contemporary practice* (pp. 331–358). Mahwah, NJ: Lawrence Erlbaum, pp. 349–350.
73. Watson, T., & Noble, P. (2007). *Evaluating public relations: A best practice guide to public relations planning, research and evaluation* (2nd ed.). London, UK: Kogan Page, p. 14.
74. Macnamara, J. (2016). *Organizational listening: The missing essential in public communication.* New York, NY: Peter Lang.
75. Edwards, L., & Hodges, C. (Eds.). (2011). *Public relations, society and culture: Theoretical and empirical explorations.* Abingdon, UK: Routledge, p. 3.
76. Edwards, L. (2018). *Understanding public relations: Theory, culture and society.* London, UK: Sage Publications.
77. Taylor, M. (2018). Reconceptualizing public relations in an engaged society. In K. Johnston & M. Taylor (Eds.), *The handbook of communication engagement* (pp. 103–114). Hoboken, NJ: Wiley Blackwell.
78. Ibid., p. 108.
79. Cornelissen, 2017; Van Riel, C., & Fombrun, C. (2007). *Essentials of corporate communications.* New York, NY: Routledge; Zerfass, A. (2008). Corporate communication revisited: Integrating business strategies and strategic communication. In A. Zerfass, B. van Ruler, & K. Sriramesh (Eds.). *Public relations research* (pp. 65–96). Wiesbaden: VS Verlag für Sozialwissenschaften.
80. Van Ruler, B., & Verčič, D. (2005). Reflective communication management, future ways for public relations research. In P. Kalbfleisch (Ed.), *Communication yearbook, 29* (pp. 238–273). Mahwah, NJ: Lawrence Erlbaum.
81. Aarts, N., & Van Woerkum, C. (2008). *Strategische communicatie* [Strategic communication]. Assen, Holland: Van Gorcum; Holtzhausen, D., & Zerfass, A. (Eds.). (2015). *The Routledge handbook of strategic communication.* New York, NY: Routledge.
82. Schoeneborn, D. (2011). Organization as communication: A Luhmannian perspective. *Management Communication Quarterly, 25*(4), 663–689.
83. Vásquez, C., & Schoeneborn, D. (2018). Communication as constitutive of organization. In R. Heath & W. Johansen (Eds.), *The international encyclopedia of strategic communication* (pp. 1–12). Malden, MA: John Wiley & Sons.
84. Schoeneborn, D., Kuhn, T., & Kärreman, D. (2019). The communicative constitution of organization: Organizing and organizationality. *Organization Studies, 40*(4), 475–496.
85. Mumby, D., & Kuhn, T. (2019). *Organizational communication: A critical introduction* (2nd ed.). Thousand Oaks, CA: Sage Publications.
86. Johansson, C. (2007). Research on organizational communication: The case of Sweden. *Nordicom Review, 28*(1), pp. 93–110, p. 93. Retrieved from https://www.

degruyter.com/downloadpdf/j/nor.2007.28.issue-1/nor-2017-0203/nor-2017-0203.pdf
87. Cornelissen, 2017, p. 5.
88. Grunig, J. (Ed.). (1992). *Excellence in public relations and communication management*. Hillsdale, NJ: Lawrence Erlbaum; Toth, E. (Ed.). (2007). *The future of excellence in public relations and communication management: Challenges for the next generation*. Mahwah, NJ: Lawrence Erlbaum.
89. Grunig & Hunt, 1984, p. 6.
90. Cornelissen, 2017, p. 4.
91. Page Werder, K., Nothhaft, H., Verčič, D., & Zerfass, A. (2020). Strategic communication as an emerging interdisciplinary paradigm. In H. Nothhaft, K. Page Werder, D. Verčič, & A. Zerfass (Eds.), *Future directions of strategic communication* (pp. 5–23). Abingdon, UK: Routledge.
92. Holtzhausen, D., & Zerfass, A. (Eds.) (2015). *The Routledge handbook of strategic communication*. New York, NY: Routledge.
93. Page Werder et al., 2020.
94. Hallahan, K., Holtzhausen, D., van Ruler, B., Verčič, D., & Sriramesh, K. (2007). Defining strategic communication. *International Journal of Strategic Communication, 1*(1), 3–35, p. 9.
95. Hallahan et al. 2007, p. 3.
96. Ibid., p. 13.
97. Holtzhausen, D. (2005). Public relations practice and political change in South Africa. *Public Relations Review, 31*(3), 407–416.
98. Deetz, S. (1992). *Democracy in an age of corporate colonization: Developments in communication and the politics of everyday life*. New York, NY: State University of New York. In this text, Deetz advocates that communication should involve engagement with and participation of those addressed (i.e., be two-way), but also notes that in some circumstances a focus on effectively achieving persuasion of others (one-way) is justified.
99. Mintzberg, H., & Waters, J. (1985). Of strategies, deliberate and emergent. *Strategic Management Journal, 6*(2), 257–272; Mintzberg, H., Lampel, J., Quinn, J., & Ghoshal, S. (2003). *The strategy process: Concepts, context, cases* (4th ed.). Upper Saddle River, NJ: Prentice Hall.
100. Falkheimer, J., & Heide, M. (2015). Strategic communication in participatory culture: From one- and two-way communication to participatory communication through social media. In D. Holtzhausen & A. Zerfass (Eds.), *The Routledge handbook of strategic communication* (pp. 337–350). New York, NY: Routledge.
101. Torp, S. (2015). The strategic turn in communication science: On the history and role of strategy in science from ancient Greece until the present day. In D. Holtzhausen & A. Zerfass (Eds.), *The Routledge handbook of strategic communication* (pp. 34–52). New York, NY: Routledge.

102. Murphy, P. (2015). Contextual distortion: Strategic communication versus the contextual nature or nearly everything. In D. Holtzhausen & A. Zerfass (Eds.), *The Routledge handbook of strategic communication* (pp. 113–126). New York, NY: Routledge.
103. King, C. (2010). Emergent communication strategies. *International Journal of Strategic Communication, 4*(1), 19–38.
104. Murphy, 2015.
105. Buhmann, A., & Likely, F. (2018). Evaluation and measurement in strategic communication. In R. Heath & W. Johansen (Eds.), *The international encyclopedia of strategic communication* (pp. 1–16). New York, NY: Wiley-Blackwell.
106. Heath, R., Johansen, W., Hallahan, K., Steyn, B., Falkheimer, J., & Raupp, J. (2018). Strategic communication. In R. Heath & W. Johansen (Eds.), *The international encyclopedia of strategic communication* (pp. 1–24). Hoboken, NJ: Wiley-Blackwell, p. 12.
107. Everitt, A. (2018). The rise of social purpose and its impact on brand success. *Journal of Digital & Social Media Marketing, 6*(3), 221–227. Retrieved from https://www.ingentaconnect.com/content/hsp/jdsmm/2018/00000006/00000003/art00004
108. Fink. L. (2019). Purpose and profit. The 2019 Larry Fink letter to CEOs. BlackRock. Retrieved from https://www.blackrock.com/corporate/investor-relations/larry-fink-ceo-letter
109. Business Roundtable. (2019). Statement on the purpose of a corporation. Retrieved from https://opportunity.businessroundtable.org/wp-content/uploads/2019/08/Business-Roundtable-Statement-on-the-Purpose-of-a-Corporation-with-Signatures.pdf
110. Arthur W. Page Society and Business Roundtable Institute for Corporate Ethics. (2009). *The dynamics of public trust in business—Emerging opportunities for leaders: A call to action to overcome the present crisis of trust in business*. New York, NY. Retrieved from https://knowledge.page.org/report/the-dynamics-of-public-trust-in-business-emerging-opportunities-for-leaders
111. Ibid., n.p., Foreword.
112. Macnamara, J., & Gregory, A. (2018). Expanding evaluation to progress strategic communication: Beyond message tracking to open listening. *International Journal of Strategic Communication, 12*(4), 469–486.
113. Guth, D., & Marsh, C. (2007). *Public relations: A values-driven approach* (3rd ed.). Boston, MA: Pearson, p. 70. While Guth and Marsh and others make this claim, critics point out that Bernays represents an American concept of public relations and that the practice pre-dates Bernays and has existed in other countries in various forms.
114. L. Held (personal communication [interview], 28 August 28, 2019).
115. Macnamara, J. (2012). *Public relations theories, practices, critiques*. Frenchs Forest, NSW: Pearson, p. 448.

116. Grunig & Hunt, 1984, p. 9.
117. Bailey, R. (2019, September 3). *Review: Rethinking public relations*. London, UK: PR Academy, para. 5. Retrieved from https://pracademy.co.uk/insights/review-rethinking-public-relations
118. Ibid., para. 6.
119. Moloney, K., & McGrath, C. (2020). *Rethinking public relations: Persuasion, democracy and society* (3rd ed.). Abingdon, UK: Routlege.
120. Kelly, A. (2017, June 9). Alan Kelly on PR's hidden truth: It's competitive and nobody wants to admit it. *The Measurement Standard*, para. 8. Retrieved from http://www.themeasurementstandard.com/2017/06/alan-kelly-on-prs-hidden-truth-its-competitive-offensive-and-nobody-wants-to-admits-it
121. Ibid., para. 10.
122. Ibid., para. 4.
123. Ibid., para. 9.
124. Ibid., para. 11.
125. A. Kelly (personal communication [interview], May 27, 2019).
126. Hall, S. (2018, July 6). Speech to Bledcom, Slovenia, para. 5. Retrieved from http://www.sarahhallconsulting.co.uk/blog/2018/7/6/a-world-in-crisis-the-role-of-public-relations
127. Edwards, L. (2018). *Understanding public relations: Theory, culture and society*. London, UK: Sage Publications, p. 198.
128. Peacock. C. (2019, September 22). Expert says PR needs an ethical upgrade. *RNZ* [Radio New Zealand], para. 13. Retrieved from https://www.rnz.co.nz/national/programmes/mediawatch/audio/2018713710/expert-says-pr-needs-an-ethical-upgrade
129. Ibid., paras 18–19, 24.
130. Saks, W. (2012). Defining a profession: The role of knowledge and expertise. *Professions and Professionalism*, 2(1), 1–10. There is wide debate on the criteria that constitute a profession, but most agree that factors beyond knowledge and expertise are required.
131. Hall, 2018, para. 12.
132. S. Bruce (personal communication [interview], September 6, 2019).
133. Public Relations and Communication Association (PRCA). (2019). My life as an ethics girl in PR [Web log post]. Retrieved from https://www.prca.org.uk/MyLifeAsAnEthicsGirlInPR
134. Norwegian Communication Association. (2019). New ethical principles for communicators. Retrieved from https://www.kommunikasjon.no/fagstoff/nyheter/nye-etiske-prinsipper
135. T. Manus (personal communication [interview], October 2, 2019).
136. Wanja, C. (2019, November 14). Government set to invest Kshs 350 million for officers training. *KBC*. Retrieved from https://www.kbc.co.ke/government-set-to-invest-kshs-350-million-for-officers-training

137. Wynne, R. (2016, January 21). Five things you should know about public relations. *Forbes*, para. 1. Retrieved from https://www.forbes.com/sites/robertwynne/2016/01/21/five-things-everyone-should-know-about-public-relations/#19bae2382a2c
138. Magri, E., Mandanna, N., Najak, K., & Singh, R. (2019, Spring). Are public relations associations sustainable? *Public Relations Dialogues*. Toronto, Canada: Seneca College, p. 20.
139. Wright, D. (2019). Comment in Magri et al. (2019), p. 20.
140. A. Gregory (personal communication [interview], August 14, 2019).
141. Field, A. (2018, August 7). PR and the problem of truth decay: It's a matter of trust. Institute for Public Relations [Web log post], para. 5. Retrieved from https://instituteforpr.org/pr-and-the-problem-of-truth-decay-its-a-matter-of-trust
142. Ibid., para. 6.
143. Ibid., para. 8.
144. Ibid., para. 5.
145. T. Manus (personal communication [interview], October 2, 2019).
146. Stefan Kloet (personal communication [interview], November 11, 2019).
147. Friestad, M., & Wright, P. (1994). The persuasion knowledge model: How people cope with persuasion attempts. *Journal of Consumer Research*, *21*(1), 1–31.
148. Macnamara, J. (2014). *Journalism and PR: Unpacking 'spin', stereotypes and media myths*. New York, NY: Peter Lang, p. 57.
149. GE. (2019). *GE Reports*. About us. Retrieved from https://www.ge.com/reports/about
150. Cappetta, M., Collins, B., & Ling Kent, J. (2018, November 16). Facebook hired firm with 'in-house fake news shop' to combat PR crisis. *NBC News*. Retrieved from https://www.nbcnews.com/tech/tech-news/facebook-hired-firm-house-fake-news-shop-combat-pr-crisis-n936591?utm_campaign=The%20Interface&utm_medium=email&utm_source=Revue%20newsletter
151. NTK Network. (2019). About us. Retrieved from https://ntknetwork.com/about-us
152. ASA and CAP. (2019). About ASA and CAP. Retrieved from https://www.asa.org.uk/codes-and-rulings/advertising-codes.html
153. Committee of Advertising Practice and Competition and Markets Authority. (2018). *An influencer's guide to making clear that ads are ads*. London, UK. Retrieved from https://www.asa.org.uk/resource/influencers-guide.html
154. International Chamber of Commerce. (2019). ICC Advertising and Marketing Communications Code. Paris. Retrieved from https://iccwbo.org/publication/icc-advertising-and-marketing-communications-code
155. Direct Marketing Commission. (2008). The DMA Code. London, UK. Retrieved from https://www.dmcommission.com/the-dma-code
156. American Marketing Association. (2019). Codes of conduct. Chicago, IL. Retrieved from https://myama.force.com/s/article/Codes-of-Conduct

157. Australian Direct Marketing Association. (2018). *ADMA code of practice 2018 released*. Sydney, NSW, para. 7. Retrieved from https://www.adma.com.au/compliance/adma-code-of-practice-2018-released
158. N. Nikolova (personal communication [interview], November 5, 2019).
159. Van der Meer, T. (2017). Democratic input, macroeconomic output and political trust. In S. Zmerli & T. van der Meer (Eds.), *Handbook on political trust* (Chapter 17, n.p.). Cheltenham, UK: Edward Elgar.
160. The Open Government Partnership Practice Group on Dialogue and Deliberation. (2019, June). *Informed participation: A guide to designing public deliberation processes*, p. 4. Retrieved from https://www.opengovpartnership.org/documents/deliberation-getting-policy-making-out-from-behind-closed-doors
161. Macnamara, J. (2017). *Creating a 'democracy for everyone': Strategies for increasing listening and engagement by government*. London, UK: The London School of Economics and Political Science, p. 25. Retrieved from http://www.lse.ac.uk/media@lse/research/CreatingADemocracyForEveryone.aspx
162. Arnstein, S. (1969). A ladder of citizen participation. *JAIP*, *35*(4), 216–224.
163. International Association for Public Participation. (2016). *The IAP2 public participation spectrum*. Retrieved from https://www.iap2.org.au/About-Us/About-IAP2-Australasia-/Spectrum
164. The Open Government Partnership (OGP) Practice Group on Dialogue and Deliberation. (2019, May). *Deliberation: Getting policy-making out from behind closed doors*, p. 6. Retrieved from https://www.opengovpartnership.org/documents/deliberation-getting-policy-making-out-from-behind-closed-doors
165. The Open Government Partnership Practice Group on Dialogue and Deliberation, 2019, June, p. 7.
166. op. cit., p. 5.
167. Ibid., p. 7.
168. Gregory, A. (2012). UK Government communications: Full circle in the 21st century? *Public Relations Review*, *38*(3), 367–375.
169. Macnamara, J. (2016). *Organizational listening: The missing essential in public communication*. New York, NY: Peter Lang, p. 210; Macnamara, 2017.
170. Paid panels are composed of people who sign up to participate in research, such as surveys or focus groups, in return for payment. Many paid panels are not constructed using probability sampling and response rates can create further bias.
171. Social Science One. (2019, December 10). Public statement from the co-chairs and European Advisory Committee of Social Science One. Retrieved from https://socialscience.one/blog/public-statement-european-advisory-committee-social-science-one
172. Latonero, M. (2018). *Governing artificial intelligence: Upholding human rights & dignity*. New York, NY: Data and Society Research Institute, p. 1. Retrieved from https://datasociety.net/wp-content/uploads/2018/10/DataSociety_Governing_Artificial_Intelligence_Upholding_Human_Rights.pdf

173. Ibid., p. 2.
174. Finkel, A. (2018, July 24). What kind of society do we want to be? Address to the Human Rights Commission 'Human rights and technology' conference, Sydney, NSW.
175. Couldry, N., & Mejias, U. (2019). *The costs of connection: How data is colonizing human life and appropriating it for capitalism.* Stanford, CA: Stanford University Press, p. 196.
176. Ibid., pp. 203–204.
177. Ibid., pp. 205–206.
178. West, D. (2017, December 18). *How to combat fake news and disinformation.* Washington, D.C.: Brookings Institution, n.p. Retrieved from https://www.brookings.edu/research/how-to-combat-fake-news-and-disinformation
179. Wheeler, T. (2017, November 1). Using 'public interest algorithms' to tackle the problems created by social media algorithms. Washington, D.C.: Brookings Institution *TechTank* [Web log post]. Retrieved from https://www.brookings.edu/blog/techtank/2017/11/01/using-public-interest-algorithms-to-tackle-the-problems-created-by-social-media-algorithms
180. Chen, A. (2019, October 2). Three threats posed by deepfakes that technology won't solve. *MIT Technology Review.* Retrieved from https://www.technologyreview.com/s/614446/deepfake-technology-detection-disinformation-harassment-revenge-porn-law
181. R. Jensen (personal communication [interview], May 28, 2019).
182. During the 2016 US presidential election campaign, Alt-right activists claimed that e-mails by Hilary Clinton's campaign manager published on WikiLeaks contained code words that connected high-ranking Democrat officials with human trafficking and child sex rings and the conspiracy was spread on social media sites including The Real Strategy.
183. Legum, J. (2019, November 6). An explosion of fake news on Facebook. *Popular Information.* Retrieved from https://popular.info/p/an-explosion-of-fake-news-on-facebook
184. Center for Media Literacy. (n.d.). Media literacy: A definition and more. Malibu, CA. Retrieved from http://www.medialit.org/media-literacy-definition-and-more
185. Mihailidis, P. (2014). *Media literacy and the emerging citizen.* New York, NY: Peter Lang, pp. 42–43.
186. National Literary Trust. (2018). *Commission on Fake News and the Teaching of Critical literary in Schools final report.* London, UK: All Party Parliamentary Group on Literacy, p. 4. Retrieved from https://literacytrust.org.uk/research-services/research-reports/fake-news-and-critical-literacy-final-report
187. Livingstone, S. (2018, May 8). Media literacy—Everyone's favourite solution to the problems of regulation. *Media Policy Project* [Web log post], para. 6. Retrieved from https://blogs.lse.ac.uk/mediapolicyproject/2018/05/08/media-literacy-everyones-favourite-solution-to-the-problems-of-regulation

188. P. Fray (personal communication [interview], September 12, 2019).
189. Fray, P. (2019). Alan Knight Media Series seminar, Sydney.
190. Kruger, J., & Dunning, D. (1999). Unskilled and unaware of it: How difficulties in recognizing one's own incompetence lead to inflated self-assessments. *Journal of Personality and Social Psychology, 77*(6), 1121–1134.
191. McIntyre, L. (2018). *Post-truth*. Cambridge, MA: MIT Press, p. 51.
192. McCorkindale, T. (2019). *2019 IPR disinformation in society report*. Gainesville, FL: Institute for Public Relations. Retrieved from https://instituteforpr.org/ipr-disinformation-study, p. 3.
193. Daniel Kahneman is widely credited with identifying and explaining System 1 and System 2 thinking in his book *Thinking Fast and Slow* (2011, Farrar, Straus & Giroux, New York). However, two systems of cognition described as 'central' and 'peripheral' were explained in Petty, R. & Cacioppo, J. (1986). *Communication and persuasion: Central and peripheral routes to attitude change*. New York, NY: Springer. Also, the concepts were described as 'systematic' and 'heuristic' in Chaiken, S., Liberman, A., & Eagly, A. (1989). Heuristic and systematic information within the beyond the persuasion context. In J. Uleman & J. Bargh (Eds.), *Unintended thought* (pp. 212–252). New York, NY: Guildford Press.
194. Pennycook, G., & Rand, D. (2019). Lazy, not biased: Susceptibility to partisan fake news is better explained by lack of reasoning than by motivated reasoning. *Cognition, 188*, 39–50, p. 48.
195. Ibid., p. 39.
196. The term 'gatekeeper' was coined by social psychologist Kurt Lewin. It was used to refer to editors, producers and journalists who control access to and content of media by David Manning White and a number of other media scholars since. See Lewin, K. (1947). Frontiers in group dynamics II: Channels of group life, social planning and action research. *Human Relations, 1*(2), 143–153; White, D. (1950). The gatekeeper: A case study in the selection of news. *Journalism Quarterly, 27*, 383–390. Reprinted in L. Dexter & D. White (Eds.) (1964). *People, society and mass communications*. New York, NY: Free Press.
197. Based on *apo* means alongside, *apomediaries* refers to others who can call out, question, or correct misinformation and disinformation, as an alternative to intermediaries who stand between users and content, commonly referred to as 'gatekeepers' in media literature, such as editors. See Eysenbach, G. (2008). Credibility of health information and digital media: New perspectives and implications for youth. In M. Metzger & A. Flanagin (Eds.), *Digital media, youth and credibility* (pp. 123–154). Cambridge, MA: MIT Press, p. 130.
198. Guess, A., Nyhan, B., & Reifler, J. (2018). Selective exposure to misinformation: Evidence from the consumption of fake news during the 2016 presidential campaign. European Research Council. Retrieved from https://apo.org.au/sites/default/files/resource-files/2018/01/apo-nid126961-1162776.pdf

199. Nyhan, B., & Reifler, J. (2010). When corrections fail: The persistence of political misperceptions. *Political Behaviour, 32*(2), 303–330, p. 303.
200. Novella, S. (2018, January 4). Backfire effect not significant. *Neurologica* [Web log post], para. 2. Retrieved from https://theness.com/neurologicablog/?s=backfire+effect
201. Wood, T., & Porter, E. (2019). The elusive backfire effect: Mass attitudes' steadfast factual adherence. *Political Behavior, 41*(1), 135–163, p. 135.
202. Ecker, U., O'Reilly, Z., Reid, J., & Chang, E. (2019). The effectiveness of short-format refutational fact-checks. *British Journal of Psychology* [online pre-print]. Retrieved from https://onlinelibrary.wiley.com/doi/full/10.1111/bjop.12383
203. N. Nikolova (personal communication [interview], November 5, 2019).
204. Australia's surprising disregard for free speech. (2019, June 15). *The Economist*, para. 2. Retrieved from https://www.economist.com/asia/2019/06/15/australias-surprising-disregard-for-free-speech
205. Knaus, C. (2019, June 6). Whistleblower protections 'a sham', says lawyer whose leaks led to ABC raids. *The Guardian*. Retrieved from https://www.theguardian.com/media/2019/jun/06/whistleblower-protections-a-sham-says-lawyer-whose-leaks-led-to-abc-raids
206. Ibid., para. 1.
207. Lyons, J. (2019, June 8). I live-tweeted the AFP's every move as they raided the ABC's Sydney headquarters. *ABC*, Back Story, paras, 1–4. Retrieved from https://www.abc.net.au/news/about/backstory/investigative-journalism/2019-06-08/federal-police-raid-abc-office-john-lyons-live-tweeting/11192898
208. Fray, 2019.
209. Attard, M. (2019, September 10). A crisis for professional journalism. Presentation to Affinity Alan Knight Media Series seminar, Sydney.
210. Jones, J., & Salter, L. (2012). *Digital journalism*. London, UK: Sage Publications, p. 74.
211. P. Fray (personal communication [interview], September 12, 2019).
212. McChesney, R. (2013). *Digital disconnect: How capitalism is turning the internet against democracy*. New York, NY: The Free Press, p. 201.
213. P. Fray (personal communication [interview], September 12, 2019).
214. Fray, 2019.
215. Center for International Media Assistance. (2019). What is media development? Washington, D.C. Retrieved from https://www.cima.ned.org/what-is-media-development
216. UNESCO (United Nations Educational, Scientific and Cultural Organization). (2019). Media development and the IPDC. Paris. Retrieved from https://en.unesco.org/themes/media-development-and-ipdc
217. Castells, M. (2015). *Networks of outrage and hope: Movements in the internet age*. Cambridge, UK: Polity.

218. Coleman, S. (2017). *Can the internet strengthen democracy?* Cambridge, UK: Polity, p. 118.
219. Castells, M. (2015). *Networks of outrage and hope: Movements in the internet age.* Cambridge, UK: Polity; Gerbaudo, P. (2017). *The mask and the flag: Populism, citizenship and global protest.* London, UK: Hurst & Co.
220. Hachten, W., & Scotton, J. (2012). *The world news prism: Challenges of digital communication* (8th ed.). Malden, MA: Wiley-Blackwell, p. 135.
221. Macnamara, J. (2014). *The 21st century media (r)evolution: Emergent media practices.* New York, NY: Peter Lang, pp. 219–220.
222. Deluca, K., Lawson, S., & Sun, Y. (2012). Occupy Wall Street on the public screens of social media: The many framings of the birth of a protest movement. *Communication, Culture & Critique, 5*(4), 483–509, p. 489.
223. Tormey, S. (2015). *The end of representative politics.* Cambridge, UK: Polity.
224. Dvorak, P., & Khan, N. (2019, June 13). Hong Kong protesters adjust tactics with lessons from 2014 Umbrella Movement. *Wall Street Journal.* Retrieved from https://www.wsj.com/articles/hong-kong-protesters-adjust-tactics-with-lessons-from-2014-umbrella-movement-11560448247
225. Pao, J. (2019, June 17). 'Two million' protest against HK extradition law. *Asia Times.* Retrieved from https://www.asiatimes.com/2019/06/article/hong-kong-grinds-to-a-halt-as-extradition-law-protest-estimated-at-two-million
226. Cohen, I., & Jacob, H. (2019, March 19). Youth demand climate change action in global school strike. *Harvard Political Review*, para. 1. Retrieved from http://harvardpolitics.com/united-states/youth-demand-climate-action-in-global-school-strike
227. Khomami, N. (2017, October 20). #MeToo: How a hashtag became a rallying cry against sexual harassment. *The Guardian.* Retrieved from https://www.theguardian.com/world/2017/oct/20/women-worldwide-use-hashtag-metoo-against-sexual-harassment
228. Sampson, T. (2012). *Virality: Contagion theory in the age of networks.* Minneapolis: University of Minnesota Press.
229. Laughland, O. (2019, August 20). 'I can't breathe': NYPD fires officer who put Eric Garner in chokehold. *The Guardian.* Retrieved from https://www.theguardian.com/us-news/2019/aug/19/eric-garner-daniel-pantaleo-nypd-officer
230. Chen, J. (2019, June 25). Shareholder activist. *Investopedia*, para. 1. Retrieved from https://www.investopedia.com/terms/s/shareholderactivist.asp
231. Kenton, W. (2019, June 25). Ethical investing. *Investopedia*, para. 2. Retrieved from https://www.investopedia.com/terms/e/ethical-investing.asp
232. Davis, A. (2019). *Political communication: A new introduction for crisis times.* Cambridge, UK: Polity, p. 208.
233. Bennett, W., Wells, C., & Freelon, D. (2011). Communicating civic engagement: Contrasting models of citizenship in the youth Web culture. *Journal of Communication, 61*(5), 835–856.

234. Fenton, N. (2012). The internet and social networking. In J. Curran, N. Fenton, & D. Freedman (Eds.), *Misunderstanding the internet* (pp. 123–148). Abingdon, UK: Routledge, p. 142.
235. Coleman, S. (2013). *How voters feel*. New York, NY: Cambridge University Press, pp. 4, 192.
236. Chase, S., Ruttenberg, S., Nourse, E., & Given, W. Jr. (1950). *The social responsibility of management*. New York, NY: New York University.
237. Elkington, J. (1998). *Cannibals with forks: The triple bottom line of 21st century business*. Gabriola Island, BC, Canada and Stony Creek, CT: New Society Publishers.
238. Holcomb, J. (2005). Public affairs in North America: US origins and development. In P. Harris & C. Fleisher (Eds.), *The handbook of public affairs* (pp. 31–49). London, UK: Sage Publications, p. 40.
239. Business Roundtable. (2019). Statement on the purpose of a corporation. Retrieved from https://opportunity.businessroundtable.org/wp-content/uploads/2019/08/Business-Roundtable-Statement-on-the-Purpose-of-a-Corporation-with-Signatures.pdf
240. Berger, P., & Luckmann, T. (1966). *The social construction of reality: A treatise in the sociology of knowledge*. New York, NY: Doubleday.
241. Couldry, N., & Mejias, U. (2019). *The costs of connection: How data is colonizing human life and appropriating it for capitalism*. Stanford, CA: Stanford University Press, p. 196.
242. Wood& Porter, 2019, p. 135.
243. Ecker, U., O'Reilly, Z., Reid, J., & Chang, E. (2019). The effectiveness of short-format refutational fact-checks. *British Journal of Psychology* [online pre-print]. Retrieved from https://onlinelibrary.wiley.com/doi/full/10.1111/bjop.12383
244. Government Communication Service. (2018). RESULT: Counter disinformation toolkit. London, UK. Retrieved from https://gcs.civilservice.gov.uk/guidance/resist-counter-disinformation-toolkit
245. Eysenbach, 2008, p. 130.
246. Internet World Statistics. (2019). Internet usage statistics. Retrieved from https://www.internetworldstats.com/stats.htm
247. Government Communication Service. (2018). Government Communication Service (GCS) handbook. London, UK, p. 1. Retrieved from https://gcs.civilservice.gov.uk/wp-content/uploads/2015/09/GCSHandbook.pdf
248. Federal Trade Commission. (2019). Advertising and marketing. Washington, DC. Retrieved from https://www.ftc.gov/tips-advice/business-center/advertising-and-marketing
249. Federal Trade Commission. (2015). Enforcement policy statement on deceptively formatted advertisements. Washington, D.C. Retrieved from https://www.ftc.gov/system/files/documents/public_statements/896923/151222deceptiveenforcement.pdf

250. Rich, J. (2016, April 7). Consumer protection 2016.0: Challenges in advertising. Paper presented to the Association of National Advertisers conference, Orlando, FL, p. 7.
251. Federal Trade Commission. (2019). Disclosures 101 for social media influencers, p.1. Retrieved from https://www.ftc.gov/system/files/documents/plain-language/1001a-influencer-guide-508_1.pdf
252. Gov.UK. (2019). Marketing and advertising: The law. London, UK. Retrieved from https://www.gov.uk/marketing-advertising-law/regulations-that-affect-advertising
253. Ofcom. (2018, August 2). Communications market report, London, UK. Retrieved from https://www.ofcom.org.uk/__data/assets/pdf_file/0022/117256/CMR-2018-narrative-report.pdf
254. Australian Competition & Consumer Commission. (2019). *Australian Competition and Consumer Act 2010*. Retrieved from https://www.accc.gov.au/about-us/australian-competition-consumer-commission/legislation
255. S. Bruce (personal communication [interview], September 6, 2019).
256. Hickman, A. (2019, June 24). PR image problem: 92% think PROs "hide the truth" and lie: Majority don't understand industry. *PRWeek*. Retrieved from https://www.prweek.com/article/1588555/prs-image-problem-92-think-pr-pros-hide-truth-lie-majority-dont-understand-industry
257. Chan, J. (2018, November 22). GDPR is not enough: The world urgently needs a global data governance regime. *Apolitical* [Web log post], para. 2. Retrieved from https://apolitical.co/solution_article/gdpr-is-not-enough-the-world-urgently-needs-a-global-data-governance-regime
258. Flew, T. (2019). Platforms on trial. *InterMEDIA*, 46(2), 24–29, p. 25. Retrieved from https://www.iicom.org/intermedia/intermedia-past-issues/intermedia-july-2018/platforms-on-trial
259. Wesner, K. (2019, May). Compelling bot speech: An analysis of California's new bot disclosure law. Paper presented to the International Communication Association (ICA) conference, 'Communication Law & Policy: Reign in Your Robot Algorithms, Governance, and Hacking' session, Washington, D.C.
260. Anne Gregory is professor of corporate communication in the Huddersfield Business School at the University of Huddersfield in the UK and immediate past chair of the Global Alliance for Public Relations and Communication Management, a peak communication industry body representing 280,000 members worldwide. She is also an adviser to the UK Government Communication Service.
261. A. Gregory (personal communication [interview], August 14, 2019).
262. Sean Larkins was deputy director of the UK Government Communication Service before joining the WPP group as director of consulting and capability in its Government and Public Sector Practice division and then as global CEO of Kantar Public Consulting. He leads WPP's executive education faculty at the Lee Kuan Yew School of Public Policy at the National University of Singapore and is the author of

The *Leaders' Report: The Future of Government Communication* based on interviews with senior communication practitioners in 40 countries worldwide.
263. S. Larkins (personal communication [interview], May 29, 2019).
264. Stigler Center for the Study of the Economy and the State. (2019, September). *Stigler Committee on digital platforms final report*, p. 15. Retrieved from https://research.chicagobooth.edu/-/media/research/stigler/pdfs/digital-platforms---committee-report---stigler-center.pdf
265. European Commission. (2019, June 14). A Europe that protects: EU reports on progress in fighting disinformation ahead of European Council. Press release. Brussels. Retrieved from https://ec.europa.eu/digital-single-market/en/news/europe-protects-eu-reports-progress-fighting-disinformation-ahead-european-council
266. Her Majesty's Government. (2019, April). Online harms white paper. London, UK, p. 6. Retrieved from https://www.gov.uk/government/consultations/online-harms-white-paper
267. Ibid., p. 7.
268. Australian Competition and Consumer Commission. (2019). Digital platforms inquiry: Final report. Canberra, ACT. Retrieved from https://www.accc.gov.au/publications/digital-platforms-inquiry-final-report
269. West, D. (2017, December 18). *How to combat fake news and disinformation*. Washington, D.C.: Brookings Institute. Retrieved from https://www.brookings.edu/research/how-to-combat-fake-news-and-disinformation
270. Pietsch, B. (2019, July 25). Explainer: What Google, Facebook could face in US antitrust probe. *Reuters*. Retrieved from https://www.reuters.com/article/us-tech-antitrust-explainer/explainer-what-google-facebook-could-face-in-u-s-antitrust-probe-idUSKCN1UJ2Z3
271. European Commission. (2017, June 27). Antitrust: Commission fines Google €2.42 billion for abusing dominance as search engine by giving illegal advantage to own comparison shopping service. Retrieved from https://ec.europa.eu/commission/presscorner/detail/en/IP_17_1784
272. Vaidhyanathan, S. (2019, July 26). Billion-dollar fines can't stop Google and Facebook. That's peanuts to them. *The Guardian*, Opinion. Retrieved from https://www.theguardian.com/commentisfree/2019/jul/26/google-facebook-regulation-ftc-settlement
273. Stigler Center for the Study of the Economy and the State, 2019, p. 18.
274. Napoli, P. (2019, April 18). What would Facebook regulation look like? Start with the FCC. *WIRED*, paras 3–4. Retrieved from https://www.wired.com/story/what-would-facebook-regulation-look-like-start-with-the-fcc
275. Ibid., paras 5–6.
276. What became the internet was based originally on ARPANET developed by the Advanced Research Projects Agency and funded by the US Department of Defense, and the World Wide Web was developed by the European Organization for Nuclear Research, known as CERN.

277. Kemp, T. (2019, April 1). Singapore prepares sweeping law to fight 'online falsehoods'. *CNBC*. Retrieved from https://www.cnbc.com/2019/04/01/fake-news-singapore-prepares-law-to-fight-online-falsehoods.html
278. Suderman, P. (2018, September 13). The slippery slope of regulating social media. *The Business Times*. Retrieved from https://www.businesstimes.com.sg/opinion/the-slippery-slope-of-regulating-social-media
279. Is Singapore fighting fake news or free speech? (2019, April 5). The *Washington Post* [Editorial]. Retrieved from https://www.washingtonpost.com/opinions/global-opinions/is-singapore-fighting-fake-news-or-free-speech/2019/04/05/ccb42ca0-5701-11e9-814f-e2f46684196e_story.html
280. R. Tench (personal communication [interview], September 20, 2019).
281. Flew, 2019, p. 28.
282. Ibid., p. 29.
283. New, J. (2019, September 23). *How to fix the Algorithm Accountability Act*. Washington, D.C.: Center for Data Innovation. Retrieved from https://www.datainnovation.org/2019/09/how-to-fix-the-algorithmic-accountability-act
284. New Zealand Government. (2019, October 16). Government algorithm transparency and accountability. data.gov.nz, para. 4. Retrieved from https://data.govt.nz/use-data/analyse-data/government-algorithm-transparency-and-accountability
285. Vaidhyanathan, S. (2019, July 26). Billion-dollar fines can't stop Google and Facebook. That's peanuts to them. *The Guardian*, Opinion. Retrieved from https://www.theguardian.com/commentisfree/2019/jul/26/google-facebook-regulation-ftc-settlement
286. Popken, B. (2019, May 9). Facebook co-founder says Zuckerberg 'not accountable', calls for government break up. *NBC News*, paras 2, 3. Retrieved from https://www.nbcnews.com/tech/tech-news/facebook-co-founder-says-zuckerberg-not-accountable-calls-government-break-n1003606
287. Ruiz, R., & Dougherty, C. (2014, March 19). Take Google to court, staff report urged FTC. *New York Times*. Retrieved from https://www.nytimes.com/2015/03/20/technology/take-google-to-court-staff-report-urged-ftc.html
288. Schleifer, T. (2019, June 4). Why does Washington suddenly seem ready to regulate Big Tech? Look at the polls. *Vox.com*. Retrieved from https://www.vox.com/2019/6/4/18652469/washington-antitrust-regulate-amazon-google-facebook-look-at-polls
289. *Cornell University Law School Legal Information Institute. (2013). First Amendment, Constitution of the United States of America. Archived. Retrieved from* https://www.law.cornell.edu/constitution/first_amendment
290. Lyons, J. (2019, July 15). AFP raid on ABC reveals investigative journalism being put in same category as criminality. *ABC News*, Analysis. Retrieved from https://www.abc.net.au/news/2019-07-15/abc-raids-australian-federal-police-press-freedom/11309810

291. Ibid.
292. Miller, N. (2019, July 11). 'Be better than North Korea': Amal Clooney warns Australia on press freedom. *Sydney Morning Herald*. Retrieved from https://www.smh.com.au/world/europe/be-better-than-north-korea-amal-clooney-warns-australia-on-press-freedom-20190711-p5264e.html

6

Conclusions

There is clearly more that can be said and done in relation to the challenges described. No one book and no one author can provide all the answers. But find answers we must. In that context, it is hoped that this discussion has contributed in some theoretical as well as tangible practical ways. In summary, this analysis leads to three key propositions that, in turn, require a number of strategies that have been outlined in Chapter 5 and are summarized here.

Three key propositions advanced in this analysis that identify a requirement for and form the basis of the strategies outlined are as follows.

Complicity

We are all complicit to some extent in fake news, disinformation and the slide towards post-truth.

Understanding of the media and public communication ecosystem as it exists today, and the many players and interests that interact in and shape it, is important to move beyond finger-pointing at a few individuals or groups based on the doctrine of selective depravity and a view of others—not us—as the evildoers.

The conclusions of a 2019 Institute for Public Relations (IPR) report on *Disinformation in Society* are an exemplar of finger-pointing and ducking responsibility in that they make no mention of public relations (PR), but instead identify "the biggest culprits" responsible for creating disinformation as "fake social media accounts" (55%), "politicians" (45%), "Trump" specifically (40%), and "the Russian Government" (33%).[1] As discussed in Chapter 5, the industry leaders and educators in PR and related fields of practice such as corporate communication and public affairs need to engage in reflection and critical thinking.

Advertising, having come crashing down to earth after the halcyon days of massive budgets that paid for extravagant campaigns and Porsches and Ferraris for their creators, is seeking every way possible to extract and use data to target people as consumers and to deceptively disguise its commercial messages as information or entertainment for financial gain or political power. Political campaign managers also use every trick in the book and every tool available to win at all costs.

Research firms such as Nielsen, Kantar, Ipsos, GfK, IQVIA (formerly Quintiles IMS), Comscore and others, and data warehouses and "data-logic platforms" such as Palantir (https://www.palantir.com) are falling over themselves to provide data to advertisers and marketers to aid them in their corporatization of communication and cultivation and exploitation of human needs and desires.

The new media oligopolies—Google, Facebook, Amazon, Apple, and their subsidiaries such as YouTube—are happy to distribute live video of a fanatical white supremacist murdering dozens of innocent people praying in mosques and deliberately falsified videos that undermine the credibility of an opposition politician as free speech. Such claims are not what the moral crusaders who fought for the First Amendment to the US Constitution had in mind. Such instances are nothing more than immoral greed-driven tactics to gain clicks that they can monetize.

Even civil service communicators working for democratic governments are adopting marketing techniques and treating people as customers instead of citizens who pay their salaries and to whom they and their political masters are ultimately accountable. The mantra of marketing restricts communication to persuasion and the narratives propagated are those of big corporations and government. Citizens have digital targets projected on their backs and *vox populi* is reduced to customer feedback after policies, products, and services are produced and marketed.

Journalism needs and deserves our support and we need it. But in its lemming-like stampede to satisfy populist tastes in sensationalist tabloids and its blurring with opinion in partisan publications and networks, journalism has failed to fulfil its important role as a watchdog and as a speaker of truth to power. In a stirring and frank address upon being inducted into the Logies Hall of Fame in Australia for service to journalism, in which he levelled criticism at politicians and institutions, ABC journalist Kerry O'Brien said:

> We the journalists have to share the responsibility for the great failures of our time … For instance 40 years after powerful evidence first kicked in that human-caused climate change threatened the world with an existential disaster, we're still stuck in the mire of drab, dishonest arguments that *will* come at great cost to future generations and we the journalists have not cut through the fake news effectively. We have not properly held politicians to account [original emphasis].[2]

Journalism needs to respond to the challenges identified and each of us needs to support quality, independent journalism. As Lee McIntyre asks in his analysis of post-truth: "Where did we get the idea that this [fact-based nonpartisan reporting] should come at no cost to us and that we are not required to be active participants in ferreting out the truth?" He adds: "Maybe we should buy those subscriptions to the *New York Times* and the *Washington Post* after all, instead of relying on 10 free articles a month."[3] McIntyre's views are echoed by veteran journalists and editors such as Peter Fray. We expect to be paid, and even paid well, for the products and services we produce. However, we expect journalists to serve society, but be paid in most cases by someone else, such as commercial advertisers with all their vested interests. The public's support for journalism is not high and attitudes need to change if journalism is to survive and be revived beyond taxpayer-funded public broadcasters, according to the *Reuters Institute Digital News 2019* report. This revealed:

> Despite the efforts of the news industry, we find only a small increase in the numbers paying for *any* online news—whether by subscription, membership, or donation. Growth is limited to a handful of countries mainly in the Nordic region (Norway 34%, Sweden 27%) while the number paying in the US (16%) remains stable after a big jump in 2017.[4]

As well as supporting quality journalism, media users and consumers must also take responsibility in other ways. This is not an attempt to pass blame. As stated above, many so-called professional communicators and professional communication industry bodies have to step up to the plate. But misinformation, disinformation, and attempts at deception and manipulation spread through society because individuals post, retweet and share spurious content, often without any effort to fact check and sometimes in a perverse disregard for truth. Citizens also give up personal data with little thought and often carelessly. First Draft's Australian bureau editor Anne Kruger, strongly supports "cross-generational media literacy education", as well as calling for the public to "support quality journalism."[5]

Recognition that we are all complicit, if not actively involved, in *post-communication* is essential for making change. Rather than thinking that "somebody ought to do something," or hoping for a silver bullet solution, we have to accept complexity, responsibility, and co-operability. We have to work together, reflecting on our own actions, respecting the interests of others, and cooperating, collaborating, and compromising to find mutual ground. In a moving speech to accept the 2019 Barlow/Pioneer Award from the Electronic Frontier Foundation, Data and Society Research Institute founder and president, danah boyd, asked the audience to honour her by "stepping back and reckoning with your own contributions to the current state of affairs" as society faces what she called "the Great Reckoning." She said "no one … is an innocent bystander. We have all enabled this current state of affairs in one way or another. Thus, it is our responsibility to take action."[6]

The strategies proposed for improving public communication seek to address the challenges faced in an inclusive multi-disciplinary way.

A Troubling Technology Track Record

We arrive at this point in history with a track record of perpetrating disinformation, deception, and manipulation with today's technologies, as outlined in this analysis. Of course, communication technologies have brought much good to society. After initially being controlled by the Church, the printing press was the first great communication revolution.[7] It brought information and education to the masses. The invention of the telegraph separated communication from transportation, thereby overcoming the tyranny of distance and opening up new opportunities at every level of society. The internet has democratized information and knowledge even further. E-commerce has accelerated our way through transactions from grocery shopping to arranging international travel. Some of us find our life partner online. But the *cyberoptimism* that greeted the World Wide Web in particular has been tempered by a continuing digital divide, corporate colonization, dataveillance, data harvesting and sale to the highest bidder, cybercrime, clustering of users into *echo chambers*, and the emergence of new media oligopolies with even more dominance that the media empires of the 19th and 20th centuries. A number of writers have referred to the web as an online Wild West.[8] We must face the reality that our track record in using communication technologies is a chequered one. We need to do better in the next few decades than we have the past few decades.

A Tipping Point

The third key proposition advanced in this analysis is that we are arriving at a point in technological development at which powerful new communication tools are coming on stream, such as advanced data analytics, widespread use of algorithms, and rapidly expanding use of artificial intelligence. Given our track record, we are arriving at this point without values, principles, standards, and regulations that can guide that development in ethical, socially responsible ways. Acquiescence to post-truth is resulting in our swords and shields abandoned or put aside and reducing us to passive game players in a 21st century digital Game of Thrones. We arrive at this point with weakened independent media and regulators struggling to keep up and often far behind. How will we go forward in a world of ever-more sophisticated data analytics, surveillance, automation, and AI?

This analysis is not an attack on free enterprise, or business, or even capitalism. It is based on a premise that mutual benefit is a realistic expectation—what John Elkington referred to more than 20 years ago as "triple bottom line."[9] How do we use new technologies and conduct communication in the public sphere in ethical ways for *mutual benefits*—i.e., social good as well as commercial gain?

As warned in Chapter 4, we are putting advanced and potentially weaponized technologies into the hands of criminals and children with few restrictions or controls.

We have foxes guarding the hen house in Google, Facebook, Amazon and the like.

This is not *NeoLuddism*—an anti-technology stance. Far from it. I use many of the technologies and platforms discussed. This book could not have been written without online research via the internet, search engines, e-mail, VOIP (voice over the internet protocol) services such as Skype and Zoom, digital recording, and data analysis. Rather, this is a call for data science to be integrated with social science.

The technologies discussed can bring much good to society. The affordances that they create depend on how they are used. If we continue on the path of post-communication towards post-truth, ever more powerful communication technologies will cause great harm. If we can apply them within frameworks of ethics, self-regulation, social responsibility, and self-responsibility, we have the potential to create better societies—where better means social, cultural, environmental, and political as well as economic well-being.

10 Strategies to Address Post-Communication

Rather than prescribing a single simplistic solution, this analysis focuses attention on some strategies that have been applied in the past, at least to some extent, as well as offering some new suggestions. The central argument is that traditional approaches to enabling democracy and social stability through participation, consultation, and dialogue must be bolstered and some additional steps must be taken by government and by industry. Specifically, this analysis has identified 10 key strategies. A '10-point plan' might seem contrived. At one stage in this research, seven key strategies were outlined, but interviews with researchers and leading media and communication professionals, as well as reviewing research literature including recent studies, informed an even broader approach. No doubt there are still other strategies and initiatives needed, and these should be welcomed and carefully considered. But, this analysis leads to at least 10 key important strategies to establish a communicative society as follows:

1. *Self-regulation by professional communication practitioners* in marketing, advertising, PR, and corporate, government, and political communication, such as through codes of practice and codes of ethics implemented by professional associations and institutes, as well as professional development and leadership;
2. *Media and communications company corporate responsibility* including the major digital and social media platforms, particularly Google, Facebook, Amazon, and Apple in relation to collection and use of data, privacy, algorithms, and the increasing use of AI;
3. *Increasing media literacy* among media consumers to critically examine content and look for corroborating sources, as well as media literacy of production to challenge and refute misinformation, starting in schools but also including adult education;
4. *Supporting public media* with adequate funding to balance commercial and powerful political interests and include diverse and marginal interests, not only populist causes;

5. *New forms of activism and social movements* that give voice and influence to marginalized groups, minorities, and youth rather than reliance on traditional institutions such as political parties that are in decline, referred to in this discussion as the relocation of democracy;
6. *Corporate responsibility and social purpose* within business and other types of organizations, including genuine engagement with stakeholders and governance rather than *greenwashing* (false claims in relation to environmental impact) and *purpose-washing*, a term coined by Steve Barrett in a *PRWeek* blog post to refer to false and exaggerated claims of social benefit by corporations;[10]
7. *Academic research* to continue to seek solutions and strategies and present critical analysis as well as recommendations to government, industry, the professions, and the community;
8. *Refuting and resisting* fake news, misinformation, and particularly disinformation by official and voluntary fact-checking organizations and units;
9. *Self-responsibility* by individuals including seeking verification of information, speaking up to call out disinformation and attempts at deception, manipulation, and abuses of privacy and human rights. Self-responsibility also should include paying for quality news and analysis to support its production;
10. *Government regulation and legislation* to enforce ethical and socially responsible behaviour in media, business, and communication practices including severe penalties for breaches of regulations. Rather than fines, which often represent a drop in the ocean for mega-corporations, penalties could include disbarring responsible directors and senior executives from holding similar positions in future.

Some thought has been given to the order of these strategies, but they should not be seen as chronological or ranked by priority. One might argue that corporate responsibility by business should be an expectation before relying on activism and social movements to effect change. Normatively, yes. But, practically, entrenched business practices and decades of neoliberal thinking are unlikely to change without external pressure. What is significant is that the proposals involve both bottom-up as well as top-down initiatives, even to the point of being a near even mix of each. This is considered important and intrinsic to the overall theme of this analysis. We are all in this together. We all have responsibilities in terms of creating a society in which we can live safe and satisfying lives and in which there is fairness and equity. To achieve that, we need social responsibility and justice applied by governments, institutions such as the courts and regulators, and corporations, as well as pressure for change from outside the systems and structures of power by independent researchers, activists, social movements, and active citizens.

A multi-pronged approach as suggested here is designed to trap disinformation, deception, and manipulative practices in a pincer movement. No one strategy on its own is likely to be effective. But combined action such as increased social responsibility by media platforms (traditional and social), backed up by appropriate legislation and severe penalties if they fail to act responsibly; a renaissance of independent reporting and analysis in journalism; support for public media free of commercial interests; increased access to and promotion of fact-checking tools; more reflective and ethical behaviour by marketing, advertising, and PR professionals; and increased media literacy within the population will go a long way to reversing the corruption of the public sphere that has occurred in the past decade.

These initiatives also need to be supported by self-responsibility at every level. People need to be encouraged to speak up and call out false information and those who produce and distribute it. In the least, individuals need to act responsibly by ensuring that they do not become part of the problem by distributing information that appears suspicious or is known to be false.

This multi-dimensional transdisciplinary approach is agreed as necessary by most scholars and media and communication industry leaders interviewed. For example, Barry Leggetter, head of a number of global PR firms and a major international communication industry association for more than a decade,[11] said: "I do believe that it is necessary to address fake news and disinformation and that it has to be a multi-pronged approach."[12] This approach also supports Couldry and Mejias's conclusion in relation to data colonization in which they say:

> … we need a way to tie together the isolated acts of resistance and technical fixes … and organize them into a larger project for dismantling data colonialism by collectively acquiring knowledge about its manifold manifestations and the alternatives they suppress.[13]

This analysis has focussed on public communication and argues that this aspect of contemporary life warrants close attention given the centrality of communication to democracy and society as noted by John Dewey, James Carey, and many others since. This is not to deny or underestimate the importance of addressing broader economic, social, and cultural issues that are also impacting and shaping politics and society in ways that are disadvantageous to all but economic and political elites. The environment in which disinformation spreads like wildfire and manipulation bears fruit is largely shaped by socio-economic conditions.

Donald Trump would never have been elected without the disenfranchised and disillusioned residents of the American Rust Belt[14] and the poor South. It might seem ironic and even perverse that a billionaire was voted into power by those with neither money nor power. But Trump presented himself as a maverick, as anti-Establishment, and appealed to the desperation and fears of under-funded, under-educated, and under-recognized citizens. Socio-economic conditions also directly contribute to the creation of disinformation. While much publicity has been given to social media sites and bots created by government-funded hackers in Russia and those operated by the Israeli intelligence firm Psy-Group in Macedonia, the reality is that most online sites dedicated to fake news and disinformation are operated by private individuals who have no political affiliations but are living in poverty in countries or regions with high unemployment and simply want to make some money. They eke out a living from posting sensational headlines and claims that generate high volumes of views and link to other sites that pay them a few cents per clickthrough. Many started out posting relatively harmless clickbait about celebrities, but have followed the gravy train as politics has careered into a new era of aggressive digital campaigning.

Political, government, and corporate leaders who have championed and nurtured neoliberalism need to redress the growing elitism in societies in which a relative small number of people control vast quantities of wealth and power, while millions of others languish. It can only be hoped that leaders with a social conscience and morality will emerge and real political and social change will occur before societies reach a point of revolt and revolution as has occurred in the past when extreme gaps in power and privilege became entrenched.

At a theoretical level, this analysis seeks to re-anchor communication in the humanities and sociology, rather than in systems theory and positivist psychology focussed on persuasion and manipulation, or marketing theory in which public communication through advertising, PR, and political campaigns are so often grounded.[15] It draws on Polish sociologist Stanisław Ossowski's claim that "sociology belongs to the humanities."[16] If this itself sounds colonizing, at least human rights and values must figure larger in sociology and in political science. Drawing on 20th century social and cultural theory such as that contributed by eminent Chicago School scholars like James Carey and the seminal writing of Robert Craig on communication theory, this analysis is shaped by a view that sociology and related studies such as political science must resist the contemporary *cause célèbre* of economics and the persuasive powers of behavioural psychology to focus more on human well-being, social equity, and social justice. Folding communication back into sociology and the humanities returns communication to its fundamental role in society and human life, rather than being colonized for achieving the objectives of capitalism and capital P politics. Such an endeavour contributes to a new sociology of communication and proposes more authentic ways of talking about communication (Craig's *metadiscourse* of communication) and more authentic ways of practicing communication.

Our Shared Responsibilities—An Action List

Table 6.1 breaks down the 10 strategies to identify key actions required by various actors for these strategies to be effectively implemented. This highlights the holistic and collaborative approach that needs to be taken and attempts to move debate beyond problem identification and conceptual solutions to concrete actions.

Table 6.1. A shared responsibility approach to addressing disinformation, deception, and manipulation

Responsible actor	Actions
Communication industry organizations: • Journalism • Advertising • Marketing • Public relations • Corporate/business communication	1. Establish and maintain codes of ethics 2. Establish and maintain codes of professional conduct 3. Provide professional development education and training that includes ethics, social justice, diversity, and responsible use of new technologies 4. Implement certification of practitioners
Professional communicators: • Journalists • Advertising and marketing executives • PR practitioners • Corporate communication executives • Political communication specialists	1. Commit to codes of ethics 2. Commit to codes of professional conduct 3. Attend professional development education and training 4. Undertake accreditation or certification as available
Media organizations including social media platforms	1. Self-regulate through codes of practice, self-monitoring, transparency, and responsive complaints processes

Responsible actor	Actions
Government (Legislature, executive, and judiciary)	1. Enact legislation on major issues such as protection of privacy, transparency of information sources, etc. carefully balanced with freedom of speech and media 2. Enact regulatory frameworks for social media platforms with appropriate penalties 3. Implement anti-trust action in the case of anti-competitive monopolies or oligopolies 4. Provide support for and independence of public media 5. Provide support for education (school and university)
Corporations and organizations (including government agencies, NGOs, and non-profit organizations)	1. Enact corporate social responsibility 2. Adopt social purpose 3. Engage in dialogic communication and consultation with stakeholders (i.e., listening and speaking)
Educators	1. Conduct independent research and critical analysis at university and research institute level 2. Implement media literacy education in schools (particularly critical media consumption skills)
Citizens	1. Acquire critical media consumption skills 2. Fact check (e.g., Snopes sites) 3. Call out disinformation as *apomediaries*[a] 4. Pay for quality journalism (e.g., subscribe or donate) 5. Speak up. Find spaces between the hubs and nodes of dominant discourses; resist
Activists and public interest groups	1. Provide monitoring, investigation, and fact checking 2. Refute false claims and disinformation 3. Advocate 4. Protest and lobby policy makers

[a] See Eysenbach, G. (2008). Credibility of health information and digital media: New perspectives and implications for youth. In M. Metzger & A. Flanagin (Eds.), *Digital media, youth and credibility* (pp. 123–154). Cambridge, MA: MIT Press, p. 130.

Notes

1. McCorkindale, T. (2019). *2019 IPR disinformation in society report*. Gainesville, FL: Institute for Public Relations, p. 4. Retrieved from https://instituteforpr.org/ipr-disinformation-study
2. O'Brien, K. (2019, July 1). Don't ever again allow politicians to diminish the public broadcaster. *Crikey*, transcript of speech, paras 9–10. Retrieved from https://www.crikey.com.au/2019/07/01/kerry-obrien-logies-speech
3. McIntyre, L. (2018). *Post-truth*. Cambridge, MA: MIT Press, pp. 104, 119.
4. Newman, N., Fletcher, R., Kalogeropoulos, A., & Kleis Nielsen, R. (2019). *Reuters Institute digital news report 2019*. Oxford, UK: Reuters Institute for the Study of Journalism and Oxford University, p. 9. Retrieved from http://www.digitalnewsreport.org
5. A. Kruger (personal communication [interview], September 20, 2019).
6. boyd, d. (2019, September 14). Facing the great reckoning head-on. Speech to Electronic Frontiers Foundation 2019 Pioneer Awards, September 12, San Francisco, CA, para. 20. Retrieved from https://onezero.medium.com/facing-the-great-reckoning-head-on-8fe434e10630
7. Carey, J. (2009). *Communication as culture: Essays on media and culture*. New York, NY: Routledge, p. 146. (Original work published 1989)
8. Fitch, K. (2009a). Making friends in the wild west: Singaporean public relations practitioners' perceptions of working in social media. *Prism*, 6(2), 1–14. Retrieved from http://www.prismjournal.org/fileadmin/Praxis/Files/globalPR/FITCH.pdf
9. Elkington, J. (1998). *Cannibals with forks: The triple bottom line of 21st century business*. Cabriola Island, BC: New Society Publishers.
10. Barrett, S. (2019, April 5). Purpose principles are right in PR's wheelhouse. *PRWeek* [Web log post], para. 4. Retrieved from https://www.prweek.com/article/1581276/purpose-principles-right-prs-wheelhouse
11. Barry Leggetter was CEO of global PR agencies including Porter Novelli, Fleishman Hillard, and Golin Harris during an extensive career in public relations before serving as CEO of the International Association for Measurement and Evaluation of Communication (AMEC) for more than a decade. He retired in 2019.
12. B. Leggetter (personal communication [interview], June 3, 2019).
13. Couldry, N., & Mejias, U. (2019). *The costs of connection: How data is colonizing human life and appropriating it for capitalism*. Stanford, CA: Stanford University Press, p. 210.
14. The Rust Belt refers to states in the mid-West and near the Great Lakes in the United States that was once prosperous due to steel production and heavy industry, but which has suffered severe economic and social decline.

15. Craig, R. (1999). Communication theory as a field. *Communication Theory, 9*, 119–161; Craig, R. (2015). The constitutive model: A 10-year review. *Communication Theory, 25*(4), 356–374.
16. As cited in Bauman, Z., & Donskis, L. (2013). *Moral blindness: The loss of sensitivity in liquid modernity.* Cambridge, UK: Polity, p. 3.

Bibliography

Argenti, P., & Forman, J. (2002). *The power of corporate communication: Crafting the voice and image of your business*. New York, NY: McGraw-Hill.
Bassel, L. (2017). *The politics of listening: Possibilities and challenges for democratic life*. Basingstoke, UK: Palgrave Macmillan.
Bauman, Z., & Donskis, L. (2013). *Moral blindness: The loss of sensitivity in liquid modernity*. Cambridge, UK: Polity.
Baxter, L. (2011). *Voicing relationships: A dialogic perspective*. Thousand Oaks, CA: Sage Publications.
Bickford, S. (1996). *The dissonance of democracy: Listening, conflict and citizenship*. Ithaca, NY and London: Cornell University Press.
Bimber, B., Flanagin, A., & Stohl, C. (2012). *Collective action in organizations: Interaction and engagement in an era of technological change*. New York, NY: Cambridge University Press.
Blumler, J., & Coleman, S. (2010). Political communication in freefall: The British case—And others. *International Journal of Press/Politics, 15*(2), 139–154.
Blumler, J., & Gurevitch, M. (1995). *The crisis of public communication*. Abingdon, UK: Routledge.
Boatright, R., Shafer, T., Sohieraj, S., & Young, D. (2019). *A crisis of civility: Political discourse and its discontents*. New York, NY: Routledge.
Bohm, D. (1996). *On dialogue* (L. Nichol, Ed.). New York, NY: Routledge.
Bradshaw, S., & Howard, P. (2018). *Challenging truth and trust: A global inventory of organized social media manipulation*. Oxford, UK: Computational Propaganda Research Project, Oxford Internet Institute. Retrieved from https://comprop.oii.ox.ac.uk/research/cybertroops2018
Breakenridge, D. (2008). *PR 2.0: New media, new tools, new audiences*. Upper Saddle River, NJ: Pearson Education.

Brunton, F., & Nissenbaum, H. (2015). *Obfuscation: A user's guide for privacy and protest.* Cambridge, MA: MIT Press.

Canel, M., & Sanders, K. (2012). Government communication: An emerging field in political communication research. In H. Semetko & M. Scammell (Eds.), *The SAGE handbook of political communication* (pp. 85–96). London, UK: Sage Publications.

Caplan, R. (2018). Algorithmic filtering. In P. Napoli (Ed.), *Mediated communication* (pp. 561–583). Berlin: De Gruyter.

Carey, J. (2009). *Communication as culture: Essays on media and culture.* New York, NY: Routledge. (Original work published 1989)

Castells, M. (2010). The new public sphere: Global civil society, communication networks, and global governance. In D. Thussu (Ed.), *International communication: A reader* (pp. 36–47). London, UK and New York, NY: Routledge.

Castells, M. (2015). *Networks of outrage and hope: Movements in the internet age.* Cambridge, UK: Polity.

Coleman, S. (2013). *How voters feel.* New York, NY: Cambridge University Press.

Coleman, S. (2017). *Can the internet strengthen democracy?* Cambridge, UK: Polity.

Cornelissen, J. (2017). *Corporate communication: A guide to theory and practice* (5th ed.). London, UK: Sage Publications.

Couldry, N. (2010). *Why voice matters: Culture and politics after neoliberalism.* London, UK: Sage Publications.

Couldry, N. (2012). *Media, society, world: Social theory and digital media practice.* Cambridge, UK: Polity.

Couldry, N., & Hepp, A. (2017). *The mediated construction of reality.* Cambridge, UK: Polity.

Couldry, N., & Mejias, U. (2019). *The costs of connection: How data is colonizing human life and appropriating it for capitalism.* Stanford, CA: Stanford University Press.

Craig, R. (2015). The constitutive model: A 10-year review. *Communication Theory,* 25(4), 356–374.

Cronin, A. (2018). *Public relations capitalism: Promotional culture, publics and commercial democracy.* Basingstoke, UK: Palgrave Macmillan.

Crouch, C. (2000). *Coping with post-democracy.* London, UK: Fabian Society.

Curran, J. (2012). Reinterpreting the internet. In J. Curran, N. Fenton, & D. Freedman (Eds.), *Misunderstanding the Internet* (pp. 3–33). Abingdon, UK: Routledge.

Dahlgren, P. (2009). *Media and political engagement: Citizens, communication and democracy.* Cambridge, UK: Cambridge University Press.

Davies, N. (2009). *Flat earth news.* London, UK: Random House.

Davis, A. (2013). *Promotional cultures: The rise and spread of advertising, public relations, marketing and branding.* Cambridge, UK: Polity.

Davis, A. (2019). *Political communication: A new introduction for crisis times.* Cambridge, UK: Polity.

Davis, E. (2017). *Post-truth. Why we have reached peak bullshit and what we can do about it.* London, UK: Little, Brown.

Demetrious, K. (2013). *Public relations, activism, and social change.* Abingdon, UK: Routledge.

Dewey, J. (1927). *The public and its problems.* New York, NY: Henry Molt & Co.

Diamond, L., & Plattner, M. (Eds.). (2015). *Decline of democracy.* Baltimore, MA: John Hopkins University Press.

Dietrich, G. (2014). *Spin sucks: Communication and reputation management in the digital age*. London, UK: Que Publishing (an imprint of Pearson Education).

Dobson, A. (2014). *Listening for democracy: Recognition, representation, reconciliation*. Oxford, UK: Oxford University Press.

Edwards, L. (2018). *Understanding public relations: Theory, culture, society*. London, UK: Sage Publications.

Edwards, M. (2014). *Civil society* (3rd ed.). Cambridge, UK and Malden, MA: Polity.

Ewen, S. (1996). *PR: A social history of spin*. New York, NY: Basic Books.

Fawkes, J. (2014). *Public relations ethics and professionalism: The shadow of excellence*. Abingdon, UK: Routledge.

Flew, T. (2018). *Understanding global media* (2nd ed.). London, UK: Macmillan.

Gillespie. T. (2018). *Custodians of the internet: Platforms, content moderation, and the hidden decisions that shape social media*. New Haven, CT: Yale University Press.

Graves, L. (2016). *Deciding what's true: The rise of political fact-checking in American journalism*. New York, NY: Columbia University Press.

Gregory, A., & Willis, P. (2013). *Strategic public relations leadership*. London, UK: Routledge.

Habermas, J. (1996). *Between facts and norms*. Cambridge, UK: Polity.

Habermas, J. (2006). Political communication in media society: Does democracy still enjoy an epistemic dimension? The impact of normative theory on empirical research. *Communication Theory, 16*(4), 411–426.

Held, D. (2006). *Models of democracy* (3rd ed.). Cambridge, UK: Polity Press.

Ireton, C., & Posetti, J. (2018). *Journalism, fake news & disinformation: Handbook for journalism education and training*. Paris, France: UNESCO. Available online at https://unesdoc.unesco.org/ark:/48223/pf0000265552

Jan, A. (2003). *The end of democracy*. Canada: Pragmatic Publishing.

Kavanagh, J., & Rich, M. (2019). *Truth decay: An initial exploration of the diminishing role of facts and analysis in American public life*. Santa Monica, CA: RAND Corporation.

Keane, J. (2009). *The life and death of democracy*. London, UK: W.W. Morton & Co.

Kent, M. (2013). Using social media dialogically: Public relations role in reviving democracy. *Public Relations Review, 39*, 337–345.

Kent, M., & Taylor, M. (2002). Toward a dialogic theory of public relations. *Public Relations Review, 28*(1), 21–37.

L'Etang, J. (2008). *Public relations: Concepts, practice and critique*. London, UK: Sage Publications.

L'Etang, J., McKie, D., Snow, N., & Xifra, J. (2015). *The Routledge handbook of critical public relations*. London, UK: Routledge.

Lipovetsky, G. (2005). *Hypermodern times*. Cambridge, UK: Polity.

Littlejohn, S., Foss, K., & Oetzel, J. (2017). *Theories of human communication* (11th ed.). Long Grove, IL: Waveland.

Macnamara, J. (2012). *Public relations theories, practices, critiques*. Sydney, NSW: Pearson.

Macnamara, J. (2014). *Journalism and PR: Unpacking 'spin', stereotypes, & media myths*. New York, NY: Peter Lang.

Macnamara, J. (2016). *Organizational listening: The missing essential in public communication*. New York, NY: Peter Lang.

Macnamara, J. (2017). *Creating a 'democracy for everyone': Strategies for increasing listening and engagement by government*. London, UK: The London School of Economics and Political Science. Available at http://www.lse.ac.uk/media@lse/research/CreatingADemocracyForEveryone.aspx

Macnamara, J. (2018). Towards a theory and practice of organizational listening. *International Journal of Listening, 32*(1), 1–23.

Macnamara, J. (2019). Explicating listening in organization-public communication: Theory, practices, technologies. *International Journal of Communication, 13*, 5183–5204. https://ijoc.org/index.php/ijoc/article/view/11996/2839

Marsh, I., & Miller, R. (2012). *Democratic decline and democratic renewal: Political change in Britain, Australia and New Zealand*. Cambridge, UK: Cambridge University Press.

Mason, P. (2015). *Postcapitalism: A guide to our future*. London, UK: Allen Lane.

McChesney, R. (2013). *Digital disconnect: How capitalism is turning the internet against democracy*. New York, NY: The Free Press.

McIntyre, L. (2018). *Post-truth*. Boston, MA: MIT Press.

McNair, B. (2017). *An introduction to political communication* (7th ed.). London, UK: Routledge.

Morozov, E. (2011). *The net delusion*. London, UK: Allen Lane.

Mosco, V. (2004). *The digital sublime: Myth, power and cyberspace*. Cambridge, MA: MIT Press.

Mosco, V. (2009). *The political economy of communication* (2nd ed.). London, UK: Sage Publications.

Mouffe, C. (2005). *On the political*. London, UK: Routledge.

Norris, P. (2011). *Democratic deficit: Critical citizens revisited*. New York, NY: Cambridge University Press.

Ott, B., & Dickinson, G. (2019). *The Twitter presidency: Donald J. Trump and the politics of white rage*. New York, NY: Routledge.

Pickard, V. (2020). *Democracy without journalism: Confronting the misinformation society*. New York, NY: Oxford University Press.

Przeworski, A. (2019). *Crisis of democracy*. New York, NY: Cambridge University Press.

Rampton, S., & Stauber, J. (2006). *The best war ever: Lies, damned lies and the mess in Iraq*. New York, NY: Tarcher.

Rosanvallon, P. (2008). *Counter-democracy: Politics in an age of distrust* (A. Goldhammer, Trans.). Cambridge, UK: Cambridge University Press.

Runciman, D. (2018). *How democracy ends*. New York, NY: Basic Books.

Scammell, M. (2014). *Consumer democracy: The marketing of politics*. Cambridge, UK: Cambridge University Press.

Shipman, T. (2016). *All-out war: The full story of how Brexit sank Britain's political class*. London, UK: William Collins.

Stauber, J., & Rampton, S. (1995). *Toxic sludge is good for you: Lies, damn lies and the public relations industry*. Monroe, ME: Common Courage Press.

Stauber, J., & Rampton, S. (2003). *Weapons of mass deception: The uses of propaganda in Bush's war on Iraq*. New York, NY: Tarcher/Penguin.

Streeck, W. (2016). *How will capitalism end? Essays on a failing system*. London, UK: Verso.

Sunstein, C. (2018). *#Republic: Divided democracy in the age of social media*. Princeton, NJ: Princeton University Press.

Taylor, M., & Kent, M. (2014). Dialogic engagement: Clarifying foundational concepts. *Journal of Public Relations Research, 26*(5), 384–398.
Tilly, C. (2005). *Trust and rule.* New York, NY: Cambridge University Press.
Tormey, S. (2015). *The end of representative politics.* Cambridge, UK: Polity.
Turkle, S. (2011). *Alone together: Why we expect more from technology and less from each other.* New York, NY: Basic Books.
Uslaner, E. (Ed.). (2018). *The Oxford handbook of political trust.* New York, NY: Oxford University Press.
Wahl-Jorgensen, K., & Hanitzsch, T. (Eds.). (2020). *Handbook of journalism studies* (2nd ed.). New York, NY: Routledge.
Worthington, D., & Bodie, G. (Eds.). (2017). *The sourcebook of listening research: Methodology and measures.* New York, NY: Wiley-Blackwell.
Zmerli, S., & van der Meer, T. (Eds.). (2017). *Handbook on political trust.* Cheltenham, UK: Edward Elgar.
Zuboff, S. (2019). *The age of surveillance capitalism: The fight for a human future at the new frontier of power.* New York, NY: Hachette.

Index

A

ABC. *See* Australian Broadcasting Corporation
Abrams, Jenna, 126–127
Achmea, 198–199. *See also* Kloet, Stefan
Activism, 15, 19, 163, 223–231. *See also* social movements
Ad Standards, 201
advertising expenditure, 4–5
Advertising Self-Regulatory Council (ASRC), 200. *See also* BBB National Programs, Inc.
advertising standards, 125, 201
Advertising Standards Authority (ASA), 125, 201
Advertising Standards Authority (Broadcast) (ASAB), 201
Advertising Standards Bureau, 201
advertorial, 103–107. *See also* native advertising. *See also* pay to play

AFP. *See* Australian Federal Police
agnotology, 12
agora, 14, 71
AI. *See* artificial intelligence
learning, 9, 17, 39, 148, 152–154, 157
Algorithm Charter (New Zealand), 248
algorithmic accountability, 247
Algorithmic Accountability Act (USA), 247
algorithmic governance, 154
algorithmic impact assessments, 209
algorithms, 7, 9, 17, 128, 148, 151–157, 198, 213–214, 241, 244, 247
alternate facts, 15, 36–37, 44, 67–68, 131–132
Alt-Right, 49–50, 126, 229–230
Amazon, 145, 152, 155, 163, 208, 213, 244, 272, 276–276
AMEC. *See* Association for Measurement and Evaluation of Communication
American Academy of Advertising, 147

American Marketing Association (AMA), 202
American Petroleum Institute, 99
Android, 144, 243–244
anti-trust action, 208, 244, 248, 281
apomediaries, 216, 237
Apple, 145, 208, 241, 244, 272, 276
artificial intelligence, 7, 9–10, 96, 155, 157–159, 209–210
Association for Measurement and Evaluation of Communication, 125, 196
astroturfing, 101, 112–113, 155
Attard, Monica, 221
Australian Association of National Advertisers (AANA), 201
Australian Banking Royal Commission, 113–114
Australian Broadcasting Corporation, 113, 130, 219–222, 249
Australian Competition and Consumer Commission (ACCC), 240, 243
Australian Direct Marketing Association (ADMA), 202
Australian Federal Police, 219–221, 249
automation, 122, 151, 157, 179, 275

B

backfire effect, 19, 217, 236
Bagnall, Richard, 125
Bakhtin, Mikhail, 46
Banking Royal Commission. *See* Australian Banking Royal Commission
BBB National Programs, Inc., 200
BBC. *See* British Broadcasting Corporation
behavioural economics. *See* behavioural insights

behavioural insights, 10, 109–111
Behavioural Insights Team (BIT), 110
belief persistence, 18–19. *See also* confirmation bias
Bell Pottinger, 111–112
Bennett, Lance, 175, 230
Bernays, Edward, 45, 99, 183. *See also* Held, Lucas Bernays
bias, 153, 157, 176, 216
   AI related, 157
   algorithmic, 153, 244
   confirmation bias, 18–19
   data-driven, 153. *See also* data-driven discrimination
   default bias, 243
   media, 176
   political bias, 118–119, 218
big data, 6, 145–149, 157, 198
big tech, 244
big tobacco, 98–99, 203
Bimber, Bruce, 48
BIT. *See* Behavioural Insights Team
Black Lives Matter, 78, 228–229
black PR, 103 *See also* propaganda. *See also* public relations
bloggers, 124–125. *See also* social media influencers
Blumler, Jay, 77
Bohm, David, 46
Bot Disclosure and Accountability Act, 156
Bot Disclosure Law S.B. 1001, 156
Botornot, 156
bots, 7, 9–10, 98, 125, 127–128, 154–158, 161, 213, 234
Bourne, Clea, 158
boyd, danah, 12, 147, 149, 274
Brand, Russell, 34–35
Brexit, 5, 8, 10, 12, 20–21, 31–34, 38, 54, 78–80, 118, 122. *See also* EU referendum
British Broadcasting Corporation, 34, 102, 126, 162, 220, 221

Broadcast Committee of Advertising
    Practice (BCAP), 201
Bruce, Stuart, 194, 241
Buber, Martin, 46
Business Roundtable, 190, 232
Buzzfeed, 159

C

Cadwalladr, Carole, 6, 33
Cambridge Analytica, 6–7, 12,
    150–151, 244
Campbell, Alistair, 102
Care.data, 6
Carey, James, 8, 46, 49, 96, 174, 278, 279
Castells, Manuel, 145, 223
Cathcart, Robert, 9, 93–95
CCTV, 146, 147, 211
Center for Data Innovation, 247
Centre for Media Transition, 177, 180
Chartered Institute of Public Relations,
    111, 112, 193–194, 240
churnalism, 115–116
CIPR. *See* Chartered Institute of Public
    Relations
Citizens for a Free Kuwait, 101–102
civility, 51–52, 54
clickbait, 67, 130–132, 143, 177,
    180, 279
climate change, 5, 37, 98–100, 118, 176,
    203, 226–227, 273
Clooney, Amal, 249
closed circuit television. *See* CCTV
codes of ethics, 194, 201. *See* ethics
Coherence theory, 69
Coleman, Stephen, 34–35, 43, 72–73,
    77–78, 124, 162, 223
Committee of Advertising Practice
    (CAP), 201
Communications Council, 201

complicity, 11–12, 104–105, 271–274
Computational Propaganda Research
    Project, 126, 127
confirmation bias, 18–19
co-regulation, 246. *See also* regulation
Cornelissen, Joep, 187, 198
Coronavirus. *See* COVID-19
corporate communication, 114, 182,
    186–189, 198–200, 233, 272, 280.
    See also public relations
corporate corruption, 113–114
corporate responsibility. *See* corporate
    social responsibility
corporate social responsibility,
    231–234, 281
correspondence theory, 69–70
Couldry, Nick, 8, 12, 15, 149–150,
    209–210, 235, 278
COVID-19, 2–4
Craig, Robert, 46, 174, 279–280
Crawford, Kate, 147–149
CrossCheck, 178, 216. *See also* First Draft
Crouch, Colin, 72, 84
CSR. *See* corporate social responsibility

D

data, 5–9, 12, 17, 103, 120,
    144–151, 163, 198, 202, 210, 213,
    218, 234–235, 241–246, 272, 274,
    276. *See also* data analytics. *See also*
    big data
analytics, 6–7, 10–11, 16, 80–81, 120,
    146, 148–150, 275
colonialism, 12, 15, 149–150, 210, 278
journalism, 178–179
mining, 80, 82
protection, 7, 147, 241. *See also*
    privacy
responsibility, 203
velocity, 145

veracity, 145
volume, 145
Data and Society Research Institute, 7, 12, 161, 209, 274
data-based marketing, 202
data-driven discrimination, 153
datafication, 7, 15, 250
Davies, Nick, 102, 115, 176, 182
Davis, Aeron, 3, 8, 13–14, 77
Davis, Evan, 10
deepfakes, 159–163, 211. *See also* fake text
Defense Advanced Research Projects Agency (DARPA), 161
Definers Public Affairs, 200
Deibert, Ronald, 38, 127
deliberation, 40, 52, 79–80, 204–205
democracy, 2, 4, 13–15, 32, 33–35, 43, 46–47, 49, 54–55, 71, 75–76, 78–79, 101, 122, 175, 191, 206–207, 219–223, 230–231, 277, 278. *See also* post-democracy
  cancer on, 118
  crisis of, 13, 67, 123–124
  end of, 4, 10, 67, 73–79, 123–124
  movements, 223–230
Democracy Index, 72, 224, 249
democracy types
  agonistic, 14
  deliberative, 14
  liberal, 14, 73, 82, 238
  monitory, 82–83, 238
  participatory, 14
  representative, 14, 82
Deuze, Mark, 179
Dewey, John, 8, 46, 49, 123, 174, 278
dialogic communication, 14, 94–95, 158, 160, 174, 281. *See also* dialogue
dialogue, 9–10, 20, 46–48, 49, 53, 94, 96, 120, 174, 189–190, 276. *See also* dialogic communication
Digital Platforms Inquiry, 243

Direct Marketing Commission (UK), 202
Directorate-General for Communication (DG COMM), 20
disengagement, 4, 6, 15, 35, 47–50, 72–73
disinfodemic, 2. *See also* disinformation. *See also* infodemic
disinformation, 2, 9–17, 19, 36–38, 114–119, 125, 130–132, 193–195, 197–198, 208–209, 210–218, 242–243, 271–272, 277, 280–281
  Action Plan Against Disinformation, 242
  by Bell Pottinger, 111–112
  in Brexit 'leave' campaign, 33, 54, 112
  by Citizens for a Free Kuwait, 101
  through deepfakes and fake text, 159–163
  by fake accounts and trolls, 126–129
  refuting, 216–217, 236, 277
  resist, 236, 282
  by tobacco industry, 98–100
distrust, 2–6, 39–50
Dunning-Kruger effect, 214–215

E

earned media. *See* media, earned
echo chamber, 18, 39, 152, 208, 216, 218, 244, 274. *See also* filter bubble
Edelman, 3, 84, 107. *See also* Edelman Trust Barometer
Edelman Trust Barometer, 3, 84
Edwards, Lee, 11–12, 185–186, 193
end of democracy, 4, 10, 73–79. *See also* relocation of democracy
Endless Mayfly, 127
engagement, 43, 47–49, 185, 189–205, 277. *See also* disengagement
Erickson, Tamara, 48

ethics, 8, 12, 16, 45–46, 53, 54, 80, 95–96, 105, 107, 111–112, 115, 117, 130–132, 149, 151, 160, 163–164, 174–175, 184–185, 187, 190, 194–199, 202–203, 234, 275–276, 280
   codes of, 194–197, 201
   investments, 230
EU. *See* European Union
EU referendum, 5–6, 20, 31–34, 54, 79, 121, 129, 150
European Association of Communication Directors, 195
European Commission, 5, 7, 20–21, 241–242. *See also* Directorate-General for Communication (DG COMM)
European Union, 20–21, 31, 74, 79, 122, 242
Exactis, 7

F

face recognition, 17, 149
Facebook, 6–7, 11–12, 112, 127, 130, 143–145, 150, 155–164, 200, 208–213, 244–245, 248, 272, 275–276
fact checking, 13, 44, 105, 130, 160, 178, 216, 236–237, 240, 277–278. *See also* CrossCheck. *See also* FactCheck. *See also* PolitiFact
FactCheck, 13, 216
fake accounts, 112, 126–129, 155, 211
fake news, 8, 12–13, 15, 33, 36–37, 44, 116, 128, 131–132, 160, 193–196, 200, 210, 214–216, 244–246, 273, 277
fake text, 155, 159–163
Federal Trade Commission, 6, 107, 200

Ferrarotti, Franco, 75
filter bubble, 18, 152, 216. *See also* echo chamber
Fink, Larry, 190
First Draft, 130, 178–179, 236, 274
Fixers 229
Flew, Terry, 241, 246–247
Fox News, 115, 118–119, 219, 221
Fray, Peter, 37, 128, 176–178, 214, 221–222
freedom of speech, 72, 161, 199, 220, 238, 248–250, 281
FTC. *See* Federal Trade Commission
Fukuyama, Francis, 2, 31, 75–76, 83

G

gatekeepers, 66, 216, 237
GCS. *See* Government Communication Service
General Data Protection Regulation (GDPR), 7, 147, 241
Global Alliance for Public Relations and Communication Management, 242
Google, 11, 144–145, 161, 163, 178, 208–209, 211, 213, 237, 243–244, 248, 272, 275–276
Government Communication Service (GCS), 20–21, 94, 103, 121–123, 236
greenwashing, 108–109, 277
Gregory, Anne, 103, 196, 242
Grenfell Action Group, 55
Grenfell Tower, 55
Grunig, Jim, 53, 183–184, 191

H

Habermas, Jürgen, 14, 52, 71, 79

Halpern, David, 110. *See also* Behavioural Insights Team
Haraway, Donna, 70
Harsin, Jayson, 66–67, 81
Hartsock, Nancy, 70
Heath, Bob, 53, 94, 186, 189
Held, Lucas Bernays, 16, 191
Hill, John, 98
Hill & Knowlton, 98–99, 101–102
Hix, Simon, 74
Hodges, Caroline, 185–186
Huckabee Sanders, Sarah, 115
Hughes, Chris, 248
human data, 5
human rights, 101, 112, 164, 209–210, 225, 235, 238, 249, 277

I

ICT. *See* information and communication technologies
influencers. *See* social media influencers
infodemic, 2. *See also* disinfodemic
information and communication technologies (ICTs), 8, 15, 17, 22, 38, 94, 96, 143–164
inoculation, 19, 213, 215–216
Instagram, 125, 144, 248
Institute for Public Relations, 53, 98, 194, 195, 272, 282
International Association for Measurement and Evaluation of Communication. *See* Association for Measurement and Evaluation of Communication
International Communications Consultancy Organization (ICCO), 195
Internet Research Agency, 126
IPR. *See* Institute for Public Relations

J

Johnson, Boris, 31–32, 48, 77, 79, 112, 122, 129–130
journalism, 11, 15–17, 36–38, 81–82, 105, 115–119, 131, 160, 164, 175–182, 219, 221–222, 243, 249, 272–274, 280–281. *See also* post-journalism
citizen, 179
civic, 179
computational, 178–179
data, 178–179
futures, 175–181
interactive, 179
networked, 179
participatory, 179
partisan, 38, 117–119, 131, 160
yellow, 36, 131
Jensen, Bob, 128, 162

K

Kahneman, Daniel, 109
Keane, John, 82
Kelly, Alan, 192–193
Kent, Michael, 48
Kloet, Stefan, 198–199. *See also* Achmea
Kogan, Aleksandr, 150
Kruger, Anne, 178–179, 274

L

Larkins, Sean, 242, 245
Latour, Bruno, 70
Leggetter, Barry, 278
legislation, 15, 16, 41, 147, 149, 156, 164, 195, 197, 208, 211–212, 237–250, 277–278, 281. *See also* regulation

listening, 20, 35, 47, 52, 54–55, 83, 121–123, 149, 174, 185, 190, 203–204, 206, 281. *See also* organizational listening
  lack of, 54–55, 83
Livingstone, Sonia, 214

M

machine learning, 7, 9, 39, 148, 152–153, 157, 161. *See also* natural language processing
Macnamara, Jim, 20, 115, 176, 181, 219
Manjoo, Farhad, 13
Manus, Therese, 147–148, 181, 191, 195, 198
marketing, 4, 6, 9, 11–12, 15–16, 47, 52, 80, 96, 105–109, 119–126, 143–151, 157, 190, 195, 199, 276, 278, 280
  by government, 121, 203–204, 272
  deceptive, 112, 125, 195, 201, 211
  regulation, 238–240, 276
  standards, 200–203
marketization, 17, 121–122
Mason, Paul, 83–84
May, Theresa, 32, 54, 79, 118, 121
McChesney, Robert, 182, 222
McCorkindale, Tina, 197, 282
McIntyre, Lee, 9, 13, 33, 71, 99, 119, 273
media content types
  earned, 80, 108
  owned, 80, 108, 177, 181, 199–200
  paid, 80, 108
  shared, 80, 108
media development, 223
media gatekeepers. *See* gatekeepers
media literacy, 11, 15, 16, 155–156, 163, 213–218, 223, 236, 243, 274, 276, 281

media monopolies, 143–145, 180, 208–209, 245
media raids, 15, 219–221, 249. *See also* Australian Federal Police
  for consumption, 215–216
  for production, 216–217
mediatization, 76
Mejias, Ulises, 8, 12, 15, 149–150, 174, 209–210, 235
merchants of doubt, 98–101
merged media, 107–108. *See also* native advertising
MeToo, 78, 228
micro-targeting, 119–120, 149. *See also* targeting
Minty, Ella, 111–112
misinformation, 9, 12, 36–38, 96, 116, 125, 128, 216–217, 237, 244, 276–277. *See also* disinformation
  refuting, 216–217, 236, 276–277
  resisting, 236, 276–277
motivated reasoning, 18–19, 215–216
muckraking. *See* yellow journalism
Murdoch, Rupert, 118–119, 221–222

N

Napoli, Philip, 245
National Advertising Review Council (NARC), 200
National Health Service (NHS), 6
native advertising, 17, 37, 80, 104–107, 239
News Corp, 76, 118–119, 176, 221–222, 249
Nikolova, Natalia, 203, 218
NLP. *See* natural language processing
Norris, Pippa, 40

298 | *Index*

Norwegian Communication Association, 147, 181, 191, 195, 198
NTK Network. *See* Definers Public Affairs

O

Obama, Barack, 44, 76, 81, 159
Occupy, 78, 82, 225
OfCom, 107, 201, 239
OGP. *See* Open Government Partnership
Olasky, Marvin, 11
Online Harms White Paper, 242
Open Government Partnership (OGP), 3, 122, 203
organizational listening, 20, 185, 205. *See also* listening
    definition of, 54
    lack of, 54–55, 83
owned media. *See* media, paid

P

paid media. *See* media, paid
pandemic, 2, 147. *See also* COVID-19
Pappacharissi, Zizi, 51
partisanship, 35, 38–39, 44, 50, 54, 164, 175, 177, 180, 212
pay to play, 103–105, 126. *See also* advertorial. *See also* native advertising
Pelosi, Nancy, 159
PESO. *See* media content types
philanthropy, 222–223, 232
Pinterest, 144
Pizzagate, 37, 211
polarization, 15, 35, 38–39, 44, 50, 69, 77, 152, 164, 209, 221, 244
police raids. *See* Australian Federal Police
PolitiFact, 13, 37, 44, 177–178, 216. *See also* FactCheck

populism, 15, 69, 74, 78, 180, 277
post-capitalism, 4, 83–84
post-communication, 8–9, 11, 93–98, 125, 132, 160, 163, 174, 274, 276–277
post-democracy, 4, 71–79, 83–84, 163
post-journalism, 81–82
post-media, 79–81
post-politics, 83
post-representation, 82–83
post-society, 4, 84–85, 163, 207
post-truth, 2–3, 8–10, 13, 15, 33, 65–67, 70–71, 81, 96, 116, 119, 130–132, 163, 193, 197, 271, 273, 275–276
    and advertising, 130
    and journalism, 116, 180, 214, 273
    and media, 119. *See also* New Corp. *See also* Fox News
    and politics, 33, 76
    and postmodernism, 70–71
    and PR, 130–132, 193, 197
    regimes of, 81, 180
PR. *See* public relations. *See also* PRization
privacy, 16, 17, 144, 147, 149–150, 164, 238, 241–243, 247, 276–277, 281
    and algorithms, 247
PRization, 116, 175, 181–194
Proctor, Robert, 12
profiling, 80. *See also* targeting
promotional culture, 12, 181, 192
propaganda, 10, 19, 37–38, 45–46, 81, 94, 96–97, 101, 103, 118, 123–128, 130–132, 191, 204, 250. *See also* black PR
    and PR, 191, 204
Protection from Online Falsehoods and Manipulation Bill (Singapore), 245–246
Public Broadcasting Service (PBS), 218

public diplomacy, 5, 51–53
  new, 51–53
public funding of media, 218–222, 281.
  See public media
public media, 218–222, 281
public relations, 5, 12, 16, 19, 45,
  53, 77, 94, 97–99, 100–101, 107,
  111–112, 120, 158, 182–198,
  240–241, 271–272, 280–281. *See
  also* black PR. *See also* corporate
  communication
Public Relations Consultants' Association
  (PRCA), 158
public relations expenditure, 5
Public Relations Institute of New
  Zealand (PRINZ), 158
Public Relations Society of Kenya
  (PRSK), 195
public sphere, 4, 5, 11, 14, 16, 18, 20,
  50–52, 71–72, 84, 119, 130, 149,
  160, 164, 173–175, 180–181, 278
public sphericles, 14
purpose. *See* social purpose

Q

QQ, 144

R

Rancière, Jacques, 83
RAND Corporation, 11, 35, 50, 67,
  176, 197
reactance, 19
Red Havas, 107, 126. *See also*
  Wright, James
Reddit, 144
refuting, 216–217, 236, 277.
  See also resist

regulation, 7, 15, 16, 95, 109, 120, 126,
  128, 149, 164, 174, 192, 198,
  237–250, 277, 280–281. *See also*
  legislation
  co-regulation, 246
  of advertising, 200–203, 238–240
  of public relations, 240
  of social media, 208, 241–247
relocation of democracy, 76–79, 83, 206
reputation, 42, 47, 98, 103, 105, 112,
  230, 240
resilience, 84, 194, 213, 215
resist, 236, 281. *See also* refute
*RESIST: The Counter Disinformation
  Toolkit*, 236
resistance, 215, 221, 236, 278
rhetoric, 3, 9, 81, 93–95, 205,
  210, 227
  invitational rhetoric, 94
  manipulative rhetoric, 81, 176
Runciman, David, 10, 74
Rushdoony, R.J., 11
Russian disinformation, 37, 38, 199–200,
  244, 272
Russian trolls, 22, 38, 67, 126

S

scepticism, 43, 49–50, 236
Schudson, Michael, 179
Scottish independence referendum, 32
selective depravity, 11, 160, 196, 271
self-regulation, 16, 95, 111, 120, 128,
  163, 175, 196–203, 239, 240–241,
  246–247, 276
  of communication professionals, 175–208
  public relations, 196–199, 240
  publishers and platforms, 208–213
self-responsibility, 16, 207–208,
  236–237, 277, 278
shared media. *See* media, paid

shareholder activism, 230–231
Siapera, Eugenia, 81–82
Sinnreich, Aram, 153
Sky News, 119, 221. *See also* News Corp
Snapchat, 144
Snopes, 13, 216, 281
snoping. *See* Snopes
social media influencers, 17, 124–126, 239
social movements, 75, 78, 206–207, 223–231, 277–278. *See also* activism
social purpose, 190, 209, 231–233, 277, 281
spin, 3, 9, 16, 38, 47, 52, 66, 96–98, 99–129, 130–132, 175–176, 181–182, 204
spin doctor, 97, 102, 118, 175
strategic communication, 20, 21, 94, 120, 150, 186, 188–191. *See also* public relations
sugar industry, 100, 203
Sugar Research Foundation, 100
Sunstein, Cass, 109
surveillance, 17, 80, 147, 213, 217–218, 221, 275
synthetic media, 162. *See also* deepfakes. *See also* fake text

T

tabloidization, 66
Tandoc, Edson, 37
targeting, 39, 47, 54, 119–120, 147, 149, 202. *See also* micro-targeting
Taylor, Maureen, 48, 185. *See also* Kent, Michael
technologies. *See* information and communication technologies (ICTs)
Tench, Ralph, 128, 155, 246

Thaler, Richard, 109
Thatcher, Margaret, 84, 111
third person effect, 19, 214–215
Thurman, Neil, 178
Tilly, Charles, 43
Tobacco Industry Research Committee, 98–99. *See also* big tobacco
toxic sludge, 100–101
transmission, 46, 120, 143, 174. *See also* transmission model of communication
transmissional model of communication, 93, 174, 188
transparency, 6, 13, 22, 114, 153–154, 157, 173, 178, 195, 197–200, 221, 243, 247, 281
  of publishers and platforms, 207–210
troll farm, 10, 38, 126
trolls, 22, 67, 126–129, 214
Trump, Donald, 2, 5, 8, 10, 21, 22, 31–33, 36–38, 43–44, 48, 65–69, 74, 77–80, 110, 114–115, 116, 126, 130, 159, 164, 229, 279
trust, 3–4, 6, 20–22, 39–50, 77–78, 116, 128, 181, 190, 200–205. *See also* distrust
  barometer. *See* Edelman Trust Barometer
  crisis of, 39, 241
  generalized, 39–40
  particularized, 39
  political, 40–42
  social, 39
  war, 44
truth, 67–71. *See also* truth decay
  postmodern, 69
  semantic theory of, 69
truth decay, 35, 50, 67, 176, 197
Tumblr, 144
Twitter, 116, 126–127, 144, 155–156, 199, 208–209, 211, 224, 228

U

Umbrella Movement, 78, 82, 225–226
uses and gratifications theory, 19
Uslaner, Eric, 39–40

V

van Ruler, Betteke, 174

W

Wardle, Claire, 178
weapons of mass destruction, 97, 102–103, 122
WeChat, 103, 144

Weibo, Sina, 103, 144,
WHO. *See* World Health Organization
Wilson, Rebel, 117
World Health Organization, 2
Wright, James, 107–108, 126

Y

yellow journalism, 116–117
Youku Tudou, 144
YouTube, 129, 144, 199, 208, 227, 244, 272

Z

Zuckerberg, Mark, 6, 144, 244, 248

Printed in Great Britain
by Amazon